HABITS OF COMPASSION

WOMEN IN AMERICAN HISTORY

Series Editors
Anne Firor Scott
Susan Armitage
Susan K. Cahn
Deborah Gray White

A list of books in the series appears at the end of this book.

MAUREEN FITZGERALD

Habits of
Compassion

IRISH CATHOLIC NUNS AND
THE ORIGINS OF NEW YORK'S
WELFARE SYSTEM, 1830–1920

UNIVERSITY OF ILLINOIS PRESS

URBANA AND CHICAGO

Library of Congress Cataloging-in-Publication Data
Fitzgerald, Maureen, 1959–
Habits of compassion : Irish-Catholic nuns and the origins
of New York's welfare system, 1830–1920 / Maureen Fitzgerald.
p.   cm. — (Women in American history)
Includes bibliographical references and index.
ISBN-13: 978-0-252-03034-5 (cloth : alk. paper)
ISBN-10: 0-252-03034-6 (cloth : alk. paper)
ISBN-13: 978-0-252-07282-6 (pbk. : alk. paper)
ISBN-10: 0-252-07282-0 (pbk. : alk. paper)
1. Public welfare—Religious aspects—Catholic Church—History.
2. Public welfare—New York (State)—New York—History.
3. Nuns—New York (State)—New York—History—19th century.
4. Irish-American Catholics—New York (State)—New York—History.
I. Title. II. Series.
BX1795.P83F58   2005
271'.9007471'09034—dc22   2005013684

To my mother,
Joan McNicholas Fitzgerald,
who instilled in me a love of history,
and to my father,
Thomas Fitzgerald,
who instilled in me a love of argument.

And in memory of my grandparents,
Anne Burke McNicholas and Martin McNicholas
and
Florence Cavanaugh Fitzgerald and Thomas Fitzgerald.

Contents

Acknowledgments

I have incurred innumerable debts over the years during which this project has moved into its current form. Its origins lie in the heady mix of 1980s politics, activism, and history that livened my graduate school days in the Women's History Program at the University of Wisconsin-Madison. I want to thank Gerda Lerner, Jeanne Boydston, Paul S. Boyer, and especially Linda Gordon, whose work on family violence inspired my search for ways to uncover working-class women's agency in history. My cohorts in Madison, especially Kathy Brown, Nancy MacLean, Joyce Follet, Susan Smith, Laura McEnaney, Leisa Meyer, Andrea Friedman, and Leslie Reagan, provided challenge, solace, laughter, and—not least important—a sense of purpose that still gets me through the dog days. Mary Peckham Magray and Betsy Clark helped keep the focus on religion a sane endeavor. Dissertation fellowships from the University of Wisconsin and the Woodrow Wilson and Charlotte Newcombe Foundations helped fund the work, and Joan Ragno, Barb Freda Thomas, and Sheila Fitzgerald Mathis provided ever-ready couches in New York. Peggy Garrett and Sharon O'Brien were cheerfully supportive at just the right times.

Colleagues and the graduate students with whom I worked in the history department at the University of Arizona helped shape the book in many ways. I especially thank Karen Anderson, Kathryn Morrissey, Laura Tabili, Jack Marietta, Sherri Goldstein Cash, Fran Buss, Michael Rembis, and Yolanda Leyva for the opportunity to learn with and from them. A year at the Harvard Divinity Women's Studies Program proved a godsend, and although I met and benefited from the advice of too many people to thank I am especially grateful to Constance Buchanan, Ann Braude, and Virginia Brereton for their support of this project. Archivists in New York helped me locate and think about convent materials in creative ways. My thanks to Sister Mary Golden, RSM, and Sister Marguerita Smith, OP, and especially Sister Anne Courtney, SC, and Sister Rita King, SC.

Many readers have over the years made this book possible and better. Although some remain unknown to me, Suellen Hoy, Susan Cahn, Gwendolyn Mink, Kathryn Kish Sklar, and Leisa Meyer have aided me immeasurably. Laurie Matheson and Mary Giles helped me through the final process with their careful reading and advice.

To my family, Tom and Joan Fitzgerald, and Jim, Tom, Sheila, Dan, and Pat Fitzgerald, thanks for asking and not asking about the book and when it will be done. To all the "girls" from Dickinson, you are my proverbial rock. And to my partner, Leisa Meyer, who has not merely read and reread every version but has also made every version possible, my undying gratitude and respect.

Introduction

> We must not cease from exploration
> and the end of all our exploring
> will be to arrive where we began
> and to know the place for the first time.
> —T. S. Eliot

On Monday morning, August 17, 1896, a simple black hearse pulled by a single horse traveled through the streets of New York City. The hearse carried the body of Sister Mary Irene Fitzgibbon and was followed by four hundred of the three thousand Catholic nuns active in the city.[1] Like Sister Irene, most of the sisters hailed from Irish backgrounds, the children of Irish famine refugees. Thousands of mourners, including Protestants and Jews as well as Catholics, watched from the sidewalks and followed the hearse as it passed by their workplaces and through their neighborhoods, until the procession was estimated at twenty thousand. Secular and Catholic newspapers alike marked her death with prominent articles; the *New York Times*'s headline read simply "Sister Mary Irene Is Dead." The *Times* called her "the most remarkable woman of her age in her sphere of philanthropy," and other non-Catholic newspapers agreed. The *Herald* characterized the massive yet simple procession that marked her death as unprecedented: "Never in the history of New York has such a tribute been paid."[2]

Over the weekend before 3,500 mourners paid their respects at the Foundling Asylum, Sister Irene's crowning achievement, an institution she had founded and then supervised for twenty-seven years. The Foundling Asylum housed an average of six hundred women and 1,800 infants at a time and also provided day care for working mothers, a maternity hospital for poor women, a children's hospital, and a shelter for unwed mothers. With an annual budget of $250,000 derived from *city taxes*, secured initially through Irish Catholic men's control of Tammany Hall, the Foundling Asylum was the largest institution of its kind in the country and the only one in New York City to guarantee care for all children and women who came to its doors, regardless of religion, race or ethnicity, marital status, or ability to pay for care.

"New York Foundling Asylum: Sister Irene and Her Flock," ca. 1890. (Museum of the City of New York, The Jacob R. Riis Collection [#94])

The tribute paid to Sister Irene, although remarkable in itself, becomes more so when we consider that Sister Irene Fitzgibbon is virtually unknown to historians of women in the United States. She was but one of approximately two thousand Catholic nuns then active in New York City charities and whose charitable work was dependent primarily or exclusively on public funding. Telling Sister Irene's story, and the many stories of other women religious that follow, is not a matter of adding their biographies to current histories of American women but of fundamentally critiquing and rethinking the premises of an American women's history that has rendered their work invisible or inconsequential.

This study focuses not just on Catholic nuns but especially on Irish Catholic nuns, and the desirability of convent life for Irish and Irish American women must be understood in the specific context of nineteenth-century Irish Catholic culture.[3] For reasons discussed later there was a conspicuous fit between the Catholic institutional ascetic option and the postfamine Irish gender system that praised women for celibacy and singleness. In the United States between 1830 and 1900, and during the period of substantial Irish immigration, Catholic women established 106 new foundations of women religious and grew to a collective workforce of approximately fifty thousand. In New York City alone, the number of women religious rose from eighty-two in 1848 to 2,846 in 1898, not only increasing their own numbers exponentially but also composing the majority of the church workforce.[4] While men and women joined the church in New York City in relatively equal numbers at mid century, the number of nuns grew to almost triple that of the combined number of priests and brothers by 1898.[5]

Irish and Irish American women, moreover, changed the nature of convent life even as they embraced it. Through the immigration experience, the most conspicuous change they wrought was to transform convents from institutions run by elite women to those composed of and administered by women who had been poor or were from the working class. Convents thus became a primary means through which working-class Irish Catholic women gained public power. Moreover, convents provided the Irish Catholic working class with the means to articulate and make manifest its political agendas and social vision.

Irish Catholic nuns considered protecting women and children in their group from the ravages of poverty, dislocation, and racial oppression to be central to their work, and they often did so through direct confrontation with Protestant middle-class women. The most derided and vulnerable of Irish Catholic women in nineteenth-century America was the destitute mother with children; she became the archetypal image of a woman whose mothering in poverty necessitated drastic societal intervention. Because they viewed poverty in the nineteenth century, as today, as a moral problem with roots in particular cultures, Protestant reformers believed that the best strategy for eradicating it was to intervene in motherhood so as to alter the reproduction of moral traits associated with poverty. According to the logic of Protestant reformers, Catholicism either exacerbated or was wholly responsible for the tendency toward dependency, and even alcoholism, evident in the behavioral patterns of the Irish Catholic poor. The sooner children could be removed from the influence of such a mother, community, and religion, the better the chances for thwarting the reproduction of a dependent class in America.

Central to the struggles between Irish Catholic nuns and Protestant native-born women was the question of who would have control over cultural reproduction in the emerging welfare state, and thereby which culture would be reproduced. From the early 1850s through the mid-1870s, Protestant elite reformers removed tens of thousands of poor immigrant children from New York City streets and homes and sent them to Protestant homes in the Midwest. Protestant female reformers were prominent in this movement, and their maternalist politics were central in constructing policy. The practice of taking urban poor children away from their natural parents rested on the normative belief that the American Protestant nuclear family, guided by the maternal devotion of the American woman, was the only proper setting for child-rearing in the American republic. Arguing that poor immigrant women's mothering, left undisturbed, would result in the reproduction of a permanent dependent class, male and female native-born Protestant activists (the "child-savers") legally transferred rights to mother from poor immigrant women to their more fortunate native-born "sisters."

A large workforce of Irish Catholic nuns in concert with a city political machine dominated by Irish Catholic men was able in the 1870s and 1880s to construct Catholic institutions that directly offset such programs. Sisters funded these institutions, moreover, through city taxes. In the name of the "parental rights" of the poor, nuns housed tens of thousands of children in danger of being placed out. By 1885 they directly controlled most of New York City's public child-care system, rearing more than 80 percent of its dependent children while Jews and Protestants controlled 10 percent each. Nuns alone housed fifteen thousand children at a time; perhaps most important, they constructed what I have termed a "revolving door" policy. They took children into their institutions at the initiation of poor parents, and on a temporary basis only, to be returned when parents themselves thought they were financially able to provide for them.[6]

Because Catholic and Jewish children together accounted for 90 percent of children in poverty, immigrant aggressiveness in expanding control over their own children effectively ended native-born Protestant reformers' unquestioned dominance in policy issues. Until native-borns again gained control of city politics in the early twentieth century, Catholic and Jewish activists retained the right to make policy on the institutional level, and they refused to allow native-born reformers to construct a city bureaucracy that impinged on their autonomy.

The two competing systems of child care funded by and incorporated into New York City's public welfare system were fundamentally gendered, reflecting divergent gender systems and values. Both the placing-out system supported by the Protestant middle class and institutionalization supported by Catholics depended on the unpaid labor of women in their respective groups. The placing-out system required the labor of tens of thousands of mothers in nuclear families throughout the country, whereas Catholic children's institutions expanded as offshoots of convents. Women in the Protestant middle class defended their rights and duties in the state as outgrowths of their role as mothers in the home. In contrast, Irish Catholics hailed nuns, including the great majority from working-class backgrounds, as having public authority superior to that of Catholic mothers. In the religious and sexual systems of the Irish in particular, chastity within the church was valued above marriage or motherhood. Women religious commanded a public authority comparable in degree, if not in kind, to that of Protestant mothers seeking public power through their role as moral guardians.

By the mid-1880s tensions between the state's support of these competing systems of child care escalated in city, state, and national debates about the relative merits of the "family plan" versus "institutionalization." Although the debates clearly reflected the class, ethnic, and religious tensions between these competing cultures, they also highlighted, and were fundamentally shaped by, the very different gender systems through which the state expanded social services.

As Protestant and Progressive reformers complained, Catholic institutionalization encouraged dependence on public charities because there was no shame or stigma associated with the institution, and institutions did not means-test their applicants to distinguish between worthy and unworthy poor, the great delineation thought critical to proper methods of Scientific Charity. The result was a massive expansion of public appropriations for private charities. New York City, for example, was expending by the turn of the century ten times more to care for dependent children than any other city in the country.[7]

Irish Catholic nuns used the language and institutional apparatuses of Catholicism to further their own self-interests as well as the interests of Irish Catholics as a group and the city's poor more generally. These sisters did not organize themselves as "working-class" per se but rather manipulated particular traditions in Catholicism to support the poor and resist internalization of middle-class ideology that blamed the poor for poverty. Disparate ideological premises in Catholicism and Protestantism allowed Catholic nuns to support the poor in ways that Protestant Scientific Charity reformers could not.

Part of a community that had survived the famine and also desperate poverty in the United States, nuns, like Irish Catholics as a group, were likely to blame English colonialism and the emerging capitalist economy for the relentless poverty of immigrant communities. The poor, in other words, were not the cause of poverty. Nuns organized their work according to medieval notions about duty to the poor. To deny charity was cruel and "un-Christian," not the hearty tonic Protestant reformers believed necessary to compel the poor to change their moral habits and behavior. Although Catholics supported expansion of the welfare state regardless of the causes of individual misfortune, Protestants as a group feared a large welfare state would, like Catholicism itself, breed dependence and laziness. The extent and kind of reverence by the poor evident at Sister Irene's funeral was in no small way prompted by the fact that nuns were reputed to be more generous and compassionate than other social reformers.

When I began this project I was not only without knowledge of Irish-Catholic nuns but also without an analytic framework for understanding why and how Sister Irene became so powerful, why and how such massive public funding for New York City charities was allotted to a group of young immigrant Catholic women, and why and how they derived such extraordinary public support for their work in the emerging welfare state. I had studied the public activism of many prominent middle-class and elite Protestant women who moved into the public sphere over the nineteenth century and emerged at century's end as social reform leaders active in radical and mainstream activities.[8] Their trajectory over the century was entirely progressive in the historical sense, albeit sometimes troublesome, because their cultural and religious backgrounds often detracted from their ability to understand the struggles of Catholic and Jewish European immigrants.

An occasional story about immigrant nuns was in evidence, suggesting that they, too, participated in some local charitable work. Yet the framework for the expansion of the welfare state in its entirety, particularly women's role in it, has been organized according to the assumption that Progressive welfare politics are explained by the linear, ever-greater visibility and power of white, Anglo-Saxon, middle-class, and elite Protestant female reformers. That Irish Catholic nuns had the kind and extent of public support and power I have indicated remains inexplicable, and that they fundamentally shaped what we have come to call the "welfare state" seems at this point a bizarre, perhaps blasphemous, assertion.

This book, therefore, does more than detail the particular stories and triumphs of Irish Catholic nuns in nineteenth-century New York City in an effort to make American women's history more "inclusive" (although in itself that might be a noble enterprise). It is also a larger call to question a framework for American women's history that renders women of nondominant cultures and poor women as objects of reform but rarely agents able to influence women and men of the dominant culture or the ideological and institutional premises of the dominant culture itself.[9]

Explorations of women's charitable work with other women and children—and, more recently, their work in the welfare state—form much of the backbone for what we think we know about women's public activism in the nineteenth and early twentieth centuries. I began this project in an effort to understand the motivations and activities of a nondominant group of women who provided services for poor women and children in New York City, as did the white, Protestant, middle- and upper-class women presumed to be the central, often exclusive, agents in welfare work. My analytic approach to studying Irish Catholic nuns was, from this project's inception, profoundly shaped by African American women's history, especially regarding questions of cultural resistance, religion as oppositional consciousness, and the strength of nondominant gender systems able to withstand the assimilating pressures of the dominant culture.[10] I assumed that Irish Catholic nuns' activism would be distinct from, perhaps even antagonistic to, that of Protestant elite women, especially because the majority of the nuns in America hailed from working-class backgrounds and worked with women and children of their own religious and ethnic culture. Perhaps principally because of my subjective standpoint as a woman raised as an Irish Catholic New Yorker, I was convinced that a distinctively "Irish Catholic" subculture managed to survive the assimilationist onslaught directed against it since the mid-nineteenth century. I wanted to know whether—and then how and why—nuns played a role in that resistance. Knowing almost nothing about nuns historically before starting the project, I found more evidence of active and deliberate cultural resistance than I dreamed possible. Yet much more surprising was my slow realization that I no longer understood explanations of causality or change over time regarding Protestant middle-class and elite women, except in relation to the activism of Irish Catholic nuns.

The erasure of nuns' activism from American historical memory is a problem linked not only to women's invisibility but also to the assumption that Catholic women generally, nuns in particular, were more oppressed by men in their group than were Protestant and secular women. From the vantage point of the early-twenty-first century we might imagine nuns' position in nineteenth-century American popular imagination as roughly analogous to that of Islamic women today. Whether stated explicitly or not, there exists an ideological hierarchy in which American or Western secular women are considered most "liberated"; religious but not "orthodox" women are less so; and the most religiously orthodox women, whether Catholics, Jews, or Muslims, the most oppressed. Even when these "most oppressed" women insist that they derive power in their societies and cultures in ways that remain unavailable to the "liberated," their protests are dismissed as either naive or the result of "false consciousness." As innumerable works by and about non-Western women have made clear, such a powerful colonialist construct rationalizes the continued subordination of cultures presumed to oppress women.[11]

A similar dynamic was in operation in nineteenth-century America, and we have grown substantially in our ability to understand this tension in relations between Protestant elite and middle-class, native-born female reformers and the Native American, African American, and immigrant women they attempted to "reform."[12] When considering the history of Catholic nuns it is useful to realize that women of nondominant groups have means to private and public power that often remain invisible to the dominant culture. We should be especially careful not to accept uncritically the assessments of their Protestant middle-class and elite contemporaries, who were often disdainful of Catholic women's, especially nuns', allegiance to their larger ethnic and religious culture. Catholic nuns provided many nineteenth-century American Protestants with the most vivid examples of women thought to be better off if "liberated" from the confines of the peculiar gender system that structured their lives. Convent burnings and the popular literary genre detailing the harrowing tales of "escaped nuns" confirmed for American Protestants that Catholic women needed to be saved from the brutality of men in their group. This is not to say that nuns did not struggle for power with

Catholic men but rather that the assumption of their chronic and total victimization by Catholic men masks the dynamics of those gender struggles and does little or nothing to further historical understanding of Catholic nuns or Catholic women.

Much of the literature now available about Catholic sisters makes clear that nuns' marginalization in general Catholic histories has reflected a "victor's history."[13] Men in the church, particularly bishops, have been credited for much of the work, political vision, and commitment to the poor that inspired Catholic expansion of charities over the past century and a half.[14] This is not only, or even primarily, an issue about who has the right to take credit for such work. The work itself, as an expression of nuns' values, theology, and worldview, emanated from a decidedly female perspective. To the degree that nuns lost power in the church, Catholicism was increasingly defined from exclusively male viewpoints. Sister Irene's commitment to poor women and her chastisement of the larger community that punished women for "passion and poverty" reflected a viewpoint distinct from that of Catholic men and Protestant women. Simply put, when women had more power in the church, Catholicism reflected that power. Therefore, it was a different Catholicism than most twentieth-century American Catholics experienced.

Part of the reason that nuns have remained virtually invisible in nineteenth-century women's history is that the measures, or signposts, of their public power do not fit the framework constructed for understanding the public power of Protestant middle-class and elite women during the same period. Nuns' strengths were centered in areas of Protestant female reformers' relative weakness. Both white and black Protestant middle-class women derived public power through associational organizations and claims to public voice, especially through their role as mothers. Nuns' effectiveness, however, was based on an ability to live together and organize themselves as large bodies of single women who lived apart from marriage and domesticity. Convents became powerful collectives for activist labor through the sisterhoods' combined labor power in educational and welfare institutions, their centuries-long apprenticeship traditions and systems in nursing, teaching, and charities, their feme sole legal status and accumulation of wealth under exclusively female control, and their freedom from mothering and the direct controls of husbands. It was a form of public organization for welfare work, moreover, that most Protestant women were unable to construct until the turn of the twentieth century.

Indeed, if we concentrate on the spectacular growth of Catholic convents in America through the late nineteenth century, the dominant narrative of Protestant women's work in social reform through the Progressive Era begins to take new shape. Although histories of "women's" constructions of nursing, teaching, and social work rarely acknowledge the influence of Catholic female traditions in these areas, the roots of these "professions" are nonetheless everywhere entwined with the work of nuns. Settlement work in particular is deemed an extraordinary departure from all tradition in that it allowed Protestant women to live together, apart from marriage and within immigrant neighborhoods, and from that base construct charitable programs. The parallels to convent life are so obvious that the compelling question is not whether the convent served as a model for settlement life but why this parallel goes unanalyzed.[15] That such a connection is not thought conspicuously absent is made possible primarily by our construction of frameworks that render nuns historically invisible.

Yet Protestant women in settlements were not forced to derive power through contestations with men in the Catholic hierarchy. The limits and threats to nuns' power, in other words, were also often distinct from those that threatened Protestant women. Over the course of this study, nuns' relative power to men in their group was threatened most directly by the rationalization of bishops' authority over religious orders in their dioceses. That process of rationalization, however, was uneven. Because the nineteenth-century American Catholic church was unorganized and chaotic, and also because most nuns did not owe allegiance or obedience directly to men, convents and the women in them operated for the most part independent of priests and bishops. A critical factor determining whether or for how long nuns could deflect male control, moreover, was their ability to gain financial independence from the hierarchy. In this study, the public funding of nuns' charitable work helped orders delay substantial loss of autonomy until the early twentieth century.

The study that follows, therefore, cannot be characterized as a "progressive" narrative. Unlike the mainstream narrative of American middle-class women's "progress" from the nineteenth through twentieth centuries, the story of Catholic nuns from the early to late twentieth century shows a substantial loss of autonomy, increased hierarchical male controls, and less public visibility and moral authority. In the early twenty-first century, Catholic women no longer view the convent as a means to substantial public power with relative freedom from men. Catholic women, including former nuns, now judge that they can attain public power; live economically apart from marriage; and devote themselves to teaching, nursing, and social work without submitting to male Catholic institutional oversight at all. Yet tens of thousands of nineteenth-century Catholic women, especially Irish Catholics, paid similar attention to overall context—the costs and benefits of choosing marriage, life as a single woman, and/or the convent—and judged the convent a preferable means to articulate religious and political commitment.

I focus on actors who lived and worked in New York City, making this project a case study in the most obvious sense of the term. Yet the findings of this study go beyond local significance for several reasons. First, the city was the hub of European immigration and a critical center of developing ethnic consciousness and immigrant community life. New York's native-born, Protestant reformers took to heart the notion that America's "gateway" of European immigration placed them in the position of not only controlling the local population but also of "protecting" the country as a whole. New York was thereby central in reform efforts aimed at assimilating and controlling the immigrant population, whether inside or far beyond the city's borders. Although eastern seaboard cities such as Baltimore, Philadelphia, and Boston were the sites of struggles common to those I will explore, New York's sheer size and centrality in the immigration process made those struggles more intense.

Second, the two great "social control" movements conducted by nineteenth-century Protestant reformers, the common school movement and the "child-saving" movement, each met sharp resistance from the Irish Catholic community in New York, resulting in the development of the Catholic parochial school system and expansion of Catholic charities for children. New York's Irish Catholic community, the largest concentration of Irish Catholics in any city in the country, provided national leadership aimed at nurturing resistance to Protestant reformers' efforts to assimilate and control the largely immigrant Catholic population. To do so, Irish Catholics relied not only on nuns as the primary initiators, administrators, and workforce in education and charities but also on the political support of Irish Catholic men in the most notorious of Irish political machines, Tammany Hall.

Third, Protestant reformers from New York City were especially influential in developing national welfare policies in the Progressive Era and beyond. Charles Loring Brace, Josephine Shaw Lowell, and Homer Folks, for instance, all of whom were active primarily in New York City, are seemingly omnipresent figures in the literature on the development of the American welfare state in its entirety. Female Protestant women active in New York City charities through the Progressive Era, moreover, had significant influence on the development of national welfare policy, especially programs for women and children, through the first half of the twentieth century.[16]

Constructing this project as a local study was critical to understanding the interactions and tensions among these groups. The national Progressive forums in which Protestant reformers became powerful at the turn of the century were almost entirely exclusive of the non-elite. The political and cultural power bases of New Yorks' immigrant leadership in charities were located firmly in local, not national, arenas. Indeed, moving decisions about New York City's welfare system at first to the New York State Legislature and next to national forums was a conscious strategy by Protestant reformers to diminish the relative power of non-elite groups that challenged their policies. Gaining prominence in national forums in the Progressive Era not only gave New York's Protestant reformers considerable power in influencing national welfare policy but also made local resistance to their work far less visible and threatening.

The Irish Catholic community in New York City never appeared or acted exactly like its counterpart across the Atlantic, nor did it operate in ways that were replicable elsewhere in America. Irish men's power in New York's Tammany machine was considerable, and Irish Catholic nuns were often ingenious and just plain lucky in thwarting the designs of elite Protestants in shaping the provision of public charities. Although I do not expect that the same story can be told about other cities, I have also come to believe that many Progressive narratives heard thus far might mask as much as they reveal.

1 Republican Mothers and Brides of Christ

> Whereas mothers derive status from their relationships
> with their children down through the kinship structure,
> virgins . . . derive their status by stepping outside the
> bounds of family into public culture. While they may
> not be dependent on their fathers, or be available for
> marriage, their power now rests, within a patriarchal
> society, directly on the extent to which they serve either
> the church hierarchy or the state.
> —Mary Condren

For students accustomed to debating whether the separation of church and state is foundational to the American republic, emphasis tends to center on whether the disestablishment of churches was significant enough to fully divest public and civil society from particular churches' influence. The focus, in other words, is on whether rights to vote, hold office, and exercise individual conscience remained contingent on membership and status in a specific church. Although few would assert that stipulated constitutional rights to freedom of religion created a society in which all religions were accorded equal respect and prominence, many could (and do) argue that the foundation of the American republic ushered in an era of increasing separation of church and state when compared to Puritan theocracies or the establishment of Anglicanism in colonial Virginia.

When we study women's role in state formation of the period, however, the overall trend appears quite different. In America as well as Ireland, women began to organize themselves collectively through groups that used particularly religious rationales to legitimate activism and establish authority in civil society. As the state then incorporated the work they did, especially by providing public funding and legal frameworks for charities run by women, these religious groups were also incorporated into the state. That what we call "the state" changed over time and took on many responsibilities over the next centuries that it had not claimed at the founding of the republic makes the standard church/state debate more complex. By focusing on women and their role in state formation, analyzing the degree to which church and state are linked considers not only what the church/state relationship had been but also how the state itself changed and the degree to which religious ideas, institutions, and people influenced that change.

When we ask why Irish Catholic women became nuns, why American Protestant middle-class women organized themselves in voluntarist groups and as mothers, and why and how both groups shaped the formation of state charitable policies we must look not to Enlightenment ideals or state theory but rather to religious cultures. In Ireland and the northeastern United States between 1800 and 1860 both religious cultures were undergoing rapid and seismic transformation. Women began in each to claim power to shape those transformations in ways that were wholly unprecedented. Culture was for each group of women never merely an ephemeral articulation of values and ideas but rather a shifting constellation of collective traditions and aspirations that could be shaped into material resources and forms. Because Irish Catholic sisters and American Protestant mothers became part of the state, their values became policy, their homes and convents became reformatories, and their modes of authority became the foundation of state bureaucracy. Thus, religion did not become more separate from the state during the nineteenth century but was instead integral to its inception.

Nation, Culture, Religion, and Gender

Although there are innumerable definitions of "culture," the primary focus in this project is culture as associated with group identity and thus those cultural activities that produce and reproduce the group or "culture." As Bruce Lincoln has argued, "Both group [identity] and culture are products of human activity and, what is more, each one is simultaneously product and (re)producer of the other." Among the most important characteristics of "culture" in its relation to community formation is that it "manifest[s] behavior and show[s] a sensibility that those who constitute themselves as members of the group (1) recognize as their own; (2) recognize in themselves; (3) recognize in those people with whom—*as a result*—they feel bound by sentiments of affinity; and (4) recognize as lacking in those from whom—once more, *as a result*—they feel themselves estranged."[1] Members of any community are, moreover, engaged constantly in a cultural process because culture, like community formation, is never static but always in transformation.

Women in both the American and Irish communities of the period were critical to "cultural reproduction," by which I mean those activities, processes, and institutions through which a particular culture and group are reproduced. As in other systems of labor, men and women were expected to accomplish distinct cultural work. Sometimes cultural reproduction included the categories of reproductive work traditionally associated with mothering, including caring for, feeding, teaching, and nurturing children or in general providing the physical labor through which a populace is reproduced. Such kinds of work were especially necessary in caring for poor children, whether reared in convents or individual homes. More broadly, however, cultural reproduction entailed the cultural work evident in constructing large-scale charitable and educational systems capable of reproducing a particular culture even as it was contested externally and internally. Both Irish Catholic nuns and Protestant mothers were thereby involved not only in reproducing a form of culture that was derivative of others' ideas and activities but also at the center of determining precisely what Irish Catholic or Protestant American culture was, and, more important, what it should be, for the goal of reproduction is always focused on the imaginative construct representing the future.

The interrelationship among nation, culture, and religion was at the heart of the dramatic transformations in the United States and Ireland in the early nineteenth century. Americans and Irish were both in the process of creating group identities capable of forming ties for emergent and unified nations or "imagined communities."[2] In the aftermath of the Revolution, Americans attempted to define a common national culture that was simultaneously strong enough to link what had been historically antagonistic or fragmented communities and adaptable enough to withstand the economic and social transformations of the industrial age. The Irish, in turn, were emerging from, and seeking to overthrow, a traditionally colonial state. That both Americans and Irish defined themselves in part against British colonialism might suggest solidarity between them. Because of the politics of religion, however, and its relation to each nation and culture, that was anything but the case.

Irish Catholic women religious of the early nineteenth century were above all at the center of a nation that existed only in the imaginations of those committed to an Ireland free of British rule.[3] The Irish nationalist myth tends to blur distinctions among classes and paint nineteenth-century Irish nationalism as deriving strength primarily from the peasant, Gaelic majority of the population. Yet formal, institutional Catholicism rose in tandem with an anglicized, not Gaelic, culture and from its inception constructed itself in relation to and against both British Protestantism and Gaelic peasant life. Adherents of the new nationalism tended to shape "Irish Catholicism" as a label and culture that could, by virtue especially of Catholics' common antipathy to British Protestantism in Ireland, unify disparate entities into a collective cultural foundation for a future nation. "Irish Catholic" as a hyphenated cultural label thus had most resonance in the nineteenth century in defining people as what they were not. The term signified their refusal, to varying degrees, to pledge cultural and political allegiance to British and Protestant colonizers. In Ireland as well as America, the label *Irish Catholic* spanned divisions between the rich and profoundly poor, English and Gaelic speakers, the avowedly religious, secular and indifferent, men and women, and radical revolutionaries and extreme conservatives. In both contexts the projection of cultural and political unity fashioned by Irish Catholics—and mirrored in the rhetoric of their Protestant adversaries—masked deeply divided populations in constant conflict over exactly who and what should shape the ideological and institutional foundations of communities.

Irish Catholic nuns were at the heart of this cultural project and reshaped it as many emigrated to the United States. Consider, for instance, Mother Mary Augustine, born Ellen McKenna, who joined the Sisters of Mercy in New York in 1849, approximately three years after a small contingent of the order had set off from their motherhouse in Dublin to establish themselves in the city. From the earliest days of her childhood McKenna was encouraged by her family to support the development of Catholicism as a gesture of solidarity with other Irish and against British colonialism.[4]

The link the McKennas perceived between religious and political identity was not new, but the form it took in the mid-nineteenth century was distinct from earlier periods. For centuries before the development of the Irish Catholic nationalist movement in the pre-famine era the British colonial system linked these elements through the Penal Laws instituted after Oliver Cromwell's conquest of the island in the seventeenth century. Under them, Catholics in Ireland were legally barred from worship in Catholic churches, voting, holding public office, or passing on property to heirs. By 1750 Catholics owned only 5 percent of all the land in Ireland.[5] The Protestant Ascendancy, moreover, developed ideo-

logical rationales for colonization and Protestant rule that linked race
to religion. The Irish were judged an inferior race over which dominion
was justified because of the strength of Catholic "barbarism" among its
people.[6] Although individual Irish people could avoid the worst effects of
the Penal Laws by converting to Protestantism, few did. "Allegiance to
Catholicism," the Irish historian Kevin Whelan writes of the eighteenth
century, "became the badge of this historical grudge, and Catholicism
became almost a vast trade union representing the shared interests of
this dispossessed group."[7]

Although avowedly Catholic, the McKenna family shared the class
status and cultural interests of the growing Irish urban and rural middling
classes and thus a distinctive type of Catholicism. Unlike the cultural
milieu of Gaelic-speaking peasants, this wealthier group supported development of an anglicized, formal institutional Catholicism. Not until the
mid to late eighteenth century, when the market economy had nurtured
the rise of English-speaking Irish middle classes in and around the port
towns of southern and eastern Ireland, did the church begin to supplant
Gaelic culture with a new, aggressive formal structure and hierarchy that
would eventually pervade and dominate Irish society. The level of formal
Catholic practice in pre-famine Ireland, including attendance at mass and
participation in the sacraments, was strongest in those areas that were
most anglicized and least dependent on traditional Gaelic culture and
language.[8]

For this middle-class leadership, therefore, cultural resistance as
expressed through commitment to Irish Catholicism was never separate
from cultural accommodation.[9] Indeed, for most of its middle- and upper-middle-class adherents, the support and development of nineteenth-
century institutional Catholicism was an assimilating, accommodating
experience and had dual functions.[10] On the one hand, Catholic leaders
encouraged a unified identity for all classes of the Irish and against British Protestant hegemony. On the other, the promotion of values and institutions supporting a particular version of Irish Catholic middle-class
respectability fortified ideological support for the Catholic elite's right
to rule in Ireland.[11]

Unlike most of the Irish peasantry who remained Gaelic-speaking, illiterate, and only nominally tied to the institutional church, for instance,
Ellen McKenna was sent to school in Waterford at an early age and shared
the classroom with the daughters of families from the highest echelons
of Irish revolutionary politics.[12] Her father was close friends with Dan-
iel O'Connell, and for some time he headed the Catholic Association,
a broad-based and cross-class effort to link the disparate Irish cultural

groups against British and Protestant rule. Unlike the Irish Protestant and Catholic alliance that had been apparent in the Irish uprising of 1798 against British rule, the pre-famine Catholic Association and anti-tithe movements focused more on a cross-class alliance between the Catholic peasantry and the newly formed Catholic middle class. The McKennas' support of nationalist movements against British Protestantism as a co- lonial institution was thus as important to defining their Catholicism as sacramental devotion. In her family's home as in her subsequent life as a woman religious, Ellen lived with the unalterable conviction that to support one was to support both.

Just as modern institutional Catholicism was largely a creation of the Irish middle class and elite, so, too, was Irish convent life. Although the convent served for much of the medieval period as a center for women's education, wealth, and public leadership, Catholic and Protestant efforts to diminish the relative power of nuns through the Reformation and early modern era all but abolished Catholic convents in Ireland. After the Council of Trent in the early sixteenth century, all Catholic nuns were required to make solemn, lifelong vows and observe papal cloister or enclosure, thereby severely restricting their mobility, rights to property, and ability to transact business or interact directly with the larger popu- lace. These contemplative orders, distinguished from "active" orders by enclosed status and a focus on prayer and meditation, were more likely to exist when and where wealthy women could bring sufficient dowries to convents to fund lifelong seclusion.[13]

In the late eighteenth century a shift in Vatican practice created a way for Catholic women to exploit convent life as a means to public power. Although the restrictions on nuns' practice of convent life remained, Catholic women in Ireland and the United States began to form active "religious institutes" sanctioned by the pope but not regulated by the Vatican until the turn of the twentieth century. Because the women did not call themselves nuns but rather "sisters" or "women religious" and made annual, or what they termed "simple," vows, they were not sub- ject to the same regulation of convent life that governed contemplative orders.[14] Catholic women transformed this opening into a cultural and political mechanism for collective organization and public authority.

Ellen McKenna's desire to enter a Catholic sisterhood was not an attempt to leave the world and its strife but rather an effort to play a leading role in shaping nationalist institutional Catholicism. The rise of institutional Catholicism in nineteenth-century Ireland was, perhaps above all, a cultural project in which Irish Catholic nationalists attempted to supplant the institutional structures of British colonialism with institutions of their own. Education and charities, because they decreased dependence on British National Schools and the British Poor Laws, were as central to that nationalist vision as the building of parishes. By 1840, although having a workforce of only 1,600 sisters (in a population of eight million), 81 percent of Irish Catholic convents had instituted facilities and programs for the poor, including sick and prisoner visitation, free schools, meal and clothing distribution, houses of industry, and visitation of workhouses among other activities.[15] Of the convents in Ireland, 84 percent ran schools by 1864.[16] Thus women religious created and administered the central institutions through which a particular version of Irish Catholic culture was produced and especially *reproduced.* The middle class increasingly defined itself through allegiance to such institutions and through them attempted to control and "uplift" the peasantry.[17] Some men in religious orders oversaw the education and care of boys, especially older boys, but charities, as in New York, were to become the almost exclusive province of nuns.

Although from a prosperous family, Ellen McKenna nonetheless experienced the trauma and catastrophe of famine by the mid-1840s, and emigration proved her greatest burden and constant inspiration. When the famine struck just after her father died, she aided the impoverished until the McKennas' own poverty became so great that they were forced to emigrate. Ellen deemed that experience a political "exile" as coerced as a political deportation.[18] And yet she "offered it up" as penance, invoking the forced exile of St. Columba from Ireland:

> Dear St. MacCartin, fearful was the sorrow
>   I offered at thy shrine as penance dread
> Upon this day, long, long ago, for Willville
>   And home, and hope, to seek strange lands instead
> God, merciful and patient, oh! accept it—
>   This hard Columban penance—thus away
> From our sweet motherland, our native country,
>   To wear out life. Oh! aid me still, I pray.[19]

Ellen was no longer in Ireland but neither was she about to "wear out life." When her mother died in New York City in 1849, Ellen and her sister, Julia, both joined the Mercy Sisters in New York.[20]

Called Sister Mary Augustine in religious life, Ellen worked immediately in the House of Mercy, the shelter for female famine migrants, where she interacted with thousands of starving Gaelic-speaking women who had fled peasant areas in western Ireland. At every point in her life thereafter she helped move the order into uncharted areas of charitable work, including the establishment of a home for destitute girls in 1860.

As mother superior of the order after the Civil War she also aggressively sought, and won, public funding through Tammany Hall, thereby enabling the order to branch out into work with children on an unprecedented scale. Ireland, however, was never far from her mind, nor were the British, whom she struggled to "forgive" as an act of charity. The continuing migration of the Irish to North America was for her a constant reminder of the deprivation and cultural losses the Irish were forced to endure and the responsibility she felt for reproducing that culture. As she characteristically observed to another Sister of Mercy in 1878, "It grieves me when the children we bring up know little about [St. Patrick] and about St. Brigid, the glory of Irishwomen; not little, but nothing, I might say about Ireland itself; ignorant of the land to whose martyr courage they owe their faith. . . . Two hundred Irish girls landed together lately to work in the New-England factories."[21]

When Ellen McKenna left Ireland during the famine she joined almost two million other Irish on a cultural journey that would prove distinct from the trials of those she left behind. By the end of the famine Irish Catholics, whether in Ireland or New York City, shared a common history, and the substantial postfamine emigration continued to keep Ireland visible and relevant to Irish American community formation. Yet the Irish in County Mayo and those New York City were also situated in radically different material and political contexts. The Catholic middle class in Ireland found it relatively easy to dominate the surviving peasant culture, but New York City's Irish population at mid-century was dominated by those of peasant origins. What an "Irish Catholic" identity meant in this American urban context was both derivative of Irish culture and wholly new, transformed by a populace that was often interacting with the formal church for the first time and whose political vision could be manifested neither in middle-class ideologies nor simple obeisance to the institutional church.

Among the most important distinctions between Irish Catholic community formation in Ireland and New York was that the Catholic community was not only Irish but also diverse, ethnically and racially. Although the Irish ascendancy in the church's workforce was dramatic, the population's ethnic and racial diversity posed distinct challenges from those faced in Ireland. By 1860 the Irish accounted for 1.6 of the 2.2 million Catholics throughout the United States, thereby dwarfing the French, German, and Anglo Catholic communities. The strength of Irish cultural and ecclesiastic power in New York City was premised in part on the proportion of the church's workforce that was Irish.[22] Fifty-nine (55 percent) of 107 male clergy in 1845 were born in Ireland.[23] By

1865, twenty-three of the thirty-two Catholic parishes in New York City were Irish, distinguished from the rest by the English language spoken by priests.[24] The organization of the city's women religious also reflected Irish dominance as the Sisters of Charity, the Sisters of Mercy, and the Sisters of the Good Shepherd, established in New York City in 1817, 1846, and 1859, respectively, became more Irish over time. Each existed outside parish structures, in contrast to others such as the French Holy Cross Sisters and the German Sisters of Notre Dame that were attached, respectively, to French and German parishes, where they taught and ran charities. The Sisters of Mercy, founded in Dublin, continued to recruit Irish-born and Irish American sisters. The Charity and Good Shepherd Sisters, founded respectively as American and French orders, depended increasingly on recruits in New York who were Irish-born or the children of Irish immigrants.[25]

That the Irish numerically dominated the New York church, however, is not to suggest that all or even most Irish in the city adhered to church authority. The percentage who actually participated in the formal church in New York during the antebellum period has been estimated at roughly half of those who called themselves Catholic.[26] Comparable to the situation in Ireland, the more "respectable" classes were more likely to attend mass, participate in the sacraments, and in general be engaged in active religious practice; the poorest were least likely to be church-going. In part that reflected the religious practices of Irish Catholics before immigration. Yet the poor's indifference to formal Catholicism also reflected class biases built into the American church. The pew rent system in America, for instance, directly excluded the very poor from participation in Sunday mass. For a time at least, poor Catholics crowded the church doors on Sunday morning but were not allowed to enter unless they could pay 10 cents for a seat, some pastors going so far as to rope off empty pews so the poor would not fill them.[27]

The class structure of New York's Irish Catholic community also belied an easy mimicry of nationalist strategies across the Atlantic. Without a substantial middle class to foot the bill for churches, charities, and education, and with an ever-growing number of destitute people from peasant backgrounds constituting the laity, the church was poor and resources were scarce. Prioritizing how best to use the resources of the community, especially its labor and funding, was a constant and unresolved tension, and Catholic sisters were often at the center of such battles.

As they expanded their convents and resources throughout the century it became clear that nuns would provide the primary labor force and leadership in expanding Catholic education and charities. Controlling and supporting the work of women religious was thus critical to designing strategies of cultural resistance in America. Catholics interested in promoting charity and those interested in promoting Catholic education would often be at odds. The scarce funds and labor of the Catholic population made competition a constant tension, often reflecting class tensions within the Catholic community itself. Nowhere was it felt more acutely than in individual sisterhoods, particularly those formed initially to work primarily among the poor.

Not least important, American Protestant nativism and anti-Catholicism reached crisis proportions in the decades before the Civil War and proved among the greatest unifying factors in Catholic, and Irish Catholic, community formation. American antebellum anti-Catholicism was a complex phenomenon and never a simple reflection of what Catholics did or said. Perhaps most important, anti-Catholicism unified Protestants of varying denominations into a nationalist religious culture that transcended the very important, potentially divisive, theological and ideological differences among competing groups. Puritans, Baptists, Quakers, Anglicans, Pietists, Methodists, Catholics, and Jews fought sectarian battles through the colonial period and understood their religious distinctiveness as representing competing worldviews. In the early national period, however, the disestablishment of state religions throughout the United States simultaneously encouraged a pan-Protestantism. In the midst of the Second Great Awakening, when Americans were embracing new religious sects, founding utopian communities, and sponsoring massive evangelical revivals, the label *Protestant* was among the most powerful in defining a nascent "American" cultural identity in real and constant danger of fragmentation. Linking the nation's survival with a democratic impulse born of and sustained through Protestant theology and fear of institutional corruption, major religious figures such as Lyman Beecher could rally crowds and voluntarist groups to frenzied activity on behalf of national cultural security. And, of course, the primary thread linking Protestants across sects and denominations was their emphatic insistence that they "protested" against the Catholic church. By the 1840s and 1850s the massive migration of the famine Irish and the Mexican War provided many Americans with concrete targets for purging the nation of threats to its cultural foundation and manifest destiny.

Thus both the Protestant American community and Irish Catholics defined themselves fundamentally through each other as a negative referent. Americans were Protestant, and truly American, because they were not Catholic; Irish Catholics were Catholic, and truly Irish, because they were not Protestant. Despite disparity and tensions widespread and rife in each community, combating the "other" was a unifying force and activity.

Promoting the distinctive gender system of each culture, moreover, was central to how each community defined itself and imagined its future. Women of each group used religious ideologies to assure their place in relation to family and nation and to enlarge their influence over the public and in the state. When those distinctive cultures met, however, these groups of women would find themselves most frequently at odds, as Protestant, native-born women strove to reproduce a community that was anything but Catholic, while Irish Catholic women held that the survival of their increasingly desperate community depended on allegiance to Catholicism.

Anti-Nun Discourse

Irish Catholic sisters had to contend with anti-Catholicism of all types, but anti-nun literature and Protestant assumptions about nuns' victimization certainly framed their struggles through the century. Specifically, anti-nun discourse constituted anti-Catholicism's most explicit discussion of the superiority of the Protestant gender system, with "liberation" to be found within the home as wives and mothers. In its common forms, nuns were depicted as deluded victims and thereby incapable of understanding their self-interests; their "liberation" from Catholicism, convents, and ascetic life, therefore, was always characterized as a positive good. Like other forms of the pervasive anti-Catholicism of the period, anti-nun rhetoric was premised on the implicit assertion that to Protestantize was to liberate. Anti-nun literature and prescriptive literature defining normative, native-born, middle-class, Protestant womanhood were mutually reinforcing genres, one describing the horrors to which women would be subject should they renounce normative womanhood, horrors not unlike those faced by prostitutes, and the other asserting the glories of lives as wives and mothers.

Protestants had, of course, always used convent life as a negative referent in constructing a normative Protestant womanhood. Reformation Protestants redefined gendered notions of sexual purity to reject celibacy as a desired option for either men or women and certainly not a condition required of the ministry. Rejecting the Catholic insistence on living one's vocation out of the world, ascetically removed from its pleasures and joys, Protestants insisted that vocation must be lived in the world. For men, that meant vocation being centered in work, and, for women, in motherhood. The "holy household" thus constructed made sex, and procreation within it, not a blemish on the soul or character but the means through which "sacred" parenthood, especially mother-hood, could be realized.[28] Protestantism was thus inseparable from a new emphasis on the household as the primary institution through which a gendered distribution of civic and moral authority was ordered. Women were integrated into Protestant societies as mothers, daughters, wives, and aunts—in other words, through their relationship to the male head of household.

In the United States during the early and mid-nineteenth century a shift in gender relations tied to industrialization prompted reorganization and reaffirmation of the holy household. This Anglo, Protestant, middle-class promotion of a newly emergent normative culture was heavily de-pendent upon the ideological gendering of public and private spheres.[29] In industrializing urban areas, white men and women of the Protestant middle-class constructed figurative boundaries that defined and more clearly delineated appropriate forms of male and female work and mas-culine and feminine nature. Male work patterns in urban areas shifted as factories took middle-class as well as working-class men away from home and left women, especially those of the middle class, prescriptively consigned exclusively to the domestic sphere.

The "home as haven" was defined by its difference from the public market where worldly corruption, competitiveness, and chaos reigned. In turn, conceptions of normative femininity and masculinity were in-creasingly defined by the attributes of these ostensibly distinct spheres. Masculinity was associated more emphatically with individualism, com-petitiveness, aggression, and rationality, whereas femininity was increas-ingly constructed as a balance to market attributes. Women were to be nurturing, warm, selfless, irrational, and the moral guardians who, es-pecially through mothering, would provide stability against an outside, public world seemingly devoid of the moral principles Americans were thought to value. Women's exclusion from the public sphere was con-sidered by men *and* women as necessary to protect them from the moral contagion of life outside the domestic haven and therefore ensure their own, and their families', moral and sexual purity. Protestant Americans were to learn moral and religious values less through institutional church structures and more through mothering within the home, thereby femi-nizing the reproduction of religious culture and sacralizing the nature and perception of motherhood itself.[30]

At mid-century these middle-class values were not yet hegemonic, meaning simply that they were not commonsensical to the majority of the American population, and certainly not to groups deemed by racial and class status to be entirely incapable of conforming to them. Promoting this new order whereby Protestant middle-class values were to become the standard against which all people were judged, including women, required a great deal of work. And it was forged not just through proclamation but through contestation.

The massive influx of Irish famine immigrants at mid-century made New York City one stage among many for such contestation. Irish women, whether nuns, sewing women, or domestic servants, neither conformed to the gendered prescriptions of the emergent Protestant middle class nor professed a desire to do so. Their refusal to accept and emulate the gender system of the dominant culture constituted active and deliberate cultural resistance to the value system of the Anglo-Protestant middle class. Irish nationalist consciousness inspired Irish nuns, as well as other Irish women, to flaunt their "deviance" and reproduce in America a culture at odds with the values of the Protestant native-born. That challenge inspired the vitriolic surge of anti-convent and anti-nun literature in antebellum America.[31]

Although the ghost writers of the tales of "escaped nuns" were often known publicly to be overzealous Protestant ministers, the belief that convents were brothels for the use of priests, in which women were tortured and raped, was not limited to a fringe of nativist fanatics. The most popular American version of the immorality of convent life, that contributed by Maria Monk in her *Awful Disclosures of the Hotel Dieu Nunnery of Montreal*, was published originally in 1836 and sold more than three hundred thousand copies by the Civil War, making it second only to *Uncle Tom's Cabin* in antebellum book sales.[32]

Aiding and avenging the abuse of an "escaped nun" was the justification given by the mobs that burned the Ursuline convent in Charlestown in 1834 and attacked the Carmelite convent in Baltimore in 1839. In the early 1850s mobs attacked convents in New Orleans, Galveston, Charleston, and Providence. In Michigan, Massachusetts, Pennsylvania, and Sullivan County, New York, Know-Nothing parties passed or attempted to pass convent inspection laws, and some petitioned for the immediate release of all young American women "incarcerated" in convents.[33] Throughout the 1850s, moreover, "escaped nuns" proved a great attraction for the nativists' lecture circuit, a practice some would resurrect in the 1890s when anti-Catholicism again became widespread in America.[34]

Awful Disclosures set the tone for much of this discourse. In it, Monk declared that she had just escaped from the Hotel Dieu nunnery in Montreal and told a tale of murder, torture, rape, and infanticide in the convent. Young, unsuspecting women, she claimed, were victimized by priests who seduced and impregnated them. The mother superior did not protect them; instead she emphasized their vows of obedience as all-encompassing, requiring them to submit sexually should a priest demand it. Priests, she told the young novices, were incapable of sin. Nuns who objected to sexual coercion would likely be tortured or murdered, and, if pregnant, they would soon preside over the strangulation of their baptized infants, who would be buried on convent grounds. When Maria Monk realized she was pregnant with Father Phelan's child, she wrote, she escaped in order to avoid killing it—or being murdered herself by the priest or mother superior who suspected resistance.[35]

Always implicit, and sometimes explicit, in these tales was a dichotomous opposition between private and public that warned women not to leave the "protection" of the nuclear family or the individual father or husband who held power within it. To willfully leave the domestic setting and enter the public sphere was to invite sexual and moral corruption of unlimited proportions. Just as prostitutes and nuns were linked in reformation literature as cultural deviants who chose not to be defined through a male head of household, antebellum nuns were similarly presumed to invite sexual chaos and victimization through their vow of celibacy.

Burning convents, avenging "escaped" nuns, and demanding convent inspection laws throughout the United States during the 1850s were all premised on an abhorrence of women's public space, free from male control. The "solution" to nuns' quandaries was to unite them with potential husbands or family members. In keeping with the romantic novels of the day, anti-nun literature often focused on the "rescue" of the unfortunate woman by a male suitor who saved her from a life of loneliness and depravity so she could marry him and have his children and through that life find true pleasure and happiness.[36] By portraying nuns as consummate victims, Protestants demanded paradoxically that women conform to imperatives for domesticity in order to find liberty. They were to subordinate themselves legally to some men so as not to be abused by others.

Each major theme in this literature and discourse, moreover, distracted attention from the decisive attack that Protestant middle-class women were making in the emergent women's movement on the premises of the middle-class gender system. Their entry into the public sphere through abolitionist and charitable activities—their fight to retain property in marriage, achieve greater access to divorce, and have access to financial gain so as to live and work apart from marriage—were demands that would grow more urgent as the century continued.[37] At mid-century it was relatively easy for most women to leave convents but very difficult for wives to leave marriages. "Escaped nuns" created a sideshow through which the insolubility of the marriage contract was proven a blessing not a burden. Nuns' ostensible vows of obedience to priests made married women's vows of obedience to husbands seem a better option.[38] And the chaos and brutality nuns faced in the public sphere made the home circle a desirable, if limited, nest of protection from such disorder.

In much of America at mid-century, Protestants, including those who may have rejected nativism and this type of hysterical anti-Catholicism, nonetheless found it difficult to understand nuns. A characteristic depiction of the Sisters of Mercy in New York, for instance, came from an 1871 guidebook of charitable institutions in the city. "However much one may criticize their work, or pity their delusions, they are certainly abundant in self-sacrifices, untiring in toil, and rank among the best of their denomination," lauded John Francis Richmond, a Protestant minister. No doubt meaning to further complement the sisters, Richmond concluded that "if disrobed of the habit of the order, and dressed for the drawing-room, a few of them would be pronounced handsome."[39]

Irish Catholic sisters were, as Richmond's comment suggests, at the very least inscrutable. Their daily lives, dress, behavior, and value systems did not reflect a "true womanhood" in which domesticity and motherhood rhetorically defined duties to family and nation. Nuns' "delusions" invoked Richmond's "pity" because their commitment to Catholicism, through which they established independence from individual men, made them literally incomprehensible as women.

The Politics of Chastity

Why then would Ellen McKenna choose life in a convent? When asked that question on applications for the Sisters of Mercy in New York, McKenna's cohorts were likely to state that they aspired to life in a sisterhood "for the greater Glory of God."[40] Yet such an assertion reveals relatively little about the reasons for the growth of convent life in nineteenth-century Ireland or why so many Irish women chose that life compared, for instance, to women in other Catholic cultures. For several reasons, however, nineteenth-century Irish women on both sides of the Atlantic made such a choice on an unprecedented scale. They, like Ellen McKenna, were likely to see opportunities and possibilities in the life of a religious that rendered other options less desirable.

At the heart of the choice was a willingness to make vows of chastity, poverty, and obedience. Making such vows seems a simple ritual on its surface, but each was made in the context of larger cultural shifts, and none was ever simple. Much of the politics of convent life (by which I mean the contestation of power both within and without convent boundaries) can be understood as efforts to negotiate what it meant to make those vows and to attempt to live by them. In the experience of women committed to life in a sisterhood the vows were not discrete but often in conflict. Negotiating their relative weight and balance in any situation or circumstance was at the heart of convent politics. Analytically separating the vows and what they meant nonetheless highlights the general contours of life in a convent and detractors' complaints against them.

Catholic women made vows of chastity in direct renunciation of the familial roles as wives, mothers, and daughters. The vows enabled nuns to cast themselves as special women sanctioned by the social and religious culture to live apart from the familial obligations most women were expected to honor. Nuns did not derive status because they were women but because they denied themselves the pleasures and fruits of the female body, especially sex and motherhood.[41] And yet the vows were not only experienced as renunciation but also as liberation. As Rose-Mary Reuther has argued, "In its rejection of marriage and motherhood as the Christian norm, asceticism paradoxically suggested that women might now be liberated from their definition by these roles. . . . Women dedicated to asceticism could count on the support of the Church in making decisions against their family's demands that they marry and bear children."[42]

Like Protestant women, Irish Catholic nuns used a legitimating language that drew from their culture and theology to argue for increased power in the public sphere. The "support of the Church," moreover, made it possible for large groups of women, not just individuals, to leave households and support themselves independent of a father or husband. Nuns often described the familial conflicts that became apparent when women wanted to enter the convent as religious in nature, thereby justifying the sisterhood's housing and defense of women as Catholic refuge for zealous souls in spiritual danger. Throughout the Mercy Sisters' annals, for instance, young Protestant women's conversion to Catholicism is noted repeatedly as a reason for tension between fathers and daughters and for daughters choosing convent shelter abruptly to escape the wrath of their fathers.[43]

Such conflicts, moreover, were common to women of lower-class as well as upper-class backgrounds. Within a month of the arrival of the Sisters of Mercy in New York in 1846, for instance, seventeen-year-old

Elizabeth Dirgen pleaded for shelter in the convent, citing her stepfather's "Deism" and hostility to her own and her mother's Catholicism. The father first attempted to take Elizabeth from the convent by persuasion but left "in a rage" when Elizabeth convinced the sisters she would kill herself if forced to go with him. The following day the Mercy Sisters were served with a writ of habeas corpus and forced to appear in court on false imprisonment charges. Dirgen testified that she wanted to remain in the convent, and her mother supported her wishes. The judge ruled that she was of an age to choose where to live. Dirgen joined the order as a postulant in the following year but left shortly thereafter.[44]

Because the substance of nuns' religious vows was oriented toward the cultural legitimation of women's choice to live apart from a patriarchal family, Catholic parents often resisted relinquishing control over daughters as vehemently as Protestants. Conflicts between parents and postulants were expected, and applications for admission to orders asked explicitly if there was parental resistance to the woman's entrance.[45] On the one hand, an applicant could use religious rhetoric to explain that resistance and enlist the convent's support. Convent leadership was, on the other hand, likely to support parental claims and deny entrance to a novice if they believed that aged parents were dependent on that woman's wages or relied on her caretaking for their health. Ascetic selflessness in such cases was considered best expressed in filial devotion.[46]

Church leaders encouraged Irish Catholics to believe that a son or daughter's entrance into the church was a great honor for the family in general, yet Catholic parental resistance was often overt. When the founder of the New York convent of the Sisters of Mercy, thirty-year-old Mary O'Connor, decided to leave Dublin for New York in 1846, her mother beseeched the Dublin male hierarchy to interfere with her daughter's and the Mercy order's decision and convince her to stay in Ireland instead. A Trappist monk consoled and remonstrated the mother before O'Connor's departure: "Dear Mother, did not your Father in heaven favor you most highly in giving you such a child. . . ? He sent to claim His betrothed at your hands, and you surrendered her, with a maternal pang, perhaps, but yet with a ready will . . . from the moment your blessed child crossed the threshold of the temple she ceased to be yours, and became His. . . . Will you not cheerfully suffer her divine Spouse to lead her whithersoever He will?"[47]

The spiritual connection as a "Bride of Christ" was clearly meant to rhetorically legitimate nuns' shift in fidelity from worldly men to the male Christ and male Father. Just as Protestant, middle-class women repeatedly invoked their duty to mother to legitimate a host of activities for which they would otherwise have had little support, nuns' employment of such language was a strategy for power. Yet it was also a capitulation to male dominance. Like Protestant women who accepted the premises of their own gender system but used it to expand their power, nuns ultimately conceded that women should be subordinate to men, whether spiritually or in material ways. Neither Protestant mothers nor Catholic nuns argued that they should be accorded political power as women. Each conditioned their claims on the degree to which it was useful to others, to children and to the male Christ, or in both cases to the larger "nation."

Such strategy was very successful in particular contexts, and yet it could backfire quickly. The question of who had cultural authority to know the wishes of the male Christ and the male Father, or what was best for children, changed over time. In this case the Mercy Sisters, not men of the church, controlled the decision-making process that prompted Mary O'Connor to embark on her journey. Yet the monk's admonition that her mother must "cheerfully suffer her divine Spouse to lead her whithersoever He will" suggested that the journey was not O'Connor's idea but rather an appropriate act of obedience and selfless duty. Although that "worked" for Mary O'Connor in 1846, Catholic men a century later would use the same rhetoric to severely restrict the autonomy and scope of convent life.

Among the most important reasons that so many Irish women chose to become women religious was that committing to a life of celibacy was not a radical break from the sexual patterns evident in much of Ireland. Before and especially after the famine, marriage patterns among the rural middle classes became increasingly distinct from those of the Irish peasantry. Until the famine, the highly communal peasantry resisted pressures either to emigrate or otherwise leave kin and community despite land shortages, overpopulation, and ever-greater poverty. Instead, the peasantry partitioned the land they rented into tiny five-acre plots. These plots were capable of sustaining large families, primarily because the newly imported and relatively nutritional potato could provide a bare level of subsistence to a large number in a small space.

Because of excessive partitioning and a reliance on the potato, peasants were able to set up households fairly easily, and they married young. The rising rural middling classes increasingly distinguished themselves from the peasantry by placing enormous emphasis on consolidating land holdings. Instead of the rampant subdivision characteristic of peasants, only one daughter and one son in each family would be dowered or receive land; to provide for more threatened to dissipate holdings and thereby impoverish the family. Few women in this class could marry in Ireland, and those who did might have to wait through early adulthood for a dowry to become available or for a potential husband's parents to relinquish control of the farm or die.[48] Those deemed superfluous, moreover, such as a second or third daughter, understood from an early age that they would not be given a dowry and therefore had few options for marriage.[49] As this pattern accelerated in the aftermath of the famine the proportion of people who remained unmarried in Ireland through most or all of their lives became very high by international standards despite high levels of emigration.[50]

Depopulation, not reproduction, was the organizing principle in gender and sexual relations in postfamine Ireland. One million deaths from starvation and disease and urgent emigration decreased Ireland's population from more than eight million in 1841 to 5.8 million in 1861. By 1921 Ireland's population was at 4.3 million, roughly half the 1841 census.[51] Subdivision and population growth were unthinkable, given their role in making the poor so vulnerable to the potato crop's failure and contributing to what all classes believed was the death of Ireland as they knew it.[52] For many, sex itself was the culprit in Ireland's ruin, and demonizing sexual behavior outside, or even inside, marriage became a critical foundation for Irish Catholic sexual culture.

Thus as the nineteenth century wore on the respectability of all Irish Catholic women was contingent upon maintaining a sexually chaste lifestyle. Unlike American Protestant middle-class culture, however, Irish Catholic dependence on Catholic ascetic tradition worked in tandem with cultural shifts to position mothers and wives on relatively low rungs of a hierarchy of sexual respectability. In the Irish Catholic schema, "virgins" and nuns came first; widows, second; and wives, because of their continuing sexual experience, third. Once a woman lost her status as a virgin in Irish Catholic society, even within marriage, she would never regain it, nor would her position as mother offset the loss of status entailed by heterosexual experience.[53]

Protestant women, in contrast, continued to be labeled as sexually "pure" so long as their sexual experience was contained within the institution of marriage. American Protestant and Irish Catholic cultures similarly relegated women who had heterosexual experience outside of marriage to the lowest rungs of humanity. Irish Catholics' emphasis on celibacy as a prerequisite for purity, moreover, continued in the American context and was neither a simple reflection of Irish culture nor a simple derivation of Catholic theology. The social context in which Irish Catholic women in New York weighed the relative costs and benefits of marriage prompted many to reject it as a worldly danger, not just or even primarily a question of religious or cultural significance (chapter 2).

For nuns, the vow of chastity was never only one of renouncing heterosexuality but always simultaneously a commitment to live in a community of women throughout one's lifetime and according to rules, and with cultural power, governing convent life. Women's ability, desire, and willingness to make a lifelong commitment to live and work with other women provided the social foundation of a sisterhood. Convent rules were often written with proscriptions against "particular friend-ships," meaning any attachment of particular nuns to each other that might interfere with the general harmony of community life, including exclusive attachments or favoritism, or friendships that led to sexual relations. There is no evidence in extant and accessible New York convent records that particular nuns had sexual relations with each other or that anyone believed they did.[54] Yet the proscriptions themselves suggest that most nuns believed that the nature of convent life was in some respects conducive to sexual intimacy between women, necessitating, for instance, conversations ridiculing postulants for choosing convents based on "infatuations" with women in specific houses.[55]

Lifelong and very close friendships in convents were not just tolerated but assumed and encouraged. Sometimes two or three natural sisters would join the same sisterhood simultaneously.[56] Women who could count favorite aunts or cousins as role models often followed them into convent life and sometimes into the same convent.[57] Friends often entered convents together, as did Catherine Seton and Sister de Walsh of the Sisters of Mercy, who were friends for decades before entrance.[58] Sisters of Charity Irene Fitzgibbon and Teresa Vincent together founded and administered the Foundling Asylum, their partnership/friendship providing the core of continuity through nearly three decades of work and activism.[59] Mother Mary O'Connor and Mother Mary Austin Horan entered the Dublin Mercy convent together and then spent thirteen years in partnership in the New York convent until O'Connor's death in 1859. The two were so close that when Austin died in 1874, O'Connor's body was dug up, and the two were placed together in the same grave.[60]

The Politics of Poverty

The vow of poverty was a complex and even paradoxical one, and balancing that vow with the others was a constant struggle for the orders committed to work with the poor. At base, the vow of poverty was not intended to impoverish women religious but rather to encourage identification with "Christ's poor" in their work and spiritual lives. At times that meant suffering through very real poverty, but at other times women religious risked their work with the poor if they squandered or did not reproduce the wealth they had. Nor did all women religious embrace the same kind of commitment to poverty. Even within orders, poverty was often an unequal experience.

Belying a simple equation between becoming a nun and embracing poverty, entrance into a convent allowed women the opportunity to collectivize wealth with other women and apart from men. Some who formed sisterhoods in pre-famine Ireland were very wealthy, certainly more so than Irish women religious in the postfamine period and much wealthier than the poor and working-class women who joined convents in the United States.[61] Their collectivization of women's wealth made sisterhoods perhaps the most powerful and rich female institutions in pre-famine Ireland. The act of joining a sisterhood moved an individual's wealth to the larger collective, and thus any individual lost their wealth as such. Yet through that action women also removed wealth from the control of men by placing it outside standard patriarchal inheritance structures. When those who dedicated their wealth to the sisterhood died, relatives could not claim an inheritance; the property remained in the hands of the present and future sisterhood.

The premise of sisterhoods' financial autonomy was augmented by the American legal system; nuns maintained feme sole legal status throughout their lifetimes. Married women of the period, who were defined through feme covert, or "covered" in marriage, generally did not hold property individually; the property was assumed to become their husbands'. Key demands of the early women's rights movement focused on married women attaining rights to their own property and wages, to sign contracts, secure loans, or in general transact business. Married women had historically participated in these economic activities as surrogates for their husbands, but in most circumstances they could not yet claim the right to do so without the husbands' permission, and all gains from such transactions remained his exclusive property.[62]

Nuns, conversely, by virtue of their feme sole status, could and did collectivize wealth, incorporate institutions under exclusively female control, derive revenue from business transactions, sign contracts, and secure loans. No men in the church, furthermore, had either legal or cultural claims to such wealth. Their collective financial and legal power thereby enabled women religious to establish female-run and female-owned public institutions at a time when the most radical woman's rights activists in Protestant America rarely lived apart from marriage or owned property of their own. Catherine Beecher herself, the chief advocate of American marital domesticity, noted in 1843 that Catholic nuns had means to power that she did not. "The rich and noble have places provided as heads of great establishments," she wrote, "where in fact they have a power and station and influence which even ambition might seek."[63] That Catholic nuns lived and worked in the public sphere in all-female enclaves long before such organization was perceived as a social or political possibility for Protestant middle-class women was for Beecher self-evident.[64] As an ambitious unmarried woman who spent her adult lifetime with no clear channels through which to engage her talents and education, Beecher lamented that Protestant culture did not allow her to live and work together with other women in a women's community.

Not all sisters shared equally in that wealth and power. European orders, including those of Irish origin, were divided into lay and choir sisters, the latter the more wealthy postulants. At mid-century, poor women who entered sisterhoods would most likely make vows as a "lay sister." Lay sisters were expected to perform the tasks of domestic servants in convents, thereby freeing the choir sisters for "higher" pursuits. In the American context, however, these distinctions quickly eroded, both because there were so few wealthy women with a requisite choir sister's dowry (approximately five hundred pounds) and because lay sisters actively protested against this caste system. As nuns ran greater numbers of educational and charitable institutions throughout the city, they were likely to gain recruits from those institutions.[65] As convent financing shifted from reliance on dowries to reliance on wages and revenue produced collectively by the sisterhood, and on state funding for charities, the ratio of nuns from working-class and poor backgrounds increased proportionately. As Mother Mary Tobin explained the Mercy Sisters' quandary to the archbishop in 1862: "[I]n a country where so few ladies have fortunes to offer . . . either we must keep to the letter of the Rule which says that none shall be received without sufficient dower, and then we die out—or we receive suitable members and support them by means of a school."[66]

Working-class women who entered convents in New York often made clear through intra-convent struggles that their motivations for entering convent life were centered on upward mobility. When they found a rigid ceiling limiting their choice of work, educational opportunities, and overall status within the community they resisted in a variety of ways. Besides frequent verbal protests within the sisterhoods, individual sisters also appealed to the male hierarchy. One Good Shepherd sister complained that lay sisters in the New York convent had "work[ed] day and night like slaves for twenty, twenty-five, and some thirty years." Citing general condescension and separation of choir and lay activities on every level, she held that "when I came here I thought that religious were earthly angels, but I soon found out my mistakes."[67] Three lay novices left the Mercy convent in 1867 in protest of the disparate educational training of lay and choir sisters, prompting considerable tensions in the community for several decades. "Sister Joseph" had asked for time in her novitiate to learn to write. When refused by the mistress of novices, she declared that lay sisters had as much right to continue their education as choir sisters. The convent leadership made clear that lay sisters' future labor required no formal education and that they would not be allowed to teach, but Sister Joseph was labeled as a trouble-maker and asked to leave the convent soon after. Two more novices left in her support, citing abhorrence of the lay/choir distinction in general and Sister Joseph's treatment in particular.[68]

In order to avoid these community tensions and delay a more fundamental resolution of the problem, the Mercy superiors went on periodic recruiting trips to Ireland, where class differentiation within convents remained rigid and lay and choir distinctions were upheld through the 1960s.[69] Presumably, a poor girl born and raised in Ireland was schooled in knowing her place and not making trouble. Similarly, women born and bred in Ireland who wanted to enter convent life but could not comply with standards for choir sisters came to the United States to enter convents. The assumption was that their status in the order would be higher, and their work less restricted, than if they entered a convent in Ireland.[70] Informal mechanisms for distinguishing between higher- and lower-status sisters and work continued in modified forms, with the level of education before entrance rather than class per se most often used as the distinction. Twin sisters who had joined the Mercy convent in 1868 without substantial formal education, for instance, left in 1883 in protest that they were required to run the workroom of a children's institution and could not aspire to positions of higher status.[71]

Despite the resistance of many choir nuns to changing practices and value systems within convents, the overall trend through the nineteenth century was to make class distinctions within orders far less rigid and more flexible than they were in Europe. New York's Mercy lay sisters were successful in gradually winning the abolition of outward indications of class status. In 1878 they were no longer required to wear a distinctive apron that set them apart from choir, and by 1895 community records no longer referred to any single member as choir or lay, even if they were professed as such.[72] Individual work schedules of the New York Mercy Sisters show that while some women worked consistently in high-status or low-status jobs, such as academy teaching or kitchen work, there was often considerable flexibility in work assignments for women over a lifetime. One sister worked alternatively as a first- and fourth-grade teacher in the select school, a kitchen worker, and sewing worker in the boys' home over a ten-year period. Others alternated between sewing, kitchen, teaching, and administrative duties throughout their lifetimes.[73]

Poverty was understood broadly as an ascetic life, denying pleasure and comfort. It also meant, however, critiquing the values and temptations of "the world." As Elaine Pagels writes of early Christians, the identification drawn among asceticism, celibacy, and freedom contained a paradox. The self-restraint required in the vow of celibacy, for instance, seemingly curtailed human freedom.[74] And yet freedom *from* the world, rather than *in* the world, allowed women public legitimacy in offering a critique of society. In 1857, for instance, the Sisters of Mercy recorded a lecture on "the liberty enjoyed by Religious." According to the annalist, Reverend Starrs "showed that real independence is possessed by God alone, that those who have broken away every tie but the loved ones which bind them to Him are in possession of the highest degree of human freedom." As the Mercy annalist wrote, the death of the "self"—the "false self" as nuns called it—also freed one from "a miserable servitude to the customs, fashions and worries which it imposes."[75]

Whether in Ireland or America, legal systems could be similarly characterized as the work of the fallen, and the Mercy Sisters of the nineteenth century often refused to uphold systems they believed to be at odds with their own moral values. The practice of Catholicism, for instance, was illegal in Ireland during the lifetimes of most of the pioneers; their commitment to it was not lessened because of its illegality but intensified as a righteous struggle against oppression. Similarly, the starvation of the Irish by the British during the famine was an entirely "legal" enterprise but nonetheless morally indefensible. As the Irish poor swelled the prisons in New York City and the Sisters of Mercy and Sisters of Charity undertook daily prison visitations, they frequently befriended men and women characterized as irredeemable by native-born Protestants. Catherine Seton, daughter of Elizabeth Seton, the founder of the Sisters of Charity, joined the Mercy Sisters almost immediately upon their arrival and focused her attention for the next four decades on prison visitation. In one instance she became attached to a young man who spent time variously at Sing Sing, the Tombs, and the city penitentiary. After his failed attempt at armed robbery, Mother Seton sent him $5 to aid in his escape and promised to care for his wife and children. When another of her proteges died, she inherited the tools he used for breaking and entering, including jimmies and pistols.[76] That such stories were included in the Mercy Sisters' published annals suggests an unwillingness to accept uncritically the notions of the native-born middle class about exactly what constituted criminality, respectability, or viciousness. In classic Irish fashion it also made for a good, funny story in the midst of tragedy.

For those orders committed to work with the poor in New York City and throughout the United States, financial pressures constantly vied with individual sisterhoods' efforts to keep their work and "mission" focused on those in poverty. Because sisterhoods in America were uniformly poorer than those in Europe, they could not rely on the dowries and legacies of individual nuns to keep convents and charitable systems afloat. In the United States, therefore, all charitable sisterhoods had to devise a means of income capable of sustaining both the order itself and its charitable work. The most common strategy was to create an elite school in which tuition was charged and then use that tuition for the convent's upkeep and charities.[77] The Sisters of Charity calculated the ongoing income from an elite school into their constitution. Although the constitution was on the whole modeled after that of the French Daughters of Charity, Elizabeth Seton and her advisors understood that the order would perish in the United States if it included the French order's prohibitions against working with the elite.[78]

Despite reluctant acceptance of an elite school as a financial necessity in the American milieu, nuns in charitable orders often rejected a focus on the elite while the poor's needs went unmet. Both the Sisters of Charity and the Sisters of Mercy experienced internal disputes when the orders ran elite schools. Many members contended that doing so was at odds with the "spirits" of the particular orders and justifiable only when sheer poverty demanded it. Between 1822 and 1825, for instance, the Sisters of Charity ran a free school and an academy at New York's St. Patrick's to support their work in the city's only Catholic orphan asylum. Yet when a substantial profit from the academy was not forthcoming and sisters were needed to staff the free school and orphanage, they closed the academy.[79] By the mid 1860s the Mercy Sisters' New York superior explained that "opposition to boarding schools is very great, even by those Communities of the Order engaged in them." When one American Mercy community attempted to achieve papal sanction for the exclusion of elite curriculums in all Mercy schools, New York's Mother Tobin protested. She argued that seeking such sanction was "thereby tacitly condemning all who differ from that one house." Moreover, she feared it would mean financial ruin.[80] Yet once the city's Mercy Sisters could rely on substantial public funding for their charities in the 1870s, Mother Elizabeth Callahan closed the order's two academies, "though both were in the height of their prosperity."[81]

One Sister of Charity explained the larger political component of these internal struggles. Nuns' work in the public sphere was expected to convey their values by example and in view of the larger Catholic public. In this way it would mold the Catholic laity's personal and political priorities. According to Sister Mary Dolorita, for nuns to work with the elite while the poor's needs went unmet was tantamount to discouraging the Catholic laity's compassion for the poor. "Years ago, when the Community was struggling with a legion of difficulties," she observed, "the pay school was a necessity." Although she taught at the Mount Saint Vincent Academy for two years "from obedience," she held that "the Academy is frequently a source of disunity among the Sisters; often tends to foster wrong ideas in pupils; and is opposed to the spirit of St. Vincent de Paul. . . . It is a significant fact," she concluded, "that the greatest kindness is shown to the infirm where Academies either do not exist, or are least flourishing."[82]

The Politics of Obedience

Until the mid 1840s, women formed and joined convents in the United States and Ireland with the understanding that women's orders were parallel, separate entities that coexisted with but were not subordinate to local or national male ecclesiastical structures. Convents and monasteries were subordinate to the pope and maintained hierarchies within their respective orders, but most were not subject to the bishops in the dioceses in which they worked. Between their foundation in New York in 1817 and 1846, for instance, New York's Sisters of Charity, like other local convents of the Sisters of Charity, was accountable to their motherhouse at Emmitsburg, Maryland. The motherhouse retained ultimate control of sisters who worked in any specific diocese, and the wishes of local bishops, priests, and laity were considered secondary to the demands and needs of the order at large. Within the motherhouse, a mother general was considered the head officer, followed by assistant mother, bursar, mistress of novices, and various grades of sisters, including professed sisters, novices, and postulants.[83] In each city in which the sisters worked, moreover, internal convent hierarchies were replicated.[84] When nuns established institutions in which they lived apart from the main local convent, particular sisters, usually called sisters superior or head sisters, would be given ultimate charge of the specific institutions. Although the rationalization of the order allowed nuns in localities distant from the motherhouse to govern their own lives and activism in ways responsive to local contexts, they remained ultimately responsible to the motherhouse.

Motherhouse rule was the linchpin in convent autonomy, and through it sisters were able to control the kinds of work they did, their religious lives, and, most important, their ability to make vows of obedience to other women, not to men. Until 1846 the Sisters of Charity did not make vows of obedience to the church at large, but rather to the order to which they belonged, specifically to the mother superior and other female leadership. Obedience, moreover, was interpreted more broadly than simple subordination to specific people. It included the utilization of individual conscience to determine if a superior's actions were in accordance with the larger "mission" or apostolate of each distinctive sisterhood. Dedicating the order and collective lives of nuns to charity, for instance, and to a particular group in poverty—whether orphans, prostitutes, or unwed mothers—meant that those who made vows of obedience were dedicating themselves simultaneously to a religious lifestyle and a lifetime of work. A postulant would learn about the "spirit" or "mission" of the order through intensive study and contemplation of the reasons for the order's foundation, especially through writing by and stories about the founding superior.

When individuals or groups in a community felt that the superiors of an order took action that pitted their obligations to the mission against those to the convent's leadership, community discord could be great enough to induce the majority of professed sisters in the community to impede the reelection or encourage resignation of convent officers.[85] All members of a community, including its leadership, were expected to respect a broad definition of "obedience" that acknowledged the entirety of convent life as shaped around particular "spirits" and "missions" and was based on the community's collective experience, education, and mutual obligations.

On an individual level, women religious who rejected the tenor or politics of convent life could simply leave. Despite the dramatic "escapes" so vivid in anti-nun literature, no active orders were "enclosed," and therefore no women within them were barred from leaving at will. Sisters in active orders took yearly "simple vows," not lifelong vows, and therefore could leave convents without a formal repudiation of those vows. In practice, however, the system of novitiate, postulancy, and final profession, which lasted anywhere from three to five years, was expected to weed out those who either did not want to commit to the order for a lifetime or were considered unacceptable by the professed sisters, who would have the final vote in chapter meeting to recommend continuance or expulsion.

Because both lay and choir sisters were expected to perform hard manual labor in the American context, poor health prior to profession of final vows could invite expulsion in a rather abrupt manner. Lay and choir sisters might also be considered either not "zealous" enough in their spiritual lives or too zealous, considered by communities as imbalanced in their religious and charitable commitments. Women who wanted to lead an ascetic life to the degree that their health suffered made poor workers and were considered inappropriate for charitable communities' labor needs. Sisters sometimes left in groups and in specific protest of their treatment or the general direction of the sisterhood's activism.[86] Personality conflicts or particular temperaments also might ensure a community's rejection of a novice. In 1851 the Sisters of Mercy asked a young postulant to leave "owing principally to an occasional outburst of temper which [was] often found to interfere with peace and charity."[87]

It was more rare for nuns to leave, or be asked to leave, after full profession, yet virtually every convent in New York experienced such departures. Some found the overall stress and amount of labor too great, as did Mother Superior Mary Tobin of the Sisters of Mercy, who left without notice in 1864 after years of struggling with poor physical health and the sisterhood's near bankruptcy.[88] A wide range of what nuns deemed poor mental health also appears as the reason for particular sisters' expulsion or voluntary departure, but labels of "lunacy" and "melancholia," for instance, were so vague in the nineteenth century that they easily veiled personal and political disputes. One Sister of Charity spent years contesting the order's expulsion of her on charges that she was "crazy." She claimed instead that her frequent disagreements with the superiors of the convent prompted them to accuse her unjustly.[89]

On both an individual and collective level, obedience demanded a selflessness that required extraordinary ascetic discipline. As Mother McKenna advised young Sisters of Mercy about to make their vows in 1873, that sacrifice was intended to benefit both the soul and others in the world:

> The easy way is the hard way, paradox though it seem. When we don't spare ourselves, when at any cost we do right, God helps us sensibly; we revel in grace and, consequently in spiritual happiness . . . I pray God that

your heart and soul may be devoted to the poor, sick, and that serving the Lord in His poor, He may make you rich in graces and blessings. . . . On this wondrous eve of your holy profession (April 16, 1873) my heart will not rest unless it speaks some of its thoughts. . . . In God's name, let this one grand act of your life be complete. . . . [T]he sacrifice of the soul . . . has to be made piecemeal, though offered entire. Inch by inch this sacrifice is exacted by little trials, more galling than great ones. To say nothing when we would naturally say something sharp; to do simply as we are told, without objection or remonstrance, for the sake of the sacrifice obedience involves; to seem cheerful when the heart aches, to be kind in return for unkindness, to save others all the pain and trouble possible, to bear and forbear—these efforts will be sacrifices.[90]

Yet Mother Augustine McKenna was also supremely conscious of the need to balance obedience against ambition and assertiveness, particularly when that ambition was in the name of others who needed her help. As the chief architect of the order's work with children, then Sister McKenna wrote out a separate promise to herself and God in 1860 and placed it at the back of the book that held her original vows. She showed it to no one, but other Sisters of Mercy found it and buried it with her.[91] Knowing that even a suggestion that the order would move into work with poor children would provoke the archbishop's anger, Mother McKenna wrote:

In the name of our Lord and Saviour, Jesus Christ, and under the protection of His Immaculate Mother, Mary ever Virgin, I, Sister Mary Augustine, for the love of His Sacred Heart, do resolve, but not vow, to suffer all the blame, shame, and humiliation, toil, trial, and trouble, that it may be God's will to permit, in order to establish a home for homeless children. I protest that, in all that concerns it, I rely solely on the assistance of God and the guidance of the Holy Spirit, especially in what will be required by this resolution; and further, that I will not do anything in relation to it except in obedience.[92]

As Mother McKenna's resolution suggests, obedience was hardly passivity. Yet by invoking the wishes, as she understood them, of God, Jesus Christ, the Virgin Mary, the Sacred Heart, and the Holy Spirit, Sister McKenna was obedient to those and to what she determined mattered most. Her obedience to the spiritual authorities above was constructed in such a way to ready herself for the worldly battles to come. And yet Mother McKenna did not share her resolution, even with those in her order who were similarly committed to this kind of work, much less to the larger Catholic public. To whom or what one was obedient thereby changed over time and shifted in particular contexts; only in the most restrictive of environments did it constitute an unthinking and inexorable submission to another's will.

And yet few even in the Catholic community understood fully what either Mother McKenna or other sisters did and thought on a regular basis. Indeed, the single most salient political limitation affecting sisters' overall power in nineteenth-century America was their relative lack of public voice. Whereas white, Protestant, middle-class women increasingly legitimated their claims to public power through a set of rational discourses promoting their cause as women or as mothers, nuns were reluctant to promote their causes through public discourse.[93]

The effect of that limitation was both far-reaching and paradoxical. The most powerful women in the church, including the founder of the Foundling Asylum, Sister Irene Fitzgibbon, demanded that they be treated, and nuns under their guidance should treat themselves, as "old shoe[s]."[94] Consistent with an ethic of ascetic selflessness, Sister Irene's pronouncements should not lead historians to assume that these ostensible "old shoes" lacked substantial power. And yet their reluctance to claim that power as such, especially in public and to the larger community, proved decisive in public arenas in which the Catholic hierarchy or Protestant native-borns contested that power. Women religious were thus most vulnerable when discussion of themselves or their work moved to public arenas. Nor did this limitation affect only nuns. Because they were the female leaders in the Irish Catholic community, their unwillingness to spar publicly with Catholic men or Protestant native-borns made the relative power of Irish Catholic women as a group, and the causes they championed, similarly vulnerable to their posture of collective selflessness.

The Politics of Anti-Catholicism

On its surface, it might seem that all Catholics, and certainly all Irish Catholics, had equal stakes in combating anti-Catholicism in America. Yet the process of choosing battles and appropriating resources constantly engaged diverse and sometimes antagonistic components of the Irish Catholic community and ultimately was both shaped by, and reshaped, power within the community. The first major battle illustrating such a dynamic, and involving sisters, religion, and the state, stemmed from the "school wars" of the early-to-mid-1840s. Because Archbishop John Hughes wanted to construct a system of Catholic schools entirely separate from the public school system, he appropriated resources, not least important being the labor of the Sisters in Charity, in order to further that goal. Although many in the New York Catholic community were critical of the anti-Catholicism evident in the public school system, far fewer were willing to prioritize building a privately funded educational system in order to offset its influence.

The Catholic community's collective critique of public schooling developed in earnest by the 1830s. Both public schooling and the burgeoning charities of the city were influenced by the pan-Protestant activism evident in the early nineteenth century. Until that time, schools in New York City were publicly funded but religiously distinct, so Catholics received funding for their schools on an equal basis with Quakers or Anglicans. The "Common School" movement was at its heart an effort to create an education for children that was acceptable to most groups along the Protestant spectrum and thus carve out and reproduce through children a national religious culture capable of unifying and transcending religious discord. When funding was rescinded from particular religious schools in New York City to fund the Public School Society, the rationale given was that to fund any one church was "sectarian" and thereby at odds with the separation of church and state.[95] In contrast, funding a school with religious teaching agreeable to many Protestants was constitutional because the school was deemed "nonsectarian" because it did not reflect the beliefs and practice of any specific Protestant sect. No one imagined that religious teaching would be absent in children's publicly funded education but merely that the religious substance of their education should not privilege a particular Protestant sect or denomination.

Such a construction of religious neutrality, however, rarely sat well with Catholics. As Irish Catholics immigrated en masse, many found its contours analogous to the mandatory British Protestantism taught in Irish national schools, not least because the state increasingly required children to attend. Targeting poor immigrants and their children, New York's city council passed a resolution in 1832 making attendance mandatory for the children of all families partaking of city charitable relief. Referring specifically to the immigrant population in New York, the trustees of the Public School Society supported the sentiment, asserting that without an education, children could not learn the values of responsible citizenship in a democracy, and thus parental rights must be curtailed accordingly. "[I]t becomes a serious and important question, whether so much of the natural right of controlling their children may not be alienated," they argued, and made secondary to the state's interest in rendering children "safe and consistent members of the political body."[96] The society assured the public that such a requirement would "affect but few native citizens." The law was directed instead at European immigrants, the trustees citing the "objectionable manner in which these children are employed on their arrival here" as the primary reason for the law.[97] Presaging the advent of the truant officer, evangelical volunteers canvassed poorer neighborhoods and searched for vagrant children, whom they brought to the public schools with or without parental consent.[98]

Catholics, however, were anything but united on how best to address this cultural threat or whether and how the material resources of the community should be allotted to it. Some Catholic parents and priests in New York City protested that explicit ridicule of "papists" and "popery" made Catholic children unwelcome in schools and turned them against the religion and culture of their parents.[99] Others held that the active role of the state in compelling their children's education under a state-controlled public school system smacked of state Protestantism in both the German and Irish homelands, something they were unwilling to suffer through again in America.[100] Poor Catholics often resisted sending their children to public schools for economic, not necessarily ideological or religious, reasons, arguing that their children's labor was needed to supplement the family economy.[101] Few among poor Irish-born parents had received even a modicum of formal education. In Ireland in 1830, for instance, fewer than 40 percent of all children had been at school at all, even for very limited periods.[102]

The great irony of the anti-Catholicism expressed during the school wars, and Archbishop John Hughes's orchestration of the community's response to it, was that each helped Hughes shore up a profoundly conservative Catholic agenda for decades to come. Anti-Catholicism itself was perhaps the most powerful tool John Hughes had in unifying and ordering New York's Catholic community, and he worked hard to sustain it, inflame it, and make it visible publicly. In many respects that was not difficult because Hughes was avowedly committed to the type of Catholicism that informed Protestant nightmares. As an ultramontanist, he believed that all church authority flowed from the top down, from popes to bishops, bishops to priests, and finally to the laity. (That women religious did not have a clear place in this hierarchy would soon compel Hughes to contest such an anomaly.) As a bishop in Philadelphia, Hughes made his mark before coming to New York by destroying a trustee system whereby the laity had direct input into church governance.

As bishop and then archbishop of New York, and through controversies such as the school wars, Hughes became a master at antagonizing Protestants in order to drum up support for policies that the Catholic community would have otherwise rejected. Lessening anti-Catholicism was often at odds with his larger goals in that he feared Catholic assimilation into Protestant America and thus held that compromise and cooperation were in themselves dangerous. Hughes refused, for instance, to cooperate with the Public School Society when it finally invited Catholic input on the expurgation of references to "papists" and "popery" in school textbooks.[103] Despite his initial insistence that "neutrality" of religious influence would be acceptable, he later refused to support a school system that some proposed should be entirely free of religious education, charging that such a system would be "Godless" and promote the interests of "irreligion."[104]

Hughes's purpose was certainly not to make public schools amenable to Catholics but rather to convince Catholics that their only option was to keep their children apart from public schools. "Whether we shall succeed or not in getting our proportion of the public money," he wrote in 1840, "at all events the effort will cause an entire separation of our children from those schools—and excite greater zeal on the part of our people for Catholic education."[105]

Hughes's prediction was optimistic. A substantial portion, perhaps a majority of Catholics, refused to support his efforts to develop a separate Catholic school system. Only a third of New York Catholic voters, for instance, supported Hughes when he organized the Catholic Party in the fall of 1841 to influence state educational legislation. Catholic public school supporters then argued that the very success of Catholic efforts to eliminate bias and more firmly control the education of Catholic children made the burdens of supporting a separate Catholic school system unnecessary. In wards that had a strong Catholic majority, public schools were soon taught and administered by a majority of Irish Catholics who provided an educational environment that was less explicitly anti-Catholic.[106] Given the education that could be had for free in public schools and the enormous difficulties of maintaining a school system dependent entirely on private funds, some priests refused to maintain a Catholic school at the expense of other needs of the parish.[107] Calling a school "Catholic" and having it run by Catholics, moreover, did absolutely nothing to lessen poor parents' reliance on children's wages, and parents often ignored Hughes's pleas to send the children to Catholic schools.[108]

Hughes nonetheless began to steer all possible community resources toward the development of a Catholic school system. Critical to this effort was his attempt to staff the schools. Throughout the late 1830s there was no male religious order in the city and only one female religious order, the Sisters of Charity, that ran several small select and free schools in addition to doing charitable work.[109] Stymied by the absence

of a labor force to run the schools, Hughes set his sights on administrative control of the Sisters of Charity. By 1841 he began to contest
the jurisdiction of the motherhouse over the Sisters of Charity within
the New York diocese and proposed that they be made subordinate to
his authority. Hughes broached the subject with, among others, Mother
Xavier Clark, superioress at the motherhouse of the Sisters of Charity
in Emmitsburg, Maryland, priests throughout New York, and the archbishop of Baltimore.[110] By 1844 the Sisters of Charity in New York were
abuzz with rumors about organizing an independent order in the city
under Hughes's direction, and Hughes boasted to Mother Xavier that he
believed that Rome would support his governing the Sisters of Charity
according to the needs of the diocese.[111] Finding absolutely no support
for his proposal, however, the rumors remained just that.

Ultimately, the sisterhood's reluctance to defend itself to the public
in ways that could be interpreted as self-promotion undermined its ability to maintain autonomy, as Hughes broadcast his complaints about
motherhouse rule to the larger local and national community. The direct issue that began the public controversy was a circular distributed by
the Emmitsburg motherhouse in 1845 to Sisters of Charity nationwide,
directing that they withdraw from the care of male orphans. Like many
other constitutions for communities of women religious, especially those
of French origin, their rule stipulated that they work only with members
of their own sex. The motherhouse was considering affiliating directly
· with the Daughters of Charity in France, which required that their rules
be consistent with the French order. In the schools in which the Sisters of
Charity worked in New York they taught girls only and were thereby in
accord with the provisions of their constitution. In reference to orphans,
the Charity Sisters in many cities, including New York, had historically
ignored their rule on this point because there were no male religious to
do such work.[112] Most Sisters of Charity in the United States responded
to the circular by hiring extra matrons to care for boys and retaining administrative control over their respective orphanages.[113]

Upon hearing of the circular, however, Hughes reframed the issue for
public consumption, arguing that the rule of the motherhouse threatened
charitable works in the New York diocese.[114] "The report that the male
orphans are to be ejected from the Asylum, is heard with consternation
by the Catholics of this city," he wrote to the motherhouse, thereby
accusing the sisterhood of literally throwing the male orphans on the
street, a suggestion made or contemplated by no one. As a solution and
a seemingly secondary concern, Hughes again suggested "retaining the
sisters now in this diocese (who choose to remain), with the consent of

their superiors to a transfer of their obedience to the [bishop]" so that "those who owe obedience shall be more immediately under the supervision of those to whom it is due." He continued, "That this supervision can extend from Emmittsburg to New York in any practical or efficient sense, is impossible," and "unauthorized interference, even when the object is a sound one . . . often does more harm than good, and at best anomalies and anarchy are its natural results."[115]

In the ensuing months the motherhouse attempted to retain authority through a variety of tactics and appealed to other priests and bishops for aid. Hughes's rationale for the subjugation of the order under his jurisdiction was far more threatening than his direct influence over the sixty Sisters of Charity then working in New York. Citing himself as the authority to whom obedience was "due" was a logical extension of Hughes's ultramontanist views in that women religious were now to have a place in the hierarchy below bishops. As such his claim made the Sisters of Charity nationwide immediately vulnerable to subordination under local male hierarchies everywhere. "[W]e consider this step of yours as calculated to inflict a deep and dangerous wound on the community" wrote Father Deluol, adviser to the motherhouse, "and if the example be imitated (every bishop in the Union has the same right), we would consider it mortal."[116]

Priests in New York were also critical of Hughes and emphatic that his claim to jurisdiction was entirely without precedent. Father Nicholas O'Donnell of Brooklyn conveyed to Mother Etienne the substance of the meeting Hughes held with New York priests on the subject. "The bishop would wish to have the sisters dependent of himself so that he should be the centre of power and authority to which they must have recourse. . . . [H]e cannot insist on it," O'Donnell maintained, "without arrogating a jurisdiction which no other bishop claims."[117] Emmitsburg declared that they would allow the sisters to stay in New York, but only under the condition that Hughes accept their authority without interference, claiming that his previous behavior was "at variance with common justice in regard to the Mother House."[118]

Hughes's genius was in using the specter of anti-Catholicism in his public charge that motherhouse rule would result in sending boys directly to "Protestant" charities. Hughes warned the motherhouse that he would take no blame for the disaster, and should the motherhouse accuse him, he promised, "I shall be able to prove myself acquitted."[119] He thereby framed the debate in a binary fashion, with sectarian dichotomies organizing his rhetoric. His rule was good for Catholics, and motherhouse rule, even if well-meaning, was good for Protestants. In regard to the question of jurisdiction, he stated his objections and terms once again: "Unless there be some change in the way of understanding between the bishops and [the sisters'] superiors, much of the good they have done will come to nought, perhaps eventuate in evil."[120] Motherhouse rule was thus variously described as disorderly, anomalous, anarchic, and "evil," all of which were to be made good when Hughes had control.

Mother Etienne's only response to Hughes in regard to jurisdiction was to affirm the community's rights under the accepted norms of religious life. She held that "it is not in accordance with the spirit of our Rules and Constitutions to consult the several bishops under whom our sisters may be placed when we deem it necessary to remove them." And "since it has never been the practice," she remarked further, "I hope you will pardon us for adhering to the spirit of our Holy Founder."[121]

Hughes responded to the motherhouse's further efforts to administer the New York sisters by demanding that all the Sisters of Charity in New York leave the archdiocese immediately. "This kind of business," he stormed, "has gone far enough." He further noted, "I shall tolerate no officer of a religious community, male or female, exercising without my previous advisement and consent, powers of disturbance and embarrassment, such as have been exercised, conscientiously no doubt, in my diocese of late."[122]

Hughes could allude to no specific act of disobedience, given that the sisters did not owe obedience to him. He held, nonetheless, that the very nature of the motherhouse's independent action, the very autonomy on which female convent life was based, was the point of contention: "When they give a meaning to their Rules which implies that I shall modify, change, almost overthrow works of charity with which they have been connected, I must complain. When they threaten to withdraw them and throw all such works on my hands by a given day . . . I have additional reason to complain. When they assume a tone of dictation, which I cannot admit except in a lawful superior, I must resent it. All this they have done."[123]

The motherhouse of the Sisters of Charity finally lost the battle, as other motherhouses were to lose similar contests over the course of the century. The sisterhood's leadership feared Hughes's ability to sway public opinion and the likelihood of bishops nationwide being brought into the debate more than they feared losing control over the New York convent. In early December of 1846 the motherhouse recalled the sisters to Emmittsburg but granted dispensations from vows of obedience for any who chose to remain in New York.[124] Roughly half of the sixty-two

Sisters of Charity in the New York archdiocese remained to form a new community under Hughes: "the Sisters of Charity of New York."[125]

Archbishop Hughes's larger intent in the takeover became clear quite soon after the new order was established. On December 31, 1846, Hughes presided over the elections in his new community, which formally abided by the rules and customs of the Sisters of Charity of Emmitsburg except that their vows of obedience were made directly to him. This transfer of obedience not only made the sisters accountable to the archbishop but also truncated the larger connection between the community's commitment to "mission" and vows of obedience. Despite his insistent rhetoric in 1846 equating motherhouse rule with the "wreck of charities," Hughes's agenda was always more centered on the development of Catholic education than on charitable work. In 1849 he objected to a second term of office for Mother Elizabeth Boyle, who had been both the superior of the New York mission and the leader in the order's charitable work with children in New York, and relegated her instead to "the last place in the community."[126] He then replaced her as superior of the order with Sister Mary Jerome Ely, who had worked for seventeen years in St. Peter's elite school and is credited in convent histories with expanding the sisterhood's role in Catholic education. Mother Jerome, moreover, was reelected seven times and held the position of mother superior of the order for twenty-four years, or until Hughes's death, a practice at odds with the Sisters of Charity's original constitution, which stipulated, as did many others, that mother superiors could not serve for more than two consecutive terms of three years each.[127] Throughout Mother Jerome's tenure, and despite the unprecedented and severe poverty of the city's Irish famine immigrants, the order became almost exclusively involved in education, staffing the girls' departments of 80 percent of the city's Catholic free schools in addition to running tuition-based academies. When an interviewer asked a young Sister of Charity in the mid 1860s about the order's work she mentioned some charitable work but stated unequivocally that their "mission" was centered on teaching.[128]

In the larger politics of combating anti-Catholicism, shifting the Sisters of Charity's labor toward education disproportionately addressed the needs and concerns of middle-class and elite Catholics for several reasons. Those who were wealthier could afford tuition and thus had access to academy training, whereas poor children had access only to Catholic "free schools." What resulted was a tiered system that Jay Dolan contends "tended to separate Catholic adolescents along class lines."[129]

Perhaps more obviously, the inability of an educational strategy to meet the needs of poor Catholic immigrants was glaring and became more so as famine immigration began. What had been a relatively poor immigrant population became a painfully destitute and miserable congregation of famine survivors, and Hughes's efforts to funnel Catholic funds and labor power into the Catholic educational system seemed to Protestants and many Catholic observers a heartless dismissal of the depth of misery around him.

What he failed to perceive or acknowledge was that the hundreds of thousands of destitute Irish who arrived at the New York port through the famine decade held only the most tenuous ties to the formal Catholic church, and his intransigence in ignoring their needs only distanced them further. Not least important, steering the community's labor power and funds toward education and away from charities left charities, particularly work with children, open to native-born, Protestant reformers. From the vantage point of the mid-to-late 1850s, the threats that Catholics, especially poor Catholics, perceived in the mandatory public schooling of their children seemed in hindsight like petty annoyances compared with the dangers the "child-savers" posed to civil and religious rights.

As the motherhouse had expected, the controversy had resonance far beyond New York City, revealing sisterhoods' vulnerability and suggesting a strategy for bishops to employ should they desire more immediate control over women religious in their diocese.[130] Women religious in orders in which motherhouses were still authoritative found themselves vulnerable to separation from the motherhouse for the pettiest of complaints by priests and bishops.[131] Bishops also actively recruited "diocesan" communities, meaning those who had no recourse to motherhouses but were instead under the authority of individual bishops. In order to deter these groups from any larger associationalism or collective organization, bishops restricted their mobility outside each diocese. When the Josephite Sisters attempted in 1847 to have a meeting of their various communities in the United States, the bishops of Buffalo, Philadelphia, Brooklyn, and Wheeling kept sisters from attending. Each group then became a distinct diocesan community.[132]

The Sisters of Mercy in New York and nationwide found themselves in similar circumstances. Without a central motherhouse, they attempted in 1873 to communicate with other Mercy convents throughout the United States to establish a "uniformity of Customs." When the New York Mercy Sisters attempted to leave the city for the meeting, Archbishop John McCloskey, Hughes's successor, sent back word to the convent through their advisor, Father Clowry: "Tell the mother . . . to mind her own House and let other Superiors mind theirs."[133]

Conservative bishops' agendas to promote a separate, parish-based Catholic educational system and subvert the autonomy of female orders were mutually reinforcing and framed charitable nuns' struggles throughout the century. Women religious in charitable orders were always in a more tenuous position than were sisters who were affiliated with educational orders. Overall, there is no evidence that orders whose missions were centered on education were pushed reluctantly into charitable work, yet there are countless examples of charitable workers pushed into education. The push to education, moreover, was rarely in terms that would augment the collective power of sisterhoods. In elite schools founded and administered by nuns, the orders retained administrative and financial control over these institutions. Parish-based education, however, subordinated nuns to priests, especially to pastors who headed each parish, thereby integrating nuns into the lowest rungs of the male church hierarchy. Any funds that sisters received to do such work, moreover, were sufficient only to pay for individuals' most basic costs of living and thereby did not provide a substantial financial base either for charitable work or convent maintenance or expansion.

In 1883–84 the national Third Plenary Council of Bishops, usually regarded in Catholic histories as the turning point in establishing a national "ultra-conservative" agenda for decades thereafter, announced two resolutions that made female orders' autonomy in charitable work more precarious.[134] The first was the demand that every parish in the nation establish a parish school within two years, thereby necessitating nuns' use as cheap labor without which the plan would be financially impossible. Second, the council asserted that all new orders founded within the United States or coming from Europe were to be governed as "diocesan" communities and were thereby under the jurisdiction of local bishops.[135]

————————

The subordination of the Sisters of Charity of New York under episcopal rule made clear to sisters throughout the country that they were vulnerable to the church's male power. Yet it also taught them a lot about strategies to protect themselves against similar assaults. Few bishops were as aggressively bent on subordinating women religious as John Hughes, in no small part because famine migration and Catholic migration from Germany would keep the church chaotic and growing. That chaos created a substantial gap between the potential and real control of women religious, and sisters did everything possible to enlarge the gap, wrest control from bishops, and expand their charitable activism. The Sisters of Charity of New York, for instance, became an extensive phalanx of charitable workers who would shape charities and then the public welfare system itself in remarkable ways. Using their educational system, they nurtured an expanded convent workforce that after the Civil War would integrate itself into the city's public welfare system. The shift made them subordinate to men in the state, but it also proved, for a time at least, a much better bargain than dependence on private funding and men in the church.

Certainly, when Ellen McKenna considered which order to join in 1849 the work that each was able to do was of primary concern. Sister Mary Augustine McKenna took vows as a Sister of Mercy in New York, who, unlike the Sisters of Charity, were able to focus on famine migrants, especially single women. In doing so Sister Mary Augustine placed herself at the center of Irish Catholic cultural reproduction because ties between "single" women buttressed the economic, cultural, religious, and physical survival of the Irish people. For McKenna as for most of the Irish, the famine, the severe and unrelenting suffering of millions of people, and the sheer magnitude of energy exerted to survive as a people and a culture, took center stage.

2 Good Girls, Bad Girls, and the Great Hunger, 1845–70

> The Catholic maiden of advanced age has a place as
> secure, and a sphere of action as respectable in Catholic
> society as the married woman, nay the very spirit and
> effect of her religion is to ensure for her increased respect
> on account of her vocation to celibacy. . . . If she is
> favored with a vocation to a religious life . . . affection,
> honor, and countless opportunities for the exercise of
> angelic virtues and charities await her!
>
> —*Catholic World*, 1871

No event in modern Irish history was more important than the famine, and no group of people was more important in escaping it than Irish single women. By the end of the decade of the Great Hunger a million Irish people had starved to death; up to another two million, a quarter of Ireland's pre-famine population, had left Ireland forever.[1] More Irish-born people lived in New York City by 1855 than in any city worldwide, including Dublin, and many more moved through the New York port on their way to other destinations. Unmarried women were the central actors in this saga of how a desperately poor and starving people were able to leave a ravaged country; embark on a dangerous journey across the Atlantic; and find jobs, housing, and ways to send money home to stave off the starvation of friends and kin.

At first glance, characterizing women who were unmarried and without children as central to a people's physical and cultural reproduction seems a strained assertion. Understanding this phenomenon requires that we not interpret Irish women's singleness as a divestiture of familial obligation but rather as a particular kind and set of obligations. Unlike American Protestant women, who were characterized as "spinsters" or "women adrift" because they seemed disassociated from the roles of wife or mother, single Irish Catholic women were encouraged to stay single, dissuaded from marrying, and expected as single women to care for an extended roster of family and friends.[2]

From 1846 through the Civil War, Irish Catholic sisters and the greater Irish Catholic community in New York City, despite its extraordinary poverty, supported charities for single women above all others. The Sisters of Mercy arrived in 1846 to care for single young women of "good character," and the Sisters of the Good Shepherd began their work with Catholic "fallen" women of the city in 1859. Neither of the orders, moreover, received public assistance until after the Civil War but relied instead on private donations from a community that was on the whole extremely poor.

This prioritization was not due to the belief that single women were more vulnerable than other famine migrants but rather to the hope that aiding single women would spiral into support for others. At mid-century, Irish Catholics believed their charities for single women were among the best investments they could make. Support of one domestic servant who had internalized strong obligations to her family, church, and nation grew into providing for and influencing the larger community as few strategies would. "Bridget," as the mythic scenario went, would bring over, one by one, friends and family incapable of migrating without her help. She would then integrate those family members into jobs and housing in New York City and encourage them to honor their obligations to become active Catholics. Those in Ireland who did not want to emigrate would rely on her periodic remittances to pay the rent on the family plot and avoid eviction. When all family obligations were complete she would contribute to the literal construction of Irish Catholicism in New York by enthusiastically augmenting the building fund of the local parish priest.

The same gender and sexual ideology that supported nuns' leadership also structured the lives of celibate Irish Catholic laywomen. Indeed, their lives of selflessness and celibacy were touted as sure roads to eternal salvation, second only to lives in a convent. An Irish Catholic married woman's lot, by contrast, was characterized increasingly as fraught with pitfalls, ambiguity, and danger to her immortal soul.

Irish Women and Migration

The centrality of Irish women in the migration process throughout the nineteenth century distinguished the Irish from other contemporary immigrant groups. The proportion of women in migration streams usually fell far below half of the total because men were the first or primary migrants or families migrated together. In their search for work, Chinese and Italian men, for instance, far outnumbered women because each group migrated primarily through male job networks. Many intended to return to their families once they had saved cash enough to secure futures at home. East European Jews, however, were likely to migrate as families because they wanted to leave Eastern Europe permanently. In contrast, as the Catholic poor from southern and western regions of Ireland began to dominate in famine migration, the number of women among them rose in tandem. Constituting a third of emigrants in the 1820s, the proportion of women who left Ireland rose to half by 1845 and increased thereafter.[3] Between 1851 and 1910 women constituted 53 percent of those who migrated from Connaught, the poorest, most stubbornly Gaelic province of Ireland.[4]

Dependence on chain migration through the famine helped shape this female-dominated migration stream. The extreme poverty of the Irish peasant populations before the famine meant that once it struck there were so few who owned substantial material goods that getting out so as not to starve to death required an extraordinary group effort. The poor could not migrate as families, only as individuals who were each a link in the human chain. Families would pool assets to send a pioneer. Once that individual arrived and found work, he or she would be responsible for getting cash to the next link, and responsibilities would thus be handed down successively until all were safely out of Ireland.

Widespread utilization of chain migration deepened dependence on women's wages, especially those of unmarried women. Poor Irish women, including wives and mothers, had been expected throughout the nineteenth century to contribute cash earnings in addition to substantial unpaid labor to family economies.[5] Chain migration soon made the imperative of speed in obtaining a position very meaningful. In New York City it was easier for an unskilled single Irish woman to find a job than it was for an unskilled male. Irish men were warned to migrate in the spring, certainly no later than October, and at that time might find day labor through the harvest season. Women willing to work in domestic service, however, could immigrate in any season and were more likely to find a job immediately after disembarking than were immigrant men.[6]

From all accounts, most domestic service positions were also year-round, not like the sporadic, seasonal nature of sewing work or day labor for men, and remained safe even through periods of depression.

Young Irish women without children flooded and expanded the domestic service industry in New York once the famine struck. Given the urgency to get cash to Ireland so as not to break the migration chain, domestic service was particularly useful. Food and board were usually part of the wages, and single domestic servants could ostensibly save their monthly stipend of $4 to $8 without threat to their own survival and thus be prepared to buy the $10 to $12 ticket for the next migrant's passage within months.[7] In 1846 the Irish accounted for between seven and eight thousand of the ten to twelve thousand domestic servants in the city.[8] By 1855 the servant population in the city more than tripled; the Irish-born composed 74 percent; Germans, 14 percent; and African Americans, 3 percent.[9]

Because the massive immigration injected tens of thousands of unskilled workers into the city's labor market, moreover, employment options for unskilled women became more restricted over time. As Carole Groneman concluded in her study of Sixth Ward families, if an Irish woman under twenty arrived after the start of famine immigration she was "six times more likely to be a servant" than had she arrived before 1847.[10]

Irish women also entered the sewing trades, but it was much harder to save cash for one's self or one's family as a result, owing especially to the industry's vulnerability in depressions and the work's seasonality even when the economy was strong. Still, approximately a third of Irish working women in New York under the age of thirty labored in the sewing trades in 1855.[11] By the late antebellum period those skilled enough to work a sewing machine might make top dollar—$3.50 a week—but that would require six twelve-hour days in a factory, a schedule impossible for most who had children. Food and board were, of course, to be paid from these wages, and thus saving cash was extremely difficult. As Christine Stansell points out, the wages for most sewing women fell significantly below what contemporaries viewed as a minimal standard of comfort. The *Times* estimated in 1853 that a minimal "workingman's" annual income sufficient to obtain basic food and shelter should approximate $600.[12] In the same year the *Daily Tribune* estimated annual earnings of a sewing woman, if fully employed, at $91.[13]

Irish male laborers were likely to make from 50 cents to $1.50 per day when they could find work. Moreover, much of the work they did—including farm labor, construction work, and sewing—was seasonal.

Most who worked outside could expect only two hundred days per year of employment even when all was well with the economy. In order to maximize days of employment Irish men migrated in and out of the city to work on the railroads or at similar large-scale projects.[14] As was true for women who sewed for a living, food and board took up most of the men's cash earnings.

Chain migration, however, depended not only on money but also on trust that someone would make extraordinary sacrifices in order to save and that they would then readily hand the money to others. The expectation among the famine migrants that single women, more than any other group, should and would devote their youths, perhaps their lifetimes, to such obligations was not a simple reflection of the job market. Rather, the Irish increasingly did not expect men or married women to sustain the chain as faithfully as single women. Irish Catholics on both sides of the Atlantic helped shape a distinctive prescriptive portrait of the selfless, unmarried Irish maiden who supported kin in Ireland, the church in New York, and through extraordinary deprivation emerged as a heroic figure who saved her people. Nor was such trust misguided. Single Irish women sent the greatest number of remittances back to Ireland, contributing substantially to the tens of millions of British pounds sent from America through the famine and postfamine years.[15]

The House of Mercy

The Sisters of Mercy in New York had little sense when they arrived in New York in 1846 that their convent would prove a central way station in this massive migration. New York's Archbishop John Hughes traveled to Ireland in 1845 specifically to recruit the Sisters of Mercy, convinced that young female migrants landing at the New York port were in need of a House of Mercy like that in Dublin, where domestic servants or other poor women could find shelter in a similarly dangerous urban environment.[16] The house, according to Hughes, would be for the "women of Ireland arriving in this city, young, pure, innocent, unacquainted with the snares of the world, and the dangers to which poverty and inexperience would expose them in a foreign land."[17]

Neither Hughes nor the seven Sisters of Mercy who arrived in 1846 foresaw the catastrophic famine of the following decade. Because the order's pioneers were predominantly from wealthy backgrounds, they were initially as removed from and shocked by the "ignorance" and cultural traits of the poorest Irish in New York as their Protestant, native-born counterparts. Once settled at Houston Street, for instance, their first project was to establish a circulating library of "great" Catholic works in English, hardly an effective strategy in aiding the masses of starving and illiterate migrants, many of whom were Irish-speakers only.[18]

The sheer enormity of the famine crisis, however, brought the Mercy Sisters out of their convent and changed their mindset, prompting them initially to provide ad hoc help in a variety of fields. By November of 1850 they had visited at least eight hundred of the sick and dying poor in their "cellars and garrets."[19] A contingent of Mercy Sisters also visited the burgeoning population of male and female Irish Catholic prisoners in the Tombs twice a week.[20] They opened the convent regularly to the poor to dispense clothing, shoes, food, and other miscellaneous items in addition to providing religious instruction to those who applied.[21] Yet all this work paled in comparison to their primary work, which began with the establishment of the House of Mercy in 1848.

In large and small ways the Sisters of Mercy shaped the services they provided, including nursing, shelter, food, letter writing, job training, and job placement, so the house functioned as a conduit in chain migration. Many who arrived at the New York ports were very ill, having barely survived the famine and the diseases that spread through the country or the Atlantic crossing itself on the "coffin" ships.[22] The sisters would nurse the newly arrived so they would be healthy enough to perform hard labor in a few weeks' time. Those who were not ill and able to work would be placed in a job immediately. Because so many migrants could neither read nor write English, the Sisters of Mercy also received and wrote letters for women who requested the service, thus ensuring that money was sent to the right people and notes from Ireland were delivered and read in New York. This was not merely a banking service but often the only means of communication between those in Ireland and those in the city. A letter to or from home was an event in lives devoted to the care of people an ocean away. The Mercy Sisters also extended their networks through the city, in part to undercut the isolation of Irish women placed as domestics in individual homes. Irish-born Mother Mary Augustine McKenna founded the Sacred Heart of Jesus confraternity as a regular prayer meeting and social gathering of single women who had lived for any time in the House of Mercy. Composed predominantly of domestic servants, the confraternity met on the one weekday night when they were not required to remain in their employers' houses.[23]

The Mercy Sisters were most visible in providing shelter and job placement. By November of 1850 they had sheltered and provided food and training for at least 750 of the poorest women in the House of Mercy and placed 2,500 in either sewing or domestic service positions.[24] By March of 1853, when the Mercy community in its entirety numbered only thirty members, 1,656 women had been sheltered and 7,365 placed in "respectable situations."[25] Six years later, more than twelve thousand had been placed in domestic service positions.[26] By the late 1860s, ten thousand women had found temporary shelter with New York's Mercy Sisters.[27]

Training for domestic service usually required a month or more at the House of Mercy, depending on whether trainees were healthy, could speak English, or had marketable skills for employment. The better-paid domestic positions—those of a cook, ironer, or household laundress—required skills that peasant women most likely did not possess before immigration.[28] In the House of Mercy, women were taught "laundry work, cooking, and needlework and, in addition, how to tend the sick and make themselves highly useful in a home."[29] Workrooms were set up to teach basic domestic skills and bring in funds for the support of inmates, although profits from laundry and sewing were never a primary part of funding.[30]

The Mercy Sisters did not receive public assistance until after the Civil War. They relied instead on private funding, including that provided by Archbishop Hughes and by supportive laity. In 1848 Hughes had collections taken up in every parish in New York, Brooklyn, and Jersey City for the construction of a permanent House of Mercy.[31] Half of the jubilee alms collected at the ascension of Pope Pius IX in the same year were allotted for the same purpose; the other half went to aid famine victims in Ireland, making clear the high priority given to aiding single women and the interrelationship between doing so and aiding famine immigrants overall.[32] Long-term funding of the House of Mercy, although constantly difficult and requiring strategizing by the sisters, was further guaranteed by Hughes's requirement that all parishes in the city contribute to an annual collection each May. Catholic laywomen of the sisters' auxiliary, most of whom were from the middle and upper classes, helped organize citywide fairs when funds were scarce.[33]

From the start of the sisters' work after the famine struck they characterized their aid to single women as part of a larger nationalist cause in which the survival and reproduction of Irish Catholic people and culture were at stake. In their published annals, the Sisters of Mercy cited three archetypes as frequent inmates of the House of Mercy: the most severely destitute peasant who came to New York with no money or skills, the newly poor middle-class woman who had become destitute during the famine but found it distasteful or dishonorable to earn her own support, and the "pioneer" migrant who came to New York to support kin in Ireland or bring over family through chain migration. Among the most destitute was a young Irish woman who, upon showing herself at the convent door, offered a letter of recommendation from Sisters of Mercy in Ireland, who asked that she be immediately sheltered and vouched for her "good character." The girl had been only six in the worst year of the famine. Her two younger brothers had died by the time their mother risked stealing a loaf of bread. The mother was caught and sent to prison, and because she refused to be separated from her daughter, both were thrown into a cell and the girl grew up in the prison. The Sisters of Mercy in Ireland, who visited the prison regularly, effected her release once the mother died and also paid for her passage to New York.[34] Because the woman was so clearly a victim of the famine and of the legal system that penalized the poorest Irish for attempting to survive it, aiding her was an act of compassion as well as evidence of the larger Irish Catholic nationalist ethos in the sisters' work.

The Mercy Sisters' second archetype was a previously wealthy woman who was vulnerable to men who promised marriage, or leisure, and imagined that she would be one of the few women who could survive the famine without deigning to do very hard work. Some middle-class or elite women who came to the House of Mercy in New York had not always been poor, but they suffered because their family fortunes had been eaten up with the devastation of the Irish economy or family members had fallen sick in the epidemics that plagued the country during the famine. All women in the House of Mercy were trained, regardless of their former class status, to survive on their own incomes.

The Mercy Sisters and the Good Shepherd Sisters insisted that economic independence was critical to women's sexual virtue. Training women in either domestic service or the sewing trades, the sisters assumed that skilled female workers could live independently and therefore avoid trading sexual services or entering prostitution for survival. Neither the Good Shepherd nor Mercy Sisters assumed that either moral reformation or encouraging women to marry would themselves constitute a defense against the pressures on poor women to enter prostitution.[35] Stories about middle-class women such as these stressed that unless they accepted that they must earn their own wages they lived in moral peril. They could easily be "seduced" by well-dressed men feigning interest in marriage, for instance, only to be abandoned and without support once they had consented to sexual relations.[36] Their love of dress and leisure, moreover, might make prostitution seem an easier route than the hard work required in supporting themselves "honestly."

The Mercy Sisters' third archetype, a selfless single woman devoted to family and kin in Ireland, became over time the dominant image of single female migrants. The story of Hanna Flynn and her relationship with the Sisters of Mercy in New York also illustrates the ways in which the Mercy Sisters' work was integrated into the larger family survival and migration strategies of Irish immigrants. Hanna Flynn arrived in New York in 1859, spoke primarily Irish but knew some English, and had volunteered to come to America to "pay her father's rent" when the family was faced with eviction.[37] After training in the House of Mercy she was sent to service in a home in the city. A month later she returned to the Mercy Sisters to have them write a letter home to accompany the wages she was sending her family, ostensibly denying herself even a penny of her earnings. When she found out soon after that the family had nonetheless been evicted and sent on the road to beg, she quickly sent passage money for her sister so both could work to earn enough "to make a man of our brother Peter, poor fellow."[38] Before she could earn enough for her father to make the journey, however, he died in Ireland. Her sister, moreover, once in America, decided she would not spend her life "slaving out" and supporting family in Ireland. Instead, she married a German and left Hanna to support those at home.[39]

Hanna's choice to live as a single woman was not a challenge to Irish Catholic gender norms and values nor a mark of her independence from cultural expectations. Rather, Hanna's selfless duty to her family was meant to prop up gender order in Ireland and "make a man" of her brother, whose financial well-being was privileged as more important than her own. Hanna's "singleness" should therefore be understood as capitulation to expectations that she spend her adult life caring for others. In contrast, her sister's decisions not to spend her life "slaving out" and then marry were, in this context, seen as a selfish acts.

The Good Girl

It was Hanna's story more than the others that predominated by the 1860s in prescriptive literature about single Irish women. "The great ambition of the Irish girl is to send 'something' to her people as soon as possible after she has landed in America," John Maguire wrote in 1868. That "ambition," moreover, was not a short-term commitment but involved an adult lifetime of self-denial. She would risk her own health and "deny herself innocent enjoyments, womanly indulgences . . . such is the generous and affectionate nature of these young girls."[40]

Single women's "families" were understood to be those of origin, including parents, siblings, nieces, nephews, and grandparents, not those into which they might marry. They were also extensive, meaning that single women were to take on responsibilities that others could not, including parenting or financing the needs of others on an ad hoc basis. Maguire thus characterized a mythic aging servant sending her remittances home after years of hard labor: "[T]he soft fair face lost its maiden bloom, and hardened into premature age, marked with lines of care and toil, as year after year this unconscious martyr to filial duty surrendered everything to keep the roof over the head of father or of mother, . . . or to pay for the support of a young brother or sister, or perhaps the orphan child of a sister who had confided it to her care with her dying breath."[41] For these services Irish women should expect no recompense, even after family members were financially able to pay them back. "She regards everything she has or can make as belonging to those to whom she has unconsciously devoted the flower of her youth," reported Maguire, "and for whom she is willing to sacrifice her . . . dearest hopes."[42]

Family members were instead to exhibit gratitude by allowing single women to lead the family through the perils of assimilation by connecting them directly with the Catholic church. "[T]he faithful girl seeks to draw them within the influence of religion, in which, as in her passionate love of her family, she has found her safeguard and her strength."[43] Single women were also lionized for devoting "surplus" earnings to the church. "The girls who live out have been called the church-builders," wrote George Deshon, "and it is a glorious title for them."[44]

Catholic sisterhoods also increasingly drew recruits from this network of single women, needing the labor of single, chaste, pious women as their charities expanded after the war.[45] Regular attendance at sodalities or confraternities, exemplary piety, and clear commitment to aiding the church and the poor were each patterns of behavior that might mark a young woman as one having a "vocation" for religious life.[46] And yet even those who wanted to enter the Mercy convent as postulants were discouraged from doing so if family members, especially parents, could be said to depend on them.[47]

Although we should be careful not to assume that all Irish women conformed to such expectations, we should also acknowledge that stories like those of Hanna Flynn or countless other single Irish female migrants were popular and had resonance for the Irish because many women tried to live up to these ideals. Like the prescriptive literature that middle-class Protestant women read, Irish Catholic accounts of success in migration dramatized the lives of poor women, casting them as heroines whose daily lives and choices mattered not just to themselves but to their communities as a whole. Through this literature and storytelling, poor Irish women were able not merely to clean a house and feign subservience to employers but through that work and behavior to save their families, church, and nation.

Praise for single women's sacrifices was never far removed from instilling guilt that any in Ireland suffered at all. The backdrop of the Irish poor's starvation and despair was prominent in literature that dramatized Irish single women's heroism in embracing drudgery for the sake of kin and community. In Mary Sadlier's *Bessy Conway; or, The Irish Girl in America* (1863), Bessy is a hardworking, pious domestic in New York. After years of service and savings, she hears that her family will soon be evicted. Sadlier brings readers to Ireland, where the family huddles on straw mats while Ellen, Bessy's "bright-eyed" younger sister, is dying of starvation. Bessy's mother cries as she boils a handful of oatmeal that she knows will not be enough to feed the family, much less save her daughter. Having not heard from Bessy in a great while, Mrs. Conway turns to her husband, "Isn't that girl of ours cruel and hard-hearted not to answer any of our letters?"[48] When Mr. Conway speculates that Bessy must not have received the letters (which, of course, turns out to be true), Mrs. Conway cuts him short: "I tell you there's no excuse for her."[49]

The praise and respect Irish single women were told to expect with unceasing self-sacrifice was always laced with the threat of condemnation if they placed their own needs ahead of any on the extensive list of those who might benefit from their resources. "What a delight it is to think of the happiness she has caused at home," wrote a New York priest, "when she gets a letter filled with love and blessings from those who are so dear to her. Is not this far purer and sweeter than if, with cold-blooded selfishness, she had loaded all her money on her own back, to parade the streets and make a show of herself?"[50]

Fortunately for the starving Conways, Bessy's filial devotion is exemplary, and she rushes to Ireland in time to save her family. In a triumphant appeal to Irish dreams of social justice she appears at the door—just as bailiffs cart off the evicted family's few belongings and the starving Conways sob uncontrollably. Bessy then not only pays off the rent but also regales the neighbors as she orders the bailiffs about indignantly, demanding that they replace the furniture with care. Sadlier joins in the delight: "It was something altogether new, and they relished it exceedingly." The neighbors, meanwhile, shouted congratulations to Mr. Conway, "Thanks be to God, Denis! . . . you can hould up your head now like a man!"[51] Bessy funds a feast not only for her family but also for the starving neighbors, who gather at the Conway house. All are enthralled in the laughter and good cheer that seems to obliterate, for the evening at least, the worries of these desperate people.

Such stories of triumph, however, were always countered by the equally dramatic depiction of the tragedy experienced by women who chose to marry. Running throughout Irish Catholic prescriptive literature on the "good girl" was a very explicit critique of women's experience in marriages, particularly marriages to poor men, and a critique of the romanticization of marriage in Protestant narratives. "Novels represent a husband as in the place of God to us. It is not so," cautioned Father George Deshon in his *Guide for Catholic Young Women.* "If you place your supreme good and happiness in the love of your husband, you will surely be disappointed."[52]

For Catholic commentators on the "woman question," the "odium and contempt" heaped upon an "old maid" in Protestant society was the single most important factor in driving all Protestant women into a dangerous rush toward marriage. Catholics of all descriptions charged that even Protestant woman's rights supporters, who identified marriage as the central institution in shaping women's oppression, feared their daughters' singleness more than their sexual, economic, religious, and political oppression as wives. Although advocating more liberal divorce laws to free some women from the bonds of wifely oppression, most women's rights supporters did not imagine a society that supported young girls who chose lives apart from marriage. "Hence the dread entertained by the girl in Protestant society for a single life," a Catholic woman wrote, "and the universal impression that to be married is the first great object of her existence. . . . Verily, the Catholic maiden need not despair if she has no vocation for matrimony! She knows she does better in remaining single than she would in entering the married state without such vocation."[53]

Catholics often characterized Irish Catholic women's choices to live independent of marriage as the easier road to salvation. Marriage was purportedly only for women who clearly had a "vocation" to endure its many demands, not the least odious of which were the husband's sexual and moral tastes. "Marriage is not a lottery; but it is mere willful blindness to forget that in all its higher aspects it may be woefully inverted or appallingly debased," noted a Catholic writer in 1859. "The formal union of two persons is no guarantee whatever for a will ennobled, or affections enlarged and cleansed. And the faith which so works by love can make a sunshine in a shady place, without an infant's or a husband's eye to look into. The harmonies of a developed and transfigured womanhood have been set many a time to other music than that of wedding bells."[54]

In critiquing marriage, however, the community at large was more likely to point to worldly suffering than other-worldly matters. In deciding to marry, Irish Catholic women sometimes gained privilege but frequently lost it as well. For married women who were poor, the activities and accomplishments for which Irish Catholic women won praise—remaining celibate, supporting family in Ireland, aiding in migration, and supporting the church and its charities—were difficult or impossible. Warnings about the perils of marriage evoked horrific visual imagery that contrasted sharply with the romantic notions of domestic and maternal bliss promoted by the Protestant middle class. "Who is that bloated, coarse-looking woman who has not apparently, combed her hair in a week, with a lot of ragged children bawling and fighting and cursing around her in her miserable, dirty hovel?" New York's Father George Deshon queried. "That was, a few years ago, a pretty, modest girl who was innocent and light-hearted, earning an easy living in a quiet, pleasant family."[55]

Irish women resisted romanticizing the conditions and benefits of wifehood and motherhood in antebellum New York City for good reason. Whether one's children or self would survive migration and life in the city's poorer districts was always an issue. With the world's highest known death rate at the time and at least a third of all infants and more than half the children between infancy and age five dying annually, motherhood for the poor in New York City was often a wrenching experience of loss and despair.[56]

As was true for free African American women of the same period, marriage to poor men in their group provided Irish women with neither access to a family wage nor freedom from wage labor. In 1855, 85.2 percent of the Irish men in New York worked within the lowest, least remunerative ranks of unskilled labor.[57] It was therefore expected among the poorest Irish that married women work, and those with children took in sewing, laundry, or boarders to make ends meet.[58]

Even if they wanted to marry there nonetheless remained a substantial surplus of Irish women over Irish men in New York City. The 1860 Census listed the number of Irish females there at 117,120 and the number of Irish males at 86,580; more than 57 percent of the city's Irish-born were women.[59] Extensive migration of Irish men in and out of New York, a high accident and death rate among those engaged in frequently dangerous occupations, "desertion," and a relatively low rate of remarriage for Irish widows all contributed to making Irish women at least twice as likely to be heads of households than either German or native-born women.

In Sadlier's fictional depiction of Irish women's lives in New York, Bessy Conway, the diligent servant, is contrasted repeatedly to women who married poor Irish men with disastrous results. Mary Murphy, "the prettiest girl about Ardfinnan, ay! and the merriest, too!" marries Luky Mulligan, who joins the U.S. Army and is sent to Mexico. Mary has a daughter after his enlistment and tries to get by financially by leaving the child at home while she works for wages. One day while Mary is out, the child starts a fire and is killed. Mary turns to drink and dies shortly thereafter at the prison on Blackwell's Island.[60] Sally, a servant who at one point works with Bessy and spends her wages on dress and leisure so as to court and marry handsome Jim, meets a similarly gruesome fate. Jim turns out neither to like wage work nor to abstain from spending on drink. Bessy reunites with Sally when the latter comes begging at the door of Bessy's employer, surrounded by starving children: "So, that is the end," Bessy muses, "of all Sally's dancing and visiting and dressing up . . . now she has to put up with everything and ask her bit from door to door, in misery and dirt and rags, with her drunken brute of a husband watching to take what she begs for herself and her children."[61]

In Sadlier's novel as throughout the larger literature, women who reject lives of servitude and celibacy are depicted as subject to great worldly suffering. Sally and others are chastised as being responsible for finding themselves in such a predicament because their love of "finery" and their selfishness ultimately lead to renunciation of filial duty and poor marriage choices.[62] Sally, for instance, cannot recover from her chance encounter with Bessy: "It tore open again the bleeding wounds half healed by custom, and seared into callous indifference. It reminded her of what she once was, and what she might have been—of the good example and the good advice by which she never profited—of all she had lost, and of all she had sacrificed for the worthless wretch whose specious promises had lured her to ruin."[63] Despondent, Sally resists her husband's blows when she comes to him empty-handed, and a policeman arrests him for assault. After crawling home, Sally lapses into sickness and dies shortly thereafter. Her children are taken in by a Protestant mission and never heard from again.

It is in this overall context that the prescriptive norm for single Irish women in New York became closely identified with the life of a nun. As a domestic servant, a single Irish woman's life was supposed to be characterized by hard work, obedience, celibacy, and prayer. Her feme sole status allowed her to save and accumulate what wealth she could, free from the concern that a husband would appropriate it. But also like nuns, the single Irish woman was praised to the degree that her financial resources were used for the greater good of the community. The ethos of her daily existence should be unflinching self-sacrifice and self-denial for the benefit of family, community, and church. Asking nothing in return for her labor, she was in essence making a vow of poverty perhaps even more costly than a nun's because no one was committed to caring for her in sickness and old age. Her rewards, however, were great. Like a nun, the life she led would guide her securely to eternal salvation. Musing on the superiority of the life of ascetic hermits, Deshon asks, "Outside of a convent, whose life is most like theirs? That of a good girl who earns her own living at some honest employment . . . who can spend her days in work and prayer, . . . and work out her salvation with comparative ease."[64]

Bad Girls

Nothing, in fact, was easy about the lives of poor Irish women in antebellum New York City, and many women could not, or did not wish to, conform to Irish Catholic prescriptions for sainthood. Throughout the 1850s intensive de-skilling in the sewing trades, a rising cost of living, and a severe depression and bank panic in 1854 and 1858 threatened the ability of poor Irish women to scratch out bare subsistences. In the almshouse, lunatic asylum, and city hospital, Irish women constituted the majority of all women housed from the late 1840s through the Civil War period.[65] They also filled the city's jails and accounted in 1860, for instance, for more than two-thirds of the female inmates of the city's penitentiary, prison, and workhouse. Almost all the women incarcerated (96 percent) reported that they had worked in domestic service or the sewing trades before commitment.[66] Four-fifths of the female inmates in the penitentiary had been convicted of petty, not grand, larceny, often a strategy for domestic servants to obtain food and cash for their families and one they defended as just compensation for incessant work and extremely low wages.[67] Fully half of the inmates convicted on charges related to prostitution, moreover, listed domestic service as their primary occupation.[68] From the period of the famine through the Civil War, Irish-born women composed the majority of those arrested for prostitution-related crimes in Boston, Philadelphia, and New York City—in fact, in all major cities along the eastern seaboard.[69]

The major group of women consistently shunned and ostracized by Irish Catholics were those who had sexual relations and children outside of marriage. The harsh treatment of unmarried mothers, "illegitimate" children, and prostitutes was apparent in peasant culture before the famine and the expansion of the nineteenth-century institutional church.[70] Such punishment constituted a kind of social death that stressed spectacle and external control and pre-dated more "modern" forms of discipline.[71]

Irish women nonetheless chose prostitution in large numbers, and some no doubt with little regret because it was a strategy for survival and gain among very limited choices. Although I would resist describing Irish prostitutes as victims only, it is also important neither to romanticize how much "choice" they had in opting for prostitution nor underestimate the social cost of that choice.[72] The famine Irish had little else but each other, their place in family and community life, and the hope of individual and cultural survival. Being identified as a woman of "ill-repute" was grounds for the community to cease interaction and therefore consign a woman to social death, to "become a perfect byword and reproach," as one author cautioned, "through the loss of that good name without which life is a burden."[73]

Irish Catholic women faced a difficult dilemma that was exacerbated by the community's treatment of women deemed "sexually deviant." They were held responsible for the economic survival of men, women, and children at a time when prostitution, especially occasional prostitution, was one of the few means Irish women had to secure a subsistence for themselves or others. There is no reason to doubt, for instance, that some portion of the millions in remittances that women sent to Ireland, and therefore the economic lifeline of chain migration, was funded through sex work. Yet Irish Catholic advice writers denied repeatedly that it was even possible for Irish Catholic women to choose this means of survival. The deliberate and relentless assertion that such Irish women did not exist was made even as they languished in the city's jails and died young of as-yet-incurable sexually transmitted diseases.

It is rare to find a description of prostitutes or prostitution in nineteenth-century Irish Catholic prescriptive literature, whether in Ireland or the United States. As Maria Luddy has shown, despite the rapid growth of prostitution in Dublin and other Irish cities and towns throughout the famine period, no public discussion of prostitution took place. Nuns and Protestant women performed rescue work "out of the public eye."[74] In literature prescribing women's duty and honor to the larger community, moreover, prostitution is always in the background of admonitions about women being economically self-supporting so as to live "honestly." Yet direct reference to Irish prostitutes is extremely rare. In Sadlier's *Bessy Conway,* for instance, women are chastised for marrying the wrong men, but prostitution remains in a literal sense an unspeakable option.[75]

Remarkably, Irish Catholic men wrote frequently of the high incidence of rape onboard passenger ships and the sexual dangers of New

York itself while simultaneously denying that Irish women fell victim to such risks.[76] In John Maguire's 1868 opus on the Irish in America, for instance, he reports that charges of "seduction" or "outrages" against women were all too common on the Atlantic crossing. He complains further that victims had little or no legal recourse upon landing in New York but instead faced heightened risk of being seduced into brothels.[77] For that reason combined with Irish intemperance and some Irish women's "vanity, love of dress, and perhaps individual perversity, acted upon through all the evil influences of great cities," Maguire concedes that "in some, yet comparatively few places in America a certain percentage of women of bad repute are necessarily of Irish origin."[78]

In itself, Maguire's confirmation that at least some prostitutes in America were Irish was unusual for an Irishman. Yet he then denies that Irish prostitution existed on any scale worth noting and ties Irish women's chastity directly with Irish nationalism:

> But . . . in any part of the United States, Irish women should form an appreciable percentage of the whole of the class of unfortunates, still, when compared with the Irish female population of those great cities . . . the number is small indeed. In very many places the proportion is infinitesimal; and there are cities and districts throughout the States in which there has never been known an instance of an Irish girl having come to shame—in which the character of the Irish woman is the pride and glory of all who belong to the old country, or have a drop of genuine Irish blood in their veins.[79]

Irish women chose to engage in prostitution for many reasons, the most important being that it paid well. Prostitutes are counted as having more money than any other group of working women in antebellum New York. Girls believed to be virgins, for instance, could make from $10 to $50 for their "deflowering," at the very least more than a month's salary for a domestic servant or sewing woman and at most half the annual salary of a sewing woman who worked seventy to eighty hours a week.[80] Marilynne Hill estimates that even for those in the lowest grades of prostitution, each trick yielded at least $1 to $5, and weekly incomes ranged from $20 to $30.[81] The price one could demand was related to age as well because younger girls were assumed to be more desirable and less likely to have contracted sexually transmitted diseases. The age of consent in New York City at the time was ten, so prostitutes tended to be teenagers or in their early twenties. Moreover, because syphilis, gonorrhea, and other sexually transmitted diseases were incurable, they were likely to die young as well.[82]

Although Protestant middle-class women were critical to the founding and support of charities for prostitutes, Irish women as a group did not find them especially sympathetic to their struggles overall. As Lori Ginzberg has shown, the most visible Protestant female charitable leadership in New York, as throughout the Northeast, shifted attention in the 1850s from work with women to work with poor children. In the process, reformist women shifted the tone of their work from an emphasis on middle-class and poor women's common oppression to a more explicit defense of middle-class privilege.[83] The New York Female Reform Society (NYFRS), for instance, provided regional female leadership in the 1830s by analyzing prostitution as the result of the sexual double standard and women's low-paid, low-status work and explicitly blamed men for creating the conditions that forced women into the trade.[84] By the late 1840s, however, NYFRS had changed its name to the American Female Guardian Society (AFGS), renounced its former radicalism, and rejected moral suasion and cross-class female solidarity as a viable political strategy for social change.

Moreover, those services that Protestant women did provide for poor women in New York City through mid-century were characterized by explicit anti-Catholicism and cultural condescension. The two most visible institutions were the Five Points Christian Home for Female Servants and AFGS's Home for the Friendless. The Five Points Home revealed the chasm in cultural background perceived between itself and its poor Irish clients in 1854: "We have the worst servants in the world; the most dishonest, unserviceable, unruly and changeable, and as a class they are growing worse." The proper management of inmates, the potential employees, required emphasis on the "home" and family worship. "The Christian philanthropist who makes himself their friend and patron . . . will shortly gain an influence over them which may compete even with that of the priesthood . . . employers will be insensibly conducted by the mediation of Christian love into a new relation and sense of responsibility of those who live in their households as servants, and who ought to be members with them of that holy and divine institution, the family." Should Irish Catholic women have any delusions about the home's intent, it advertised, "Among the special advantages of the Home, may be instanced, first, family devotion, morning and evening, at which (as it should be in every Christian family, whatever the Roman priesthood may say) each inmate is expected to be present, whatever her religious persuasion."[85] The Association for Improving the Condition of the Poor (AICP) concluded in 1866, "Of females in domestic service, chiefly foreign born, it need only be said that they occupy the places for which they are best fitted, and having abundant employments and very liberal wages they cherish no higher aspiration."[86]

Protestant reformers in New York were also quite hostile to Irish Catholic efforts to continue chain migration, arguing that it only exacerbated the problems of poverty in New York. In the 1850s the AICP called for increased restrictions to bar pauper immigrants from landing in the city and chastised Irish Catholics for sending what little money they had to Ireland. This practice, the AICP maintained, made the city's already destitute Irish Catholics poorer by its expense, kept a tide of penniless paupers arriving in the New York port, and left the Protestant community taxed to aid them all.[87] The short-lived Women's Protective Emigration Society, organized during the depression of 1857 by the Protestant female elite of the city and led by Elizabeth Phelps, encouraged poor women to "emigrate" to the West, where they could presumably establish their own homes.[88] Confounded by Irish women's refusal to go west, the society folded within a year.

The values of the American, native-born, Protestant middle class were also apparent in the lines drawn between legal and illegal behavior. The Irish as a group tended to be jailed for behavioral crimes such as drinking and fighting, but Irish women were almost always arrested for inability or reluctance to conform to gendered prescriptions for personal conduct. Representing 68 percent of all women jailed although constituting only 28 percent of the city's female population, Irish-born women also accounted for almost half (49 percent) of all Irish people incarcerated. In contrast, German women constituted only 28 percent of German inmates, and native-born women represented about a third (34 percent) of their group.[89] Between 1850 and 1870 more than 80 percent of all women in the city prison had been convicted of intoxication, disorderly conduct, or vagrancy, the latter charges often referring to prostitution.[90]

Irish women's refusal or inability to conform to prescriptions against intemperance highlighted their incarceration as one designed to punish public gender deviance. In 1874, for instance, women represented only 33 percent of those arrested for intemperance but 37 percent of those convicted. The police magistrates explained the high number of convictions by claiming that "public exhibitions of drunkenness in females indicate a depraved and abandoned condition."[91]

Even Irish women's participation in prostitution was marked by an inability or refusal to conform to American middle-class gendered norms. Prostitution, for instance, was not illegal in New York City, but "vagrancy" and "disorderly conduct," the very presence of women in public, were. Native-born and German prostitutes had greater access to

the cleaner and safer "parlor or private houses" where clientele were restricted and risk of arrest was slight. As Timothy Gilfoyle argues, "The
very label 'parlor house' reflected an emphasis on replicating the atmosphere, privacy, and physical environment of the middle-class home."[92]
Irish women, however, were relegated to the level of streetwalkers, those
most obviously in public and without the protection of a domestic environment. Irish streetwalkers instead met johns in public and brought
them to "Houses of Assignation," several rungs below even "public
houses" or "bawdy houses."[93]

Dependence on women's wage work was not new for the peasant
Irish; what was novel was the Protestant middle-class assumption that
such activity was shameful. The Irish often accepted as peccadilloes much
of Irish women's behavior deemed "deviant," dangerous, and criminal by
the Protestant, native-born middle class. Women's poverty, public visibility, and wage work, for instance, were unequivocally not shameful.
They were described instead as tragic. Poverty and the desperate search
for wage work were the consequences of the Irish people's oppression as
a whole, another chapter in many centuries of suffering. Even a prison
term for stealing was not necessarily dishonorable. Servants stole so often, and justified it so brazenly as compensation for too much work and
too little pay, that priests gave sermons explicitly arguing against such
logic.[94] Women's poverty might be also be exacerbated by a poor marriage
choice, a tendency toward drink, a hot temper, or just plain bad luck,
but such were the struggles and temptations of life itself, not grounds
for demonization.

Native-born Protestants, particularly women from the middle class,
were nonetheless more likely than most of the Irish Catholic community
to be active in support of charitable work for prostitutes in New York.
Disparate conceptions of women's sexuality and desire may have been
influential in such a phenomenon. The Protestant, middle-class emphasis
on women's natural "passionlessness" and men's aggression helped them
to characterize prostitutes as victims of male oppression in general. The
relative youth of the prostitutes, moreover, helped Protestant women
view them as victims of adults, including parents who had presumably
led them to such work through neglect or exploitation.

Articulating a new emphasis on childhood as a time of innocence
and freedom from labor, some among the urban middle class viewed the
expansion of prostitution in the city as a problem to be advertised and
addressed not hushed up. Irish Catholic discussions of sexuality, however, acknowledged women's passion and desire. Priests were willing to
admit that all human beings, male and female, had "an inclination to this

vice" but warned that if not controlled through one's will, it "became
. . . a horrible monster, ready to devour you if you expose yourself in the
least to its power."[95] Irish Catholics were also more likely as a group to
blame women and children for sexual activity, even if they were coerced
physically or turned to it as their only hope for physical survival. Women
who overtly and without apology chose prostitution, and profited in the
bargain, were not to be acknowledged as human, much less Irish.

The House of the Good Shepherd

Some Irish Catholic women nonetheless provided aid to prostitutes, but
engaging financial and moral support for their work proved a relentless
struggle. Sarah Ripley, a Protestant convert to Catholicism and wife of
George Ripley, founder of Brook Farms, was one of several lay Catholic
women who visited the Tombs and found that most prostitutes in jail
had little choice but to return to the brothels from which they came. In
coalition with the Protestant matron overseeing prostitutes on Blackwell's Island, she and other Catholic laywomen "implored" Archbishop
Hughes to consent to the establishment of a Good Shepherd Convent
and House in New York. Hughes stalled the work for years, at one point
denying that there could be a large number of Catholic prostitutes and
then hesitating because there were too many to aid.[96]

Both the Good Shepherd Sisters and the laywomen who aided them
insisted that shelter and vocational training would provide women with
a chance to avoid further sin, an argument that finally caused the archbishop to relent. "Suffice it to say," Hughes wrote in his pastoral of 1854,
"that the Sisters of the Good Shepherd have more than once offered to
take charge of such persons in this City; that we have been importuned
to authorize collections for the object . . . that in fact, after years of hesi-
tation on our part, we have at last been almost compelled to give our
consent to the founding of a Magdalene Asylum."[97] It took another three
years, however, before Hughes gave final approval to the establishment
and then only under the condition that laywomen accept exclusive responsibility for raising all funds necessary for the convent.[98] Neither he
nor his successors ever organized a regular annual collection as he had
for the House of Mercy.[99]

Hughes's final approval of the Good Shepherd Sisters, however,
changed neither his attitude toward the women under their care nor the
general disdain of Irish Catholics for unchaste women. After laywomen
in the community rented a house on Fourteenth Street, several Sisters
of the Good Shepherd arrived from Philadelphia to begin the order, and

a temporary superior was sent from St. Louis by the motherhouse in Angiers, France. When the motherhouse transferred a permanent superior,
Mother Coeur de Marie, from Philadelphia to replace the first, however,
Hughes forbade her from taking control of the mission. As a Good Shepherd sister remembered it, Hughes told her she was too attractive for the
position and sent her back to Philadelphia.[100]

Like the House of Mercy, the House of the Good Shepherd was an
extension of Sisters of the Good Shepherd's convent, and life in it was
taken up with work and prayer. The sisters encouraged veneration of
Mary Magdalene as a means to cultivate a spiritual connection with a
similar female victim of social shaming who was not only protected but
also respected by Jesus. The strategy of reformation the sisters developed
was further conducted "through moral means alone" and organized so
women could spiritually return to the childlike innocence they had sup-
posedly lost. While Protestants imagined the facility as the epitome of
the convent cruelties so vividly conveyed in anti-convent literature, no
corporal punishment or forced detention was permitted under their rule.
Some, but very few, women chose to stay for a lifetime and took vows
similar to those of the nuns.[101]

Unlike the Mercy Sisters, and because of their relative lack of support
among Irish Catholics, Good Shepherd nuns relied on sewing and laundry
done in the house for a major portion of their revenue. Native-born Catholic converts, not the Irish laity, made private financial donations critical
to the well-being of the House of the Good Shepherd. Henry Anderson,
for instance, provided a large piece of property on Ninetieth Street, then
the "country" in New York, on which to build their institution.[102] In the
late 1860s, when Irish Catholic men became dominant at city hall, the
order gained some financial stability through the city's provision of land
grants and per-capita payments to care for women committed through
the courts. Those convicted of crimes were the only inmates required
to stay in the house, and all who did enter had to have freely chosen it
over the workhouse or penitentiary at the time of sentencing. Prostitutes
customarily used the workhouse and convent when without housing
and the penitentiary when in need of medical treatment, particularly for
sexually transmitted diseases.[103]

Although a confining and difficult option for any woman, more tried
to get into the House of Good Shepherd than could be accommodated.
This seems a testament not so much to the desirability of the house than
to the lack of alternatives for women who wished to get off the streets. In
1867, for instance, the Good Shepherd Sisters sheltered 275 penitents but

reported that so many applied and were turned away that they could have sheltered five hundred or more, especially from the Irish community.[104]

Perhaps the most detrimental aspect of the Good Shepherd Sisters' work was that they were largely invisible to the public. Unlike any other active order of women religious in New York throughout the nineteenth century, the Good Shepherd Sisters were primarily enclosed. Only the "outside" (or what they termed "touriere") sisters, a small fraction of the total community, were ever allowed outside convent walls without special permission from their motherhouse or the archbishop.[105] Although most nuns had limited public voice and presence, the Good Shepherd Sisters had almost none at all, perhaps exacerbated by, and contributing to, the already paramount problem of social death and invisibility for Irish women deemed sexually deviant.

The sisterhood's protection of sexually deviant women relegated its work and existence to the unspeakable. As a result, any association with the Good Shepherd Sisters became cause for social stigma. When members of the male laity asked them to care for girls in the newly established Catholic reformatory for delinquent children in 1863, Hughes found out and forbade it. "[T]he idea of connecting the condition of the poor little girls with the House of the Good Shepherd . . . I cannot consent to," he wrote. "[T]heir having been protegees of the Good Shepherd, the nature of whose Institution . . . is perfectly known over the land, will be considered by some . . . as a ground of suspicion and a blemish."[106]

Catholic girls were ostensibly to be kept from understanding "the meaning that is attached to the House of the Good Shepherd," as though silence about prostitution would make the reasons for women's dependence on it disappear as well.[107] Girls who were thought to be sexually active or knowledgeable, moreover, were the only group of "delinquent" children systematically separated from all others. In 1878, for instance, thirty-one committed for destitution were transferred from the Protectory to the House of the Good Shepherd because they had "fallen" "so low . . . that it was considered unadvisable to allow them to come in contact with the other children."[108] The stigma moreover, persisted throughout the nineteenth century. Although the Good Shepherd Sisters tried to integrate women back into the larger community by placing them in domestic service positions, few could find jobs. "The fact itself that [women] have been inmates of the Good Shepherd House," wrote a New York Jesuit in 1891, "is an indelible stain on their character. No family wishes now to take them into service; no shop wishes to employ them."[109]

That services for "fallen" women under Catholic auspices were provided at all was due to some Catholic women's refusal to capitulate to those in the community who brutally cast women outside the figurative community they called "Irish." Yet the Good Shepherd Sisters' lack of public voice, public visibility, and funding severely limited their ability to change the Irish Catholic community's harsh treatment of sexually deviant women. Nuns could provide some Irish prostitutes with an island of relief from community scorn, but they were never able to challenge the stigma itself.

––––––––––––

Irish Catholic nuns' work in organizing and expanding the meager resources of the famine Irish in New York proved a boon and a burden for the Irish women who used their services. Nuns undoubtedly helped make survival possible at a time when chaos, deprivation, and profound suffering threatened the Irish people, particularly the poorest among them. Unmarried chaste laywomen, like nuns themselves, were expected to embrace a life of ascetic selflessness for the good of the larger society, to literally save an entire people from the brink of destruction. If they failed in that task, or if they chose means to do so that were at odds with Irish Catholic prescriptions for gendered and sexual conduct, they faced ridicule and ostracism from the Irish, and incarceration by Americans. Because Irish nuns' power was always premised on their place in a hierarchy of women that relegated those with sexual experience to the bottom, the relative respect and status of celibate women was always dependent on the relative subordination of sexually active women. The sublime could not exist without the degraded.

The efforts of nuns to expand their power and means of cultural reproduction were often at odds with those of the Protestant, native-born, middle class and sometimes strangely symbiotic. Irish Catholic women's cultural distinctiveness was both desired by the Irish and used by the Protestant middle class to rationalize Irish poor women's relegation to the low-paid, low-status wage work that freed middle-class women for "higher" pursuits and political power. Indeed, the example of Irish women's "deviant" behavior as domestics, prostitutes, and nuns helped to culturally define a Protestant "true woman" more precisely. Although Irish women needed wage work, native-born, middle-class women were increasingly able to define themselves as middle class by their reliance on Irish women's labor. A "true woman" or lady was defined in part by her freedom from heavy domestic labor. One or more domestic servants were as critical to defining her native-born, middle-class status as the size and location of her home. And, of course, a true woman was to be "passionless," not bothered by the constant sexual demands of her husband, in part because he could now buy sex on every New York street. In the cases both of domestic service and prostitution, Irish women did not just fill jobs that other women had performed; each of these "professions" expanded enormously with the onset of famine migration. Protestant middle-class women's power thereby rested on the degree to which Irish women took up the heavy labor and sexual services that earned for them the status of the deviant.

Yet the most frightening interaction that famine Irish women had with those of the Protestant middle class involved the question of who had the right to control and raise the children of the Irish-born. If sexually active women helped provide nuns with their claims to status as virgins, and servants and prostitutes helped bolster native-born, middle-class women's status as "true women," then poor Irish mothers' denigration as bad mothers helped Protestant, native-born, middle-class women define themselves as good mothers. Such good mothers, moreover, used their status to legitimate movement into the public sphere. Indeed, "saving" the children of the Irish-born from their mothers' supposed brutality became a means through which native-born, Protestant, middle-class women achieved unprecedented political power.

3 *Placing-Out and Irish Catholic Cultural Reproduction, 1848–64*

"How did you hear of her?"

"Miss Fairbarn . . . found them out in the course of her visitations."

"Has she parents?"

"Her father is dead, and her mother is married again. They both drink, and use up all they earn in whisky. Meantime the children are sent out begging to supply the family with food . . . in the coldest weather, no better clothed than she is now . . . and more than once they have turned her out of doors, and kept her out all night."

"A nice family to take a child from" said Miss Ward.

"I never heard of a family that is more desirable to take a child from. I should think that the sooner she was taken from them, the better."

—Lucy Ellen Guernsey

It has been computed that, at a low calculation, thirty thousand children of Catholic parents, mostly Irish, have been sent to "kind Christian homes," through "Sectarian Reformatories," and institutions of a kindred spirit. . . . [W]ho can be unconscionable enough to object to an operation so legitimate, or so strictly in accordance with the entire system of—kidnapping may be too rude a term to apply to such institutions and such men,—so we shall say, of gathering little children in.

. . . its longer tolerance by the Catholics of America, and in a special manner by those of Irish birth or descent, would be in the last degree shameful.

—John Francis Maguire

Male and female Protestant reformers launched the child-saving movement in the early 1850s, and with it began an intense battle between Protestant and Catholic charitable workers that persisted through the turn of the century. Marshaling their political power to enact legislation and secure state funding to permanently remove children from poor parents, the child savers' collective aim was to counter the cultural reproduction of the poorest of the famine Irish. They did so by transferring these children into Protestant homes outside the city, where they were to be raised according to the religious, social, political, and economic value systems at the heart of Protestant middle-class culture.

From an Irish Catholic point of view, the removal of children from poor Catholic families threatened not only the parental and religious rights of the Catholic poor but also the physical and cultural survival of the community as a whole. Child removal was initiated in the 1850s on a small scale and then magnified substantially after the 1863 Draft Riots in New York City prompted even the most apathetic of the city's upper and middle classes to fear violent class warfare. The Catholic movement to care for Catholic poor children grew in response to the very successful efforts of Protestant reformers to use the power of the state to sever children's ties to family, church, and community. Catholics and Protestants thereafter competed in determining which kind of family, church, and community would be supported through New York City's emerging public child-care system.

As Catholics began to organize cohesively by the end of the Civil War they also began to articulate a defense of poor families, particularly of parents' rights within them, that would contrast with that of Protestant groups over the next half century. Protestants at once lauded middle-class, especially rural, Protestant nuclear families as the backbone of the Republic and held that the persistence of immigrant poor families, or what they termed "nurseries of debauchery," was a profound threat to American society. What Protestants understood as the individual rights of poor children beyond duty or submission to parents, in other words, should be paramount, and thus "saving children" necessitated that parental rights be limited accordingly. Catholics instead used traditional patriarchal language and tradition, invoked the rights of parents over children, and stressed the filial duties of children to parents and kin in an effort to construct and reconstruct working-class family economies dependent on all family members. Throughout the century, Catholic championing of the parental rights of the poor proved a foundation for a child-care system (and a means of combating poverty in its entirety) that was fundamentally at odds with that of Protestants.

Race/Ethnicity and Class in Famine Migration

Those who worked to alleviate poverty in New York City during the 1850s and 1860s were overwhelmed by the number of immigrants and their relative destitution. Never before had the city been the center of such extensive poverty nor host to so many extremely poor immigrants. The population grew at unprecedented rates; in 1845 it stood at 370,000, and by 1860 it had surpassed eight hundred thousand. European immigration accounted for most of the increase. In 1845 the foreign-born composed just over a third of the city's population; by 1855, however, the majority was foreign-born (52.3 percent)—28.2 percent of them from Ireland and another 15.7 percent from Germany. African Americans, in contrast, represented only 2.7 percent of the total population.[1]

Irish poverty through the famine, moreover, was of a type and degree that white Americans had historically escaped due to a relatively greater access to land and other resources. The peasants who fled western Ireland were largely illiterate; deeply traumatized by their experience in the famine; openly hostile to Protestants; and, unlike many previous immigrant groups, unwilling to enthusiastically embrace the values and expectations of the dominant culture in America. Existing charitable systems were wholly incapable of meeting their needs.

By 1850 there were three separate yet interdependent systems of charitable relief for the poor in New York City: the Commissioners of Emigration, the city's institutional system, and private charity. New York State established the Commissioners of Emigration in 1847 and with it assumed jurisdiction over immigrant paupers for the first five years after their arrival in New York City. The commissioners were instituted as a means of checking the abuses to which immigrants were subject on arrival and to relieve the Irish Catholic Emigrant Aid Society and German Emigrant Society, both small private groups that were overwhelmed by the massive immigration after 1845.[2] At Ward's Island the commissioners set up forty separate institutions to house the poor and sick upon arrival, and in 1855 they took over Castle Garden, the first official immigrant depot. Although they managed to enact various reforms that protected immigrants from potential pick-pockets, swindlers, and petty thieves, the commissioners were limited in their ability to either stem the tide of impoverished immigrants or care for them adequately after arrival.[3]

City and state public charitable systems were more extensive and yet constructed in the early antebellum period for a population that was smaller, more homogeneous racially and ethnically, and not quite as poor as a group. The public system consisted primarily of a loose network of institutions, including the Department of the Outdoor Poor, the alms-house, Bellevue Hospital, the lunatic asylum, a nursery on Randall's Island, the city prisons, the penitentiary, the House of Refuge reformatory, and, by the mid-1850s, a workhouse.

Almshouses, the center of the system, were constructed throughout the Northeast during the Jacksonian period as an alternative to giving outdoor relief (direct aid) to individuals in the community. Influenced in part by British ideas and reforms enacted as a series of "Poor Laws" in the late-eighteenth and nineteenth centuries, this system contrasted rather sharply with America's preindustrial charitable systems. In the colonial period, aid to the poor, infirm, and widows, although often meager, was judged a neighborly responsibility and obligation of their social betters and an act of Christian charity through which the elite benefited in their quest for salvation.

The shift in the philosophy of charity in early-nineteenth-century America was linked with industrialization, urbanization, and the formation of a middle class as the number of poor people and the extent of poverty grew in tandem. Underlying reformers' fear of generous outdoor relief was their assumption that the causes of poverty were traced not to God or misfortune but to such individual moral deficiencies as excessive vice, laziness, and intemperance. The almshouse, therefore, was meant to be more punitive and less desirable than outdoor relief, because the latter was believed to encourage idleness rather than help the poor to reform morally in order to escape poverty. Like the almshouse, the penal institutions and House of Refuge were organized first to remove individuals from the environment of moral contagion and then to impart the values of industry, punctuality, cleanliness, and orderliness through strict discipline and routine.[4]

Private charitable organizations, with the Association for Improving the Condition of the Poor (AICP) at their apex, were at mid-century often run by men but increasingly staffed by women as well. The AICP was an umbrella group that rationalized and ordered the city's private charities. Like other mainstream Protestant charities, it attributed poverty to individual causes, particularly the moral failings of the poor. Although the AICP gave material aid to the poor, it also attempted to limit such allocations by maintaining a strict distinction between the "worthy" and "unworthy" poor. The former were deemed industrious, thrifty, and possessed of self-control, but they faced poverty during a period of recession, unemployment, or illness. They deserved charity, therefore, because they were not thought chronically dependent. The unworthy, or "paupers," were those who were always poor. They did not deserve charity and were thought to be hurt by it because it ostensibly furthered their tendency toward dependence. The AICP gave its purpose in 1845 as being "to discountenance indiscriminate alms-giving"; end "street-begging and vagrancy"; extend "appropriate relief" when necessary after visitation of the poor in their homes; and "through the friendly intercourse of Visitors, to inculcate among [the poor] habits of frugality, temperance, industry, and self-dependence."[5]

Issues of culture were inextricable from Protestant reformers' analysis of the causes of poverty and the determinants of class status. Until the late 1840s the emerging Protestant, native-born, middle class believed it had, or could nurture, substantial cultural links with even the poorest people in New York. Even the Irish in America were often Protestant and from artisanal or farming backgrounds, much like many of the white poor among the native-born community who found themselves downwardly mobile and working class. Germans migrating in the 1840s and 1850s provided Protestant, native-born reformers with an example of "good immigrants," those culturally and behaviorally similar enough to native-borns to warrant praise and welcome. Only a minority of German immigrants were Catholic or Jewish, and most were not extremely poor upon entrance. Germans in New York, therefore, were far better prepared to participate in the industrial market, thus confirming native-born notions that proper cultural backgrounds determined economic well-being. The peasant Irish, in contrast, had been very poor in Ireland, arrived very poor in New York, and tended to stay very poor. Most tried to find work in unskilled labor and provide for kin and friends struggling through the famine and its aftermath.

Protestant reformers' emphasis on culture simultaneously explained the relative well-being of native-borns and Germans and the misery of the Irish. The Irish, according to reformers' logic, were among the unworthy poor, and their desperate, chronic, and very visible poverty encouraged native-borns to racialize the categories of worthy and unworthy so Germans and native-borns were more likely to be considered worthy.[6] The Germans, AICP leader Robert Hartley claimed, were "the opposite of the Irish, being generally a self-reliant, sober, frugal, thrifty people."[7] Of the Irish, however, he was pessimistic: "Since many of them evince too little force and energy to be the arbiters of their own destiny. . . . So pauperized in spirit and inefficient is the great mass. . . , to say nothing of the ignorance, and physical and mental imbecility of many of them, that they cannot be made profitable laborers even in our Almshouses."[8]

As native-born reformers were quick to point out, the Irish swelled relief rolls and dominated those who depended on private and city charities, whereas Germans were underrepresented relative to their population as a whole. In 1850, 1855, and 1860 the Irish accounted for more than 60 percent of almshouse residents; Germans accounted for about 5 percent, and native-borns accounted for one-quarter.[9] Combining indoor and outdoor relief given by the city, averaged over six years from 1854 to 1860, the Irish accounted for 69 percent of the recipients.[10] Irish dependence on public health facilities, moreover, was even greater proportionately than their dependence on the almshouse. They accounted for 70 percent of the patients at Bellevue Hospital in 1850, 74 percent in 1855, and 66 percent in 1860. Throughout the 1850s the Irish also made up about half of the lunatic asylum's residents.[11] In the same decade at least half of those who received aid from New York's primary private dispenser of outdoor relief, the Association for Improving the Condition of the Poor, were Irish-born.[12]

Many of New York's prominent reformers believed that the most serious threat the famine Irish posed was in their potential to form the core of a permanent dependent class in America. New York City's unique position as the hub of European immigration, warned Robert Hartley, "has brought with it, not only the wealth, and skill, and labor which we want, but also a vast amount of impotent and thriftless poverty we do not want." The hardships of the Irish in their homeland and their numerical dominance over the Germans in New York, Hartley argued, could not explain the ubiquitous evidence of Irish poverty. In the city and throughout America there was "really nothing in the way of . . . thrift and social elevation, excepting [their] own incompetence, ignorance, or perverseness" or their "addiction to intemperance."[13] "Of a large number of Irish immigrants," Hartley wrote, "it may be said that they are but little disposed to change their thriftless habits with a change of country. . . . They are prone to stay where another race furnishes them with food, clothing, and labor. . . . Unlike immigrants of other nationalities, they have a . . . disrelish for migration into . . . the 'far west' [which] appears to decide the impracticability of relieving our city of this class in this way; for if they will not go, where is the power to coerce them?"[14]

For the most part, native-born reformers quickly judged the adult Irish to be irredeemable. They were impervious to proselytization, inured to fighting and drinking, and refused to "go west" to better their prospects for upward mobility. Nor could reformers imagine a legal system that would "coerce" adults into leaving. By 1851 the AICP declared that "more decisive measures than heretofore have been adopted in respect to the debased poor" were needed. They were "too numerous and dangerous a class to be allowed to increase."[15] Characterizing the families of the poor as cradles that would nurture and reproduce a permanent dependent class in America, Hartley held that "to keep such families together is to encourage their depravity. . . . These nurseries of indolence, debauchery, and intemperance," he held, "are moral pests on society and should be broken up."[16] Because reformers believed that the moral environment of the adult Irish had nurtured their deviance, they also believed that removing an "innocent" child from the same moral environment would increase that child's chances of escaping poverty. Adults were thought to live in poverty because of moral deficiencies; children, however, could be saved.

Maternalism, Class, and Culture

Historians of women in modern Europe and the United States have emphasized that welfare states in industrialized nations would be incomprehensible historically without the leadership of middle-class women in constructing so much of what we now call welfare. Maternalist movements and ideas were especially powerful in the United States and Britain, where a relatively decentralized state relied through the nineteenth century primarily on private charities rather than on public, state-run bureaucracies. To paraphrase the definition offered by Seth Koven and Sonya Michel, maternalism constituted a range of political strategies and discourses through which middle-class women expanded and legitimated their public power by claiming that they needed such power to better perform their private duties, namely their obligation to mother well.[17]

Maternalism, moreover, did not represent a coherent ideological outlook. The commonality in variants of maternalism historically is that the women promoting such strategies accept to some degree the premise that their duty to "mother" is their most important contribution to family and nation. Accordingly, they seek to increase mothers' power, not necessarily women's rights. Although the rhetoric of maternalism often purports to speak for a universal alliance of all mothers, it simultaneously defines through a normative system which mothers are considered good and which are considered bad. Maternalists have thereby been located historically on the left and the right; they have both resisted and reinforced class, racial, and gender hierarchies in society at large. The spectrum of those who have used maternalist strategies is as diverse as left-leaning socialists, fascists, African American middle-class women, and white women in the Ku Klux Klan.[18] Each group has promoted contending notions of good mothering, their political similarities resting only on the degree to which they claim political power in accordance with their proclaimed status as good mothers.

Maternalists in the placing-out movement in nineteenth-century New York melded two premises of Protestant middle-class gender, racial, and class ideology at mid-century to create the link enabling them to argue for increased public power. First, they accepted the premise that a collective morality or culture was the major determinant in a group's relative success or poverty. Second, they also emphasized motherhood and the home as the primary means and site of cultural reproduction. In contrast to older Calvinist assumptions about the inherent wickedness of children derivative of original sin, the Protestant middle class at mid-century increasingly promoted the idea that children were born innocent, a tabula rasa upon which mothers could instill positive morality through nurturance and gentle discipline. Good mothering could therefore take center stage in efforts to reform the culture of the poor significantly enough to thwart the reproduction of poverty itself.

Protestant middle-class women were among the first to see and use this connection and expand their relative public power in order to mother the children of the immigrant poor. In New York City, middle-class Protestant women's entrance into and, in many cases, creation of charitable fields were marked by championing policies that transferred the right to mother from immigrant women to themselves. Female Protestant middle-class reformers in the American Female Guardian Society (AFGS), for instance, took the lead in urging New York State to adopt legislative support for child removal. In a meeting of the AFGS in September 1849, they resolved to "petition our Rulers to pass an act, whereby dissipated and vicious parents, by neglecting due care and provision for their offspring, shall thus forfeit their natural claim to them, and whereby such children shall be removed from them, and placed under better influences."[19]

The AFGS then used its central headquarters in New York City, and auxiliaries throughout rural and small-town New York State, to encourage other women to petition the men in the state legislature to support their work. "Christian sisters and fellow-laborers," they began in the appeal, "here is a long-neglected work calling imperatively for action—but a work that our own feeble arm is too short to compass except by faith and prayer. If done it must be done by our rulers. . . . The power, the resources are theirs," they conceded, "but the right of petition, this is ours. . . . We may come before them as their mothers, their companions, their sisters—as the friends of fallen humanity, and make our respectful but long and strong appeal." They characterized their ensuing struggle to achieve such legislative power as one that would substantially enlarge their field of action and "turn the hearts of the fathers and guardians of the nation to the children of the nation, and thus avert the fearful alternative of 'smiting the earth with a curse.'"[20]

The AFGS took responsibility and credit for piecing together the discrete forms of legislation on which the system of child removal and placing-out would be based. By 1849, before enactment of legislation laying the groundwork for large-scale placing-out, the AFGS secured power from the state legislature to "bind out" children and begin a placing-out system.[21] Thereafter they refused to take any children into their mission unless parents agreed that the child could be placed permanently in a Protestant home.[22] In 1852 the AFGS reported that of the 187 children received into the Home for the Friendless, 157 were placed in Protestant homes outside the city and only twelve were returned to parents or relatives.[23]

By 1853 the AFGS took credit for the passage of the state truancy law, which, it reported, provided legal machinery for child removal. Under the law, parental approval of their children's permanent placement in homes outside the city was no longer required. The AFGS printed the following article in its annual report to clarify the new possibilities: "Heretofore a great obstacle has existed in the inability to get hold of the idle, vagabond boys and girls, unless they were detected in crime; but now the law provides for their arrest and commitment. Even those children who are simply neglected by their parents, and who do not attend school regularly, or are not regularly employed in some proper way, come under these legal provisions, which, however, are not so much penal in their character as reformatory."[24]

The truancy law allowed any citizen, and commanded any police officer, to arrest a child on the street during school hours. The child was then taken to a private mission such as that run by the AFGS, and workers there had no obligation to contact parents. If the parents found their children they could retain custody by promising to keep them in school. Those not found, or those arrested a second time, would be committed for the length of their minority to a Protestant institution such as the Home for the Friendless run by the AFGS or after 1854 to the Children's Aid Society run by Charles Loring Brace. "It is a bold but wise measure of the State," wrote Robert Hartley of the AICP, "which, by assuming the position and responsibility of a parent to the child, not only secures the right to guard itself against evils from this source, but to save as well as to punish."[25]

The AFGS was certainly not alone in this campaign. The AICP and the Children's Aid Society, established in 1853 after the AFGS's legislative success, threw substantial funding and political influence behind programs that aggressively usurped the rights of the poor to parent their own children. Nor was the legal concept of parens patriae, declaring that the state assumed the rights of the parent, unprecedented. The state had, since colonial times, protected its vested interest in children who were abandoned or parented in such a manner as to threaten the interests of the larger populace. Reformatory institutions such as New York's House of Refuge, established in the 1820s for children who had committed crimes, were premised on separation of children from parents during the period of reform. Reformers' increasing belief that the moral environment to which children were exposed tainted their "innocence" translated into reform strategies that abrogated parental authority. Delinquency was viewed as more directly attributable to parental neglect than any other source. The House of Refuge, for instance, insisted that parents surrender the child for the length of his or her minority and limited visiting days to the Wednesday or Friday of every third month.[26]

What was new in the AFGS approach, and in others throughout New York in the 1850s, was emphasis on prevention and the near-conflation of poverty with criminal behavior. The AICP's first step in addressing the problem of children's delinquency was to help establish another institution in 1851, the Juvenile Asylum, a privately run but publicly funded institution similar in organization and administration to the state-run House of Refuge. In each, inmates were subjected to strict discipline, routine, isolation, and corporal punishment for periods usually not exceeding two years. Unlike the House of Refuge, however, the Juvenile Asylum was intended for children who were found on the streets, seemingly orphaned or vagrant. Vagrancy and destitution were considered evidence that the child was a candidate for a life of criminality or chronic poverty.

What distinguished the placing-out system from the institutionalization of children in reformatories, however, was the imperative that they be placed in a "home." More specifically, children, once taken from parents, were to be "placed out" in a "Christian home." This was not merely a difference in the physical site of reform but the mid-century articulation of a Protestant, middle-class critique of older Calvinist notions of parenting based on fatherly discipline rather than motherly nurturance. Rather than the Calvinist flavor of the House of Refuge, for instance, where strict corporal discipline and routine were intended to reform, mothers in individual homes were to sympathize with poor children and nurture the individualism they cultivated in their own.[27] Children were not to be commanded into submission but compassionately guided toward self-reliance.

Protestant female reformers linked their power as mothers with a collective ability to "save children" from circumstances or homes deemed inadequate. In 1858 the AFGS reported that its statewide convention had supported expansion of placing-out efforts, and resolutions were adopted that clearly articulated the foundations of state maternalism upon which commitment to the system was based:

> *Resolved*, That in the outer circle of Christian duty, the *poor* and *destitute children* present one of the strongest appeals to every mothers's heart, and that the affection and sympathy of which her own children are the first recipients, should be so expanded, that it may . . . embrace all those friendless little ones whom God has sent to be cared for by Christian humanity . . .

> *Resolved*, That while the first duties of Christian wives and mothers lie within the home-circle, it should never be the boundary of their sympathies and efforts, but that they should seek as wide a field of Christian and philanthropic labor as their time and abilities will enable them to cultivate; remembering that to minister to the needy, to elevate the degraded, and to reclaim fallen humanity, are among the *legitimate* duties of every Christian woman.

> *Resolved*, That of all the benevolent enterprises of the present age, the most *noble*, the most *hopeful*, and the most *satisfactory*, is that which lifts the *little children* of destitution and vice up from their wretchedness into the healthful influences of this and similar institutions, and through these into Christian homes.[28]

The AFGS reported, moreover, that "nine-tenths" of the children placed out in 1856 were "of foreign birth, and a large majority Catholics."[29]

The maternalist foundation of the welfare state was consistent with the sacralization of motherhood then evident in middle-class Protestant culture and with a new emphasis on childhood itself as a portion of the life-cycle when children should be sheltered from labor or even from knowledge of the "sinful" male, adult, and public world. Religion and questions of morality were shifting from institutional church settings to the home and domesticity, and Protestant middle-class women as moral guardians of the nation, would construct the home as a haven against the chaos and immorality of the public sphere. Children found on the street had crossed a boundary into the immoral public sphere that threatened the moral balance that the Protestant middle class presumed would ensure that moral adults would be reproduced. Instead of life on the street, the new Protestant home became the setting, and Protestant women the redemptive agents, in reforming poor immigrant children.

The placing-out system, not institutionalization in public reformatories, became the branch of child-saving through which Protestant middle-class and elite women were able to expand direct public power in charities. It is important not to overstate the gendered division of labor in these child-care systems. A few Protestant women worked in the Juvenile Asylum and House of Refuge, and some men became quite powerful in the placing-out system, particularly Charles Loring Brace of the Children's Aid Society, and male reformers such as Homer Folks later in the century. Yet the placing-out system gave Protestant female reformers more direct control over children and charitable work than the system of institutionalization had allowed. Each reformatory institution, which would remain the dominant Protestant-run public children's reformatories in New York City throughout the century, was overseen by men. Very few women worked in them except those employed as paid matrons. In contrast, the placing-out system's expansion was dependent on the unpaid labor of women activists and mothers in the homes where children were placed.

Although the placing-out system was designed as a radical reorientation of children culturally, female and male child-savers were nonetheless indignant when Catholics and Jews contended that the system was anti-Catholic, anti-Semitic, and at odds with the legal and cultural principles separating church and state. Placing-out agencies such as the Children's Aid Society and the American Female Guardian Society, although composed of Protestants and not including any Catholics or Jews, claimed they were not "sectarian" organizations.[30] Because they represented many Protestant groups and not one exclusively, they asserted, they were promoting broad-based Protestant principles for rearing and reforming children. Catholic and Jewish groups, Protestants argued, were sectarian because they represented the views of only one church or sect. Protestant-run "nonsectarian" organizations deemed themselves incapable of proselytization because no specific Protestant denomination or sect profited directly from such vague conversions. Reformers argued as well that their policies were consistent with those of the House of Refuge and Juvenile Asylum, where the large majority of children housed was Catholic but from which Catholic priests were barred until 1888.[31]

Placing-out advocates attributed the frequent protests that Catholic parents made to the forcible removal of their children as evidence that the Catholic poor were duped by "priests' power."[32] The term *priests' power* referred to a general set of assumptions to the effect that priests exerted undue influence over the thoughts of parishioners and had interests always and exclusively focused on extending church power. Characterizing poor parents' protests of the placing-out system in this way tended to dismiss their perspectives as ignorance and misguidedness, the very characteristics of poor parenting that placing-out advocates sought to vitiate through the larger system. Instead, Protestant placing-out advocates were sure that granting children access to the gospel, unmediated by priestly interpretation, was a liberation priests feared primarily because any child so liberated would naturally reject priests' authority. The AFGS defended itself against "the charge of bigotry" by arguing that the "outsider" who "objected to its painstaking to place the children . . . where the commands and precepts of the gospel may reach" was evidence that "Satan had come down in great wrath." Members were assured that "manifestations of [Satan's] rage in any form need not surprise us. . . . They may call us bigoted, but remember what Christ was called."[33] Charges of bigotry or anti-Catholicism were thus dismissed as yet another burden that child-savers must endure, if only to emulate the suffering Christ.

Charles Loring Brace, himself a Methodist minister, nonetheless encouraged a break from proselytizing methods prominent in the antebellum period:

> We would not breathe a word against the absolute necessity of Christianity in any scheme of thorough social reform. . . . To attempt to prevent or cure the fearful moral diseases of our lowest classes without Christianity, is like trying to carry through a sanitary reform in a city without sunlight.
>
> But the mistake we refer to, is too great use of or confidence in, the old technical methods—such as distributing tracts, and holding prayer-meetings, and scattering Bibles. The neglected and ruffian class which we are considering are in no way affected directly by such influences as these. New Methods must be invented for them.[34]

Placing-out advocates tended to focus on Europe and the ever-more-frequent threat of revolutionary working-class movements to indicate what might happen in New York. From the outset, the AFGS highlighted its child removal and placing-out system as designed to inhibit the formation of a potentially violent proletarian subculture that would, if left undisturbed, soon threaten the elite with violence. "Let it be neglected," the AFGS contended in 1848, "and the number of paupers and vagrants continue to multiply in the same ratio as at present, and the time may not be distant when the division of classes—the poor arrayed against the rich—may give us a revised edition of such scenes as have been once and again enacted in the streets of Paris."[35] Brace courted the men of the Protestant upper class of New York City with comparable rhetoric, securing substantial private and public funding as well as ideological support for the placing-out system as a buttress against class warfare. "The greatest danger that can threaten a country like ours," he observed in 1855, "is from the existence of an ignorant, debased, permanently poor class," particularly "if this class be of foreign birth."[36]

Irish "whiteness," or more precisely white skin color, mattered a great deal in this debate in two ways. The first was in reference to rights of citizenry. Irish immigrants were deemed legally white and therefore eligible for naturalization and full rights of citizenship. In contrast, the Chinese-born were barred from naturalization because they were deemed non-white. Native Americans and African Americans were not explicitly guaranteed the rights of citizenship until 1926 and 1868.[37]

The legal imprimatur of Irish whiteness was no small factor in reformers' consideration of the Irish Catholic threat because it allowed Irish men full participation in American politics and the ability to create political machines. Through those machines the Irish Catholic community and other European immigrant communities were to gain substantial power in American society. Collective protest from the immigrant poor, Charles Brace warned, would soon threaten the principles upon which the American republic was based. Poor children might seem harmless, but some would soon wield the same political power as native-borns. "They will vote. They will have the same rights as we ourselves though they have grown up ignorant of moral principle, as any savage or Indian." Issuing an ominous warning he would reprint after the outbreak of the Civil War Draft Riots, Brace remarked, "Then let Society beware, when the outcast, vicious, reckless multitude of New York . . . come to know their power and *use it!*"[38]

Irish whiteness mattered as well in the solution that advocates proposed. The placing-out system rested on the presumption that children would so visibly physically integrate into new families that their origins as Irish Catholic, German, or Jewish would either not be known or be ruled insignificant. In contrast, African American, Native American, or Chinese children were never discussed as appropriate candidates for placing out during the nineteenth century despite the obvious poverty of each group. The goals of boarding schools for Native Americans were similar to the placing-out system, but strategies for assimilation were distinct. Native American children were first taken from their parents and then forced to renounce their languages, religions, and larger cultural values and replace them with Christianity, English, and, in general, the emergent Protestant American culture's value system. Moreover, Native American children of the nineteenth century were rarely placed with native-born Protestant families, although there is mounting evidence that some missionary families took them in as boarders. There was, however, no large-scale program for integrating Native American children into the white population.[39]

The predominantly unspoken assumption that placing-out was a strategy appropriate only for white children kept African Americans virtually invisible in reformist literature. Child-saving literature is, if anything, marked by a conspicuous lack of concern about African American poverty and an absence of fear that the poor of this group would threaten the social order, whether through acts of criminality or proletarian violence or the attainment of significant political power. Care for poor African American children remained segregated and traditional. Although Anna Shotwell and Mary Murray, white Quakers, established the Colored Orphan Asylum in 1836, it remained small, housing no more than 150 at a time, and was meant for orphans only. The city's African American population of approximately ten thousand was more likely, however, to integrate orphans, whether half or full, into extended kin networks, as did the Irish.[40]

The placing-out system's origin in private charities is not analytically comprehensible if we assume that private charities constituted some entity separable from the state. All major child-saving groups in New York City by 1865, including those run by women, depended on Protestant, native-born, middle-class, and elite use of state power and funding, whether in city or state government. The 1853 truancy law granted city and state funding for the "expenses of providing and maintaining such place for the reception, clothing, support, and instruction of such children."[41] Instead of the roughly $100 per year that the city paid for institutionalizing a child in private Protestant reformatories, placing-out was fairly cheap, estimated at about $10 for each child's transportation costs.[42]

The CAS, AICP, AFGS, and the Five Points House of Industry also derived substantial annual allotments from the state and city and larger grants sporadically. All of these nonsectarian organizations, moreover, relied on the relative political power of the city's native-born, middle-class, and elite to enact legislation, influence judicial appointments, demand police enforcement, and in general provide substantial state support for their agendas and policies.

The Children's Aid Society, because it was so focused on placing-out and because Charles Loring Brace so successfully expanded and rationalized the system, became influential in city, state, and national arenas, including other East Coast cities in which the European immigrant population grew substantially during the period. Brace's defense of placing-out would soon become gospel in most Protestant child-saving organizations, and his theories formed the basis of New York's state charity laws.

Before the Civil War, the New York Orphan Asylum, the American Female Guardian Society, the Five Points House of Industry, the city children's institution on Randall's Island, and the Juvenile Asylum, among others, each placed out children regularly.[43] Yet many Protestant male and female leaders in city and state charities after the war regarded their volunteer experiences with the Children's Aid Society as formative in their ideological and practical approach to charity work. Although the CAS encouraged many reform activities that did not include placing-out, among them industrial schools and family visitation, most volunteer energy was directed toward what was termed "deportation." "The great duty . . . of the Visitor, to which all his other efforts tend," Brace explained, "is to get these children of unhappy fortune utterly out of their surroundings, and to send them away to kind Christian *homes in the country.*"[44]

In arguing for expansion of the placing-out system Brace was also arguing against the practice of institutionalizing children in reformatories. Explicit in his warnings were assumptions about institutionalization's effects on an individual's sense of community and class consciousness. As Paul Boyer argues, Brace was not fearful of the poor as individuals, but he was haunted by the specter of collective action among the poor.[45] Institutionalization, Brace asserted, did not solve problems endemic to urban areas where the poor congregated. The congregate system allowed for the poor and outcast to mingle, and doing so would confirm their belief that they were part of the masses rather than individuals with aspirations independent of a larger group.[46] Forming a "separate population," the foreign poor lived apart from the native-born community, corrupted those around them, and if "numbers be large, times of great want or excitement may call them out in ungoverned license, to seize upon the luxuries which surround them, but which they are never allowed to taste."[47]

In the first decade of its work the CAS did not pretend that the majority of the children sent west were orphaned. The society's annual reports show that fewer than one-quarter of the roughly nine hundred children placed out annually between 1856 and 1858 had no living parent. The characterization of the "orphan train" to the Midwest was developed in later decades when the CAS loosely implied but never proved that living relatives could not be found for most children it placed.[48] It would be unreasonable, however, to accept the statistics that Brace made public.

In 1861, for instance, the society claimed that only 15 percent of children placed out were of "unknown parentage"; in other words, 85 percent had a least one known parent. The following year the number of "unknown parentage" jumped to 70 percent.[49]

The repetition of the terms *orphans* and *orphan trains* to refer to the tens of thousands of children who passed through the system or to the means by which they were conveyed worked primarily to assuage the Protestant community's conscience about the extent and intent of the placing-out system. In a public lecture in New York, John Francis Maguire, an M.P. from Cork, Ireland, denounced the proselytization and "kidnapping" evident in the placing-out system. As an 1867 editorial in *Harper's Weekly* made clear, his direct charge was likely to invoke in-credulous indignation and denial:

> The character of our institutions is the result of Protestantism. Perfect religious liberty produces all other liberty. . . . It is, of course, amusing to hear a disciple of the Roman Catholic Church, with its beloved In-quisition . . . denouncing proselytizing; and does Mr. Maguire seriously believe that the Children's Aid Society of which he speaks is in the habit of abducting children as the boy Mortara was stolen by the priests of his church in Rome? Let him know then, that no children are taken in charge by the Society who have any other home; they are never taken from parents or guardians without their consent; and they are sent to the West with the full consent of every body concerned . . . the condition of the poor in the Roman Catholic countries is not a condition into which we wish to see the poor of our own country fall; and . . . the recruits to our population from his native isle are not such as to heighten our ad-miration for the religious, political, and social influences under which they have been bred.[50]

On its face, the charges in the *Harper's* editorial seem absurd: Prot-estants cannot deprive citizens of religious liberty because they are the very source of it, Catholics have a very bad history in this regard and thus should not complain, and Catholicism is a bad influence on new immigrants, thus prompting a lessening of its influence. Perhaps most important, however, is the categorical insistence that the children were "sent to the West with the full consent of every body concerned." Reform-ers themselves would certainly not have made such a statement because the most cursory knowledge of the placing-out movement made clear the daily struggles between them and parents. And yet the beliefs behind the declarations were not unusual, even when there was abundant and very visible evidence to the contrary. It was easier for most to continue a euphemistic discussion of "orphans" and "homeless children" than fully appreciate, much less take responsibility for, the kinds of trauma the system inflicted on immigrant families.

Whether the larger Protestant community understood or acknowledged it, reformers' efforts to dismantle poor families were central to their mission from the time the placing-out system began. Moreover, the efforts were supported rhetorically by demonizing poor immigrant parents. Condemnation was often contingent on the distinct family economies that supported native-born, middle-class, Irish city life. Irish dependence on children's and women's labor made native-born Protestants unsympathetic with Irish Catholic child-rearing. As Christine Stansell has argued, poor children contributed to their families' income or managed their own survival through scavenging, huckstering, rag-picking, stealing, and begging. Slovenliness, neglect of physical appearance and comfort, malnutrition, and truancy were also cited as evidence of parental depravity.[51] The native-born interpreted children's wage work and scavenging as evidence of bad parenting because they drew children from their homes and schools and into the public sphere. Women's wage work was suspect because it either drew women out of their homes or placed the wage work within the household, thereby sullying the home's atmosphere and creating a place unfit for child-rearing.

The Children's Aid Society's published diatribes on the failings of the parents of poor children and evidence of children's hostility to their parents were designed to negate public sympathy for those who claimed the right to keep their children. As the matron in the CAS girls' lodging house reported, "A young girl in our lodging-house was relating to us, recently, how she had been attracted to another young girl there, by hearing her answer our Matron: 'No Ma'am! I don't know where my parents are. I don't care—*I hate them!*' This was a common bond of sympathy between the poor creatures!"[52] CAS reports are crammed with references to "unhappy and vicious parents."[53] A typical report of one visitor was published in 1859: "The child brings the most shocking charges against her mother, the least of which is, that she sent her to the Catherine Market to steal. . . . An effort is being made to take her from her vile mother."[54]

Poor Irish women, especially single mothers, bore the brunt of the attack in literature that emphasized the depravity of bad parenting. Hostility to these women in particular was premised on their perceived deviance from gender norms that the native-born middle class promoted with vigilance. The ideology behind the CAS and all placing-out societies was premised on a maternalism that defined true womanhood according to native-born, middle-class standards and justified the removal of poor children from their mothers by judging them according to the same standards. "Good mothers" could not exist without the corresponding example of "bad mothers."

The degree to which "bad mothering" was in evidence also legitimized the increasing political power of "good mothers" best able to fix such problems, particularly those caused by the "drunken mother."[55] That these "drunkards" could desire to keep their children, or that the children would want to return to them, was almost incomprehensible to placing-out advocates. Just as poverty was most severe for single mothers, moreover, their right to parent was also most precarious. In CAS annual reports averaged from 1856 to 1862 the number of children placed out who had a mother only was twice that of those who had a father only.[56] In 1854 the AFGS reported an exchange between one such mother and her remarkably articulate little girl: "Her intemperate mother, hearing where she was, called, and used every entreaty to induce her to leave, promising to be kind to her in future. The child replied, 'You have said so before, and when I went home you would beat me, and my stepfather would curse me every time I took a bit of bread in my mouth and put me out of the house, and when I was going out would *hurl a brand of fire after me.*'"[57]

In the full-length novel *Irish Amy,* published in New York in 1853 by the evangelical American Sunday-School Union, the twelve-year-old Amy is depicted as a child of wonder and goodness. She is treated with love and kindness by the Ryans, a Protestant family that take her into their home and off city streets. The Ryans reprimand Miss Ward, the cranky, selfish aunt, when she derides their efforts to help "these miserable creatures, who are hardly worth saving, after all."[58] The family instead judges Amy to be entirely innocent of the sins that led her parents and friends to poverty, theft, and depravity. Removing her from her family of origin is thus depicted as an act of generosity and compassion prompted by Christian charity, not a hopeless or futile gesture. With the Ryans, Amy finds for the first time in her life that others can be caring, truthful, pious, and hard-working. She misses no friends or relatives—indeed, nothing of worth exists for her before she crosses the threshold of her new home. Amy's natural mother does not love, work, laugh, sing, or pray; she exists to drink and to squander Amy's hard-won earnings. Amy is therefore reformed by women with whom she is placed, and their maternal guidance becomes the path to Christian salvation and worldly well-being.

When "Irish Amy's" stepfather appears unexpectedly at the Ryans' door he demands that she return home with him, a tragedy made ever-more painful by his reasoning and Amy's reaction. "I want her where she can help the family, . . . instead of being brought up a fine lady, and despising her own folks. I've no notion of children knowing more than their parents," he begins. When confronted by opposition, he refers to "the priest" as supporting his decision. The Ryans react accordingly. "You cannot surely think," he is asked incredulously, "that the child's soul will be any safer in such a place as yours, and with the company you keep, than here?" "Indade, and I do then," he responds, "for the priest says we have faith, if we haven't any thing else."[59] Caricatured as a mindless dupe unable to think for himself and therefore dangerous to Amy's worldly well-being and eternal salvation, he is dismissed as having no moral right to such a request. The Ryans, however, are shocked to realize that he still has legal rights to claim Amy, who is terrified:

> Oh! how can I go back there again? There's only one room . . . no larger than a pantry; and they all sleep there, and eat there, and all. And it is all full of cockroaches, and bugs, and worms: and, oh, it is such an awful place! They get drunk, and fight, and beat one another. . . . You don't know what horrid women come there. There's that Judy Dean, with her baby, not six weeks old. I saw her go out of our house, and fall down close by the water, dead drunk, and lie there for an hour, with her little baby crawling over her neck in the mud and rain. Poor little thing! There is not a pig on this farm that don't live more like decent people than they do.[60]

The dichotomy that reformers drew between immoral adults and redeemable children was at the very heart of child-saving and placing-out. Unlike those who, like Miss Ward, might ignore the suffering of these innocent children, child-savers wanted to lift children out of poverty and into what they presumed would be a much better life. And yet the cultural explanation for poverty that bifurcated the poor into guilty adults and innocent children also made child-savers almost insensibly dismissive of the needs, aspirations, and humanity of the parents of these children. To be an adult and poor was to be immoral, thereby making Irish people's survival into adulthood the mark of endless sin. Irish women's survival in numbers great enough to mother their children and reproduce their own culture exacerbated the threat beyond existing poverty to a dystopian future that would cast Americans in the violent class conflicts so visible in Europe.

Every depiction of Irish women throughout this literature is constructed so as to invoke joy in the hope offered by severing the child's every link with mother, family, and community. On the final page of *Irish Amy*, the author spells out the "design of the narrative":

[It] is to bring to the reader's view opportunities and methods of doing good. If it should make any Sunday-school boy or girl feel more interest in the poor children who go round begging in the wet and cold, with no one to care for them, or teach them to love the God who made them and the Savior who died for them, one purpose of the author will be answered. She hopes, too, that some kind-hearted family, who have abundant means and a good country home, may think whether they cannot make room and find work for a little boy or girl out of the city, and train them up to be happy and useful, instead of becoming miserable vagabonds, useless to the world, and breeding a moral and physical pestilence wherever numbers of them are brought together.[61]

Irish Catholic Resistance(s) and Survival

Throughout the famine period survival was what most concerned Irish people who were poor, in itself a form of direct resistance to the movement discussed earlier. "Charity" per se remained through the 1850s highly unorganized but nonetheless widespread. Extended parenting, whereby relatives, distant kin, or neighbors took in children, helped mitigate high mortality rates. Single women, whether young or old, had disproportionate responsibilities as heads of households, primary wage-earners, and financial linchpins that linked migrants from the south and west of Ireland to New York's streets. Job networks aided chains of Irish kin and neighbors, encompassing domestic servants of the most fashionable city districts and day laborers spread throughout the emerging national railroad system. What native-borns perceived to be an atomized, uncaring population was at base a very intricate and resourceful network that made group and individual survival possible.

Catholic nuns participated in these networks and used them in formal and informal charity work. The Mercy Sisters, for instance, distributed outdoor relief, food, clothing, medicine, shoes, and sundry supplies each week from their convent in the heart of the city's poorer district. Other convents in the city, including the various small ones of the Sisters of Charity, also provided outdoor relief from within poor neighborhoods and, like the Mercy Sisters, went into private homes to nurse the sick. In the cholera epidemic of 1849, in which five thousand New Yorkers, overwhelmingly from the poorest districts, lost their lives, Sisters of Mercy and Charity faced the epidemic as nurses in the homes of the poor. The Mercy Sisters also paid the rents of the some of the poor whom they encountered through prison and home-nursing visitation.[62] Sisters convinced, sometimes through relentless harassment, those well placed to find jobs for others not so fortunate, particularly for those who had spent time in jail or were similarly difficult to employ.[63]

Despite the myriad informal networks that Irish Catholics constructed to survive the famine, the single most salient feature of the city's formal Catholic charities through the Civil War was a lack of services for most poor people. Although some single women could access the resources of the Sisters of Mercy and the Sisters of the Good Shepherd, non-orphaned children, mothers, or men had few options other than to depend on Protestant relief. In 1856 Robert Hartley noted that 75 percent of those relieved through the auspices of the AICP were Catholic, "while not one percent of its pecuniary means . . . come from persons of that faith."[64] Poor Catholics might have agreed with Hartley in his indictment of the ends to which the church used the wealth it did have:

> All our Protestant churches are charitable institutions. . . . The same is true . . . of the Jews amongst us. But the Roman Catholics of this city, excepting the relief of a few orphans, make no corresponding provision for their poor. . . . Their adult poor and children, the sick, the aged, and the impotent, are alike neglected by them.
>
> Remonstrance with them on the subject, is uniformly met with the plea of poverty. But it does not appear how such a plea is reconcilable with . . . the millions invested in large and costly church edifices . . . while their suffering poor are left to be cared for by others, or to perish.[65]

Hartley was substantially correct in noting the degree to which the wealth of the Catholic community was invested in churches and Catholic education, neither of which met the very desperate needs of the majority of the Catholic population in the city.

Hughes greatly influenced the strategies of the community as a whole through ceaseless efforts to control religious orders and the laity in ways that promoted education and church-building. Primarily, he tended to ignore the misery of most of the two hundred Irish-born in the city. Characterizing their poverty as no worse than they endured in Ireland, he dismissed detractors who held that the church must allocate resources to meet the emergency. "It is but truth to say," Hughes explained, "that their abode in the cellars and garrets of New York is not more deplorable nor more squalid than the Irish hovels from which many of them had been 'exterminated.'"[66] To a people who had watched friends and kin die of starvation and disease being told that their environment was "not more deplorable" than before was hardly a rallying cry to run to church doors.

Archbishop Hughes, however, did not stop at disinterest; he made it difficult for any other Catholics in the city to care for the poor. His relentless concern with establishing his authority over everything "Catholic" in New York resulted in policies that severely restricted the charitable activism of the city's religious orders and laity. In 1858, when a Catholic from Boston was observed collecting donations for a Boston charity in New York, Hughes stopped him, stating that no charities outside the city would be permitted to solicit funds until St. Patrick's Cathedral was finished.[67] Hughes allowed no lay charities under even an "Irish" rubric to be organized independent of his authority. The Irish nationalist Thomas D'Arcy McGee, a rival to Hughes's authority in the New York Irish community, organized a colonization program to be funded by the Irish middle and upper classes. The Irish poor would be sent west with resources enough to start them on their own land. Hughes disguised himself in lay clothing, snuck into the meeting, and then dramatically denounced McGee and the program's supporters, effectively ending Catholic colonization programs in New York.[68] After reading in the morning paper that a lay Catholic group was organizing a special feast and gifts for the orphans in the Roman Catholic Orphan Asylum in 1858, Hughes wrote to Mr. R. Coddington, president of the Orphan Festival Society, to express his displeasure:

> The Apostle directs that all things should be done in order and this must apply to charity even for the orphans as well as to any other subject. These unhappy children are to meet the rugged strife of the world. . . . Their preparation for this lot should be more rugged than it is now under the gentle Sisters of Charity. But "cakes," "pies," and "sweet meats" . . . are out of the question for children like them. "Shoes," "Brogans," "coarse garments" would be much fitter offerings.
> . . . I have instructed the Sister Servant of the Orphan Asylum to decline receiving any gift or offering such as your humanity has prompted you to devise for the orphans, by way of a feast either at Easter, Fourth of July, Christmas or any other time. If your society can make offerings let it be to the Sisters in the form of clothing, flour, even potatoes, or perhaps best of all money—since the Sisters can lay it out for the benefit of the orphans with more tact and economy than anyone else.[69]

It was through his control over the Sisters of Charity, however, that Hughes most effectively promoted education over charities. After the sisterhood had been reestablished in 1846 under his direct control, it became almost exclusively involved in education. That shift, especially during the famine, distinguished the Sisters of Charity of New York from Sisters of Charity nationwide who maintained ties with their motherhouse in Emmitsburg. The Sisters of Charity in Buffalo, for instance, expanded their charitable networks through the 1850s and in response to the famine. Catholic charities in antebellum Buffalo surpassed those of native-borns, prompting grudging respect even from outspoken anti-Catholics.[70]

Despite his unwillingness to funnel the wealth of the community toward poor children or their parents, Archbishop Hughes was nonetheless characteristically vocal about the evil of anti-Catholicism apparent in child-savers' activities and disparaged Protestant "ladies in the street" who threatened Catholic civil rights: "Many children without being beggars, but at the same time seeking relief in a way which the law does not prohibit, have been encountered by the smiling benevolence of gentle ladies who had at their disposal stale candies and cheap calicoes," he complained. After subsequent dealings with the child, "the victim was transferred to a receiving house, then by legislative authority, transferred to another house, where it was deemed no crime to disregard all parental and natural rights of the child."[71] Like the meddling Protestant women caricatured by New York Catholic novelist Mary Sadlier, Protestant reformers, especially women, were depicted as being greedy for the souls of Catholic children.[72] That they might have genuinely wanted to aid the impoverished and were critical of Catholics for not doing so was not considered.

Organized Catholic charities for children instead remained through the 1850s extremely limited and were unable to reach more than a handful of poor children. German, French, and Irish women religious ran orphanages for Catholic children of each ethnic group, yet these were traditional facilities for orphans only, not the far greater number of poor and vagrant children targeted by the child-savers. In 1866, for instance, roughly 1,200 children resided in the city's three Catholic orphanages.[73] Comparing overall numbers reached by Catholic and Protestant child-care workers in the period, the inadequacy of the Catholic child-care system was stark. The Children's Aid Society alone claimed to have deported 1,450 in 1866 and proudly proclaimed to have placed-out more than eleven thousand children over the previous decade.[74]

The Civil War Draft Riots and the "Dangerous Classes"

The Draft Riots of 1863, still considered the bloodiest in American history, were a turning point in Catholic efforts to address the problems of poor children and counter the work of child-savers. Through the first years of the war the conditions in which poor Irish Catholics lived worsened, and organized Catholic charities became even more restricted than in the 1850s. Salaries of skilled and semiskilled workers increased and therefore kept up with or exceeded rates of wartime inflation of food staples and rent. Indeed, the success of skilled workers in approaching lower-middle-class incomes prompted groups such as the AICP to decrease charitable aid by two-thirds under the belief that few of the remaining poor were worthy.[75] Yet the unskilled found fewer jobs and lower rates of pay than in the decade before.

Instituting the draft in March of 1863 compounded the problems of the poor. Not only did they resent the infamous option given the rich—they could pay a substitute $300 to take their place—but they also feared the increased effort to arrest and imprison poor draft resistors who could not begin to collect such a sum.[76] Poor men resisted the draft not only because of the dangers of military service but also because their families were likely to suffer further impoverishment once they were sworn into the military. The city council provided emergency funds for women and children dependent on infamously irregular military allotments, but the inadequate ad hoc system combined with a rising cost of living did little to convince the very poor that service to the state would stave off ever-more intensive destitution.[77]

Despite worsening conditions, Catholic charities shrank during the war. The Sisters of Charity and Sisters of Mercy sent considerable portions of their urban workforces to battlefield areas, where Catholic nuns overall composed a third of all nurses who worked in the Civil War. Such a commitment to patriotic service, like Irish men's participation in the Union Army, was considered a strategy that would ingratiate the Irish in general, nuns in particular, to the American population.[78]

The Irish Catholic community in New York was painfully divided about what to do and who to blame for such conditions, and those divisions were obvious when rioting against the draft began on July 13, 1863. Archbishop Hughes helped inflame racism against African Americans because he was opposed to the emancipation of slaves. The *Metropolitan Record*, the official newspaper of the archdiocese, was likely to portray the rights of the Irish as conflicting with those of African Americans and refer explicitly to blacks as "an inferior race."[79]

Yet some Irish blamed each other. The predominantly Irish mob began the riot by nearly beating to death Superintendent of Police John Kennedy, who enforced strict compliance against desertion or evasion and in his role as provost marshal charged even those who voiced criticism of republican rule with treason.[80] On the first night of the riots Colonel Henry O'Brien of the Union Army fired his howitzer indiscriminately into a gathering mob, killing a female bystander and her child. He was apprehended and then brutally tortured and killed the following day and given last rites by Father William Clowry once the priest could disperse the crowd.[81] Thomas Fitzsimmons, although supportive of the anti-draft protest, organized a committee to guard against arson and pillaging, and saved an African American man from being lynched.[82] Two predominantly Irish Catholic city districts, including the "Bloody Sixth," remained calm, and African Americans in the district were undisturbed.[83] The largely Irish police force, national guard units, and Union Army members killed scores of Irish Catholic rioters, including many women, and were otherwise identified with suppressing not only the riots but also peaceful resistance to the draft.[84]

Placing-out advocates, however, were unlikely to see such complexity. Instead, native-borns ascribed the riots to the "Irish mob" that brutally attacked and killed African Americans and burned the homes of the rich. According to reformers, the rioters manifested not only brutal racism but also class-consciousness—and thus the very behavior that placing-out advocates had predicted. The Irish were no longer characterized as dependent and rather pathetic but rather as the racial core of the "dangerous classes."[85]

In the Irish Catholic community, the riots marked an end as well as a beginning. At the end of the week of rioting, for instance, Archbishop Hughes finally agreed to address the street crowds in an attempt to avert further violence. The group that assembled at his house was not composed of the hard-core rioters but rather of peaceable citizens who nonetheless showed sympathy with the plight of poor New Yorkers by chanting repeatedly for an end to the draft. Hughes refused to sanction that sentiment and continued to support the Conscription Act, admonishing that constitutional, not revolutionary, activity provided the only legitimate means of social change.[86]

In the long run, Hughes's posture before the crowd showed most of all the want of effective leadership in addressing the community's urgent needs. Although many in the Irish clergy and laity considered his support of the racial oppression of African Americans reprehensible, his lack of sympathy with the brutal conditions under which the Catholic poor of his own diocese lived was no less alarming. Such power that he had, he used to discourage the allotment of Catholic money or energies toward the needs of the poor. As a consequence, if the poor were disdainful of the pretended beneficence of the state in their behalf, many were similarly disdainful of the Catholic church.

Charles Loring Brace, and others who similarly had warned the public

that such violence was possible, attained more visible political prominence in the riots' aftermath. The effects on the Children's Aid Society's
placing-out system, for instance, were immediate. Brace asserted in 1864
that those "in the calm enjoyment of their comforts, and with all good
influences around them, could not believe that the fires of social revolution were slumbering just beneath their feet." It was "young men" who
were the leaders in the mob: "These sackers of houses and murderers of
the innocent, are merely *street-children* grown up." In addition, "The
number of children sent out by the Society the past year has been greater
than in any year since its foundation, and a *third* greater than in the
previous year . . . owing to the increased liberality of the public, which
has enabled us to widen our field of work . . . and thus to gather in more
destitute children."[87] No longer lulled into imagining that American
capitalist society would be free of class conflict, the native-born public
now heeded reformers' warnings of impending anarchy from an under-
class seemingly untouched by the blessings of capitalism or the moral
and political values all Americans were supposed to share.

Yet Catholic charities were for the first time organized in such a way
as to make them visible and begin to offset the policies of native-born
Protestant reformers. In April of 1863, just three months before the riots,
the Society for the Protection of Destitute Roman Catholic Children in
the City of New York was able after years of lobbying to secure a charter
from the state legislature to take in Catholic children who had been arrested for vagrancy, truancy, and other crimes.[88] Contributing from two
to five thousand dollars each, the society's members constituted the
founding board of managers for the Catholic Protectory, a reformatory
that would eventually become the largest single institution for children
in the United States. Consisting of twenty-six men, almost all of whom
were of Irish birth or ancestry, the board was a who's who of the Catholic middle and upper classes in the city and included renowned lawyers,
merchants, bankers, and judges.[89]

Structured largely as a Catholic parallel to the Protestant House of
Refuge and Juvenile Asylum, the Protectory mirrored the class and gender
composition of Protestant reformatory work although the Protectory initially received no public funding whatsoever. Unlike Catholic charitable
institutions for dependent children founded after the war, this reformatory institution was run primarily by men—both elite men in the laity
and a male religious order, the Christian Brothers. The Sisters of Charity
were recruited later in the project to care for girls because Hughes forbade
the Good Shepherd Sisters to work in the institution. "If you get a house
of reception for such creatures," he conceded, "I am willing that two, or

three or even four Sisters of Charity should undertake its management . . .
until something better can be done."[90] Unlike their role in institutions for
dependent children established after the war, the Sisters of Charity were
not deemed the legal incorporators or managers of the institution itself.

Although the first president of the Protectory's board of managers
was Levi Ives, a native-born convert to Catholicism, the board appealed
to the community at large for funding by linking Irish nationalism and
religion and tying support for Catholic charities with racial uplift. Con-
fessing a mixture of outrage and embarrassment at the condition of the
Irish poor in the city, the board of managers of the Protectory appealed
in 1864 "to . . . national pride and sympathy" in their bid for donations
and only secondarily to the protection of Catholic religious rights:

> In the *first* place we address ourselves to IRISHMEN, who constitute the
> great body of Catholics in this city, while, as we all know, the children
> of Irishmen make up by far the largest proportion of sufferers for whom
> we are called upon to provide. Vast numbers of the defenceless young
> creatures are daily wandering over the face of this great city, exposed to
> all the horrors of hopeless poverty—to the allurements of vice and crime
> in every disgusting and debasing form, bringing ruin on themselves, and
> disgrace and obloquy on the Irish name. Our object is to extend to these
> little sufferers a helping hand; to raise them from their state of degrada-
> tion and misery . . . to become, in short, instruments of good to society,
> and an honor to their race.[91]

The single most important contribution made by the Protectory's
leadership during and immediately after the war was that it articulated
a distinctly Catholic critique of the placing-out system. The Protectory's
managers, moreover, did not stress religion itself as a single or narrow
issue concerning church allegiance only. Rather, they began to focus on
what would become after the war a far-reaching critique of Protestant
reformers' ideologies, policies, and practices in attempting to mitigate
class warfare in America.

The specter of class revolution figured prominently in the rhetoric
of Catholics and Protestants after the riots but was characterized by each
group as stemming from different causes. The tide of immigrant poor
was itself at root for Protestant reformers and therefore required more
drastic and effective intervention. Catholics instead blamed Protestant
charitable policies, disdain of poor people, and willingness to break up
families with impunity for exacerbating class antagonisms and pushing
the poor to violence. "Can you expect that the poor, however depressed,
can experience such injustice and inhumanity, and have no feelings of
resentment?" asked Levi Ives. Irish Catholics, he conceded, composed

the largest segment of the poor, yet the causes of poverty were not their own. These "paupers, or their families, have been reduced to this state," Ives asserted, "by the hardships and dangers of the kind of labor to which, through Protestant cupidity, they have been subjected; and, in which the health of some, and the lives of others, have been lavishly sacrificed."[92] To add insult to injury, the elite then used state power to punish the poor for the ensuing poverty that they had created. "Let them reflect what would be their feelings," Ives contended, "should some powerful neighbor, through the power of the State, and on the very plea urged by themselves for taking away the rights of the poor, . . . deprive them by stealth of the children of their love."[93]

The plight of poor Catholic mothers under the system of family breakup and placing-out was especially prominent in literature used to encourage community support for the Protectory and for subsequent children's institutions aimed at diminishing the influence of the child-savers. The strategic, deliberate, and unrelenting effort to make poor mothers visible in this literature was meant to counter what Catholics saw as the complete absence or vilification of those women in Protestant placing-out literature.[94] John Maguire noted that the published children's letters back to the CAS virtually never mentioned a biological parent, "possibly the widow of an Irish soldier who died fighting in defence of the Union, and whose boy got beyond her maternal control."[95] Ives maintained that even women who had genuinely "vicious" husbands should not be deprived of their children because they were all the more dependent on those children for love and financial support:

> There is a little boy who nestles at her breast, or plays around her knee, and looks up with infant fondness and pity into her sorrowful face. She cherishes the hope that at some future day this child will be her support and comfort. . . . Cases . . . have, for the past few years, passed under my own eyes,—cases in which, on the plea of relieving poverty and benefitting society, a suffering mother has been cruelly deprived of her darling boy . . . that she is never, perhaps, to see him more, while he is deprived of parental guidance—is taught, perhaps, to forget her—to become callous to all sense of duty "to honor and succor his father and mother," and she, poor woman, has, in addition to a drunken husband, the wretchedness of a lost child![96]

Just as native-born reformers' public literature attempted to discourage sympathy with poor parents, especially poor mothers, Catholic literature throughout the century intended just the reverse. A poor mother who lost her children through the actions of child-savers was the single most visible figure in appeals for funding and support from the Catholic public, and she was used much more frequently than appeals to the hardships that children themselves faced in such a system.

Catholics thereby articulated a fundamentally different idea of the rights and duties of children and parents. For Catholics, filial duty was considered sacred, whether articulated in behavioral obedience or economic support, and they held that the state should enforce, not undermine, parental authority. The Irish as a group held that for children, particularly adolescents, not to labor when labor was needed was a threat to the dictum to honor their parents. As they had for the Irish peasantry for centuries, a family economy based on women and children's labor and care of the elderly in poverty and sickness provided the foundations for community life.

Catholics argued that Protestant policies that systematically denied poor people parental rights did not just encourage revenge but threw the poor into an endless cycle of chaos and desperation that threatened the rule of law. To encourage children's removal from their parents or "to lower in the eyes of children the standard of duty to their parents, or the sacredness of parental authority . . . was a fatal blow, aimed at the very foundations of the social structure."[97] The policies of the Protectory and the many Catholic institutions that would be established after the war therefore sought to reinforce, not sever, family ties critical to the Irish Catholic poor and the working-class family economies through which they survived. "Next to their duty to Almighty God, the children are taught to have regard to that which they owe their parents," wrote Ives in the first annual report. "Hence in all those cases where children of parents able to support them have been committed for minor offences, we insist upon returning them [as] soon as . . . it can safely be done."[98]

Conceptualizing Catholic patriarchy as inherently oppressive to both women and children and the Protestant individuation of poor families as liberating, Protestant reformers became ever-more convinced after the war that they needed to expand the placing-out system. Child-savers wanted to liberate children from families that they believed exploited them for their labor, a community that stressed communal survival over individual achievement, and a church that stressed interdependence rather than independent thought and action. For Protestant child-savers, the parental authority of those they viewed as the immoral poor was the very wellspring of poverty itself. Undermining such authority was essential to the larger project of stemming the reproduction of a permanent poor class in America.

Yet from the viewpoint of poor, Irish Catholic mothers, Protestants' "liberation" of Catholic children was an assault so cruelly dismissive of human dignity that it could only be explained as yet another example of Anglo-Protestants dominating and subordinating the Irish poor until they had nothing left. Like the larger Protestant colonialist logic in Ireland that "liberated" Irish Catholics from religion, land, and finally food itself, Protestant efforts to "save" Irish Catholic children assaulted the most fundamental social fabric on which the Irish poor depended.

To argue that patriarchy was good for poor mothers is to invite controversy, and yet the more common assumption that maternalist movements were good for all women because they were run by some women also needs to be questioned. The "bad mothers" discursively created through the placing-out system found few "good mothers" who would defend their interests. Instead, the increasing visibility of Catholic charities as run by the male laity and nuns, and the Catholic community's explicit championing of the rights of poor mothers, made patriarchal ideology seem a sane and compassionate option for the Irish poor. The strategic use of Catholic patriarchal ideology proved not only useful to Irish Catholic women but also a principled and sustained defense against the policies and ideological agenda of elite Protestants.

What Protestants saw as an oppressive religious ideology and institution that hindered the progress of the Catholic poor in general, women and children in particular, soon proved to poor Irish Catholics an ideological tradition that could be used to support their struggles to survive. It was also an institutional complex of charities that could protect them from the harshest policies of yet another Protestant state.

4 Saving Children from the
Child-Savers, 1864–94

[T]here is now, in the lower strata of the population, a
larger mass of ignorance, vice, and heathenism combined,
than was ever before known in our history. . . . It is the
residuum or dregs of four millions of European immigrants, including paupers, felons, and convicts, that have
landed at this port within the last twenty years. . . . Suddenly transferred to a country where the law imposes no
test either of intelligence or education for the exercise of
suffrage, they are . . . enfranchised. . . . Such a constituency, requiring, of course, a corresponding representation,
created a description of political leaders before unknown
in our municipal government.
—Robert Hartley

And whilst we cannot yield our rights to any one sect of
Protestantism, we are equally determined, while respect-
ing the rights of all Protestants, not to yield our constitutional rights to all the sects of Protestantism combined.
—Isaac Hecker

Catholic sisters in New York City began after the Civil War
to construct institutions that would eventually undermine the placing-
out system. Like women in the Protestant middle class and elite, Irish
Catholic women increased their overall power through work with poor
children, used state funding secured by men in their group to do so, and
claimed the right to instill in those children the values commensurate
with their class and culture.

Because the gender systems at the heart of the Protestant middle-
class and Irish Catholic cultures were so distinct, the form the charities

took and the substantive policies they enacted were also quite different. In a broad sense, Catholic sisters expanded convents to take in poor children, much as Protestant women received children into their homes. Through that expansion nuns and other Catholic community activists articulated a response not only to the placing-out movement but also to scientific charity enthusiasts who held that relief itself caused America's inequitable class structure. The Catholic response was to use state and city funding to inflate provisions for the poor to unprecedented levels. By the mid-1890s New York City's care of dependent children expended ten times as much as that in any other American city.

Sisters rarely participated in the general "Catholic" discussions on the origins of poverty or meaning of charity. Nor did they publish almost any written material that lays out succinctly the principles that guided their charitable work through the nineteenth century. Yet because nuns believed that their spiritual lives were centered on work as an expression of values, understanding their ideological positions in the on-going debates requires a close look at their institutions as the literal embodiments of larger policies and agendas. To do so, moreover, does not require guessing at meaning or intent. Nuns' efficacy in changing the nature of the welfare system constructed by native-borns was swift and decisive. Firmly in place by 1885, their institutions for poor children, and the values evident in constructing them, became a large part of New York City's public welfare system.

The sisters' reliance on massive public, not just private, funding influenced their charitable institutions and policies in many respects. Among the most important was the relatively limited role that the Catholic elite and middle class had in shaping nuns' policies through the period of Tammany's greatest strength. Because the nuns did not depend primarily on private funding, they had little need to conform to the ideas or perspectives of those able to give it. Indeed, as convents became the provinces of a much greater proportion of women who were either poor or of the working class, charitable work increasingly reflected the distinct concerns of those groups.

The Sisters and the Tweed Ring

After the war, Irish Catholic sisters were able to build an infrastructure of children's charities that would eventually undermine the placing-out movement for two reasons. The first was that Irish Catholic men had newly won political power in the city and state. With the foreign-born constituting more than 60 percent of total voters in New York City in

1867, immigrant control of local government was decisive.[1] By 1869 the Association for Improving the Condition of the Poor (AICP) claimed that only thirteen of the forty-eight members of the city's central representative body, the common council, were native-born and that "Irishmen" held more than a thousand of the city's government jobs. As the AICP characterized them, the Irish were "political leaders before unknown in our municipal government—cunning, shrewd, unscrupulous demagogues, intent mainly on their own selfish greed—among whom those were ever most popular and successful who pandered most adroitly to the foibles, vices, and prejudices of the masses."[2] Hostility to placing-out was, of course, among the masses' greatest prejudices.

The second factor that led to undermining the placing-out system was John Hughes's death in 1864 and the ecclesiastical leadership of his successor, John McCloskey. Archbishop McCloskey made his mark in the following two decades primarily by encouraging but not tightly controlling the political and religious activism of both religious and laity in the diocese. McCloskey's most important contribution to the development of Catholic charities was to encourage Catholic activism of all kinds and through new and creative channels. Instead of laity and religious being discouraged by (or fearful of) administrative control and priorities, the postwar Irish Catholic community seemed to thrive on a host of possibilities that the political machine, and an increasingly cohesive and resourceful Irish Catholic community, offered. The sisters who worked in charities did everything possible to take advantage of the new order.

The gender system underlying the expansion of Catholic charities during this period was different from that of the emerging Protestant middle class. Neither nuns nor Catholic laywomen, including those among the elite and of the middle class, formed associational groups comparable to the American Female Guardian Society (AFGS). Catholic mothers, as a group, had less cultural power than nuns, and those who became active in charitable activities did so primarily in auxiliary groups associated with a particular sisterhood.[3] Their status as mothers in Irish Catholic culture did not provide a way to claim public power or the right to mother beyond their individual home spheres. Middle-class men in the laity, however, formed the St. Vincent de Paul Society, which offered a parallel to "friendly visiting" from the Protestant middle class.

Numbering 933 active members in 1864, the city's St. Vincent de Paul Society (SVDP) consisted of parish-based organizations that dispensed alms and visited prisons and charitable institutions. The New York Council of the society described its members in 1864 as "men who have themselves struggled, when new comers here, to earn their living and attain the comparative ease they now enjoy. . . . They are . . . familiar with the picture of want."[4] Also composed predominantly of Irish Catholics and having an exclusively male membership, the Catholic Union, the society's elite arm, was formed in 1872 by a coalition of leading lawyers, judges, and merchants in addition to Tammany leaders Richard O'Gorman and "Honest" John Kelly. The group's primary purpose was to promote Catholic civil and religious rights in city and state legislation.[5]

Sisters then began to expand their convents in two stages. During the first, from immediately after the war until 1875, sisterhoods relied on large grants of public funds to begin building the physical institutions themselves or expanding convent buildings to take in poor children. During the second stage, from 1875 to 1885, they began to mold a system of institutions to undermine placing-out and scientific charity policies.

The Sisters of Mercy provide but one example of the first stage, when a transition from private to public funding dramatically altered the priorities of individual orders. Until 1864 the sisters depended on private funding through the church and struggled with financial problems that were growing worse instead of better. Unable to pay off the $30,000 mortgage on the House of Mercy, they found that payments took "almost the whole of the annual collection made in the Churches for the benefit of the Institution."[6] Irish-born Mother Mary Austin Horan attempted to gain parish priests' approval for a great fair, an independent project she likely would not have attempted had Hughes been alive. Mother Austin not only visited every pastor in the city individually but also called a common meeting of pastors citywide to encourage their support. Although "from the greater number she received encouragement," the convent annalist reported that "there were some whose language was really insulting."[7] Mother Austin attempted to minimize the grumbling by making a deal with the larger group. No subsequent collections would be taken up on the parish level. In doing so, the order relinquished its right to the collective parish contributions for one Sunday each spring. In return, pastors agreed as a group to support the fair. Proceeds from the event were sufficient to pay off the mortgage, but subsequent financial need put the order into debt again by the following year.[8]

By 1865, however, the Mercy Sisters began to use the Irish Catholic men in city government as a means of radically altering their prospects. In a visit to the convent in 1865, newly elected Alderman Farley, a representative on the common council, suggested that the Sisters of Mercy petition the president of the board of aldermen for "a grant of $5,000 to enable the Community to pay some floating debts contracted unavoidably." The petition was granted shortly thereafter. That same year the sisters petitioned the council to fund a new institution for destitute girls, a project they had long desired to undertake. "Rev. Mother Austin . . . talked the matter over with Alderman Farley . . . and he kindly volunteered to present a Petition to the Corporation of the City, for a place in the upper part of New York City, on which to build an Industrial Home for girls."[9] The sisters then drew up a petition, Farley supported it in the council through an eloquent exposition on the sisters' wartime service as battlefield nurses, and the sisterhood was given a large tract of land at Eighty-first Street and Madison Avenue.

By 1867 the sisters had prepared a second petition, this time to the state legislature, to ask for help toward the building fund, and they received $50,000 by year's end. The convent annalist reported that Archbishop McCloskey subsequently visited the convent and expressed "his great satisfaction at the remarkable success of Rev. Mother's applications to the Legislature and his surprise at the[ir] generosity."[10]

Protestant reformers certainly did not see such funding as "generous" but rather as fraud. By the late 1860s William Tweed had strategically placed himself on the Senate Committee on Charitable and Religious Societies in Albany, the committee that had regularly rubber-stamped requests from Protestant or nonsectarian charities for state funding. Tweed expanded state appropriations for private charities and schools and steered most of the funds to Catholics. The senate committee allotted almost $900,000 to Catholic charities while keeping appropriations for Protestant, Jewish, and nonsectarian charities at $83,000, $26,000, and $194,000, respectively.[11] In 1871 Charles Loring Brace claimed that $30,000 of the $110,000 annual state appropriation on which the Children's Aid Society (CAS) had come to depend had been lost "by frauds."[12]

The Tweed Ring also manipulated city revenues to redirect funding from placing-out societies to Catholic children's charities. In 1871, for instance, the Board of Apportionment of the City and County of New York sent notices to approximately seventy charitable organizations soliciting applications for a portion of the excise funds.[13] A. Oakley Hall, Richard B. Connelly, William M. Tweed, and Peter Sweeney—the "Tweed Ring" in all its glory—announced that they interpreted the new city charter that Tweed had secured as giving them power to decide whether individual private charities should be funded. Catholic institutions were often given as much or more than requested, and no organization that participated in placing-out received as much as in the past.[14] When Brace and others brought the Tweed Ring's activities to the public, *Harper's Weekly* and the *New York Times* published scathing articles characterizing the Ring's activities as a Roman Catholic coup.[15]

In "Church & State," Thomas Nast contrasts the separation of church and state in Europe with a depiction of the New York Irish as simian creatures shifting city funds to the Catholic church; a nun sews together two halves of a previously torn flag representing church and state. Lady Liberty remains chained to the ballot box. *Harper's Weekly*, Feb. 19, 1870. (Provided courtesy of HarpWeek LLC)

The postwar activities of the Sisters of Charity were dramatically different from those of the order during Archbishop Hughes's administration. Hughes's emphasis on education provided the sisterhood with important assets. Through the famine period the sisters produced a multitiered system of education for Catholic girls that served as the structural foundation for recruiting and training large numbers of nuns. From a total of one hundred women religious in New York City in 1848, the city's convent workforce expanded by 1865 to more than 550 nuns; the Sisters of Charity alone had 335 members.[16]

The order reallocated personnel and funding to construct and support a variety of charities throughout the city, thereby becoming an order whose work was again reflective of its name. In Brooklyn, the Sisters of Charity opened St. Paul's Industrial School in 1866 and St. Joseph's in 1873.[17] They expanded the Roman Catholic Orphan Asylum by war's end and founded St. Stephen's Home for Children by the early 1870s in addition to establishing the enormous Foundling Asylum in 1869. The Sisters of St. Dominic and the Missionary Sisters of the Order of St. Francis were among the other orders instituted in New York after the war with the goals of working with children and establishing industrial schools.[18]

The Tweed Ring's funding was substantial, but sisterhoods were perhaps more creative in harnessing private funding and a lot of help through extensive networks of both poor and wealthy women. The sodalities and confraternities organized by the Sisters of Mercy and composed primarily of domestic servants raised more than $18,000 for their children's home; the members of St. Joseph's society individually contributed 10 cents a month.[19] The annalist reported that "the Poor took much more trouble to help in paying for the building expenses than the rich . . . if we except the members of the State Legislators." Tweed himself contributed $1,000.

Sister Irene Fitzgibbon of the Sisters of Charity established the Foundling Asylum in 1869 for abandoned infants and received public grants for the building. By 1870 she had organized a "Ladies Auxiliary" of very wealthy Catholic and Protestant women, , including the wives of such illustrious Tweed Ring members as Richard Connolly, the city comptroller.[20] The group was responsible for securing legislation that brought the institution subsequent land grants and per capita payments. It also raised substantial private funding. The auxiliary's Great Fair of 1871 alone netted $100,000. Included in the illustrious group were Caroline Ewing Bouvier, grandmother to Jaqueline Kennedy Onassis, and Mrs. Paul Thebaud. Both women provided critical links to elite Catholics who had considerable political and social influence in the city and state.

As it had for Protestant women, movement into work with children substantially increased nuns' overall public power. The Tweed Ring's support was of the very best kind. They gave sisterhoods a great deal of money and put minimal stipulations on its use. The machine's primary interest, as Theda Skocpol states, was in "displaying" support for immigrant and working-class communities. It was relatively uninterested in closely controlling how the funding it dispersed would be used.[21] In conjunction with an ecclesiastical administration that encouraged but did not control Catholic charitable expansion, machine politics maximized the kind of power Irish Catholic nuns exercised.

Securing city and state funding provided relief from financial dependence on church authorities or the Catholic elite, and sisters used the opportunity to establish autonomy in legal form. For each institution founded after Irish Catholic ascendance into political power, for instance, the Sisters of Charity acted as the legal incorporators and managers over whom no one had state power. When sisters working at the Foundling Asylum decided in 1874 that the growing institution needed legal and political strategic advice from men in the laity, Sister Irene quite explicitly limited the powers of the advisory board. The bylaws incorporating the institution were amended accordingly: "[I]t has seemed proper that some of the special friends of the Asylum, men of business habits and experience should come forward and, without, in the slightest degree, attempting or intending to interfere with the exclusive control which their charter has conferred upon these benevolent ladies as the legal managers of the Asylum, should proffer their services as advisors."[22] When the Sisters of Charity took charge of a permanent girls' department at the Protectory in 1867, they brought resolutions to the board that guaranteed "that in all respects in the management of the female department the Sisters shall have the same power which is granted to the Brothers." The board accepted the resolutions, giving the Sisters of Charity the right to control all aspects of internal management.[23]

Yet the flurry of activity in the first stage of expansion did not rest on continuous funding and therefore did not fundamentally threaten the placing-out system. Until 1875 Irish Catholic men provided land grants and sporadic but very hefty monetary grants to supplement private fund-raising and help women religious begin building institutions that had enough space to house large numbers of poor Catholic children. Without funds to maintain those institutions, however, no more than a few hundred could be clothed, fed, and educated. The Sisters of Mercy, for instance, claimed only a hundred children in their 1871 petition for city funding despite the building's capacity for 350.[24] In the same year the girls' building in the

Catholic Protectory, built to accommodate six hundred, contained only 250. Besides the Protectory, moreover, the Sisters of Charity had opened St. Stephen's home in 1868 to care for destitute children but were able to maintain only a hundred at a time through the early 1870s. St. Joseph's Orphan Asylum for German children, run by the Sisters of Notre Dame, had a building that could accommodate two hundred but contained only 160 in the institution in 1871. The Holy Cross Sisters ran St. Vincent de Paul's Orphan Asylum as an industrial school and were dependent on private funds to care for the two hundred children in the institution. Other orders were instituted in the city during the postwar period with the goal of working with children and instituting industrial schools. They, including the Sisters of St. Dominic and the Missionary Sisters of the Order of St. Francis, depended primarily on private funding.[25]

Neither was the Protectory able to provide poor Irish Catholic children with an alternative to Protestant-run reformatories. In 1871, for instance, Irish-*born* children still constituted the majority of inmates in the Juvenile Asylum, and the children of the Irish-born made up a significant number of the remainder.[26] The fall of the Tweed Ring and the impending long depression of the 1870s therefore threatened to limit effects of Catholic nuns' charitable work to a valiant but feeble attempt at resistance.

Scientific Charity

During the early 1870s, elite female Protestants began to take a leadership role in charitable work as part of a larger elite urban reform movement aimed at regaining political control of the city and state lost to the Tweed Ring. "The moneyed, cultured, moral and industrious classes, who are overwhelmingly in the majority, as a rule and habit," charged one Protestant reformer, "have abandoned their posts as citizens and surrendered the care of public affairs into the hands of the vagabond element of society."[27]

The establishment of the State Charities Aid Association (SCAA), the single most important organization for Protestant women's charitable work from its founding in 1872 through the turn of the century, differed from antebellum organizations of Protestant women in several important ways. As part of the anti-Tweed, elite-sponsored, urban reform movement spearheaded by the Union League of New York City, the SCAA was concerned with checking machine politics by drawing on a larger base of Protestant native-borns throughout New York State to override the policies of an immigrant-controlled city government.[28] The SCAA's access to male power brokers in city and state government was far more direct than that attained by the AFGS. Maternalism itself was therefore not emphasized as the legitimating wedge through which they derived political authority.

The SCAA, established by Louisa Schuyler and Josephine Shaw Lowell, among others, had considerable political power from its inception by virtue of its members' status in the most elite Protestant families and through the mechanisms by which they guaranteed political access. The first SCAA victory was to reorganize the State Board of Charities in 1873 to extend its legal authority to appoint local citizens to inspect institutions under state supervision. Such legislation also gave the SCAA quasi-state authority. It was agreed before the board's reorganization that it would immediately grant SCAA members authority to investigate the conditions in all state-run charities.[29] Josephine Shaw Lowell won an appointment to sit directly on the State Board of Charities in 1876 and became the first woman to hold a position of such authority in the New York State charities system—the only one to do so for the remainder of the century.[30] Such connections augmented the power of the native-born elite, and its female members in particular, to regain authority over charitable institutions and legislation.

In its personnel and organization the SCAA was constructed as an offshoot of the U.S. Sanitary Commission. Its members were from the same predominantly female and elite group of reformers who had organized war relief efforts through their headquarters in New York City. Although leaders such as Schuyler and many volunteers in the larger organization got their start in the Children's Aid Society, the Sanitary Commission was ultimately more central to their charitable training. As Lori Ginzberg observes, the female leadership of the commission organized its work in accordance with "corporate" imperatives toward rationalization and efficiency. The commission and the SCAA thereby proved a departure in Protestant female benevolence, rejecting implicitly and explicitly the more "sentimental," less rational or "efficient" impulses that had guided female charitable work throughout the mid-nineteenth century.[31] Imagining themselves to be the "benevolent" side of benevolent capitalism, SCAA leaders were far more likely to consider themselves female counterpoints to the male capitalist (ruling) class than as middle class.

The SCAA also positioned itself as a step beyond nonsectarian and closer to the avowedly secular, concerned with the public and state rather than with private or religious matters. Lowell and Schuyler were both Unitarians and considered themselves to be only vaguely Protestant.

They explicitly restricted religious proselytization in the organizations in which they worked, including the SCAA, State Board of Charities, and Charity Organization Society (which Lowell founded in 1882). Thus they could portray themselves as being above the fray of sectarian squabbles. All SCAA members, however, were from Protestant backgrounds, and none were Catholic or Jewish.

Science rather than religion was ostensibly to guide SCAA policies and agenda. The association therefore centered its work on expanding and integrating policies that supported "scientific charity" and placing-out, the twin pillars of charitable work among the native-born after the war. Scientific charity proponents insisted that science, if properly understood and used, could discern the natural laws leading to humanity's ultimate well-being. Figures such as Lowell, whose family was deeply committed to abolitionist and reform causes, believed the old Christian dictum "the poor shall always be with you" encouraged charity workers to accept poverty as a given. Reform, in Josephine Lowell's estimation, was best aimed at eradicating poverty entirely so as to bring the poor's suffering to a definite end.

Scientific charity was similar to antebellum Protestant reform in that the moral failings of the poor were still deemed the primary cause of poverty's growth. Yet the new scientists of charity distinguished themselves from antebellum Protestant reformers likely to conform to sentimental imperatives that they be "charitable"—if only for their own salvation as Christians. Josephine Shaw Lowell argued that such weaknesses in charity work exacerbated the poor's dependence on material aid and thereby perpetuated poverty itself. More "enlightened" reformers, Lowell believed, should use science without sentiment, withhold aid except to those who would starve or perish imminently without it, and thereby work toward reforms that would eradicate poverty entirely. Directly using the work of the British theorists Charles Darwin, Herbert Spencer, Thomas Malthus, Octavia Hill, and John Stuart Mill, American scientific charity activists held that the most any able-bodied poor person should receive must be less than the very poorest worker makes lest people become dependent on charity and unwilling to struggle to survive.[32]

The Darwinian or Spencerian "struggle for survival" shaped the logic of scientific charity enthusiasts profoundly. For them, providing direct aid helped the least rather than the most fit survive, thereby damning society to the unnatural reproduction of its worst elements. Charles Loring Brace is said to have read Darwin's *Origin of Species* thirteen times and from it concluded that the greater the struggle, the better the human product produced.[33] According to Spencerian theory, the immoral habits leading to poverty were hereditary, a viewpoint that supported observations that poverty had risen in tandem with the large influx of immigrants into New York. Dispensing charity to those who were poor due to biological, therefore racial, inheritance helped people survive who would then degrade the larger biological pool. American society was therefore not obligated to reproduce such populations. Its concern for the betterment of the species, in fact, made any structural attempt to aid cultural or biological reproduction a self-destructive act. Charles Loring Brace and reformers similarly inclined were therefore among the first to link placing-out with social Darwinism.

And yet biology or race did not supersede culture in entirety. Heredity, as Protestant reformers understood it, did not make either friendly visiting or placing-out efforts as moot as they might had reformers understood heredity as being the only factor in reproducing poverty. Culture remained, in their estimation, an important factor in determining destitution or wealth. Elite contact with the poor through friendly visiting was therefore intended to "morally elevate" the poor's collective character.

Explicit in this approach was fear that the physical and cultural segregation of rich and poor in large industrial cities had exacerbated the poor's isolation from those of "better character." Because Protestant reformers still deemed character, whether inherited or shaped in cultural contexts, the critical factor determining destitution or economic well-being, the poor's continuing isolation ostensibly predetermined their cultural reproduction and therefore the continuance of poverty itself.[34]

The logic of social Darwinism convinced SCAA members among many others that renewed and ever more vigilant efforts at child removal were necessary so as to minimize cultural factors entirely. Heredity could make children more or less redeemable, but heredity combined with being raised in environments organized by their "pauper" parents, kin, and community rendered poor children a hopeless cause and therefore threatened the larger society with ever-more painful class stratification. Charles S. Hoyt, a commissioner of the New York State Board of Charities, submitted his 1877 report on the causes of poverty derived from a survey of poorhouse inmates throughout the state:

> Most cases of pauperism are due to idleness, improvidence, drunkenness, or other forms of vicious indulgence, which are frequently, if not universally, hereditary in character. Insufficient attention has been given to hereditary factors, and society must take positive measures to cope with them. Many families dependent on private charity seem to exist only to rear children like themselves. To keep such families together is

contrary to sound policy; the sooner they can be separated and broken up, the better it will be for the children and for society at large.[35]

The SCAA concurred in 1879, arguing that "when there is a hereditary tendency to evil or pauperism in the child, . . . its progress in such case can be arrested only by early, prompt, and vigorous measures . . . it is in the beginning of life, before the habits are formed, that pauperism is the most easily, economically, and effectually prevented."[36]

Such theories were brought to bear directly on any hint of hesitancy in removing poor children from their parents. William Letchworth, a member of the state board and among its most active child-saving proponents, cautioned against sympathy with poor parents, especially poor mothers, in light of his investigation of children in almshouses throughout the state: "In some poorhouses I find that the children have one or both parents with them, and the kind heart of the keeper, . . . or his amiable wife, who is a mother herself, protests against the separation of the child from the parent. But in every case that has come to my notice . . . the antecedents of the parent were such as to make it evident that the only hope of rescuing the child from a life of pauperism was to separate it from its parents."[37]

Protestant reformers in New York City found their test site for such theories in the "Long Depression" of 1873 through 1877. They became in the midst of that crisis more, not less, reluctant to aid the poor. The depression, reformers believed, was caused by the poor's dependence on charity; it was the poor's mounting belief that they had basic rights to charitable support that threatened to undermine reformers' careful adherence to the principles of scientific charity.[38]

In 1873 the Bureau of Charities, precursor to the Charity Organization Society (COS), began an inventory of aid recipients so as to rationalize disparate almsgiving by private and public sources and thereby diminish opportunities for any individual to receive aid from more than one charity.[39] The AICP lambasted those who had tried to feed the multitudes by organizing make-shift soup kitchens throughout the city. The "thirty four soup-kitchens, free lunches, free dormitories, and others of a kindred class . . . —free to all who would partake of the charity—irrespective of their need or desert" were said to be the very cause of the depression.[40] The Children's Aid Society claimed that the United States had "escaped the curse of a pauper class" but warned that "with our occasional business calamities and the unbounded benevolence of our fortunate classes, we are in frequent danger in the large cities of forming one." The winter of 1874, the severest since 1857, brought increased donations to the society, but it demonstrated prudence: "Whatever direct assistance in food and clothing and coal was given was rendered in connection with our Schools, by teachers and visitors long experienced." Most of the funds collected, the society asserted, were spent deporting children west.[41]

The SCAA, State Board of Charities, and other Protestant-run groups worked throughout the depression to ensure the contraction not only of private charity but also of the public welfare system. At the state level, the SCAA, along with the AICP and the Bureau of Charities, supported in 1874 an amendment to the state constitution that banned state aid to private charities whose funds went to any form of outdoor relief.[42] The SCAA supported the bill in part to minimize the possibility of the machine using such funds for political favors and in part to limit the distribution of outdoor relief and therefore strike at what the association believed to be at the root of the depression. The situation was further aggravated by a successful campaign led by State Board of Charities members Theodore Roosevelt Sr. and Josephine Shaw Lowell to pass a state law that abolished public outdoor relief by New York City's government. All other cities in New York State were exempt.[43] Coal continued to be distributed, but public outdoor relief was not instituted again in New York City until 1931.[44]

Scientific charity ideology held sway throughout the depression at all levels of private and public charitable systems controlled by Protestants. The contraction of public outdoor relief, for instance, did not result in the poor's greater dependence on the "last resort" of the public welfare system—entry into the poorhouse. The city's almshouse managers reported that despite widespread destitution, the number of inmates in the institution had diminished from 3,201 in 1870 to 2,075 in 1875, owing to careful adherence to principles of scientific charity: "Care has been taken not to diminish the terrors of this last resort of poverty, because it has been deemed better that a few should test the minimum rate at which existence can be preserved, than that the many should find the poor-house so comfortable a home that they would brave the shame of pauperism to gain admission to it. Acting on this principle, the per capita of 1875 was still further decreased to 12 cents . . . per day."[45]

Such efforts, however, pale when compared to the intensification of placing-out rhetoric and programs. By the mid-1870s Catholic observers estimated that ten thousand children a year were being placed out from New York City. The CAS alone reported deporting more than four thousand annually through the worst years of the depression.[46] In 1876 the American Female Guardian Society and the Five Points House of Industry were among twenty-eight separate Protestant or nonsectarian organizations in New York City that listed their primary "objects" as placing-out.[47] The managers at the Howard Mission put the issue concisely. Allowing poor immigrants to live together in an urban environment, they asserted in 1876, "cannot fail to make them feel clannish, or create the actual existence of caste in our democratic America. Disintegration is the true watchword for mission work among the destitute."[48]

As the final piece of major legislation secured by the SCAA and other Protestant reformers through the 1870s, the Children's Law of 1875 was expected to complement legislation abolishing both state funding for private charities and the city's public outdoor relief.[49] The Children's Law made the shelter of children in any poorhouse in the state illegal, and, according to the SCAA, it was intended to serve dual functions. Resting on the Protestant bifurcation of children and adults into the innocent and guilty, it was aimed both at saving children and further punishing poor parents. As the SCAA asserted, removing "a child away from the ruinous influence of a poor-house gives it the best chance of redeeming the place in society forfeited by its parents, and thus saves the State the burden of future paupers and criminals."[50] Further, it would decrease the adult poor's dependence on public relief by making less attractive "the hospitable leisure of the Poor-house" in that entrance would now be contingent upon poor parents' surrendering all guardianship rights over their children.[51] Because the poorhouse was the only institution in the city and state system to keep adults and children together, the SCAA, as well as the State Board of Charities, believed that the Children's Law would strike the final blow against transmitting or reproducing familial and institutional pauperism.[52]

The SCAA assumed that most children who were to leave the almshouses of the state would be funneled through private groups and placed out quickly. In anticipation, the Children's Law also made it easier to declare children dependent on the state and therefore under the legal control of private charitable societies. Before 1875, parents who wanted to commit dependent children were required to do so through the city's superintendents and overseers of the poor. After 1875, children could be declared dependent by any "justice of the peace, police justice or other magistrate." The law further stipulated that the state would "provide for their support and care in families, Orphan Asylums, or other appropriate institutions" and allocated approximately $2 a week to cover maintenance costs until their presumed placement in a private family.[53] The Catholic Union, however, in its first victory in the state legislature, was successful in adding a "religious clause" to the final version of the bill: "In placing any such child in any such Institution, it shall be the duty of the officer, justice, or person placing it there, to commit such child to an Orphan Asylum, Charitable, or other Reformatory Institution, that is governed or controlled by officers or persons of the same religious faith as the parents of such child, so far as practicable."[54]

The SCAA protested the inclusion of that clause "as being contrary to the traditions and usages of this country, in recognizing religious distinctions in State legislation," thereby seeing it largely as a sectarian issue but not a provision that would threaten placing-out efforts or the general intention of the bill to expand child removal to every level of public policy.[55] The clause was deleted in an amendment the following year but restored in legislation of 1878 that extended placing-out powers to private societies incorporated to take in dependent and delinquent children.[56]

The SCAA remained optimistic in 1878 that the institutionalization of destitute children was a temporary expedient until homes could be found for them: "The only question we have to meet is, how quickest and by what simplest machinery can we restore the family life of a child who has lost his natural home through the death or depravity of his parents?" The association then listed "the finding of family homes for homeless children" as the first priority of its work, followed by the goal "[t]hat children shall be guarded from any possibility of a return to pauper influences in their surroundings."[57]

Through 1878 neither Catholics nor Protestants as a group understood the full implications of this legislation. Within a few years, however, SCAA members would become the staunchest critics of the effects of the Children's Law, which in their view backfired mercilessly and created a legal and financial base upon which Catholic children's institutions under nuns' direction thrived.

The Catholic Union assumed that its successful lobby for inclusion of the religious clause was a small, albeit satisfying, victory that effected the few children then housed in almshouses throughout the state. On the convent level, however, nuns understood the law's provisions immediately. It guaranteed that public finances would be allotted for maintenance of destitute children in institutions of their own religion. It also enhanced the ability of nuns and the Catholic poor to declare children dependent and therefore entitled to public funds for housing in those institutions. New York City's nuns immediately began taking in hundreds and then thousands of children with the understanding that they were legally guaranteed funding to maintain them. The nuns refused, moreover, to place children out.

Politicizing Irish Catholic Poverty

That the male laity, or occasionally the clergy, claimed to speak for Catholics as a group did not mean they articulated a defense of Catholic charitable institutions encompassing the goals or politics of all other Irish Catholics. The Irish Catholic postwar alliance was always fragile because it depended on varied, sometimes antagonistic, components of a community deeply divided by gender, political, and especially class tensions. The Catholic middle classes may have supported charities as a form of racial uplift whereby their own respectability was tied to helping the poor achieve upward mobility. The Catholic elite was concerned, as were other elites, with minimizing the threat of revolutionary activity among the poor. The poor often wanted help but were critical of the kinds of controls that came with that help. Women in these disparate groups attempted to gain power with respect to men, children, the Catholic hierarchy, or Protestants. Yet, for a time at least, Catholic institutions' support for poor children drew these disparate groups together to fashion a nationalist discourse that linked poverty in Ireland with Irish poverty in Gilded Age New York.

Part of this discourse was focused on community defense against anti-Catholicism. Increasingly, however, Catholics investigated and distinguished among several types of anti-Catholicism evident in Protestant charities. Over time, a simple sectarian construct whereby Protestants were depicted as competing with Catholics for the souls of children was less prominent. The Catholic National Hierarchy, for instance, began their 1866 pastoral letter by lamenting, "Whether from poverty or neglect, . . . a large number of Catholic parents either appear to have no idea of the sanctity of the Christian family, and of the responsibility imposed on them of providing for the moral training of their offspring, or fulfil this duty in a very imperfect manner." Blaming poor Catholic parents in a manner similar to, if not harsher than, child-savers, they expressed concern primarily with the children's subsequent conversion to Protestantism. "Day after day," they noted, Catholic children were placed in "distant localities, where they are brought up in ignorance of, and most commonly in hostility to, the Religion in which they had been baptized." They therefore advocated building a complex of industrial schools comparable to those of Protestants "wherein . . . the waywardness of youth may be corrected, and good seed planted in the soil in which, while men slept, the enemy had sowed tares."[58]

The second kind of defense was to publicize evidence of the most egregious forms of anti-Catholicism found in charities in New York, especially in placing-out societies that received public funding. "The Heathen of New York" appeared in *The Little Wanderer's Friend*, the publication of the Home for Little Wanderers, in May 1865. "The mass of the population consists of the most ignorant, bigoted, degraded foreign Catholics, who know no higher law than the word of their priests" the article began. "Their Christianity is mere baptized heathenism." John Maguire republished this and another excerpt from a Little Wanderers annual report in *The Irish in America* (1868). There was no missing who the "Heathen of New York" were or what was to be done about them: "We are in the midst of it. Our mission is in front of one of their large churches. . . . They listen to our songs, while we witness their idolatry. They curse while we gather in the children, teach them the truth, feed, clothe, and send them to kind Christian homes. . . . Last year 155,223 persons landed here from Europe, of whom 92,861 were from poor, ignorant, bigoted, Catholic-cursed Ireland."[59]

With similar intent, the *Catholic World* published a full set of letters attained in the case of Edward Nugent, a Civil War veteran who lost contact with his two children after he was drafted and their mother died. In veterans' hospitals for years after the war, Nugent asked the SVDP in 1874 to help him locate the children. Nugent was informed that they had been taken into the American Female Guardian Society and then sent to the CAS to be placed out, his son to a family named Wilson in Dubuque, Iowa, and his daughter to a family in upstate New York. The SVDP attained the Wilsons' letters from the AFGS and CAS, warning that the boy should be sent away before the SDP could find him. A Mrs. C. Spaulding of the society advised:

> [The father] . . . is lame, he is not able to take care of his children, yet still claims he has a right to know where they are, though *we* do not feel after all these years he has any claim at all . . . it seems he is a Catholic, and has been to the priests with his story about us whom they call heretics . . . they are very persistent, and may send some one in that part of the country to ask the neighbors . . . if they can get him no other way they will steal him, so if you have become attached to the child, and would desire to save his soul from the power of the destroyer of souls, we would say to you it would be better for you to send the boy away for a year.[60]

Over time, however, Catholics tended to downplay or ignore such anti-Catholicism and focus instead on unmasking the label of nonsectarian as being designed to exclude Catholics, or promote Protestantism, through state institutions.[61] Catholics agreed that Protestant reformers could be truthful in claiming that inmates in public reformatories or placing-out societies were not taught a specific Protestantism. "They admit that Catholic teaching and practices are rigidly excluded," the Rev. Isaac Hecker observed, "and yet that the children are taught a certain religion."[62] That the Protestantism taught was not specifically Methodist, Episcopal, or Presbyterian mattered little to Catholics. As Hecker, a native-born Protestant convert to Catholicism, argued eloquently in 1873, "Whilst we cannot yield our rights to any one sect of Protestantism, we are equally determined . . . not to yield our constitutional rights to all . . . sects of Protestantism combined."[63]

And yet it was not opposition to anti-Catholicism but opposition to scientific charity policies that unified New York's Irish Catholic community across classes. American Protestant reformers' promotion of scientific charity and placing-out policies underscored commonalities in the city's heterogeneous Irish Catholic community in ways few threats could. The rhetoric scientific charity reformers used, the measures they advocated, and the theorists they quoted were profoundly implicated in the Irish famine and the "exile" of New York's Irish Catholic community. Historic memory and nationalist consciousness linked the colonialist suppression of Irish Catholicism and the severe impoverishment of the Irish people as a political effort designed not just to subordinate Irish Catholics but to eradicate them as a people.

Even elite Irish Catholics viewed the famine as a national experience that transcended class divisions, in part because the Irish Catholic elite were not implicated in enacting the poor laws that turned a crop failure into a Malthusian testing ground to control Irish overpopulation. Irish Catholics as a group were hardly likely to accept the most basic assumptions of scientific charity ideology or practice. For them to do so they would have had to believe that their collective poverty in Ireland and New York City was their own fault and believe the British were right to withhold relief while a million people starved to death and millions more were forced to emigrate. An Irish Catholic nationalist construction of the famine as political, cultural, and biological genocide thereby shaped the promotion of Catholic charitable systems and ideology as resistance to British imperialism, Irish suffering in general, and the rise of the utilitarian state.

American Catholics published a variety of works investigating the poorhouses and workhouses constructed throughout Great Britain, criticizing the liberal Protestant theorists who supported them, and emphasizing the parallels in American Protestant reformers' politics in the Gilded Age. A particularly lengthy postwar series of articles was published in the *Catholic World,* New York's Catholic literary magazine under the editorship of Isaac Hecker. In these poorhouses and workhouses in England or Ireland, one investigator claimed, the treatment of "paupers" was so degrading that the poor often purposely committed a crime so as to enter jail rather than a "charitable" institution. As one poorhouse keeper told the investigator, "I am really unfit to be a poorlaw guardian; I have some vestige of humanity left in me!" Catholic commentators used such evidence of suffering to link the poor laws, scientific charity, the famine, and Protestantism with the rule of the capitalist elite. "What this argument renders most apparent," the article continued, "is the necessity for an umpire, or mediatorial power, between collective society and the individual or family requiring aid, a power sympathetic alike with those who have more and with those who have less . . . and whose social position shall derive, from a source superior to either, a prestige which will inspire confidence . . . and give a certain authority to its decisions."[64]

The ideological malleability of Catholicism allowed Irish Catholic writers and charitable workers to choose particular parts of the Catholic tradition to defend their stance against scientific charity. It would be misleading, however, to imagine that a particular version of Catholicism was readily available for brandishing as an ideological weapon against Protestant scientific charity ideology. Rather, the process by which Catholics began to employ aspects of the Catholic tradition to support resistance was active and creative, and it took place within a specific historical context. By the turn of the century, middle-class Irish Catholics would have enough influence in the community to move discussions of Catholic social teaching closer to the scientific charity models espoused by the Protestant elite during the Gilded Age. Such strains of ideology were overshadowed in Gilded Age New York City by an emphasis on restoring the rights of the poor through resurrecting a social order reminiscent of the precolonial middle ages in Ireland.

New York's Irish Catholics relied especially on Catholic medieval social teaching as a language of resistance to scientific charity and modern capitalism. Such a strategy of nostalgia linked religion and Irish nationalism. Medieval Ireland was constructed as the true Irish society that had flourished before British colonization. Catholic medieval principles demanded that the rich appreciate their duties to the poor and in that way contribute to a harmonious and stable society. The hallmark of medieval Catholic Europe was its hierarchical and static social order, not the emphasis on individualism or upward mobility so cherished in Protestant charitable thinking. The Catholic religion was to be mediator between rich and poor, demanding of the rich that they not abuse privileges of power and wealth and of the poor that they not advocate violent revolution against the rich. Lambasting wealthy Catholics for apathy, Catholic writers charged that "communism, and the whole mass of social disorders which have lately come to the surface of the body politic . . . are principally to be traced to the abuse of power and wealth by the governing classes."[65] Characterizing Protestant support of scientific charity principles as examples of the elite's abuse of the poor, they charged that such policies would exacerbate antagonisms between classes and thereby lead to revolution. As a matter of self-interest, therefore, wealthy Catholics needed to turn attention to the expansion of Catholic charities, not just as a religious matter but as a better hope for achieving social stability and their own well-being.

At base, Irish Catholics positioned themselves as supporting charity so as to relieve suffering, not to eradicate poverty or the class structure itself. To scientific charity reformers such thinking was literally backward because it undermined their efforts to end poverty entirely and accepted the suffering of the poor as a condition that American reform and progress could not alter. Poverty or wealth, according to Catholic teaching, was a condition on earth that might be overcome or altered by individuals, but the moral qualities of the rich and poor were not deemed causal in determining who had power and who did not. Irish Catholics as a group therefore did not emphasize, as did scientific charity organizers, that aid was in itself an evil. They held instead that alleviating suffering was both their Christian duty and a bulwark against revolution.[66] Even conservative Catholics' belief that the social order was and should remain static and poverty could not be eradicated made estimation of the moral qualities of those who were poor less harsh and judgmental than those of liberals trying to reform the poor morally.

Attributing the potato blight to the supernatural but the famine itself to British poor law policies, Irish Catholics shifted the blame for Irish poverty from the Irish themselves to the Protestant elite in Ireland and America. British poor law officials who withheld aid to the starving so as to encourage them to improve their characters through hard work were characterized by Irish nationalists as deliberately genocidal. John Stuart Mill's support of the British 1834 Poor Law, under whose auspices the famine thrived, was characterized by a Catholic writer as but one example of the absolute contrast between Protestant and Catholic thinking. Mill argued that the Poor Law "prevents any person, except by his own choice, from dying of hunger" and "leaves their condition as much as possible below that of the poorest who find support for themselves." Such reasoning, one Catholic charged, "seems to arrive at the reductio ad absurdum; for the state of these poorest of the working poor . . . is too distressing for charity, acting below that level, to be of any avail. . . . Usually inclined to the most liberal and humane views, Mr. Mill has here given way to a Protestant prejudice, which regards as ill-advised the more whole-souled Catholic style of charity."[67] Another Catholic commentator noted, "The problem to be solved is, how to give the greatest amount of needful help with the smallest encouragement to undue reliance on it. Energy and self-dependence are, however, liable to be impaired by the absence of help as well as by its excess. It is even more fatal to exertion to have no hope of succeeding by it than to be assured of succeeding without it. When the condition of any one is so disastrous that his energies are paralyzed by discouragement, assistance is a tonic, not a sedative."[68]

Mediating institutions organized through the church, including labor unions, guilds, and charities, were to bridge the growing cultural and economic gap between the poor and wealthy. Institutions run by women and male religious were touted in Catholic publications as "the most perfect organs of this Christian work."[69] Unlike Protestant reformers' strategies that focused on a top-down elevation of the poor morally through contact with the elite, Catholic theology emphasized instead that the elite must learn from and embrace the struggles of the poor. Religious orders, not friendly visitors, were deemed a model of interaction between classes. Through all nuns' voluntary assumption of it "poverty itself becomes ennobled . . . and its degradation disappears."[70] By virtue of the fact that convents were increasingly the province of women from poor and working-class backgrounds, the cooperation between classes necessary for the everyday interactions in each sisterhood exemplified Catholic visions of social harmony.

Support of convents could then be made central to a strategy of resistance that was not just religious but more broadly a defense of the poor against scientific charity policies. The spread of Irish Catholicism was therefore not only a religious duty but also a buttress against such brutal oppression. Positing the suppression of convents in Ireland as the means by which the British instituted a ruthless, state-sponsored utilitarianism, some Irish Catholics held that promoting the expansion of convents and their charities would provide the means of resistance to such oppression in America:

> If Ireland had still her seven . . . or eight hundred monastic institutions, there would be no . . . famines and typhus fevers there; no need of sunset or sunrise laws shutting the people up at night to prevent insurrections; . . . no schemes for getting rid of a "surplus population"; no occasion for . . . their dying of starvation, while their ports are crowded with ships carrying provisions from their shores, and while an army is

fed in the country, the business of which army is to keep the starving
people quiet.[71]

The Expansion of Convents

By the mid 1870s, Catholic institutions for the care of children were stag-
gering under the combined pressures of the poor's demand for relief and
convents' dependence on erratic private and public funding. "The various
institutions of the city were crowded to overflowing," the Protectory's
admissions office reported, "while destitution and misery were widespread."[72] Between 1863 and 1875 the Protectory, because of its heavy
dependence on private funding, had already turned down a majority of
applications for admission; it was able to take in only nine thousand of
twenty-one thousand children who applied.[73] In the Protectory's report for
1874, appeals for state and private funding were made with unusual fervor,
acknowledging the degree to which the institution was overwhelmed and
belief that commitments would rise during the depression. "The unusual
number, this winter, of unemployed workingmen threatens to throw upon
the charity of the public a correspondingly large number of destitute and
vagrant children." In the same report Sister Mary Helena, directoress of
the Female Department, added, "In the way of appeal, it appears to us
only necessary to remind you, that we are now actually crowded, and to
ask you what we are to do with those who will apply to us for admission
in future? Must we reject them? Must we abandon them?"[74]

The lack of public funding sufficient to support Catholic children's
charities created difficulties in the early 1870s and a severe crisis after
two years of the depression. Groups of women religious throughout the
city tried to expand their services. The Sisters of Charity in charge of St.
Stephen's Home for Children set up beds in the classrooms to accommodate the overflow.[75] Others such as the Sisters of Mercy feared the
collapse of their industrial school:

> Applications for admission were so urgent that by degrees a number of
> small children were taken in though their friends could give nothing to-
> wards their support. At the same time the growing girls in the workroom
> were hardly able to earn enough for their own support, and many of the
> parents of the pupils in the school, delayed a long time before paying,
> owing to the hard times existing for business people. In this way debt
> began inevitably to accumulate, and the Mother House was obliged to
> lend all it could possibly spare to keep up St. Josephs.[76]

Other Catholic children's institutions were forced to change their
very character and make room for half orphans (those with one living par-

ent) instead of full orphans and free instead of paid charges. The majority of all children in the care of the nine Catholic institutions in New York City in 1875 were non-orphaned children of immigrants.[77] The Roman Catholic Orphan Asylum's (RCOA) board of managers attempted to limit the ratio of half-orphaned to orphaned at one to five. Keeping that ratio through the depression, however, proved impossible: "At present [1874] the number of half orphans applying for admission is eight times in excess of the number of orphans," the board of managers reported. "The number of half-orphans now in the Asylums is largely in excess of orphans; . . . it is impossible to admit all that make application for admission and to give satisfaction to the clergymen of the different parishes who make applications in consequence of the already overcrowded condition of the asylums."[78]

The Sisters of Charity at the RCOA nonetheless encouraged the board to admit more non-orphans despite lack of funding. "The accounts that we hear of Catholic orphans sent West and deprived of religious instruction urge us to make great exertions in order to take a hundred or so more under our care." They assured the board that help would follow their resolve: "The sisters unite in desiring this; and for the accomplishing of it, many of our particular friends will come forward to assist."[79]

It was in this context of widespread destitution that the Children's Law of 1875 was passed. The law, which mandated that each destitute child would be housed in an institution of his or her own religious background and that the city was bound to pay for the child's maintenance, proved to be manna from heaven. The Sisters of Mercy, for instance, were struggling to support 150 girls, aged three to fifteen, in an institution that could have accommodated 350.[80] The sisters aggressively made their institution available to children who were to be taken out of the poorhouse on Randall's Island. The sisterhood's annals noted:

> As the majority of such children are Catholics it seemed likely that many of them would be sent to us. For this reason, the Mother Superior had an interview with Mr. Kellogg, the Superintendent of the Poor, and informed him that the Institution of Mercy would take charge of any number of little girls at whatever rate the Government proposed. . . . He informed her that . . . there remained a great number of girls between the ages of three and seven, and these she agreed to take as soon as the time appointed by law came. This was the last day of 1876. The Commissioners of Charity agreed to give $8 per month for each child.[81]

Before the girls arrived in the institution, the Sisters of Mercy made yet another decision to expand both their work with children and a means of funding it: They decided to take in boys as well as girls. When 113 boys and girls arrived by ambulance from Randall's Island, St. Joseph's began expanding to accommodate them.

The Mercy Sisters thereafter integrated themselves into the court system so as to encourage judges to send dependent Catholic children to them rather than to placing-out societies. They obtained a copy of the Children's Law and sent notes to judges throughout the city to inform them that St. Joseph's was prepared to take in any Catholic girls or small boys committed as destitute. "[P]reparations were hardly complete before the children began to arrive," the annals reported. "The first of them was Lizzie Carney, a child whose mother took her from the 'Five Points House of Industry' as soon as she learned that our Sisters would take charge of little girls."[82] The "Institution of Mercy" continued to receive children committed through the courts and received 559 in 1878 alone.[83] The Sisters of Mercy then converted a building outside the city in Balmville in order to house boys. In 1880 St. Joseph's Industrial Home received more than $77,000 from the city, compared to $3,000 from private sources, to support approximately nine hundred committed children.[84]

As in the first stage of expansion, decisions to expand convents in this second stage were not top-down impositions of the archbishop or the Catholic elite but made within convents by nuns themselves. Between 1875 and 1880 four Catholic institutions that cared for children expanded to take in those committed as destitute or vagrant by the courts.[85] In addition, women religious founded seven entirely new institutions between 1875 and 1884 to care for dependent children, some by orders previously established in the city and others by those who established a convent in New York once funding for dependent children became available.[86] By 1885 nineteen thousand dependent children were maintained concurrently at the city's expense, and Catholic convents housed more than 80 percent of the total.[87]

Male religious cared for only a small minority of dependent children, primarily in the Protectory and the Roman Catholic Orphan Asylum, as they had since the antebellum period. All of the female orders except those working with prostitutes extended their child-care institutions to include boys. They usually held that they did so in order to keep siblings together.[88] By 1886 there were 365 Catholic women religious in New York City who worked primarily in child care; in contrast, just fifty-six Christian Brothers were responsible for adolescent boys.[89]

The Sisters of St. Dominic reportedly took in their first boy in 1884, when Mother Mary Ann arrived in court to take home girls and took in a brother of one of them so they would not be separated. The Sisters of the Third Order of St. Dominic, who formed a new community in

1876 specifically for the care of girls, took in boys for the first time in 1883, ostensibly for the same reason—to avoid separation of brothers and sisters. The Franciscan Missionary Sisters of the Sacred Heart had until 1879 been involved exclusively in teaching but took up work with poor children after the Children's Law was passed. After converting their school in Peekskill, New York, they began taking in court commitments in 1879 and by 1883 had expanded their services to care for young boys as well as girls. Only three institutions, St. James Home, St. Ann's Home, and the House of the Holy Family, did not take in boys because of the particular missions of these homes as focused on young girls. The latter two institutions were the domain of the Sisters of the Good Shepherd and the Sisters of the Divine Compassion, both of which saw their work with girls to be an extension of their preventive reform work with women.[90]

The "Revolving Door"

Perhaps the most important resource Irish Catholic nuns provided the poor was not labor or physical shelter but enactment of policies that bolstered the rights of the poor against family breakup. Had nuns simply kept children institutionalized they would have replicated most of the problems that the poor experienced at the hands of placing-out advocates. Keeping children within institutions indefinitely would have "saved" a substantial, but nonetheless finite, number of Catholic children from the child-savers. Yet if poor parents were to lose rights to and control over their children to Catholic or Jewish co-religionists, then their vulnerability as poor people would not have been significantly diminished.

From its inception, the Catholic "system" functioned more precisely as an immense revolving door through which poor children were to enter when parents deemed their financial need to be greatest and through which they would be returned when parents' financial struggles were less urgent. By the SCAA's estimate, only 2.5 percent of dependent children in the city's institutions in 1894 had been there for ten years, 56 percent for three years or less, and 68 percent for four years or less.[91] About three-quarters of the children in the Catholic Protectory in the same year had been there for fewer than three years, and 82 percent of those who left that year were discharged to parents.[92] By 1909, moreover, the average length of time any child spent in a Catholic institution was down to eighteen months and only a third of applications were accepted.[93] By keeping the population of dependent children moving into expanded convents and quickly out of them, nuns were able to make this strategy available to a much larger population of the poor. That the system functioned in such a manner, moreover, increased poor parents' willingness to institutionalize children when financial expedience or fear of child removal warranted.

The revolving door system is critical to understanding Catholic institutionalization as distinct from a mere sectarian countermeasure and more precisely a means through which to preserve the parental rights of the poor and reconstruct and support the family economies on which the poor depended. At base were two assumptions at odds with the logic of the placing-out system. The first was that the larger families and communities of which these children were a part should be collectively strengthened by fortifying rather than dismantling poor families. Nuns virtually never spoke in "rights" language or advocated women and children's "liberation" from the patriarchal family. They instead sought to strengthen the patriarchal family structure by minimizing stresses that made family cohesion and stability difficult among the urban poor.

Second, in attempting to maximize the capacities of poor families to survive poverty nuns attempted to reconstruct a household economy in which all members worked. Instead of an artisanal model whereby household production was organized and directed by the patriarch, however, mothers were often the organizers and directors of a family economy dependent on collective wage-earning rather than collective household production. Men, women, and children may have worked in different physical spaces, but their ability to survive was tied to a collective use of such wages. Women who headed households that lacked an adult male as a primary wage-earner depended on the collectivity of women's and children's wages to a greater extent than others with access to the "family wage" of male skilled workers. Accordingly, nuns also assumed that poor women and children needed to work and that a larger family, particularly its elders, had a legitimate moral right to a portion of their wages. Children sent back into their families and those without families were expected to leave with resources to secure work in a skilled labor position and thereby contribute to their own support or their family's. The Protectory had the best industrial training for both girls and boys, including a variety of programs in skilled labor. Boys could learn stenography, typewriting, printing, electro-typing, machinery, shoemaking, chair making, stocking making, tailoring, blacksmithing, carpentry, gardening, or a wheelwright's duties. The girls' department, although offering fewer options, nonetheless stayed at the cutting edge of industrial training and kept close watch on emerging job opportunities. By 1893 glove making, machine sewing, cooking, stenography, typewriting, and various types of work other than domestic service were taught at the institution.[94] The nuns not only refrained from blaming poor parents for depending on children's labor but also constructed a system of children's charities under which such dependence was recognized and encouraged as a legitimate moral and financial right.

Two groups of children, however, could not be returned quickly to families—those who did not have parents or family and those the Society of the Prevention for Cruelty to Children (SPCC) placed in an institution because their parents were charged with abuse. Nuns defended the practice of keeping children without families in institutions until their mid-teens by asserting, as they had in previous decades, that economic independence for women and children through job training and placement was the best defense against labor and sexual exploitation. It was also critical to women and children's moral and financial autonomy. When the sisters bragged that their charges received "high wages, because they have been trained" they were implicitly boasting as well about the moral and religious protection such skills represented. Girls who could command decent wages would be more likely to protest or change employers if faced with assault or abuse.[95]

For older children who could not be returned home, nuns generally refused either to place them out or put them into jobs or apprenticeships until in their mid-teens. Allowing girls or boys to enter homes or jobs at an earlier age, the nuns argued, would subject them to labor and possibly sexual exploitation. Nuns assumed that families took children through the placing-out system in order to use their labor rather than welcome them as family members. Children older than six or seven were not likely to be adopted or made members of any family. They were, however, likely to be exploited for their labor and be vulnerable because of their age, lack of training, and religious and cultural background to abuse and overwork. Catholic women religious made this issue a cardinal point of their work with children and resisted attempts to place out Catholic children, whether by those within the Catholic community or those without.

Church, State, and Class

Nuns' value systems guiding the promotion of industrial training and resistance to placing-out were best articulated in institutions in which they had to struggle with a male elite management in order to shape their work. The great majority of Catholic institutions were managed almost exclusively by women religious. Boards of managers connected to these institutions were either composed of a majority of religious or delegated responsibility by religious in much the manner of a relatively powerless but useful auxiliary. In the two New York Catholic institutions that had strong boards of managers, however, the Roman Catholic Orphan Asylum and the Protectory, there was substantial conflict between male middle- and upper-class board members and male and female religious who ran the institutions. The Protectory's board frequently voiced opinions and suggested programs that seemed more in line with Protestants of similar class backgrounds than with other Catholics.

Both institutions were throwbacks to antebellum Catholic charitable organization when Catholic children's charities were entirely dependent on private funding. In each, the board had considerable power; it was responsible for the overall finances of each institution and often the pri- mary source of private funding. The Christian Brothers and the Sisters of Charity worked in both institutions, and each took pains to establish autonomy relative to the respective boards.

Yet conflict between the interests and authority of church and state within the institution was literally experienced as conflicts between religious and the respective boards. Self-identified as the better, more respectable classes of Irish Catholics, board members based their au- thority on class status and specific legal powers they derived from the state as legal incorporators of the institution. This hierarchy of the state, however, contradicted the hierarchy of the church through which boards of managers, as members of the Society of St. Vincent de Paul, were to be subordinate to male or female members of the church's workforce. "[W]e must, above all, follow with docility the directions which our ecclesiastical superiors may think proper to give us," read the society's Rules in 1862. "We will extend, to a certain degree, this deference to the Sisters of Charity, or even to laymen who may have offices of charity to perform."[96]

Catholic religious orders, however, based their authority in chari- table work on having embraced a vow and life of poverty, commitment to the poor, and position in the church. When faced with conflict, for instance, Brother Justin claimed that the legal powers invested in the Protectory's board were at odds with the common understanding of the authority of religious orders. "Of course there is a Charter granted by the State Legislature and it provides for a Board of Managers," he wrote to Henry Hoguet, president of the board, "but I suppose no educated Catholic doubts that Charities and Boards for Catholic Institutions are for the purpose of complying with the Statutes of the State and for the conducting of Catholic Charities as the ecclesiastical authorities see fit and not otherwise."[97]

Throughout the 1870s, however, the boards of both institutions reacted to an escalating community demand to place children in Catholic institutions by trying to limit admissions and increase the means of placing-out. Both boards condemned Catholic parents' dependence on children's institutions and insisted that their duty as board members was to "the State," which increasingly funded the work. They saw their primary responsibility as preventing "the possibility of having the tax-payers burdened with the support of subjects unworthy of, or not entitled to, the charity of the County of New York."[98] In their report of 1881, for example, the RCOA's board condemned attempts by many destitute parents to give their children over to an orphan asylum:

> Recent developments have proven to the satisfaction of the Committee the necessity of making the most rigid examination, to prevent as far as possible, our Institutions from becoming an Asylum for the children of those who should be supported in some of the many Catholic Institu-tions receiving State Aid; this applies particularly to Half-Orphans, who in many instances the surviving parents find a bar to contemplated mar-riages; . . . domestic difficulties arising, the children become an encum-brance on one or the other and they attempt, by false representations, to make the Asylums an easy method of disposing of them.[99]

The Protectory's board instituted a special Bureau of Admissions and Discharges. P. C. Dooley, appointed as supervisor in 1876, was charged with making room for new commitments and immediately releasing any children whose parents seemed able to support them. He then concen-trated on "a careful scrutiny of the claims of every applicant for admis-sion, and, by so doing, was enabled to conscientiously refuse admission to many who otherwise would have become permanent burdens on County charity."[100] Dooley also used truancy agents, the SPCC, and visitors from the St. Vincent de Paul Society to investigate the committing parents. Within a few years he boasted that hundreds of boys and girls had been placed out. The majority were orphans, but some had parents who could no longer be located.[101]

Through the mid-1870s both boards expanded placing-out mecha-nisms and promoted agricultural rather than industrial training. This system resembled that of Protestant placing-out societies, although chil-dren had to be placed in Catholic families. In choosing the West as the best place for the expansion of their placing-out activities, the boards reflected the same romanticization of rural life as was characteristic of Protestant placing-out organizations—and the same fear of the congre-gation of urban poor. Lamenting the lack of agricultural training at the Protectory, President Henry Hoguet claimed that "the existence of a city mechanic, at best, can only be one of unceasing toil in close, unhealthy workshops, . . . these existences become lost in dissipation, and end in vice—perchance, in crime."[102]

The Sisters of Charity and Christian Brothers both held that industrial training of children for the purpose of securing them employment should be the primary purpose of children's labor in institutions and that profit from such labor should be a secondary consideration. The Christian Brothers, for instance, resisted the board's attempt to close the shoe department because they could find no market to sell shoes at the height of the Long Depression. The brothers insisted that their purpose was to train boys and not make money and that if the department ran at a deficit, it was to be calculated into the cost of the boys' education.

By 1878, however, the board usurped the brothers' exclusive control of internal management by employing a supervisor for the shoe department and giving him control over all hiring, teaching, purchases, and sales in order to make the department profitable. The board defended its action by citing its legal responsibility to manage money contributed by the state. "The present Brother rector . . . and the Brother visitor have steadfastly opposed the existing system of conducting the Shoe Department, insisting that the boys are demoralized," Hoguet complained to Archbishop McCloskey. The brothers believed "that this evil is attributable only to the presence of Superintendents and employees, not of their own choosing" and were "insisting upon a return to the old system of management."[103]

Similarly, in 1880 the Sisters of Charity resisted the board's decision to keep knitting as a vocational course. Mother Ambrosia held that training girls to knit would not help them find employment, and thus the skill was superfluous for those under her charge:

> What benefit will our little ones derive from it when they leave us? The answer is not very encouraging. It is true, the Institution has profited in a pecuniary way by the results of their labor, but the prospects for the children counterbalance all that the Institution has gained. By a continuance of it, they are unfitted for household duties or serving, [sewing, or glove-making] . . . things with which children should if possible be thoroughly acquainted. . . . [If] the above suggestion . . . should not meet with the approval of you, Honorable Gentlemen, I shall respectfully submit to your wise judgement, knowing that your tenderness for the little ones confided to your care will not permit you to consent, that they be employed in anything, which would be detrimental to their health or their future prospects.[104]

The knitting was discontinued, and Mother Ambrosia's argument became assumed logic for decades, as stated in an 1893 report by the sister in charge of the girls' department: "Our vocation lies more in the direction of industrial education for our wards than of profit from their labors. . . . We find our rewards in the future blessings these educations will bring to the children themselves."[105]

By the end of the 1870s female and male religious overtly refused to participate in efforts to place out as many children as advocated by the RCOA and Protectory boards. In 1878 there was considerable discord between the board and the Christian Brothers who ran the boys' department of the RCOA when the brother in charge refused to place a boy for whom the board had found an apprenticeship. Instead, the brother argued that the boy had yet to complete his training in the tailor shop and could not be placed until he did so.[106] In the same year, Mother Regina, who directed the girls' department of the Protectory, criticized the supervisor of admissions and placements for his failure to either supervise and protect the children once placed or locate parents and guardians before children were placed out:

> In some instances it would seem there was no one to look after them when they were placed out, tho I believe there are several salaried officers for that purpose connected with the Protectory. Our children are daily returned to the institution when down in health and spirits with scarcely clothes to cover them decently, and yet they have lived in families for two, three and even five years and during all that time not one came to learn how they were treated.
> It not infrequently happens that little girls of twelve and thirteen years are expected to do the labor of women, and when they cannot accomplish all that their considerate kind mistresses require, they are stigmatized as being saucy, stubborn and disrespectful. Poor children my heart aches for them, is it any wonder they rebel?[107]

Mother Regina, moreover, refused thereafter to allow children to be placed out unless she was assured that their families, if they had them, had been contacted and every effort made to reunite the family. As she was in contact directly with some family members of the children, moreover, she demanded lists of addresses for those already placed out. "I am very much obliged to you for the List of Children placed out," she wrote, "and for which I so frequently asked, but there are still a few more girls and all the little boys of whom you have given no account, as enclosed list will show, of William Horrigan . . . I am especially anxious to hear, as his Father is sick in Hospital and very naturally wishes to know how his child is."[108]

Supervisor of Placements Dooley defended the placing-out practice in 1879 by stating that most children placed out had no living parent, and "[i]n no instance, and under no circumstance, is the child of an industrious and worthy parent placed out, without that parent's consent."[109] By 1880, however, Dooley had become convinced that the system whereby children were placed out, even if orphaned and placed out with Catholics, resulted in the child's alienation and potential exploitation, thereby threatening children's rights. "Occasionally," he wrote in the annual report, "there may be found a genuine orphan . . . who falls into the hands of a respectable family and learns to substitute the newfound affections and duties for those it has lost; but the instances, I assert, are rare and bear an infinitesimal proportion to the total number of children deported." Dooley asserted, moreover, that the need to place children had diminished because many other Catholic institutions had expanded.[110]

Although the board's instructions to Dooley's successor were to "not retain children in the Institution any longer than their welfare demanded," the religious in the institution blocked his ability to place out children.[111] Western placements were not made at all in 1882 because "Reverend Brother Rector has been unable to select such subjects as were sufficiently prepared" for placement. By 1883 the Protectory had discontinued Western placement altogether and limited placements to sixty-five children, whereas 710 were returned to parents.[112]

By the mid-1880s the Protectory stood with other Catholic institutions throughout the city in refusing to place out any children. The board held that the policy shift stemmed from "the conviction . . . forced upon the Managers that a greater evil even arises from the avarice or money-getting spirit of the persons to whom the children are apprenticed." In addition to neglect of religious and secular education, "[A]pprentices from institutions [were] often overworked, [and] scantily fed and clothed."[113] Such economic critiques of placing-out were consistent with all other Catholic institutions in the city and brought the lay boards of the institutions in line with male and female religious and poor parents who protested the abuse of children's labor in apprenticeships. The board also conceded that "our boys take much more kindly to mechanical than to agricultural pursuits," and thus they were committed to training their wards for skilled urban labor.[114]

Sisters' Homes and Labor

By the mid-1870s, nuns in New York City had increased their numbers substantially and put mechanisms in place for recruiting and training large numbers of novices. By 1875 there were approximately a thousand

Catholic women religious in the city, and by 1885 there were two thousand.[115] Convents throughout New York recruited hundreds of young, strong women capable of doing difficult physical labor daily. In 1867, once the Sisters of Mercy were granted state funding for St. Joseph's Industrial Home, "it became necessary," their annalist wrote, "to have a large number of Sisters ready to undertake the management and work of the Institute and therefore the number of postulants admitted was greater than usual."[116] The Sisters of Charity alone, moreover, were training seventy novices in 1877.[117] Postulancy and spiritual training before taking vows no longer provided novices with a temporary reprieve from work in apostolates. The Sisters of Mercy reported that "[t]he work at St. Joseph's was so arduous that most of the Novices had to be sent there quite soon after their Reception."[118]

Those orders committed to doing charitable work, moreover, found that expanding and staffing institutions required so much physical labor that women from higher-status backgrounds could not avoid work that would have been considered anathema for European choir nuns. When the city's female orders moved into work with children in the 1870s and 1880s, for instance, they had almost no servant help.[119] In 1886 five institutions run by women religious had no servants, and the remainder used a fairly small number. Combining all children's institutions run by nuns, they averaged one servant to every three sisters.[120]

Housing, feeding, cleaning, teaching, and generally caring for hundreds of small children simultaneously, and at a time when "modern conveniences" were few, required that all nuns contribute constant, often arduous, physical labor. The work was also often dangerous; children could sometimes resist disease more easily than adults. In 1865 three of the seven Sisters of Charity in the Protectory who contracted "malignant typhus fever" died, but only one of the ninety girls who contracted the disease did so.[121] In 1887 sixty-year-old Mother Mary Joseph Devereaux, formerly mother superior of the Mercy Sisters in New York and from a wealthy background, was stationed as refectorian, or director of the kitchen, at Balmville, an institution housing approximately a thousand children. When a small boy carrying a pail of boiling water collided on the stairs with Mother Joseph, who was carrying a large plate of butter, the substances mixed, and she was covered with hot grease. She died the following day of the burns.[122] It was an industrial accident not unlike those to which the larger Irish Catholic community was vulnerable.

Convents also purchased land with revenue from private donations in nearby rural areas such as Westchester and Rockland Counties or Staten Island. Those extensions were meant to accommodate increasing numbers, expand industrial training and recreational facilities for the children, and improve health conditions. Because contagious diseases threatened when large numbers of children were congregated, most convents also built separate infirmaries and buildings for quarantine. Able to rely on a constant source of revenue for the children's maintenance, they continued to ask the Catholic community for private donations when new buildings were necessary. In the process of expansion, makeshift buildings and tents were sometimes used until accommodations were complete.[123]

The exception to the rule that the institutions were run internally, and most often externally, by religious was the Mission of the Immaculate Virgin (MIV), an offshoot of St. Vincent's Home for Newsboys instituted by the St. Vincent de Paul Society in 1870. For the year 1885 the total number of children housed was 1,525, most of them boys. The mission received $96,924 from the city, thereby making it the second largest Catholic child-care institution in the city other than the Protectory.[124] Yet the mission was never able to secure the services of adequate numbers of either male or female religious.

Their reluctance was no doubt fueled by Father John C. Drumgoole's insistence that he retain centralized power over the institution's management. In 1882 the Sisters of St. Francis agreed to work at the mission, but by 1886 only eleven were on hand to administer what had become a huge institution. In 1888 an attempt was made to educate and train a new brotherhood for the work, but it failed shortly thereafter.[125] The very high number of forty-nine paid officers and 136 paid servants (compared to 138 in all other New York Catholic child-caring institutions combined) made the institution an anomaly in the Catholic system at large. Catholics and non-Catholics often criticized the Mission of the Immaculate Virgin as promoting a "warehousing" of children and held that it replicated the worst abuses of public institutions.[126]

Another small but exceptional institution was run by the Sisters of the Divine Compassion, a group that grew from a lay Catholic women's organization, the Association for Befriending Children. Their founder, native-born Mary Caroline Dannat (called Mother Veronica as a religious) was raised as a Congregationalist and converted to Catholicism. The work the group began with children after the war was intended to offer a Catholic women's counterpoint to Protestant laywomen's work with children. Unlike other Catholic groups, however, the association tended to use rhetoric and support policies that seemed a great deal like Protestant child-saving in that poor parents were imagined as being children's greatest threat. "So plain is it that the great army of the vicious and abandoned in this city is recruited continually from the young children of degraded parents," the association maintained, "that every charitable scheme which aims to diminish this army and lessen the amount of vice and suffering must attempt to reach and reclaim the very young."[127] There is evidence, moreover, that the association was reluctant to return children to parents when it deemed the parents unfit.[128] The group remained very small and only marginally involved in the care of dependent children, in part because at some point the SPCC became reluctant to send children to them. Yet their distinctiveness from other Catholic sisterhoods places in higher relief the absence of comparable sentiments or policies expressed by other sisters or sisterhoods.[129]

That the system of institutionalization depended on nuns' labor and activism is also made apparent by comparing it to Jewish institutions in New York City. The funding system through the Children's Law made institutionalization a viable strategy for Jewish resistance to placing-out because it similarly allotted payments for children in institutions run by those of the same religious background. Because Jews did not have access to a female workforce comparable to nuns, however, Jewish institutions were administered primarily by men and staffed primarily by paid workers and servants, which made the institutions more expensive to run and more difficult to regulate. In 1886, for instance, the Deborah Nursery and Child's Protectory reported employing four officers and thirty-three servants to care for 426 children; the Hebrew Sheltering Guardian Society reported nine paid officers and thirty-four paid servants caring for 472 children.[130]

Because of such salaries, Jewish institutions relied heavily on private funding from the Jewish middle-class and elite community to supplement city and state support for annual maintenance. They could not rely, as did nuns, almost exclusively on public appropriations.[131] Although middle-class and elite Jewish women supported institutions through voluntary societies designed to bring "home influences" to bear on children, they did not live within them, nor did they provide a primary labor force.[132] As a result, and because the population of the Jewish poor was in this period fairly small, Jewish institutions were generally smaller than those run by Catholics and Jews as a group remained outside the primary battles waged between Catholics and Protestants.

The Backlash

As native-borns were soon to protest, nuns' rapid expansion of Catholic institutions had subverted the principles underlying child-saving and scientific charity in several ways. First, sending children to nuns' institutions allowed parents to enlist public support for raising them. Instead of public policy supporting the necessary loss of parental rights for those who sought help, nuns' use of state law allowed them to encourage parents to use public charity without threat to their rights over their children. Catholic and Jewish parents thus generated the push toward institutional expansion. No Catholic or Jewish groups attempted to take children off the streets, and for forty years twice as many parents attempted to institutionalize their children than could be accommodated. Poor parents' use of this system thus undermined the intents of the placing-out and scientific charity movements. As Josephine Shaw Lowell argued, "It is undoubtedly the duty of every parent to maintain his own child; there are exceptional cases where this is an impossibility through circumstances beyond his control, but if through intemperance, or other crime, the parent incapacitates himself from supporting his child and throws that burden on the public, he should not be allowed to claim the child as soon as the latter has reached an age to contribute to the parent's support."[133]

Native-born reformers complained further that the sense of "degradation" they considered necessary to keep the poor independent of charity was not in evidence. These were not, in other words, institutions comparable to the almshouse or workhouse and thereby punitive and only to be used if faced with starvation or homelessness. Lowell attested that "there is no check put upon the growth of the majority of these institutions, and in this direction they combine the disadvantages of both public and private charities, the recipients of their benefits having on the one hand no such sense of degradation as often deters persons from seeking relief in a public institution, and the managers, on the other, having no consideration of economy to force them to scrutinize with severity the claims of each applicant."[134]

Finally, instead of a system controlled almost exclusively by Protestant native-borns and geared toward assimilating Jewish and Catholic children into the native-born, Protestant, middle-class culture, the system encouraged religious pluralism and promotion of distinct Jewish and Catholic subcultures. Although Protestant reformers considered this a dangerous promotion of sectarianism and a merging of church and state, Catholics and Jews defended it as just the opposite—the separation of Protestant control over the state and a triumphant victory for the religious rights of minorities.

The state legislature organized several investigations to determine why commitments of dependent children in New York City had risen so abruptly during the 1880s. The committees, led by Josephine Shaw

Lowell, argued that investigation of cases of destitution by committing judges was lax and therefore parents able to support their children were still allowed to derive public support to do so. To reduce commitments, the committees supported the independent move of city judges in March 1880 to give the SPCC a quasi-state authority to investigate destitution and vagrancy commitments. The SPCC would then apprise the judges of its recommendations. The committees were confident that the SPCC's discernment would lower the rate of commitments. The SPCC, in turn, was to provide the state board with a list of children denied commitment either because the SPCC deemed their parents financially able to support them or found relatives willing to do so. When SPCC investigators believed that temporary poverty was a problem they also referred cases to the St. Vincent de Paul Society or the United Hebrew Charities, which provided private outdoor relief and helped male heads of household find employment.

Having invested the SPCC with legal authority to commit and regulate, however, other Protestant reformers, especially Lowell and the SCAA, were soon disappointed to find that the SPCC supported large-scale institutionalization. When the SPCC began its work in the city in 1874, the Catholic community assumed that it would, like other Protestant societies, advocate family breakup and put Catholic children in Protestant homes or charitable institutions. Catholic protests prompted the SPCC's leader Eldridge Gerry to promise that if children were taken from Catholic homes because of neglect or cruelty, he "would place all Roman Catholic children in Roman Catholic institutions."[135]

The SPCC, moreover, did not comply with stringent means-testing for admission to institutions. Between 1875 and 1902 the society investigated and declared dependent a hundred thousand children who were then admitted into the city's Catholic or Jewish institutions.[136] The SPCC was also invested with authority to collect payments from parents deemed able to contribute to a child's upkeep, especially those in reformatories. "The penalty for neglect of parental duties now falls mainly upon the child and the public," Josephine Shaw Lowell argued, "it should be placed where it belongs."[137]

Although authorizing the SPCC to collect payments for such children was assumed to further check parental dependency on institutions, the SPCC ignored the provision. In compliance with a critique of placement of children in homes as abusive, the society refused to place children out once it deemed them candidates for public support. As Homer Folks, secretary of the State Charities Aid Association for much of the 1890s, lamented in 1902, the number of children placed out by the SPCC was infintesimal compared with those placed in institutions. "Usually, they have not cooperated to any extent with placing-out societies, . . . but have rather become the feeders of institutions." In consequence, Folks wrote, the SPCC's "influence has done more to strengthen and perpetuate the subsidy or contract system, as it existed prior to 1894, than any other one factor."[138]

In frustration, counties outside the city attempted to cut off public funding and force nuns to place out children under their charge. In 1886 the superintendent of the poor of Westchester County authorized the Children's Aid Society to take children supported by public funds out of the Franciscan Convent in Peekskill to lower county costs for dependent children. After the CAS refused to assure that the children would be placed in Catholic homes, the sisters hid them in a barn and then appealed to the State Board of Charities. The board supported the sisters, arguing that the actions of the county and the CAS were in violation of state law guaranteeing that children dependent on public welfare be housed by those of their own religious background.[139] Similarly, Long Island City stopped making public payments for dependent children to the convent of the Sisters of the Order of St. Dominick once they realized the nuns refused to place out. The nuns sued and won in 1888, the court finding that the Children's Law established no limit in its provision that committed dependent children be supported by the city's public funds.[140]

Lowell, by 1884, advocated creating a Bureau for Dependent Children that would be organized under city auspices and headed by a commissioner of dependent children. Lowell spelled out the intended functions and ideological premises of the bureau as an antidote to institutionalization's promotion of religious pluralism and expansive funding for dependent children. First, no institutions receiving public funding were to be sectarian in character. Second, the bureau should be responsible for constant visitation of parents, exacting payments for children's support in institutions when possible and terminating parental rights should the child remain in the institution's custody for more than three years. As Lowell was fond of repeating, "A parent who will not perform the duties of a parent should not have the rights of a parent." Further, Lowell asserted that the bureau would be geared toward placing-out so children would "gradually but surely be cut off from the influences which have brought their parents to a condition of dependence, and be absorbed into the bulk of the population, with no memory even, if it can be avoided, of any thing suggestive of pauperism or crime." Finally, the bureau would be responsible for "regular and severe official inspection" of private institutions so a "standard is kept up by constant criticism from persons who know what they are talking about."[141]

Irish Catholic men used political power to ensure that no bureaucracy controlled by native-borns could be built with powers to regulate or diminish the authority of nuns within institutions themselves. In frustration, Lowell wrote to the archbishop in 1885, asking him to support the appointment of a commissioner for dependent children in New York: "I believe . . . such action . . . to be an absolute necessity to put a stop to very serious evils," she advised. "[I]t is certainly desirable that we should work together, if possible, and we might hit upon some plan which we could all support."[142] The archbishop, of course, refused to support the appointment.[143]

––––––––––

It is hard to understand on what terms Lowell thought compromise was possible. Every point she advocated as fundamental to the construction of the children's bureau struck at the very foundations of Catholic institutional expansion and the organizational and ideological reasons why Catholics supported it. It was clear by the late 1880s that nuns' success in charitable work had undermined the native-born charitable policies against which Catholics as a group had protested for decades; Catholic men who had power in the church or state were not about to support plans to dismantle that system.

Catholics and Jews nonetheless feared through the 1894 New York State Constitutional Convention that a positive vote on a proposed constitutional amendment banning any and all appropriations to charitable institutions of a sectarian character would mean the decisive destruction of decades of institutional expansion. By the late 1880s the State Charities Aid Association called for a state constitutional convention through which the question of public aid to private institutions could be addressed. In what they termed an effort to "decrease the burden of the taxpaying public," the SCAA contended that the state constitution must be brought in line with others that included absolute prohibitions against public aid to private institutions. The SCAA allied with the National League for the Protection of American Institutions and the Evangelical Alliance, drew up the amendment, and rallied supporters throughout the state.[144]

Both nativist and Protestant, the National League had been successful in states throughout the United States in the late 1880s and early 1890s in organizing resistance to public appropriations for sectarian organizations. In pamphlet literature, proponents of the amendment focused on the huge expenditures allotted to Catholic institutions.[145] The definition of "sectarian" was that used throughout the nineteenth century; organizations run by a coalition of Protestants were not sectarian, but those organized by only one Protestant denomination, or by Catholics or Jews, were sectarian. Catholics and Jews tried to expose the logic of the sectarian construct as one designed to exclude Catholics and Jews and favor Protestants.[146]

The first victory for Catholics or Jews at the conference was the convention's finding that public funding to sectarian institutions was constitutional, thereby lessening the ability of critics of Catholic and Jewish charities to withhold funding on the basis of an institution's sectarian character alone.

Even more important was the convention's establishment of a de facto concession stipulating that parents and children could now expect support from the state because the public welfare system had funded work with dependent children for decades.[147] From the viewpoint of the SCAA and most Protestant charitable reformers, that assertion was the most controversial in that it accepted in principle what had been asserted through practice over the previous two decades: Dependent children should continue to be supported by public funds and therefore through taxation. Because New York City was expending ten times as much as any city in the country to care for dependent children, the concession established, at least in principle, continued funding of institutions for dependent children as legitimate expenditures in the charity system. Nuns, in other words, accomplished through the literal expansion of their institutions, their political text, what they could not accomplish through public discourse.

Yet from the viewpoint of the Catholic poor, institutionalization may have proven a better option than placing-out, but it fell woefully short of addressing the more fundamental questions of poverty and social justice. Although institutionalization was a temporary stopgap that allowed poor Catholic parents the option of short-term relief, that relief was still premised on separation from their children. Nuns' ability to meet the needs of children and adults in poverty was therefore limited by the sisters' institutional framework. To the degree that convent institutions became increasingly tied to the state; moreover, the poor resented the corresponding power that nuns gained over families. As newer immigrant Catholic groups began to interact with such Irish-dominated state institutions, those groups began to consider convents as powerful engines of assimilation.

5   *"The Family" and "the Institution": The Roads to the White House, 1890–1909*

> Two hostile camps were set up, at odds and at war with each other, both set in their respective views, each out to "get the other" and, if possible, put him out of business. To the less discriminating and less tolerant of the institutional-minded, the "home-finders" became increasingly objectionable . . . they were viewed as trouble-makers and wreckers of institutions with venerable traditions. . . . The crusading evangels of placing-out, on the other hand, regarded institutional workers as harpies from whose evil clutches they must rescue suffering childhood.
>
> —Elias L. Trotzkey, 1930

> As I am a poor woman and left with six children one of which is in an institution and the others are about to follow him I hope before they do that Senator Ahearn bill will pass . . . the Societies are not willing to give me a little Hand to assist me to feed or clothes them and I am not very strong after having a young baby not nine weeks old and my heart is broke if I have to part with them.
>
> —Mrs. Dorsey to Mayor William L. Strong, 1897

Until the late 1890s in New York City, Protestant middle-class and elite reformers were often uninterested, and decidedly unsuccessful, in establishing what scholars would call a hegemonic order. Hegemony, as defined by Raymond Williams, "is not limited to matters of direct political control but seeks to describe a more general predominance which includes . . . a particular way of seeing the world . . . [and] its acceptance as 'normal reality' or 'common sense' by those . . . subordinated to it."[1] The critical question when investigating the construction of hegemonic discourse in this study, and in the Progressive Era, is to find how it became commonsensical to large portions of the population, including Catholics and Jews, that institutions were of themselves bad for children. Conjuring up Dickensian depictions of orphans brutalized and abused is insufficient, as is the assertion that the "family plan" (placing-out) was in itself somehow good for poor children.

Rather, the political processes that enabled various actors in New York during the Progressive Era to help construct a hegemonic discourse were complex and nuanced. There seemed nothing subtle about the placing-out system or scientific charity and resistance to it, but the rhetorical, bureaucratic, and legislative changes that characterized charitable work during the Progressive Era were generally veiled from the larger public. Increasingly obvious, however, was the reorganization of alliances historically based on religion to those that crossed religions and were based on class.

The most significant shift in the politics of charity in turn-of-century New York City was tied to who did or did not speak in designated forums for discussion of public policy. Almost all white leading Protestant men and women in charitable work were members of organizations in which their own relatively high class status, educational credentials, and the breadth of each group's associational organizing rendered its members legitimate voices in debating policy. By the late 1890s, conferences and public meetings sponsored by private and public charities became the prescribed spaces in which to debate policy decisions and contest the minutiae of rules and regulations.

For Protestant elite women in particular, gaining admission to such public space was a victory that culminated decades of activism pointed toward achieving access to public forums influencing the configuration of the state. Although still without the vote, younger women in such organizations or in settlements throughout the city used their college educations and class status to achieve some measure of power relative to their male counterparts. Sharing knowledge and debating policy were central to the Progressive ethic whereby science and professional experts were to educate the public in order to influence state formation. That commitment to public debate so critical to Progressive Era politics was therefore a shift that supported the greater inclusion of middle-class and elite women.

The same reorganization of public space and policy, however, excluded the most important people in Catholic charitable work: nuns. Women religious did not have either the educational or class credentials to enter formal arenas and discuss policy. Nor did they have the cultural authority to engage other activists in public policy debates. Convents may have historically provided women with access to certain kinds of public authority prohibited for Protestant women, but once critical decisions about policy in the overall system moved beyond institutions themselves, nuns found themselves increasingly proletarianized. They were applauded for their cheap and selfless labor but less able to control the political meanings of their work.

The only group in the Catholic charitable spectrum with sufficient class status to merit access to these public forums was the St. Vincent de Paul Society, which was exclusively male, middle-class or elite in membership, and likely to support charitable policies consistent with scientific charity ideology. Although the society represented a very small portion of the Catholic community, and the private funds it dispensed to poor households never exceeded a small fraction of public funds allotted to institutions, the reorganization of authority in the state pushed the St. Vincent de Paul Society to disproportionate visibility and influence. The society's interests were by no means equivalent to those of the broad coalition of Catholics that had allied in the Gilded Age. Thomas Mulry, leader of the group in New York from the mid-1890s through the mid-1910s, played a pivotal role in positioning the St. Vincent de Paul Society as a broker that organized compromise and consolidation among Protestant, Catholic, and Jewish charitable workers. During the 1890s this "Catholic" voice in charities increasingly narrowed the Catholic agenda to downplay the critique of scientific charity that had been so central to institutional expansion.

Class and Ethnicity in Catholic and Jewish Institutions

Throughout the mid-1880s, class conflict between the rich and poor in the Irish Catholic community was apparent and best exemplified through the dramatic events of the "McGlynn Affair." Father Edward McGlynn was a radical priest who had participated in the increasingly militant labor movement, Irish nationalist causes, and socialist activities for much of his tenure as a pastor of St. Stephen's Parish in New York. McGlynn publicly questioned priests' vow of celibacy, papal infallibility, the divine inspiration of the Bible, and the morality of building parish schools while the poor went hungry. Part of a larger group of priests who called themselves the Accademia, McGlynn believed the church should reflect the democratic principles of American society and thus be determined in its course by the poor. In order to do so, moreover, McGlynn and the larger Accademia argued that the church must function as a leader in social reform and social justice and not just ameliorate the worst effects of capitalism.[2]

Archbishop John McCloskey had for the most part protected McGlynn and only once relented under other American bishops' insistence that McGlynn must be disciplined lest he undermine all episcopal authority in America. McCloskey then reproved McGlynn "'for his various communistic addresses.'" Almost immediately after McCloskey's death in 1885, however, the new archbishop, Michael Corrigan, issued several warnings to McGlynn, prohibiting public speaking in favor of mayoral candidate Henry George, whom he called a supporter of "socialism, communism and anarchy." Corrigan was the child of Irish-born parents who were estimated to be the wealthiest family in the metropolitan area. Schooled in Rome, he was an ultramontanist and earned his reputation as a leading conservative bishop by advocating in the Third Plenary Council of 1883 for local bishops' increased control of priests and nuns and immediate establishment of a parochial school in every parish in the nation.[3]

After McGlynn defied Corrigan's order and spoke again at a United Labor Party rally, Corrigan suspended him temporarily from parish duties. The archbishop then issued a pastoral letter, to be read by every pastor in the diocese at Sunday mass, on the "rights of Property" as deriving from natural law. Charity, Corrigan argued, was a duty to ease the plight of the poor, but social reform was anathema. Many other American archbishops praised Corrigan's pastoral and made it their rallying cry for combating radical elements.[4]

The controversy, which stretched from the fall of 1886 through the summer of 1887, heightened the divide between disparate Catholic groups that worked in New York charities and made clear the fragility of the cross-class Catholic alliance that had supported the expansion of children's institutions over the previous decades. Henry Hoguet, a member of the board of managers of the Protectory, wrote to Corrigan, "It is with pleasure I beg to state that the Managers . . . directed that an edition of your late pastoral should be struck off . . . at the printing shop of the Institution without charge."[5] Hoguet and the managers seemed unaware of the irony of having institutionalized poor children provide the labor to reproduce a statement defending the rights of property. "The paper for twenty-five thousand copies has been privately donated," Hoguet continued, "the first five thousand of these will be delivered at your residence."[6]

McGlynn responded directly to the pastoral in the *New York Tribune* of November 24, 1886:

> You may go on forever with hospitals and orphan asylums and St. Vincent de Paul Societies, but with them you can't cure the trouble. In a right state of society there ought not to be any hospitals or asylums or charitable societies, or else very few of them. . . . Nor is there much comfort in the condescending advice to the slaves of poverty and oppressed toil to remember even that Christ proclaimed the poor blessed and bade them hope for reward of eternal happiness. . . . So long as ministers of the gospel and priests of the Church tell the hardworking poor to be content with their lot and hope for good time in Heaven so long will skepticism increase.

Ending with a proclamation that charity was the "great panacea," McGlynn sent Archbishop Corrigan into a rage, prompting him to denounce McGlynn's teachings as contrary to those of the pope and the social teachings of the church. Corrigan took further action to move McGlynn permanently to a rural outpost where he could presumably do little harm. When McGlynn refused the transfer, Corrigan asked the Vatican to condemn McGlynn's "heresy" of asserting that the priesthood was accountable to the laity and not to the hierarchy. The Vatican sent a cable to McGlynn, ordering him to report to Rome, but McGlynn refused to go and instead became even more brazen in his remarks. "[P]rivate ownership of land is against natural justice, no matter by what civil or ecclesiastical laws it may be sanctioned," he wrote to Corrigan, "and I would bring about instantly, if I could, such change of laws the world over, as would confiscate private property in land, without one penny of compensation to the miscalled owners."[7]

Public reaction to the controversy makes clear just how misguided it was for Archbishop Corrigan, or other Catholics and non-Catholics, to assume that the laity, priesthood, and women religious would bow to Corrigan's episcopal authority. Other priests refused to replace McGlynn at St. Stephen's. When Corrigan finally installed one of his right-hand men, Edward Donnelly, as pastor, the *Tribune* reported on January 17, 1887, that "the janitor refused to tend the furnace. Few altar boys or choir members took part in the services and no ushers volunteered to take up the collections." Moreover, as Corrigan confided to a friend, Bishop Bernard McQuaid of Rochester, "The servant girls were the worst. The cook would not prepare the dinner but sat for hours in the same room with [Donnelly], watching him like a thief, and saying how holy [McGlynn] was and how 'near to God.' Tonight all kind of violence was threatened."[8] When Donnelly tried to enlist the police to break up a meeting aimed at organizing mass demonstrations they refused to intervene, and a movement began to stage an economic boycott of St. Stephen's until McGlynn was restored. In addition, the planning "committee of thirty-five" composed of male and female laity attempted to meet with Corrigan the next day to demand a public accounting of the reasons for McGlynn's dismissal. The archbishop refused to see them and instead issued a written statement arguing that a "general" was not required to justify actions to "his soldiers."[9]

Women religious were involved on both sides of the controversy, although how many supported McGlynn is difficult to ascertain given that the consequences of doing so publicly were significant. The Sisters of Charity, for instance, ran the children's institution at St. Stephen's, an emblem of the controversy itself in that McGlynn had refused Corrigan's order to turn the space into a parochial school. In early April of 1887 the Sisters of Charity at St. Stephen's Home staged a ceremony in which the children performed plays and exercises in support of McGlynn. Corrigan, who as archbishop was the person to whom the sisters ostensibly owed obedience, was incensed and took immediate steps to discipline the order.[10]

Mother Ambrosia tried to mitigate Corrigan's wrath, preferring to sacrifice Sister Francis Xavier Ryan, the errant nun presumably responsible, rather than risk sanction against the entire order. "Permit me here, Most Rev. Father," Mother Ambrosia wrote, "once more to give expression to my heartfelt regret and humiliation at the thought that any member of our Community should have been so misguided as to add to the scandal now desolating our City by coming to approve of a suspended priest defying your episcopal Authority." Claiming that she believed initially "that it was a mistake; that the proposition had been made to the Home from outside, but had been declined," Mother Ambrosia pleaded forgiveness for "the thoughtless act (I cannot believe she realized the magnitude of his fault) of one of my Sisters; and accept in part atonement at least, the sorrow of the rest of our Community, as also the affectionate expression of our renewed allegiance."[11]

Within months, however, and without public fanfare, Corrigan presided over a chapter meeting of the Sisters of Charity. Sister Ryan had already been removed from St. Stephen's and reassigned to nonspecific duties at the motherhouse, Mount St. Vincent's. The August chapter meeting decided, with concurrence from professed sisters in the order, that St. Stephen's home was to be closed. The children would be sent instead to the Roman Catholic Orphan Asylum, also run by the order. Seven sisters then moved into the empty building at St. Stephen's and there opened a parochial school.[12]

It would be too simple to stress only Corrigan's archconservative practices and suppression of those who questioned his authority. Much more important is the degree to which the Irish Catholic poor believed that support of Catholicism—and support of struggles for social justice— were not only compatible but also ideologically and practically linked. Corrigan may have won the battle over McGlynn's excommunication, but he became in American Catholic society an example of a leader so out of touch with the laity that he risked prompting the Irish poor's whole-sale abandonment of the church. If the Catholic press was hesitant to support McGlynn it became far less hesitant to support the organization of labor and demands for limits to the laissez-faire economy. As James Roohan observes, "A trend that had been apparent among Catholic so-cial thinkers in the previous decade had by the nineties become a fairly well-defined position: In its premises at least laissez-faire had become as unacceptable to them as socialism. The problem was to find a satisfac-tory middle road between these extremes."[13] The American hierarchy found that middle road by convincing Pope Leo in 1891 to express, by means of a papal encyclical, explicit support for organized labor and yet condemn socialism.[14]

Catholic Charities

The Catholic middle class was increasingly likely to see itself as uniquely able to mollify tensions between the community's rich and poor and me-diate between "American" and "foreign" Catholics. By the late 1880s, increasing proportions of the dependent children housed in Catholic and Jewish institutions were Italian and East European, whereas administra-tors of the institutions remained predominantly Irish Catholic or German Jewish, respectively. Spurred significantly by middle-class, Irish Catholic and German Jewish fears that newly won and very fragile toeholds in the venues and circles of American respectability would be endangered by unassimilated newcomers, both groups set out to control and assimilate coreligionists to degrees that rivaled the efforts of their purported adver-saries among the Protestant native-born elite.

Italian immigrants to New York City never swelled the ranks of the poor or depended on private and public charity to the same degree as the famine Irish and their children. In 1880, 89.5 percent of the city's foreign-born were English, Irish, or German, but by 1890 those groups accounted for only 72 percent of the total. In their places, newer groups became more conspicuous, if not dominant. Russian Polish Jews represented 7.6 percent of the city's total foreign-born population; Austrio-Hungarians, 7.4 percent; and Italians, 6.24 percent.[15] The proportion of newer immigrant groups in institutions, however, grew over time. In 1915, for instance, a great majority were the children of immigrants; 23.5 percent of their parents were born in Italy, roughly 20 percent were born in Russia, and only 28 percent were native-born.[16] Italians' increasing presence in the city's larger church system and institutions for dependent children had by the late 1880s highlighted what some Irish Catholic church leaders were prone to refer to as the "Italian Problem."[17]

To a significant degree, Italians struggled with problems endemic among newer Catholic immigrant groups, such as Poles, Lithuanians, and Czechs, who were likely to establish "national" parishes, as had been the practice for non-Irish Catholics for decades. Distinctive languages, particular customs, and clergy and women religious of their own national backgrounds marked the independence of groups who were Catholic but, like the segregated neighborhoods from which parish life sprang, expressed and practiced Catholicism in ways distinct from Irish and "Americanized" coreligionists. Renewed complaints by German Catholics in the United States and their advocates in Europe brought the increasingly widespread critique of Catholic Americanization (or "Irishization" in America) to international Catholic audiences. Archbishop Corrigan defended the practice to the Germans' advocate Peter Cahensly in 1891 by arguing that such a strategy was necessary because "one of the greatest drawbacks to the progress of our holy faith is the taunt continually cast up to us that we are *aliens*, and the Catholic Church is a *foreign institution.*" While asserting that "[t]he prejudice is unjust," Corrigan nonetheless held that "we are continually obliged to show that we Catholics are not opposed to the institutions of this country; that we are not subjects of a foreign potentate; and are sincerely attached to the land of our birth and adoption."[18]

The Vatican connection, and the centrality of New York City in Italian migration of the period, made Italian struggles with the Irish-dominated New York church most visible to the Vatican and therefore more vexing to the Irish hierarchy, particularly those who defined authority through networks in Rome, as did Archbishop Corrigan. The Bishop of Piacenza, Giovanni Battista Scalabrini, was charged by the Vatican in the 1880s with investigating and bettering the conditions of Italians in America. He then organized Italian priests and women religious to immigrate and focus their apostolates on assisting migrants and integrating them into American jobs, housing, and churches in addition to catering to their distinctive spiritual and religious needs and demands. From New York City, Countess Mary Di Cesnola, wife of the Italian-born curator of the Metropolitan Museum of Art, lobbied Corrigan for years to establish charities specifically for Italian children. Among the most conspicuous and celebrated of the religious migrants finally secured through the combined exertions of Di Cesnola and Scalabrini was Francesca Saverio Cabrini. Mother Cabrini soon organized her newly constituted sisterhood, the Missionary Sisters of the Sacred Heart, to migrate to New York and there establish, under Italian control, a Catholic school and orphanage for Italian children.[19]

Italian demands for a separate institution for children were in many senses spurred by native-born Protestant and Irish Catholic assertions that Italians as a group were more likely than others to institutionalize their children. At base was a charge that Italians had not internalized notions that charity was to be accessed only as a last resort. Italians allegedly believed that sending children to Catholic institutions gave the children opportunities for *collegio* (education) they would not have in Italy.[20] As early as 1882 the Protectory's board, acting on an assertion by the Society for the Prevention of Cruelty to Children (SPCC) that Italians were likely to institutionalize children even when financially able to care for them at home, began to send Italian children back into their homes within three months of commitment.[21]

Increasingly, generalized anti-immigrant sentiment helped fuel the notion that "foreigners" believed they could immigrate and then instantaneously place their children in homes that the public was taxed to support. Poor immigrants were characterized as sapping resources only grudgingly provided for "real Americans." Thus the new relative respectability of the Irish was tied directly to their perceived difference from, and superiority to, Italians as a group. For the first time, the Irish as a group were, in native-born estimations, moving above the bottom rungs and were not considered the city's "dregs of Europe." Irish Catholics' increased, but by no means secure, middle-class political and financial power in the city helped facilitate the tentative shift. Yet Irish subjugation and distrust of Italians was a critical means to that relative elevation as well.[22]

In an effort to quiet Italian complaints about poor treatment by Irish Catholics, Corrigan attempted to meet Countess Di Cesnola's demands that a separate institution for Italian children be established and urged sisters in the diocese to do so. Mother Ambrosia of the Sisters of Charity told Di Cesnola in 1887 that they would train the sisters in the Italian language and then secure a home, and she hoped Di Cesnola would find such an establishment acceptable. She did not. Instead, she continued to correspond with Scalabrini, and he convinced Mother Cabrini in December of 1888 to take up the work. Scalabrini was convinced that the combination of elite funding, a house promised by Di Cesnola, and the public funding assumed available in New York, would be sufficient to support Cabrini's charities and sisterhood.[23] The sisters then set out from Italy and debarked in New York in March of 1889. Arriving in the city with virtually no money or anyone in the order who spoke more than a few words of English, they were astonished to find that no house was provided for them and met with Corrigan and Di Cesnola the following morning.

In a markedly shrewd use of strategy that alerted the archbishop that Mother Cabrini was not a woman to be dismissed, Cabrini countered Corrigan's assertion that she return to Italy by arguing that doing so would constitute direct disobedience of the pope because her mission was Vatican-controlled and supported.[24] Corrigan then authorized Di Cesnola to immediately rent a house for the order on East Fifty-ninth Street and asked the Sisters of Charity to care for them until the house was ready. He continued, however, to argue that funding for the "orphanage" would be difficult or impossible and establishing an Italian parish school at St. Joachim's would prove a much better investment of the sisters' time and money.[25] Cabrini refused, set up the house as a small orphanage, and began preparing to take in Italian children.

Corrigan relied on a great deal of subterfuge in dealing with Cabrini, the larger order, and their many supporters back in Rome. He asserted repeatedly to all concerned that no money for the care of "orphans" was derived from the public treasury and that no Catholic institutions in the city received (or would likely ever receive) such funding. He failed to disclose, however, that Catholic institutions for "dependent children," were very well funded and that if a charter specifying care of dependent children were secured from the state, the order might be put on firm financial footing almost immediately. Di Cesnola, for her part, secured a charter for an orphanage that gave her, not the sisters, entire control of its management. Moreover, she asserted that the sisters could fund the orphanage by seeking employment in the many waged jobs available to women in the city.[26] In Corrigan's effort to paint himself as entirely innocent in the orphanage's demise he enlisted the support of Josephine Shaw Lowell, still a member of the State Board of Charities, whom he hoped would impress upon Mother Cabrini the impossibility of receiving public funding from New York's state or city authorities.

When Lowell visited the order in June the sisters expressed interest explicitly in caring for dependent children and being authorized by the state and city to receive commitments through the court system. Without declaring explicitly that they would not be granted such a charter or license, Lowell threw up so many roadblocks that the sisters were unable to do more than take in four children, with whom they shared living space and food. As Lowell wrote to the state board the following month:

> I explained to them and to the vicar-general, that I thought it necessary to be very careful in acting in this matter; that it would be a dangerous precedent to grant a charter to foreigners coming here for the purpose of opening an asylum for foreign children, to be supported by money raised by taxation . . . I told them that, at present, there was a strong inclination on the part of Italians to place their children in institutions ('al Collegio,' as they called it), and that I heard in two different institutions of the practice on the part of Italians, able to maintain their children, of paying brokers of their own nation to secure admission for them . . .
>
> I make this report at present, in order to suggest that when the application is received, it be very closely scrutinized, as it will serve as a precedent . . . I would also suggest that . . . when foreign children are supported in this country by public funds, that they should be brought up as Americans, and not as foreigners.[27]

After years of struggling with the archbishop, Di Cesnola, and city and state authorities, in 1890 Mother Cabrini finally bought a house on 109th street in Italian Harlem and opened the Sacred Heart Orphan Asylum for Italian children. Catholic visitors to the new house, however, were convinced that despite the asylum having secured a legal right to receive children, those commitments were still controlled by the SPCC, which would likely not commit more than a few children. James Traynor, a general agent for the Roman Catholic Orphan Asylum run by the Sisters of Charity, reported to Corrigan two years later, "As Your Grace will understand, even under the most favorable circumstances the Sisters will not receive even one or two children in a month, as [the SPCC] will have to approve of the commitments and they have no great love for Italians."[28] Without expressing explicit support of the SPCC's attitudes toward Italians, Traynor and Corrigan "understood" that the more likely alternative was that Italian children would continue to be placed in Irish-dominated institutions. They would there be trained as Catholics, perhaps as "American Catholics," and returned to families that were likely, in their view, to benefit from the children's influence.

For both German Jews and Irish Catholics, their ability to use resources at hand, including state funding, to house non-Irish Catholics and non-German Jews enabled them to attempt to define within their respective communities, as well as outside them, what it meant to be Catholic or Jewish in America. Like Irish Catholics' treatment of Italian Catholics, moreover, German Jews often reinforced negative stereotypes of East European Jews so as to simultaneously distance themselves from them in the eyes of native-born Protestants and convey willingness to take on the job of assimilation. When Myer Stern argued in 1894 against a proposed state constitutional amendment to ban all sectarian funding of private charities, he held that the anti-Catholic and anti-Semitic sentiment behind the amendment was to be rejected entirely because it was meant to "stir up the terrible fire of religious hatred."[29] Yet Stern also maintained that continuing to fund Jewish children's institutions would enable German Jews to assimilate East European Jews expeditiously:

> You can't make a silk purse out of a sow's ear, and we can't expect a high grade of civilization from a Russian. . . . Few of you have seen Russians who are not Jews, or I would not need say to you that the unpleasant traits of those you see, are not due to the fact that they are Jews so much as because they are Russians. But we are attached to these unfortunates . . . by ties of a common religion and ancestry, and besides that, the world, while it speaks of Americans and of Russians, never recognizes a difference of nationality or origin when it speaks of Jews, so that, in self-defense, we must protect our good name, by so training the children of these emigrants that they may be a credit to their adopted country and to their brethren in faith.[30]

Within Jewish institutions for dependent children, moreover, cultural gaps between German Jews and East European Jews might have been greater than was the case in the Catholic system. Because growing numbers of Jewish poor were likely to be from East European backgrounds and New York City had become so central to East European Jewish migration, by the turn of the century 60 percent of all institutionalized Jewish children in the United States were housed there.[31] Those who ran the institutions, however, were overwhelmingly German Jewish and of the middle or upper classes. German Jews as a group therefore maintained direct input into running the institutions through the early twentieth century.

At issue were not only the overtly racial/ethnic differences manifest between the German and Eastern European Jewish communities but also the ways in which those differences were reflected in attitudes toward assimilation, religious practices, and the distinct cultural frameworks through which the two groups expressed Jewishness. In her study of Jewish orphanages through this period Reena Friedman cites New York's Jewish children's institutions as particularly plagued by tensions between what she terms the "uptown" and "downtown" components of the city's Jewish community.[32] The German middle- and upper-class community was likely to practice a Reform Judaism consistent with, although certainly not identical to, various forms of American middle-class religious culture, including emphases on individualism, professionalism, and integration into larger, non-Jewish educational, economic, political, and social networks. East Europeans came from areas where commitment to Jewish orthodoxy and resistance to cultural assimilation were deemed central to cultural survival.[33] Nor were the orthodox more likely to give up distinctive cultural practices because other Jews prompted them to do so. Like Italians, East European groups formed their own charities so as to decrease dependence on the German Jewish community. Beth Israel Hospital and Hachnosas Orchim were opened in the 1890s, and three orthodox institutions for children were eventually opened between 1914 and 1917.[34] By the 1920s and 1930s, especially after children of East European Jews were likely be their managers, the institutions began to introduce Kosher food and Bar Mitzvah training and place greater emphasis on parental visitation.

Consolidating the Elite in the "Charitable Trust"

The growing alliance between Catholic and Protestant middle-class and elite charitable workers was made possible initially by Protestant reformers' acceptance of public funding for Catholic and Jewish charities in 1894. In the short term the 1894 Constitutional Convention in Albany seemed a victory for Catholics and Jews in that the convention rejected outright the proposition put forward by the State Charities Aid Association (SCAA) and the Evangelical Alliance that all "sectarian charities" be legislatively barred from receiving public money.[35] In a rather well-played bad cop–good cop routine the SCAA stepped in to denounce the religious "hatred" that had inspired the Evangelical Alliance's hostility to Catholic and Jewish charities. The convention also concluded that public funding of children's institutions could be expected to continue, as it had for upward of twenty years. On the surface these seemed the primary issues that the Catholic alliance had historically demanded.

Yet the convention shifted rather abruptly to the question of how to determine who among the poor had a right to support. There was, moreover, significant tension among Protestant reformers over the question. Eldridge Gerry, president of the SPCC, argued that his organization believed that public payments to institutions for the support of dependent children was money well-spent. He also rejected the premises of scientific charity: "I do not believe in that so-called economy of charity which restricts the appropriation of public moneys . . . to the minimum amount required to prevent the child from suffering from absolute starvation. . . . To my mind the City of New York can well afford to spend, not $1,000,000, but, if necessary, $5,000,000, in the support, care and training of the destitute and indigent and dependent children." As to proposals to cut the level of public funding to institutions, Gerry proclaimed, "It would be one of the greatest blunders this community ever permitted if it were to try how cheaply the children of the City of New York could be supported in institutions, for it can more advantageously make the only other provision for them; that is, a proper cemetery in which they can be interred."[36]

Representatives of the SCAA held instead that the problem with institutions was not their religious character but that the state did not adequately control admissions or discharges, a practice that had allowed for the "pauperizing of a whole people." Although the state board had always investigated and regulated institutions in regard to health facilities and education, SCAA member Joseph Choate announced at the final hearing of the convention that there would "be a power in the State that has never been exercised before to go through these institutions, any year, any week, or any day, lay its hands upon this child and upon that child, and say: 'You shall not receive one dollar for that child, because its parents are perfectly able to support it.'"[37] In essence, he concluded, "The admission will be made more difficult and the exit will be made more easy."[38]

Advocating placing-out, restriction of admissions, limits on commitments, and increased state and city regulatory control, Choate submitted and won approval for a constitutional amendment. Prepared by the SCAA, the amendment made funding for private institutions contingent upon inspection and certification by the State Board of Charities.[39] The amendment further reaffirmed the SCAA's quasi-legal status and granted the State Board of Charities constitutional guarantees to its status, a provision the SCAA felt necessary to protect the board against institutions that felt threatened by it. "These institutions are very powerful," Louisa Schuyler cautioned. "No State supervisory body, dependent solely upon the Legislature for its existence, could fearlessly perform the duties required of it by law without danger of being abolished. And yet . . . no undue autocratic authority need be feared by the institutions."[40] Thus was born the first public bureaucracy with power to regulate admissions and discharges to institutions.[41]

Various reformers thereafter vied to control this city bureaucracy, either because they intended to means-test and restrict admissions or intended to allow poor parents relatively easy access to institutionalization. Yet the bureaucracy was not excessively rationalized, and policies that resulted were inconsistent and contradictory. The SCAA, for example, believed it had solved the problem by having the city hire five examiners in March 1895. They were to be accountable to the city's commissioner of public charities and charged to investigate all homes of dependent children, decrease admissions, and increase discharges.[42]

Over the next five years examiners were somewhat successful in limiting commitments. Katherine Hall, the head city examiner in 1897, reported that in the first six months of that year she had investigated the families of children in institutions throughout the city and found 1,683 improper charges.[43] Citing the reductions, the state board and SCAA both published reports in the same year and assumed they would continue.[44] The following year, however, commitments again rose, largely because the amendment had not divested the SPCC of authority to commit and the SPCC rejected the principles of scientific charity on which the policy of restriction was based. Parents denied aid by the Department of Public Charities then were able to bypass DPC authority by applying directly through the SPCC. By 1899 the SCAA reported that the number of examiners was insufficient to promote a rapid decrease in institutionalization. Although subsequent city administrations would either favor or contest poor parents' ability to declare their children dependent, the total number of children in Catholic and Jewish institutions stayed fairly constant during the next two decades at roughly twelve thousand and two thousand, respectively.[45]

Catholic middle-class men increasingly mediated between contending groups. Thomas Mulry, for example, proved to be a perfect poster boy for Irish American, middle-class, and elite assimilation. He was born in 1855, one of fourteen children of Irish famine immigrants whose father worked as a "cellar-digger" in the city and rose to prominence as a contractor who reaped the financial rewards of allegiance to Tammany. Mulry inherited his father's business and branched into real estate and banking, eventually becoming president of the Emigrant Savings Bank although he had not received a college education.[46] By the mid-1880s he augmented his voluntarism in the SVDP by joining the Charity Organization Society (COS). Mulry asked for and gained approval from Corrigan to do so as an individual, not a representative for Catholics. He thereafter saw himself as the "link" between Catholic and Protestant charitable workers, a role he cultivated assiduously by the late 1890s. Although defining himself primarily as Catholic, Mulry often worked to legitimate Protestant-run charities to the larger Catholic population by reporting on the absence of explicit proselytization in the COS and later the SCAA.[47]

The methods and goals of scientific charity so thoroughly influenced Mulry, however, that what was particularly Catholic about his politics or charitable work became increasingly difficult to decipher. As secretary for the New York Particular Council of the St. Vincent de Paul Society in 1894, for example, he characterized the friendly visiting of the society during the severe depression of 1893 in terms indistinguishable from Protestant native-borns: "Every means was tried with the consequence that often times more injury was done the recipients by giving, than would have been experienced by withholding the help altogether. The manner of giving in such cases being certain to rob the poor of their self respect and independence. Throughout those trying times the Conferences conformed, in most instances, strictly to the rules, and gained the respect and admiration of our non-Catholic citizens."[48]

Mulry's role in this new "cooperative" effort among the "Charity Trust" is perhaps best exemplified by his friendship with Homer Folks. Folks came to New York City in 1893 from Philadelphia, where he ran the Children's Aid Society (CAS) and won a national reputation for managing and reforming an enormous placing-out system. Hired by the SCAA as a paid secretary, Folks bridged the transitional period from charitable voluntarism to paid social work and was enormously energetic in rationalizing and centralizing reform efforts in charities, particularly after Republicans gained substantial political power following the enactment of the 1896 city charter. The charter passed in the state legislature redrew the city's boundaries to include suburbs in Brooklyn, Queens, and Staten Island, where Republican majorities ruled. Thereafter, the administrations in the city were likely to be either Republican or "Fusionist," a third-party coalition dependent on both Democratic and Republican votes.

City administrations had by the end of the 1890s assumed regulatory and bureaucratic control over private charities that received public funds, so particular positions in city government took on new importance, especially the job of commissioner of public charities. The commissioner headed the department from which examiners were dispatched to institutions and the homes of the poor, largely with the mission of reducing the number of children the city deemed dependent and therefore worthy of city funding.

Thomas Mulry emerged as a leading candidate for commissioner of public charities in 1897, largely because the Democratic mayoral victory convinced Protestant reformers that their control over city government

would be undermined by a return to Tammany politics. As Robert Hebberd, a Protestant member of the State Board of Charities, reminded Folks,
"Former Commissioner Brennan is looming up as a candidate, would it
not be a good thing to try to get the leading charities into line for Mr.
M? . . . He is not dependent upon politics for a livelihood and I believe
would make an honest, efficient, and fair Commissioner."[49] Hebberd cautioned, "To my mind the chief danger in the situation lies in the chance
of getting in one of the old incompetents who are opposed to reform and
to reformers and who . . . have kept New York City's charities about
fifty years behind the age."[50] Eldridge Gerry and Josephine Shaw Lowell
similarly supported Mulry, and Lowell lobbied Archbishop Corrigan to
support the appointment as well.[51]

Ultimately, these backroom machinations of reform politics functioned above all else to unify the charitable elite across religions. Perhaps the most revealing of the politics behind the appointment was that
Josephine Shaw Lowell had managed to prompt the archbishop to meet
with Tammany head Richard "Boss" Croker so as to entice him to meet
and hire Mulry.

That Protestant reformers were now introducing Mulry to the Irish
Catholic machine spoke volumes about how far he had distanced himself
from the city's earlier Irish politics. Similarly, Lowell's regular discussions
with the archbishop were based on their collective stance in opposing
the more radical class politics of the likes of McGlynn and his follow-
ers or the desires of new immigrants to attain access to or control over
Catholic charities in New York.

Both Mulry and the archbishop, however, distinguished themselves
from Protestants sufficiently to present what was, ostensibly, an oppositional point of view within the Charity Trust and therefore validate
the rhetoric of compromise and cooperation. Mulry, for example, refused
Homer Folks's invitation in 1897 to join the "Get-together Club" for
reformers: "I do not agree with the writers of the circular or invitations
sent out. I do not think the Reform government of the city has been an
unalloyed blessing to the people."[52] Similarly, when Folks emerged as the
leading candidate for commissioner of public charities under the reform
administration of Mayor Seth Low in 1901, Lowell went to the archbishop and reported back to Gertrude Rice, vice president of the SCAA.
"Saw the Archbishop today and he was friendly—said he had no candidate—wished to keep out of it but had heard Mr. Folks said he thought a
good home was all that was needed and could not see what difference the
religion made. I told him this was absolutely *false*—he said he was very

glad and would contradict it if repeated."[53] Lowell and Archbishop Corrigan were similarly content to characterize the approaches of Catholics and Protestants to children's charities as distinguished only by religious affiliation.

Mulry, moreover, saw his role as conciliator in very personal terms, encouraging and receiving considerable support from Protestant reformers who considered him a strategic ally. When Folks failed to receive a post as commissioner of charities in 1899, for instance, Mulry sent his condolences and a copy of the life of St. Vincent de Paul:

> I wish also to say that I feel drawn to you more closely than ever. There was a time when I did not have this feeling, but I consider you one of my dearest friends, and for this reason I feel a great disappointment at your failure to obtain the position you were a candidate for . . . I hope that our relations in future will be even closer than in the past—and expect that every day will bring us closer in the "point of view" with which we look at subjects in which we are interested—I want all the benefit I can obtain from your great experience and study of the questions which are continually brought to our notice.[54]

Catholic "opposition" as articulated by Thomas Mulry thus reduced in dramatic ways the richness of the historical Catholic critique of Protestant reform to its most narrow manifestations—to which church would poor children pledge allegiance? When Folks found yet another of his attempts to gain the post of commissioner threatened by Catholic opposition in the city, he wrote to Mayor-elect Low, "the [SCAA] and myself, in speech and in practice, have consistently advocated the policy of keeping children under the influence of the religious faith of their parents."[55]

Such a simplification of the issues involved did not indicate that Protestant reformers considered differences in Protestant and Catholic approaches to charities to be as inconsequential as their rhetoric suggests. Gertrude Rice of the SCAA similarly wrote to warn Low against appointing a Catholic in Folks's place. He might, she suggested, lessen Catholic opposition by appointing "a Catholic at the head of some other great department where his religious views would not be so likely to impair his judgement and by having a Catholic Deputy Commissioner of Charities for this Borough."[56] When Folks was appointed commissioner, Rice suggested to him that "it would be well for you to say that you should wish a Catholic Deputy Commissioner and one who would be acceptable to Mr. Mulry and others, and that you relied on their help and cooperation."[57]

Demonizing the Institution

Poor mothers and their children stood at the center of these warring ideological and institutional systems. For a time at least, many among the poor preferred dependence on Catholic and Jewish charities to the alternatives. And yet nuns' institutions now loomed as the greatest immediate threat to parental control over children. The decision to institutionalize a child was the only way that poor parents could receive public help should illness, unemployment, or poverty in general necessitate it. Institutions proved a safety net of sorts but a painful one for parents to employ. For poor mothers to surrender children rather than have them removed from their care, to lose control for short periods rather than indefinitely, and to rely on Catholic reconstruction of working-class interdependent family economies rather than be punished by the state for depending on women and children's wage work made reliance on institutions less risky than reliance on Protestant charity. And yet neither strategy struck at the roots of women and children's poverty, much less the greater vulnerability of poor mothers to having their children removed from their homes simply because the family was poor.

Once nuns had control over children and their families, they earned criticism from poor parents resentful of such power and suspicious of its abuse. Whatever the original purpose and political intent of institutionalization, by the 1890s institutions had become part of the state's bureaucracy and had rules and regulations that seemed more oriented toward protecting and reproducing institutions than shielding those in their care. In 1891, for example, the Sisters of Charity released Sarah Devine from the Protectory. Her relatives were appalled that she was forced to wear the same clothing she had worn into the institution eight years earlier. The officer who discharged Sarah Devine argued that "[t]he rule about clothing was made in the case of those who bring children clad in rags (which often have to be destroyed) and in a few weeks demand the discharge of the child, thus gaining a new suit at the expense of the institution."[58] One St. Vincent de Paul member observed that the poor feared the Sisters of Charity: "It is claimed that the children are badly used at the Protectory, that the sisters beat them, that they are taught little or nothing, that they come out *timid, fearful,* and *broken spirited,* and unfit to face the world or make a living . . . [and] that great efforts are made to deceive the visitors who are in authority."[59]

When two girls "escaped" from the Protectory in the same year Sister Jerome had to convince Corrigan that newspaper accounts of "the children being 'strapped down to a bed and whipped'" were "entirely false."[60]

Officially, corporal punishment of any kind was prohibited. *"Discipline should be secured by gentle measure as far as possible; kindness and reason generally will control,"* a member of the Board of Managers reported. "There are cases where punishment is necessary. Demerit marks and deprival of play are sufficient in some cases; in others increase of task, or removal from companionship of comrades."[61]

To a populace forced to rely on the sisters to care for their children, however, stories of abuse fueled speculation that the sisters cared more about public funding than the welfare of children. Mother Mary Veronica Starr of the Sisters of the Divine Compassion held that state funding had itself changed the nature of charitable work:

> Every institution in this diocese, for the past twenty years, has been running after committed children; some, founded for other purposes, have abandoned their original intentions, and some have been opened to obtain that source of revenue. . . . That it would prove injurious in the end to the religious spirit, there was little doubt. First would come the mercenary motive which is death to true charity and faith in God. Those who look so eagerly to the Government for daily bread cannot say with the spirit of true dependence, "Our Father who art in heaven." . . . Another evil, and a grievous one, is that the religious houses have lost the affection and confidence of the poor. Forgetting the good derived from the Sisters' influence, they see only that they are paid and say "no thanks to them."[62]

The poor's criticisms of nuns, however, were by no means the same as those offered by the Protestant elite. Protestant female reformers' complaints about the system's effects on children shifted considerably by the 1890s. Inspectors who visited institutions in the 1880s often explicitly acknowledged nuns' "devotion" as ameliorating the harshness of life within an institution. Given Josephine Shaw Lowell's general condemnation of the system throughout the 1880s, her continuous praise of nuns who ran the institutions was striking. "We find . . . that the evils which seem to be inseparable from so large an institution," she wrote in 1886 of the Catholic Protectory under the Sisters of Charity, "are reduced to a minimum by the constant, personal oversight of the indefatigable Sisters who are everywhere, taking charge of every thing, and converting into a natural individual life what would seem to be necessarily so unnatural and hurtful."[63] Lowell's state-sponsored investigations of individual institutions refer repeatedly to nuns' "devotion" to children, and the children's general good health and cleanliness.[64] In the SCAA's estimation, given the association's larger rubric of "efficiency" in charitable work, such devotion was not desirable because it kept public expenditures high: "Of the better class of them, it is thought that the kind hearts which have them in charge are sometimes so fond of the children . . . [they] . . . are kept too long."[65]

By the early 1890s, however, Lowell and other Protestant reformers began to depict nuns' care for children as "unnatural" as opposed to an individual mother's care in a "natural" family. Natural families, according to this discourse, produced independent, individualized, self-reliant children. Unnatural situations were those in which attention to the provision of clothing, food, and children's needs produced dependency. Lowell characterized the army of "dependents" being reared by the city in 1893:

> [T]housands of children who ought to receive the training of family life are . . . living in the unnatural isolation of a crowd of children like themselves, and subject to institution training, which must destroy in almost all the capacity to meet the difficulties and temptations to which they will be exposed as soon as they begin life for themselves. What preparation for independent action can be found in a life, the one necessity of which is absolute dependence upon and conformity to rule? What room is there for the development or exercise of energy or invention in a life where everything is ready to hand and prepared by machinery? What chance is there for a child to learn the value of property . . . where everything, even the clothing, belongs to no one individual, but to the whole community? What sense of personal love or care can be felt when the child is one of a thousand. . . . Fancy the stultification of mind and soul which must follow from such conditions.[66]

Lowell's argument drew power to persuade from three venerable traditions of nineteenth-century Protestant reform: anti-nun literature, child-saving, and urban reform. Indeed, there was very close correlation between the kind of Protestant rhetoric evident in antebellum, anti-convent literature and that of anti-institutional rhetoric in New York during the Progressive Era. The emphasis in anti-institutional rhetoric on rigidity, obedience, and a grueling lack of individuality in the form and substance of everyday life could have sprung from anti-convent literature such as that of Maria Monk. And, of course, what was institutional life for dependent children if not an expansion of convent life itself, now publicly funded on such a scale as to rear substantial portions of the community's children within its walls?

If convent life had provided antebellum native-born Protestants with an alternative gender system they feared would supplant or endanger the emergent emphasis on motherhood and domesticity among the middle class, then expansion of the institutional system in New York was even more frightening. Institutional expansion was, in the reformers' view, the fruition of a Catholic-controlled state whereby ecclesiastic hierarchies and alternatives to the normative, middle-class family system were supported through massive public funding. Instead of a bizarre but numerically and organizationally very limited manifestation of a deviant culture, the convent was now in danger of becoming normalized as an appropriate means through which to rear American citizens. The ensuing and extremely passionate debate about the relative merits of the family plan and institutionalization was always, therefore, deeply resonant of larger tensions that had fueled Protestant-Catholic conflict in America for decades, especially regarding the distinct gender systems central to these contending communities.

Yet during the 1890s anti-institutionalization was constructed as an increasingly secular discussion and rarely identifiable as explicitly anti-Catholic. Most renditions of anti-institutionalization rhetoric through the 1890s did not mention or allude to nuns. Those that did tended to patronize nuns, characterizing them as well-meaning but ignorant. When a male manager of the Protectory delivered a paper at a conference sponsored by the SCAA, Lowell took the podium to critique the presentation. Although believing "sincerely" in the "earnest desire of the managers of the Protectory and of the Christian Brothers and the Sisters of Charity to do good to the children under their charge," Lowell began, "still I believe that their system is wrong, and that they do harm where they only strive to do good."[67]

The larger rubric of "dependence upon and conformity to rule" paralleled anti-Catholic, anti-pauperization rhetoric through the century and was used repeatedly as a contrast to the encouragement of individuality, independence, self-reliance, and resourcefulness in guiding children's upbringing, whether in homes or families. Reformers who wielded anti-institutional rhetoric referred to the "conformity" or "machinery" of institutional life as a spring from which a dependent class would rise. "Children massed in institutions," claimed Sophie Minton, chair of the Committee on Children of the SCAA, "are 'singularly stupid, showing a want of pluck, dependence on others, inability to shift for themselves, characteristics which develop into the grown pauper.'" She went on to observe that "'there are many girls who are immoral from the barrack system, hardly any from foster homes.'"[68]

As in anti-nun literature, moreover, the "institution" or convent conveyed a rejection of domesticity and incarceration of mindless victims secretly longing for "rescue" and placement into the sanctity of a home circle. The contrast drawn between the family plan and institutionalization reinforced the sense of convent life and nuns' form of mothering as deviant as opposed to promotion of normative, "motherly love" in a home. What guided anti-institutional rhetoric throughout the decade was a sense of totality in creating the "institutionalized child" as a social deviant incapable of adjusting to middle-class values or adjusting to "normal" life. The placing-out system, by its very nature, could not be abusive, and the institution could not be anything but harmful. Given that construct, nuns could not, in Protestant reformers' estimation, do their work well. The reformers understood nuns' attention to children's needs as promoting dependency, whether in those children or in their parents. The only way to perform such work adequately was to not do it at all and reject the poor's applications for aid.

The proponents of institutions did not defend those run by nuns to supplant family life but to supplement it.[69] Statistics showed that parents continued throughout the 1890s to employ institutionalization as a temporary strategy for coping with poverty. Most institutionalized children spent the great part of their childhoods with their parents. As Eldridge Gerry reported in 1894, "Children are . . . discharged to their parents when the latter are able to care for them, for the child is rarely retained when the parents are able to support it and applies for its discharge; and they are discharged at all times on the order of the Court."[70]

As New York's population grew and institutions were held at totals not exceeding those of the early 1890s, the average length of time any child spent in a Catholic institution was reduced to eighteen months, and the proportion of applications accepted was down to one-third.[71] The totality of the construct of the institutionalized child was divorced from the realities of how institutions were used and what they were used against. Yet the construction of this binary debate left Catholics in the unenviable position of declaring over and over again that they did not support institutionalization as a preferred family form but only as a temporary expedient for the care of children.

The anti-institutional construct took on a life of its own through the Progressive Era and appealed to child-savers' visions of rescuing children from unspeakable cruelties. No longer focusing on "depraved" parents who produced a dependent class, child-savers characterized institutions as a strange aberration of state development that placed thousands of children at risk of becoming walking automatons. Speaking in 1898 at the National Conference of Charities, Thomas Mulry claimed that those who became intensely critical of institutions "have fairly gone crazy over this. . . . Take for example the man with what might be called 'institution-phobia.' . . . He lies awake at night, his mind filled with dreadful pictures of institution life. When he sleeps, he dreams of the institution walk, of the institution look and he talks at all times of the piece of machinery, in the shape of a human being, which the institution turns out."[72]

Such anti-institutional propaganda influenced some examiners sent to visit the institutions. The general hostility to institutional life expressed by many inspectors in the 1890s had little to do with issues of health, safety, food, and education. Seemingly schooled on anti-nun, anti-institutional rhetoric, the inspectors' accusations were so far-fetched that nuns responded with a mixture of disbelief, indignation, and amusement. On one occasion the Good Shepherd Sisters had to contend with a young female inspector who insisted repeatedly that the sisters show her their "dungeon." Shocked, the nuns replied that they never employed corporal punishment in any form and most certainly did not have a dungeon in the basement.[73]

The Sisters of the Divine Compassion complained to the state board about a rumor they heard circulated by a state inspector in 1902 after he toured their institution. As the nuns told it, a sister watching over a small group of young children was called away momentarily. The children, "to play a trick on the Sister," ran up the stairs and hid in an empty room. When the inspector passed the room he asked if any children could be in it, and, presuming it to be empty, the sister giving the tour said no. Hearing them in the room after they passed, he exclaimed excitedly that there were children "locked in a room!" The sister in charge of the children explained what had happened, as did the children, and the order thought nothing of it until they heard a rumor circulating that they had sixty children "locked up" in a small, unventilated room purposely hidden from inspection. The sisters wrote to the state board:

> Now granting what seems to be assumed as an incontrovertible fact by the State Board, that nuns are given to mendacity and frauds and stratagems, would we not have been extremely poor in resources to have ventured on such a course knowing that . . . your Inspectors would telephone to Albany for the exact number of children in the House. . . ? We have not yet learned what motive rumor assigns for this hiding away of children. If *our* word is to be taken, they were clean, healthy and cheerful, and . . . very much amused at what they considered a bold stroke on their part.[74]

Why, the sisters asked, is there an "offensive" spirit to inspections or an inspector who "creates adverse public opinion, striking defenceless women? Doubtless there are those who think it can be done safely."

The Sisters of the Divine Compassion further questioned what they termed the "inquisitorial methods" by inspectors who investigated the families of children in the institution.[75] When Josephine Lowell responded in 1900 to Mother Veronica's complaints that investigations had become "brutal," Lowell explained that there was concern about harm done to children when keeping them too long in the institution. "[W]hen you talk of 'the injury to the children by subjecting them for too long a time to the influence of institution life,'" Mother Veronica shot back, "I do not know what you mean. I do know the word is a sort of Shibboleth among certain people, but I very much doubt if they know just what they mean, themselves."[76]

Despite passionate anti-institutional rhetoric, the SCAA and COS throughout the 1890s feared expansion of outdoor relief more than they feared institutionalization. We should not, for instance, assume that Protestant reformers were suggesting in the 1890s that children should be supported by the charitable establishment and kept with their parents. As an SCAA pamphlet made clear in 1893, "The unwise admission of children means pauperized parents; their unwise detention, institutionalized children."[77] Reformers provided only two options. If enlisting the help of the state to support their children, parents necessarily lost parental rights and should agree to the children being placed out. If they refused, no funding for dependent children should be given. Reformers argued that the option of institutionalization, especially given nuns' attempts to mitigate the harshness of the experience for children, was the primary cause of the poor's greater dependence on charities for children. As SCAA member Sophie Minton observed, "[L]ooking at it from the point of view of the poor parent, how convenient is a free boarding-school, where he has confidence in the management, where his child is taught his own faith, where all care and responsibility are lifted from his shoulder, and whence he can withdraw his child at will! How easy it is for him to shift his burden to the public!"[78]

Ultimately, the great problem with institutionalization, reformers argued, was that it did not provide sufficient deterrents to keep the poor independent of charity. The fear of losing their children permanently, however, would no doubt provide that deterrent:

> It is a fact that many poor people, who would readily place their child in an institution . . . would strenuously object to have him boarded out. They have not the same confidence in the management. . . . Hence they will make every effort, both of hard-working and decent living, to keep the child, or at least to get him back as soon as possible. We are presupposing love for the child [but] alas! it is well known that with some unfortunate women there is little more tenderness than with an animal for its offspring. And, surely, in this latter case the way to cultivate the

maternal instinct is not to separate the child from the mother, but to use every means to urge her to care for it.[79]

Minton's supposed cultivation of the "maternal instincts" of poor women, therefore, was emphatically not to be achieved through material aid but by instilling fear in poor mothers that the state would take away their children should the mothers find themselves in poverty.

At no time through the 1890s did native-born female reformers support public funding for poor families, including those headed by widows. Nor did Lowell in her capacity as head of the Charities Organization Society attempt to channel any significant private funding into the homes of widows on a long-term basis. In 1891 she was alerted to a bill pending in the state legislature that would require all dependent children be taken out of institutions and kept with their mothers ("unless she is declared unfit by a judge"), supported there by public funds. Lowell opposed the bill because it was "so dangerous." "I do not," she said, "approve of the wholesale putting of children into institutions, but neither do I approve of obligatory outdoor relief."[80]

Protestant reformers nonetheless so skillfully created and promoted the specter of the institutionalized child and emphasized institutions' tendency in the short term to separate parents and children that they created a kind of backlash that was, in their opinion, more threatening than what existed. Given that institutionalization was so apparently bad for children and wrenching for parents, by the end of the decade New Yorkers of all descriptions and classes began to demand direct funding to help poor parents care for children in their own homes. Horrified, the city's charitable elite, especially those in the Charity Organization Society, State Charities Aid Association, and Children's Aid Society, had to scramble to prohibit the foundation of a massive system of outdoor relief over which they would have little or no control.

The Destitute Mother's Bill

The decisive shift in allying Protestants, Catholics, and Jews by class was that achieved through support or opposition to the Destitute Mother's Bill introduced by John Ahearn, a Tammany Democratic state senator whose Fourth District constituency on the Lower East Side was half Jewish and half Irish Catholic. The bill called for granting public payments in New York City, approximately $2 per week, to poor mothers themselves instead of institutions.[81] Without fanfare the bill passed both houses of the state legislature in 1897; only the mayor's and governor's signatures were needed to make it state law.

Scientific charity advocates were shocked that public support for the bill was so widespread, but much of the public considered it the most logical alternative to the current system that Protestant reformers derided so heartily. If the state's duty to care for dependent children was conceded in the 1894 State Convention, and institutionalization's effects on children were so objectionable, then surely funding poor families directly would be a better alternative for all concerned. Indeed, Lowell's slogan, coined in 1884, "the poorest home, unless it be a degraded one, is better than the best institution," provided a terse statement of principle seemingly consistent with the intent of the bill.[82]

Announcing that he would hold a hearing on the bill before deciding whether to sign it, the Republican mayor and reform candidate William Strong was inundated by letters from the bill's supporters as well as its opponents. Ahearn claimed that a life spent in Lower East Side neighborhoods gave him "opportunities of witnessing privation and distress" to degrees unknown by most politicians.[83] "Under existing laws," he argued, "poverty would seem to be regarded as criminal, since a good mother left husbandless without means must suffer the severest penalties in being deprived of her children, to whom she is attached by the highest laws of God and nature."[84] Using Protestant reformers' rhetoric, Ahearn maintained that "it must be admitted that such institutions, no matter how well conducted, can never take the parents' place towards the child, nor foster and develop . . . home instincts."[85] The bill, moreover, gave the SPCC the legal authority to grant direct payments instead of committing children to institutions, an alternative, Ahearn said, that "provides for the better exercise of charity, and a greater exercise of justice, in the future."[86]

Ahearn anticipated the bill's rejection on several counts, including contention over whether the SPCC was the appropriate agency in which to confer such power and the inevitable question of whether the state could or should make direct payments to individuals. Ahearn dismissed the first question as minor because the SPCC's corporate function was concerned overall with the "welfare of children," so payment of funds to keep children at home fell within its legal scope. As to the question of outdoor relief, Ahearn held that precedent had been set by granting veterans' pensions in 1888 and outdoor relief to the blind. Finally, expecting that institutions themselves would object, he told Mayor Strong that he was "sure that no consideration of selfish, financial reasons will induce the withholding of your approval."[87]

Mothers forced to decide whether to institutionalize their children wrote passionately of the agony of that choice. "I am a scrub-woman in

City Hall, where you daily come to your office," one wrote, "a widow with seven orphans and their sole support is thirty dollars per month, . . . and upon this we have to depend for shelter, food and clothing." Claiming that the family had insufficient income for coal and food through the winter, she stated nonetheless, "I would suffer every one of them to die rather than place them in a institution."[88] Others held similarly that the choice to institutionalize a child was "a sorrow or punishment worse than death."[89] One woman recalled a neighbor who placed her only son in the Protectory: "I knew of a Mrs. Lynch whom it used to cost a few dollars every time she went there and she had only one boy and she made neck ties for a living and I knew her to be night after night never to undress only sew all night to bring the boy a few things when she went to see him she could have kept him home with what she earned and $2 a week to help her along."[90] A Mrs. Peterson from Brooklyn "most earnestedly beg[ged]" the mayor to sign the bill:

> I am a widow with six Children and I have been forced to put two Boys in Snug Harbar and one girl in the Blind asylum and I have three girls at home the oldest is fifteen years old and works for 2.50 per week and the other two girls I have at home are two years and eight years old I have had such a hard time trying to keep the home together that I will have to put the two youngest that I have away as I am not able to keep them in bread. I have to support my Mother who is to old to work hoping that God put it in your heart to look with favor on it is the heartfelt Prayer of Mrs. Peterson, 68 Jay St., Brooklyn, N.Y.[91]

Democrats and Republicans alike expressed support of the bill to Strong, alluding repeatedly to the wrenching separation of mother and child and the impossibility of replicating in an institution the home care provided by a mother. One Republican from the East Side claimed that he had witnessed "many Sad Heartfelt scenes where good Brave mothers had to Part With their children and Break up the Dearest Spot on Earth. Home Sweet home. Where a Little aid Would have Saved (Even if given only for a few months) the shelter of home and a mothers Loving Care Who Can Guide Like a mother who can Protect Like her. Surely not the Cold Greedy Hand of Charity for the Sum it can grasp in Payment of a childs care."[92] "My Father died when I was young and My Mother put us in a home," Clara Jackson recalled. "There was six of us when my Mother died we do not know where any my brothers are if there was a bill like this we might have been all together. Hoping you will surely sign this bill and received an Orphan's prayer."[93] Strong vetoed the bill.

The Protestant charitable establishment took the lead in opposing the bill but ended its efforts by taking the first steps toward official support of family preservation in an effort to lessen widespread public condemnation of "so-called charities." Homer Folks urged the mayor to hold a hearing, claiming that the "provisions of this bill are so extraordinary, that one could hardly believe it was seriously proposed."[94] Protestant groups that opposed its passage included the SCAA, COS, State Board of Charities, and American Female Guardian Society as well as prominent reformers throughout the city. Lowell put the matter as she did in 1891: "The evil of keeping children shut up in Institutions is a very great one, but I believe also that Senator Ahearn's proposal, that the remedy should be to pay parents from the public funds for taking care of them, would result in even a greater evil."[95] "[T]his plan is a scarcely disguised form of outdoor relief," the Charity Organization Society reported, "and . . . 'shiftless fathers' would be quite as apt as 'destitute mothers' to claim the indulgence of the Society and the public."[96]

When faced with the choice of institutions or outdoor relief, the same people whose life's work seemed devoted to removing children from the horrors of institutions suddenly depicted the same places as being much better for the children than their own homes. State Board of Charities President William R. Stewart maintained that to offer payments directly to mothers, without threat of institutionalization as a deterrent, would greatly "pauperize" the population. Such payments came dangerously close to admitting unequivocally that parents were entitled to direct aid. As Stewart testified at the hearing:

> The admission of the principle that parents are to be paid for the care of their own children by the public would be very demoralizing, that is a duty devolving upon all parents, and if the public is compelled to pay for the support of children the parents should suffer the inconvenience of being separated from them in order that some deterrent influence should be felt by them, and the children receive the benefits of training and education which are to be derived in all well managed private charitable institutions. While we hear much of the danger of "institutionalizing" children, it must not be forgotten that in most of the homes from which destitute children go to institutions they do not learn habits of cleanliness, order or discipline, and are without the moral, educational, and other advantages which institutions extend . . . the people of the City expend nearly $2,000,000 a year for the support of destitute children in charitable institutions. Remove the fear of separation . . . and no one can foretell to what extent and volume these figures . . . will grow.[97]

Although Stewart and his cohorts had spent much of the decade attempting to dismantle institutions, he and other reformers wanted to do so in order to decrease all public expenditures for dependent children and decrease the relative power of Catholics and Jews in charitable work. Faced with the prospect of massive outdoor relief, institutions very suddenly became, in his estimation, proper places for raising destitute children.

Similarly, Kate Hall, the city investigator assigned to decrease the number of commitments to institutions, held that no "worthy mother" would seek public aid, and therefore payments would necessarily go to the undeserving. In all, Hall seemed confused. She was absolutely opposed to direct payments to mothers, committed to reducing the number of parents who could rely on institutionalization, and reluctantly complimentary about the institutions she had otherwise condemned:

> Fully ninety per cent (90 percent) of the mothers who would receive this maintenance are "Foreign Aliens."
> The worthy mother never seeks but always tries to shield the public from her needs. She very seldom parts with her children as there are several charitable societies in this City who seek and help such worthy mothers to be self-supporting, and inspire their children to be moral and upright, thereby reducing pauperism . . .
> By allowing this bill to become law it would act as an incentive to the lazy and incompetent parents and guardians to increase destitution.
> In most cases these parents are reduced to this state through their indolence, vicious and criminal habits.
> The surroundings of these children are most deplorable. They will never progress but would degenerate through such surroundings as they will be compelled to live in to derive the benefit under this law . . .
> Our charitable institutions are filled to overflowing with the legal and illegitimate children of these parents, and are idiotic, epileptic and cripples for life by ill-treatment and abuse in infancy and childhood . . . while in the institutions where dependent children are placed they protect and inculcate all that is good for the child.[98]

If "worthy mothers" never sought aid, how could private charity help them? If charitable institutions were "filled to overflowing with the . . . idiotic," how could they "inculcate all that is good for the child"? More to the point, if Hall's daily occupation was to decrease the number of poor parents able to rely on institutionalization as a strategy for coping with poverty, how would their continued and unrelieved poverty help that child to "progress" in what were admittedly "deplorable conditions"?

Catholic and Jewish charitable activists neither played a major role in the bill's demise nor joined forces with Ahearn to champion the bill. Representing the institutions themselves, the American Female Guardian Society's Home for the Friendless, the Shepherd's Fold, and the Children's Fold, all white, Protestant organizations, protested at the hearing.[99] The *Sun* and *New York Daily Tribune* reported on April 22, 1897, that opposition to the bill was voiced as well by the "Colored Orphan Asylum, the

Catholic Protectory, the Hebrew Orphan Asylum [and] the St. Vincent de Paul Society." The *New York Times*, however, also on April 22, named only the SPCC, SCAA, State Board of Charities, and city commissioners as opposed.[100]

That Catholic and Jewish leaders remained relatively invisible or silently complicit in the bill's demise, however, proved a harbinger of politics to come. By allying directly with the Charity Organization Society and SCAA in efforts to keep public outdoor relief illegal, Mulry at once increased the power of his organization, the SVDP, and moved the image or politics of Catholic charities decidedly to the right.

Compromise and Accommodation

The effects of the Destitute Mother's Bill's publicity and the general public's articulate opposition to the charitable establishment's policies were critical in prompting Protestant reformers to renounce the policies of the last half century whereby they advocated removing children from family for reasons of poverty alone. When the mayor's veto was announced, Ahearn threatened to propose the bill again the following year. Given public support for Ahearn, scientific charity reformers feared a wholesale dismantling of the charitable system as they knew it. Although Ahearn reintroduced the bill in each legislative session in 1898 and 1899, opponents used hearings before the Senate Committee on the Affairs of Cities to keep it from reaching the Senate floor.[101]

The COS and SCAA pledged to provide small amounts of outdoor relief to poor widows and their children under private, not public, auspices. Ultimately, such willingness was an attempt to control the meaning and extent of the aid. The agencies considered legislative sanction of public outdoor relief as equivalent to proclaiming an entitlement to such relief. Thereby the nature of the charitable system was changed from one based on noblesse oblige to another based on the rights of the poor. That the poor should have any rights to—or expectations of—relief was for scientific charity reformers the very worst possibility.

The agitation over the Destitute Mother's Bill, moreover, exposed the contradictions of scientific charity policies on several levels. Although poor women with children and without access to the wages of an adult male had historically been the group most vulnerable to severe poverty and loss of children, Protestant reformers' rhetoric about the sanctity of home life and mothers' care made their family breakup policy seemingly untenable, particularly for widows. If any group of women in poverty were seemingly innocent of the behavioral sins thought to plunge the poor into destitution it was widows who married, had children within marriage, and expected that their highest duty would be to refrain from wage work and care for children at home. They committed no sin worse than believing in the normative American system that promised all the blessings of prosperity and home life. Even those who considered most of the adult poor to be undeserving could find little fault with widows, who were subjected to the very worst that charities had to offer—separation from their children—because their husbands' death had robbed them of the fruits of conforming to normative behavior.

The Protestant charitable establishment could no longer ignore the widespread public resentment of such policy and the mounting political power of wide segments of the population that rejected the charity establishment's moral and political authority. The COS and SCAA therefore attempted to head off this rising sense of entitlement to cash relief by promising to take care of the innocent or worthy poor. In an attempt to encourage Strong's veto in 1897, the SCAA introduced a resolution supporting charitable relief in the homes of the poor in order to stem institutionalization. The resolution was the first of its kind in SCAA history: "Resolved, That we desire to hereby place on record our conviction that children should not be committed to institutions for the sole reason that their parents are destitute, except as a last resort, and that cases of hardship should be obviated . . . through a more effective co-operation between private relief-giving charities and committing authorities, and not through public out-door relief."[102] The fact that the SCAA gave official recognition to the idea that destitution was not necessarily evidence of moral depravity was a critical milestone in the shift from scientific charity principles.

With an eye to the larger public, Catholics, Jews, and Protestants began to publicize their willingness to cooperate on a host of issues. The placing-out system provided the easiest issue on which to compromise, in large part because it had become nearly obsolete. "There are very grave dangers involved in the placing out of children," a SCAA member declared at a 1900 conference of Catholics, Jews, and Protestants who worked in the city's charities. "Perhaps you may consider that a surprising admission from one connected with the State Charities Aid Association, for I know that many people think we are bigoted devotees of the placing-out system; but in reality we think that no one who does not fully realize these dangers and who does not take every possible precaution to avoid falling into them can possibly do good placing-out work."[103] In conjunction with that sentiment, the SCAA, COS, and CAS supported the Stranahan Act to limit placing-out and require visitation and inspection in homes. The same groups, however, induced the governor to veto a version of the bill guaranteeing that children be placed with people of the same religion as their parents. The bill was revised to read that such a stipulation was to be followed "if practicable."[104]

Catholics and Jews also began their own placing-out programs, ostensibly to exhibit the spirit of cooperation. The Catholic Home Bureau, headed by Mulry, was instituted in 1898 to place children who had no families to which they could return. Archbishop Corrigan, with rhetoric indistinguishable from that of the SCAA or COS, gave hearty approval: "The project of establishing a Catholic home bureau impresses me favorably, and seems likely to accomplish good results. In the first place, it will prevent overcrowding in our institutions and relieves us of the care of many children who are now dependent on charity, and will enable them to become self-reliant. It will relieve the taxpayers of the burden of contributing to the support of these children, and will prevent the number of public wards becoming too large."[105]

Because the group represented a small minority of children in institutions, however, the program remained very small and resulted in one placement for every thirty-two institutionalized children.[106] By 1913 the bureau had just 1,500 children under supervision and maintained a budget of only $14,000 in operating costs.[107] Like Protestant reformers' efforts to indicate willingness to compromise, such gestures were more likely to result in a superficial change in form rather than a substantive shift in policy. As Catholics had argued for decades, placing-out was objectionable except for very young children who had no family ties. Others could not be placed without violating parental rights or subjecting children to labor or sexual exploitation.

Protestant reformers also instituted new programs under the auspices of private charity to provide aid for children who remained within their own homes. The COS reported that it, "in conjunction with other societies, was obliged to oppose Senator Ahearn's bills, owing to the certainty that great moral injury would be sure to result to the character of the people by this return to 'public outdoor relief.' Yet a question arose of whether there was not much truth in the Senator's arraignment of [the system] whereby parents and children were separated in many instances for years simply because of poverty."[108] The society then set up investigations tied to the city's Department of Charities. When families wanted to commit children as dependents, a group from the society would investigate the families. For those deemed worthy (about a quarter of applicants) the COS attempted to organize the resources of various charities. It did not, however, provide direct funding. It did appoint a visitor who would direct applicants to other sources for food, coal, or cash that would presumably tide the family over.

For the first time, moreover, the society's rhetoric shifted to make theoretical exceptions to poor widows who received outdoor relief. As Josephine Shaw Lowell noted in the aftermath of the Destitute Mother's Bill, "This sort of help is not demoralizing nor pauperizing, if properly watched, because it only places the family in a natural position. Women and children ought to be supported, and there is no sense of degradation in receiving support."[109] As a representative from the COS stated, "Whenever a woman of good character is willing to do her utmost to keep her children with her she should have all the assistance in money and all the help of other kinds that may be necessary to enable her to do it. It is cruel to deprive children of the oversight and parental care which is their birthright merely because of poverty or because of the lack of friends to tide over a period of discouragement and exceptional hardship."[110]

Although such rhetoric suggested promotion of a system of private pensions comparable to the public pensions favored by Ahearn, some reformers nonetheless equated family care with a complete denial of aid. Homer Folks argued in 1901 that he and the SCAA were heartened by the fact that restrictions on admissions to institutions had since 1895 resulted in the removal of one thousand "children who were not destitute, and . . . whose parents became able to care for them and were of good character." This trend, Folks maintained, was of "the greatest benefit to children who otherwise would have been deprived of family care, and to parents who otherwise would have been allowed to shirk their proper responsibilities, and to taxpayers who otherwise would have had heavy additional burdens."[111] In 1905 the SCAA reported on the COS committee: "In the past year [1904], 677 families applying for the commitment of their children have been investigated by the Committee, and 297 families, representing 564 children, were induced or enabled to keep their children at home, thereby preventing them from becoming a public charge." In addition, "Under the present system it is difficult for parents to throw upon the city the responsibility for the care of their children, which they should themselves properly bear, or to neglect to remove their children from institutions when their circumstances improve. That the children themselves are better off is obvious, for the superiority of family life is now almost universally recognized."[112]

By 1906, however, the SCAA's rhetoric shifted so as to tentatively assume that at least some private cash relief would be allotted to poor widows deemed worthy. Perhaps most important, the SCAA finally conceded that cash relief must be augmented to make the program work: "It seems to be generally agreed that in the case of widows, mothers whose husbands are disabled, insane, or otherwise unable to support their families, it is better, if the mother is of good character and able to afford her child proper training, to assist her to maintain the home, than to break up the family and assist her by supporting the children in institutions. . . . Increasing sums should become available by private contributions for this type of relief."[113]

Throughout the first years of the century the great distinction between Catholic and Protestant rhetoric remained the former's insistence that parental rights be respected even when they conflicted with those of children. Protestants supported children's rights and only slowly and gradually recognized parental rights. The SCAA's first concession on the issue was articulated in 1897, when it held that parents who paid a portion of the costs of institutionalization could expect to maintain parental rights. Edward Devine, editor of several journals on the emerging social work profession and teacher at the Columbia School of Social Work, led the COS in the early twentieth century as Josephine Shaw Lowell retired.

Conversations between Devine and Catholic clergy and SVDP members point to widespread disagreement about what "family preservation" should entail. Devine conceded that "[p]arents who are of good character and who with a reasonable amount of private assistance can support their children at home should, as a rule, receive such assistance, and the breaking up of the family should thus be averted."[114] Catholic male leaders argued that the state should not permanently remove children in almost any instance. To parents, Vincentian Edward Butler said, "Certain rights have been accorded which no other person may abrogate, and they are charged with certain duties with which no one else may interfere."[115] Devine, however, asserted that his position was focused on the good of the child and remained reluctant to provide a consistent amount of cash help or allow children to be institutionalized for brief periods should parents be found "unworthy" of private outdoor relief. "If children are removed because their parents are morally unfit guardians for them this removal should be absolute and final," Devine declared. And, he added, "The paramount consideration should be, what is best for the child . . . when the family is an unfit place for the child, . . . the child ought to be removed and the interest of the child ought not to be sacrificed because in one case out of a hundred, or a million, the parents may subsequently change their characters and become fit guardians."[116]

Male religious in these settings were more likely than the elite laity to articulate a defense of institutionalization consistent with nuns' reasoning over decades. Father Thomas Kinkead, newly appointed superintendent of Catholic Charities in New York City and administrator of the Catholic Home Bureau, believed that only very young children should be placed out and "care should be taken not to place a child in a family where it is wanted chiefly for the service it can render. Many thus placed are made household drudges and are deprived of education. Owing to their age they are unable to protest against such treatment and effectively maintain their rights." Critical of rhetoric that idealized the family into which children would be placed, Kinkead concluded, "[W]hen applicants say they intend to treat the child as a member of the family that simply means they do not intend to pay anything for services rendered." Parental rights, moreover, included not only the presumption of maintaining custody of children during their minority but also that children would be able to help support parents in old age.[117]

It is apparent as well that various players in these debates had radically divergent views about what constituted the morality or "immorality" of the poor. In frustration at hearing continually about the immoral poor at a New York City conference in 1900, John Crane, a member of the city's SVDP, said, "I wish to correct an erroneous impression. Many people are of the opinion that there is a great deal of vice in the tenement houses. There is everywhere, but, for my part, an experience of thirty years' visiting . . . I will say that it is very seldom we find a family where the mother or daughters are suspected of immorality. There is not five percent, where there is any indication of these vice, and I firmly believe that the average morality in the tenement house district is as good as it is in any part of the country."[118]

For those reformers of the SCAA or COS, it was difficult to imagine that being poor was not itself evidence of vice and immorality. For Crane and other Catholics, "vice" per se did not have a causal relationship to poverty. Crane's assumption was that talk of vice implicated the poor, and only women among them, in sexually transgressive behavior. Despite efforts to compromise on some aspects of policy, these conferences reveal a great deal about how distant these groups were in their most basic understanding of what caused poverty and therefore what to do about it.

Perhaps the most frustrating of the charges made against Catholics at such conferences was that institutionalization was a system that tended to break up families. Catholic men argued in these conferences that the temporary institutionalization of children was always pointed toward reconstructing that family, and that Catholic private relief was allotted so as to avoid institutionalization, not increase it. "In my experience as connected with the Society of St. Vincent De Paul," John Crane declared, "I have not in the last thirty years separated a family, even where the father was a drunkard, where it was possible to keep them together and preserve the morals of the children."[119] Devine acknowledged the difficulties defenders of institutions had in deflecting such charges:

> The managers of those institutions, having in mind [destitute children] indignantly and with some justification deny that their institutions have a tendency to break up families. In their eyes the institution is like a hospital, in that it provides temporary care for one who will shortly be restored to the family but for whom proper provision cannot at the moment be made. The children of the well-to-do are sent to the boarding school, so the children of the poor are sent to the only place where corresponding opportunities are provided by the city for the poor.[120]

Yet to the degree that Mulry, Butler, and the greater SVDP membership supported restrictions to *public* outdoor relief, they did position Catholics as supporting a system whereby many poor parents had only the option of institutionalization when faced with poverty and not a reasonable expectation that they would receive adequate outdoor relief from private charities. Even the SVDP and the United Hebrew Charities, ostensibly more generous than the COS, did not have sufficient funds for adequately relieving the poor in their homes. Parents' narrow choices were either to petition private charities for meager and uncertain resources and thereby invite friendly visiting and personal reform or to place their children temporarily in institutions.

The White House Conference

The White House Conference on the Care of Dependent Children in 1909 marked a watershed in many aspects of welfare provision for dependent children, some of which were more important to the politics of charitable work in New York City than others. In many respects SCAA Secretary Homer Folks's efforts to bring certain questions to a national audience paralleled the SCAA's decades-long strategy of establishing authority in the state and having power to override New York City's more contentious urban politics. The SCAA could no longer rely on the New York State Board of Charities as a dependable ally, in part because the board now contained Catholics, Jews, and even some Protestants who resisted efforts to dismantle institutions. The SCAA therefore bypassed the vagaries of city and state politics and tried to promote consensus at a national level for policies that would not be supported by New York's voting constituencies on either city or state levels. Folks, an organizer of the conference, reportedly attempted to exclude Catholics and Jews altogether. President Theodore Roosevelt, however, argued that it could not be viewed as a national conference unless non-Protestants were invited.[121] Folks then enlisted the cooperation of Thomas Mulry and Julian Mack of Chicago; the three activists then presumably represented the Protestant, Catholic, and Jewish perspectives on questions posed at the conference.

The conference was also a milestone in bringing together many reformers, predominantly Protestant and native-born, who were active outside private or public charity itself and more inclined to do preventive work involving settlements, labor organizing, and consumer advocacy. Having avoided work in charities because of the perceived limits of alms-giving, this diverse population was likely to support insurance programs providing unemployment, injury, sickness, and death benefits to the working poor. In general they did not support scientific charity principles but worked for reform in industrial capitalism so as to ward against the possibility of workers being thrown into desperate poverty for reasons the participants acknowledged were structural or environmental and unexplained by individual deficiencies alone. Similarly, men and women among them supported the family wage ideal. If all male workers could secure wages that would decrease reliance on women and children's labor, they contended, a host of social problems, from juvenile delinquency to child labor, could be avoided and the need to distribute alms minimized.

On this national stage the debate about institutionalization versus the family plan played out very differently than it did in the New York context. The "New York system" was unlike that of any other state, and the meanings of the national debate about institutionalization were not reflective of the same religious, racial/ethnic, and class tensions informing that debate in New York City. Two distinct streams of thought motivated anti-institutional activists from areas outside New York. The first was similar to that articulated by maternalist activists in antebellum New York, namely that public institutions first constructed during the antebellum era to deter dependence on outdoor relief were not appropriate for children because the institutions were premised on punishing the poor. Poor children, innocent of their parents' sins, should not be punished similarly but given all chances to avoid parents' faults and aspire to individual achievement. The second national group against institutionalization included people such as Julia Lathrop, who as an inspector for public institutions such as Illinois' Lunatic Asylum believed patronage politics was responsible for the warehousing of the poor and sick by "incompetent" men who showed little or no interest in social work as a science. They therefore attempted to regain control of cities so as to demand compliance in public institutions with professional standards for social work. Both groups were horrified to hear how many children in New York were housed in institutions solely because they were poor.

Folks's strategy at the conference was to characterize the institutionalization of dependent children as a national problem. Yet fully a third of the country's ninety thousand institutionalized dependent and orphaned children resided in New York City. The remaining sixty thousand institutionalized nationally also included a large number in traditional orphanages, a subject entirely ignored at the conference. In a joint letter to Roosevelt a committee consisting of eight national male figures (three of whom, Folks, Mulry, and Devine, were from New York City) issued a conference call by stating, "According to . . . the United States Census there were in orphan asylums and kindred institutions on December 31, 1904, not less than 92,887 children."[122]

Although Catholics were represented among those who called for the conference, Thomas Mulry had been hesitant initially about participating from fear that only those supporting a placing-out system would be heard and the conference would then legitimate only that point of view. Mulry was right to be hesitant. The ensuing debates at the conference reflected the care taken by organizers to control and narrow discussion so all institutions for dependent children were grouped under one heading. They posed questions in the call for the conference that required yes or no answers and then structured the various sessions to address those issues. The following are examples of the nine questions the conference was to consider; only three were particularly pertinent to New York City's institutional system:

> 4. Should children of parents of worthy character, but suffering from temporary misfortune, and the children of widows of worthy character and reasonable efficiency be kept with their parents, aid being given to the parents to enable them to maintain suitable homes for the rearing of children. Should the breaking of a home be permitted for reasons of poverty, or only for reasons of inefficiency and immorality?

> 5. Should children normal in mind and body, and not requiring special training, who must be removed from their own homes, be cared for in families, wherever practicable?

> 6. So far as an institution may be necessary, should they be conducted on the cottage plan, and should the cottage unit exceed twenty-five children?[123]

The question of whether institutions should be run on the "congregate" or the "cottage" model was similarly predetermined to favor the latter. The term *congregate system* referred to large institutions wherein children were likely to live, learn, and play in large groups rather than small ones. The cottage system came into vogue during the early twentieth century as a means of encouraging more individual attention for children and generally pushing institutions closer to a model replicating family life. Catholics and Jews at the conference would occasionally protest the characterization that congregate institutional life as necessarily gloomy, rigid, and neglectful of the individual child. Yet the conference's overwhelming conviction that any mechanism promoting individual attention to children should be supported made advocacy of the cottage system inevitable. George Robinson, president of the board of managers of the Protectory, concurred with that sentiment but argued that the logistics of converting to the cottage plan at an institution such as the Protectory, which housed 2,600 children concurrently, would take fifteen years of rebuilding and restructuring. Realizing that the Christian Brothers and Sisters of Charity were not organized to function as a hundred separate groups managing twenty-five children each and that buildings constructed decades earlier could not easily be renovated to fit the new system, Robinson asked "where the teachers are to come from?"[124] Although agreeing in principle to the superiority of the cottage system, he asked for patience with institutions attempting to make the conversion.

When Michael Scanlan, SVDP member, leader in the Catholic Home Bureau, and member of the State Board of Charities in New York State, took the podium as the first speaker on question 4, he articulated what other Catholic men were to assert throughout the conference: "family preservation" was, of course, the very point of Catholic charities. "For us Catholics there can be no question where we stand. The teaching of our church has always been in favor of the preservation of family ties." SVDP member Thomas Hynes of Brooklyn concurred: "I am a strong advocate of the principle that the homes of the poor should not be broken up until all hope of keeping the family together be lost; and that weaknesses on the part of either parent, when not entirely vicious or criminal, should not be an excuse for withholding aid."[125]

Exceptions and/or particularities of various state and city contexts were downplayed in the larger project of producing a national mandate for the care of dependent children in which activists and experts vied for power in articulating policy. Almost no one at the conference defended institutions, other than Catholic and Jewish activists from New York

City, and some of them did so very poorly. The Rev. D. J. McMahan, newly appointed supervisor of Catholic Charities in New York, attempted to lessen the majority's anti-institutional zeal by articulating a defense of institutions that flew in the face of Catholic policies for the preceding half century. McMahan provided a rationale for family breakup by asserting that the conference should not "make a fetich of the family life or conceive it as so sacrosanct that all must fall before its juggernaut wheels to be crushed out of existence."[126]

What was not discussed at the conference was even more important than what was. Most notably absent from the debate was whether outdoor relief, to be dispensed to the poor in their homes, should come from public or private funds. When Hastings Hart tried to ask that question, Homer Folks cut him off, arguing that "if we go into public outdoor relief versus private relief, we are apart from our general field, and we shall never get through." Folks believed instead that "each community" must settle the question individually because it was inappropriate for national discussion.[127] He was enormously cunning in limiting this part of the discussion because New York City's prohibition against any public outdoor relief would likely be condemned by the larger group, who lived in cities, and states, where outdoor relief was legal. Folks wanted to present the institution-versus-family-care debate to the national group so as to get the obviously pro-family-care mandate. Yet he did not want family care to entail public relief.

Catholics and Jews were complicit in the silence about public relief. Neither group suggested that public funds be allotted for the relief of the poor in their homes, as they believed that their own private organizations should ultimately have control over direct outdoor relief. The Rev. D. J. McMahan even argued against public funding for the poor in their homes, holding that abuse of the system would naturally follow.[128] Thus it was perfectly reasonable for those at the conference unfamiliar with the New York system to believe that Catholic and Jewish New Yorkers who supported the institutionalization of children for poverty alone were voicing support for family breakup policies. Catholics and Jews insisted over and over that this was not the case, that family preservation had been at the heart of their charitable work from its inception. Without a corollary discussion of why New York's system developed as it had, however, participants who did not reside in New York could view their defensiveness as craven acts aimed at ensuring that their institutions continue to receive funding.

Returning to the question of hegemony, the White House Conference of 1909 provides a classic example of the work of hegemony, "a process in civil society whereby a fraction of the dominant class exercises control through its moral and intellectual leadership over other allied fractions of the dominant class." As Mark Carnoy describes hegemony, "The leading fraction has the power and ability to articulate the interest of the other fractions."[129] But the elite and dominant fractions do not appear rigid or heavy-handed in imposing their will on others. Hegemony functions best when the subordinated feel they have a range of choices and can express conflict and limited forms of resistance. The choices thereby legitimate hegemonic rule by offering the consent of the ostensibly subordinate to the rule of the elite.

Having been invited to the White House Conference, leading Catholic and Jewish activists in charitable work legitimated the conference resolutions to a much wider public than would have been possible had the event remained exclusively Protestant or composed solely of placing-out advocates. The alliance between the middle class and elites in Catholic, Jewish, and Protestant charitable work restructured questions concerning the care of poor children so by 1910 long-term tensions tied to racial/ethnic and class politics were almost absent from public debate. The poor in New York City were still overwhelmingly Catholic or Jewish, but the elite who represented these groups no longer claimed the same national background as the poor in their group, much less a similar class perspective.

Religious discourse, moreover, no longer provided a language in which to express a meaningful oppositional consciousness. Arlene MacLeod has maintained, for example, that the "limiting of discourse lies at the center of hegemonic politics . . . oppositional imagination cannot effectively engage reality."[130] In this case the limitations of the discourse were set by the forums that predetermined that only the most elite of Catholic and Jewish charitable workers could enter the debate as well as the careful control and limitation of exactly what was debated.

Try as some New York Catholics and Jews might, the specificity required to explicate in a national forum why the New York system had grown to care for so many children in institutions could find no means of expression at the White House. Neither could the reason why poor people might prefer institutional care to its alternatives. That the conference was organized according to questions articulated through the rhetoric of social science rather than Protestantism substantially undercut the ability of Jews and Catholics to argue in a national forum that their religious traditions supported alternative policies. Although for decades Catholics and Jews in New York City had been able to shape their rhetoric in dialogic relation to that of Protestant reformers, the ascension of secular social science rhetoric in charity circles left Catholics and Jews stumbling for legitimacy and authority in voicing opposition through this new language and methodology.

The circumscription of discourse at the White House Conference marked the beginning of the end of institutional care for dependent children in New York City. Historians have analyzed the conference and reasonably concluded that "institutions worked badly. Very few people could pretend any more that they gave children the love, attention, and education they needed."[131] Conflating public poor law institutions with those run by Catholics and Jews in New York City and characterizing the massive institutionalization of New York's children as a Dickens-inspired dystopia harmful to poor parents and children alike, figures such as Folks returned home with an unequivocal statement by the nation's leading experts that "institutions were bad for children." Such a sentiment masked much more than it clarified and did not indicate a shift in policy for New York's "Charities Trust." Yet in Homer Folks's hands, the result was a mandate to close city institutions for dependent children regardless of whether sufficient private or public relief could or should be dispensed to poor children in their homes.

Yet others in the city used the mandate to secure public funding for widows' pensions, an extremely constricted version of what Ahearn had advocated twelve years earlier but nonetheless the first legalized form of public outdoor relief available in the city since the mid-1870s. In this effort, moreover, Jewish women provided leadership in securing public and professional support for the pensions, relying in part on reference to Talmudic tradition and in part on the language of social science to authorize and legitimate that funding. Catholic nuns, by contrast, suffered decline in their status and authority through the ensuing transition to social work in New York City. Having come from backgrounds in which their educational attainment was meager, their working-class status prominent, and their unfamiliarity with the language of social science and "modern parenting" obvious, nuns were soon held up as the epitome of incompetence and conservatism. Progress demanded that they comply with their own annihilation.

6 The Immaculate Conception of the Welfare State, 1895–1920

> January 30, 1909
>
> Dear Sister Superior,
>
> [T]he proceedings in Washington . . . will, doubtless, increase the pressure against our institutions . . . until the force will be so great as to close them out after some time. I would, therefore, urge upon our institutions these points to prevent these constant attacks and to uphold our good name.
>
> 1. The institutions must be made as near the cottage system as possible. This can be done by the system of "Mothers," vis., certain Sisters should be appointed to act as such for bands of twenty-five or thirty children. Each band should have a kind of sitting-room (portion of dormitory fixed with chairs, pictures, etc. etc.) and after play or school time they go to it, their Sister, who acts as "Mother" to be there at such times.
>
> —D. J. McMahan

> In the beginning of the work we had no other resources and we were thankful to receive all the children that were sent to us by the city. . . . There was plenty of room, and why not? . . . So others have reasoned, and so did we. We took them, but the system is none the less pernicious. . . . There are many masters nowadays. The State Board of Charities, the Comptroller's Office, the DPC have legal rights over you, and the Society for the Prevention of Cruelty to Children, and worst of all, the Charities Organization Society. . . . We have also a Catholic Home Bureau and a Catholic Supervisor of Charities. We have had our experiences with them all.
>
> —Mother Mary Veronica Starr

193

By 1910 Irish Catholic nuns had resisted assimilation to the Protestant gender system for the better part of a century. To a large degree, nuns in New York City charities became in the later Progressive Era less able to continue such resistance, in part because a new "professional" class was fast assuming authority in charities and social work and in part because the Catholic male hierarchy increasingly asserted power over the nuns' collective apostolate.

From the sisters' perspective, Catholic male authority over them, and the city's increasing dependence on professional expertise in social work, became the "many masters" who would thereafter restrict nuns' autonomy and substantially diminish their control over charities they had founded. Catholic men were increasingly anticipating criticisms of nuns and institutions, and they used their power over nuns to demand conformance to the gendered organization of the dominant culture so as to deflect such criticism. Nuns were to suddenly transform themselves from "sisters" to "mothers"; to mask institutions' dependence on convent organization; and to refurbish their living quarters into poor imitations of middle-class domestic life and motherhood, with priests and the secular state being the embodiments of omnipresent husbands.

Predominantly from working-class and poor backgrounds, Catholic nuns in charity work had neither the class status nor educational backgrounds to claim authority as experts despite having worked in those fields for decades. Nuns' relative loss of power over the late Progressive Era, therefore, was tied to their working-class status, their subordination by men in their group, and campaigns to encourage public rejection of convent life as a suitable cultural framework for state development.

Catholic nuns had come full circle. Protestant middle-class and elite women's participation in the settlement movement, and their professionalization of nursing and social work, had depended initially on Catholic models of convent life and training. Yet a new professional model of women's work in fields that denied religious, especially Catholic, origins masked such influence. Knowledge gained through formal education and from scientific method and practice was heralded as the foundation for an ostensibly all-new approach to social work that would supplant religious-motivated charity. Many Catholic women joined the ranks of educated professionals in teaching, nursing, and social work, and some who were middle class or elite brandished maternalist arguments to support their work in the state. Other Catholic elite women established settlements that mimicked, in organization and political priorities, those run by Protestant native-born women.

The erasure of nuns' role in this dialectic constitutes the most important pillar on which the myth of the "immaculate conception" of the welfare state rests. Nuns' absence in this narrative confirmed the Protestant professional model as immaculately conceived. There is no original sin derived from reliance on Catholic models but rather a linear story of Protestant enlightenment, progress, and women's ever-greater power as a group. That linear mythology also masks the centrality of class and racial and ethnic tensions that divided women during the Progressive Era. Nuns, like less-educated Protestant women, lost power relative to the few elite women who could claim superior educational training. While establishing the option of salaried work without ecclesiastical control for some women, professionalization was also contingent on the public derision of a far greater number of women who understood their work in religious terms and contested the value systems underlying professional social work. Non-elite women could contest the power and policies of the elite through religious-based ideology and institutions during the Gilded Age, but those in the Progressive Era who tried to articulate their interests through religious rhetoric were denigrated as backward, incompetent, and unable to recognize the superior methods of the modern age.

Perhaps most important, this linear narrative also masks decades of working-class Catholic and Jewish activism in shaping private and public provisions for the poor. That parents should not lose custody of children solely because of poverty, that the poor were entitled to public aid for raising their children, and that the communities from which these children came should not be excised from their memories were each urgent demands that were asserted over decades of struggle.

When Catholic nuns were made invisible in the Progressive narrative that claimed the welfare state's immaculate conception, so, too, was working-class women's activism. When Catholic nuns continue to be invisible in contemporary narratives of the origins of the welfare state, the state is characterized as having been shaped primarily by the beneficence of the elite, whether men or women. That neither narrative is historically correct is the least of the matter. The creation and dominance of a narrative explaining the welfare system's immaculate conception was a complex and nuanced cultural process through which a professionalized middle-class and elite group was ostensibly able to "save" the poor, particularly children. Through that process it could claim unprecedented cultural authority and power in the state. The persistence of the mythic narrative, therefore, is not just reiteration of bad history but rather the cultural scaffolding that continues to subordinate the relatively non-elite in the process of state formation.

Gender, Religion, and Professionalization

To say that Catholic nuns' role in state formation was erased is not to say that those who participated in that erasure were conscious of doing so. Rather, in many fields and venues of the Progressive Era, optimism about the new, modern age and its promises overwhelmed any sense that the new was rooted in what was decidedly old. American patterns of women's professional training in nursing, teaching, and social work, for instance, had for decades depended on models of convent life and training, although those origins were rarely acknowledged.

Like Catholic ascetic celibacy's opposition to Protestantism's sacred motherhood, convent life was for modern professional women the negative referent against which a new order was constructed. One must look only slightly below the surface of the origins of Protestant women's professionalization to find the direct influence of sisterhoods— even as oppositional models. It was no coincidence, for instance, that Catherine Beecher and Florence Nightingale, among the most distinguished of Protestant single women who established professions for women in teaching and nursing, should have looked to active Catholic sisterhoods with a measure of sympathy. Nightingale, trained in nursing during the Crimean War by the Sisters of Mercy, was quite generous in attributing that training to the order. She also countered anti-Catholic rhetoric about the tyranny of convent life by addressing such concerns with rare frankness: "I have known a good deal of convents and of the petty, grinding tyrannies supposed to be exercised there, but I know nothing like the petty, grinding tyranny of the good English family."[1]

Other Protestant women were rarely as cognizant of being dependent on convents as models or as generous in assessing Catholic women religious. When the State Charities Aid Association (SCAA) was formed in the early 1870s women within it noted that the lack of qualified nurses in the city's public poor-law institutions limited their ability to significantly improve the conditions within those institutions. The SCAA therefore founded the Nurses' Training School at Bellevue in 1872 under its own direction, one of the first such facilities in the country.[2] Because no one in the elite-dominated SCAA was trained in nursing, they advertised for a trained nurse to administer the program.

SCAA member Elizabeth Hobson was stunned when a woman in "a most rigid conventual garb" knocked at her door. Hobson was then relieved that the visitor's "beautifully trained English voice dispelled the unpleasant impression."[3] Sister Helen of All Saints Sisterhood was identified as a Protestant, Anglican nun, and therefore hired as the administrator of the Nurses' Training School because she linked it with English Protestant, not Irish Catholic, womanhood.

The SCAA's subsequent promotion of the nursing program at Bellevue relied on publishing texts that excoriated nuns throughout. The first pamphlet detailing the history of nursing in Europe stated, "[A]s a general rule, the women of the religious orders are themselves of about the stamp of domestic servants." Distinguishing their vision of professional nursing from the history of Catholic nuns' work, the SCAA argued further, "The stern rules of their order forbid them to let their human affections flow out toward the helpless people in their charge," thereby making them poor nurses presumably devoid of motherly, or even "human," sympathy.[4]

Good nurses, professional nurses, were thus good because they were not Catholic nuns. The attainment of elaborate skills and bodies of knowledge would influence nurses' professional training, but their origins as professional were inseparable from their explicit rejection of connections with and dependence on the training provided by Catholic religious orders.

American Protestant women's dependence on convent life as a model for settlements was at the same time substantial and almost unconscious. Catholic nuns had lived and worked in the public sphere, whether in all-female enclaves and in immigrant and poor communities, and from these public homes organized charitable work long before Protestant reformers were able to do so.[5] Yet settlement leaders such as Jane Addams traveled to London to evaluate the all-new approach of Toynbee Hall as a model for Hull-House.[6] As Suellen Hoy suggests, she might have simply walked the streets of Chicago to see the Mercy convent there but would likely not have believed that Toynbee Hall and the Mercy convent had anything in common.[7] Elite Protestant women refused to believe that the Catholic gender system should ever be emulated, a cultural construct so ingrained that even when evidence of Catholic influence was seemingly irrefutable they would continue to see the Protestant system as an entirely new creation.

Elite women active in Progressive circles tended to see themselves as the "first women" who were active in a variety of fields in which nuns had worked for centuries. Women religious privately noted the irony of calling all such work new. As Mother Mary Veronica Starr mused in 1902, "I do not depreciate the good works of the Protestants. Why should I? They are all borrowed from the Church and there are few forms of charity in existence today that were not set in motion by St. Vincent de Paul three hundred years ago."[8]

Comparable comments were unlikely in Progressive forums. Limiting discussion of nuns' work in these fields was central to the project of professionalization in that professionals wanted to characterize their work as entirely new and therefore worth the wages sought. As Robin Muncy notes, "Professional women at the turn of the century were constrained by a culture that increasingly granted respect, financial resources, and effectiveness to those who could convince their public that they possessed esoteric knowledge on which the public's welfare depended. Thus only by rendering somebody else powerless could professionals justify themselves." The effort to professionalize social work thus promoted some women as potential experts who had intellectual and administrative capacities equal to men and simultaneously undercut the value of an exclusively female, religious, and Catholic perspective on that work historically.[9]

Professionals promoted a shift in what was considered legitimate and progressive knowledge by relying on social science and psychology instead of religion, social work instead of charities, individual casework instead of institutional solutions, and in general a discourse available through higher education and predominantly to the middle-class and elite. Those who could not or would not engage on this level were derided as old-fashioned, poorly trained, foolish, and wrong-headed. In other words, nuns' labor, generally free or extremely cheap, was ultimately characterized as inferior in quality and therefore potentially dangerous. Like the physicians' campaign of the mid-nineteenth century against midwives, the professional status and claims to expertise that nurses, teachers, and social workers sought depended on the simultaneous denigration of nuns' work or that of similar non-elite women who performed it with little or no recompense.[10]

Catholic nuns were vulnerable to accusations that they were, especially in relation to educated experts in a variety of fields, poorly educated and poorly paid. Public perception of sisters' cheap, and by implication unskilled, labor resulted in part from their vow of poverty and from decades of Catholic spokespersons' declarations that sisters provided the cheapest labor force possible, the greatest return for public money paid to care for the poor, and that no comparable workforce could be substituted without inflating the costs of charities to prohibitive levels.[11]

The Catholic hierarchy, moreover, kept the educational achievements of Catholic women relatively limited. Even Catholic middle-class and elite women were often barred from Catholic colleges and discouraged from attending Protestant schools. The first Catholic women's colleges in the United States were established in the 1890s but remained few in number and contested within the Catholic community.[12] By contrast, Protestant middle-class women could claim higher educational attainment, integration into social science networks and discourse, and professional credentials designating them experts. By 1900 women accounted for more than a third of all undergraduates and 13 percent of those enrolled in graduate schools throughout the United States.[13] Sisterhoods would expand educational opportunities for themselves and all Catholic women by the 1920s and did so in part because the glaring imbalance between opportunities for Catholic and Protestant women's education became so obvious, and harmful, by the 1890s.[14]

Many women who entered convents during the Progressive Era were indeed from working-class or poor backgrounds. Of the successful applicants to enter the order of the Sisters of Mercy at the turn of the century, for instance, only a small fraction had either a high school or a college education. Applicants listed their work before entering convents as "teacher," "artificial flower maker," "telephone operator," "dressmaker," and "nursery governess." Others had worked in "housekeeping," "silk winding," and at a "printing establishment."[15] None could pay the $500 dowry, and some could not pay for their clothes upon entrance. In New York City, nuns who ran charities were likely to be engaged in all aspects of child care, grammar and high school education, and hospital and nursing work. They fed, clothed, cleaned, held, healed, educated, disciplined, and entertained young children every day of their lives in such institutions. In other words, they were working women before they entered the convent and they remained working women thereafter.

The proletarianization of nuns' work and the simultaneous promotion of elite and middle-class professionals therefore must be understood as a class-based stratification of women's work in the state that cut across religious lines. Professional women, whether Protestant, Catholic, or Jewish, were increasingly to manage nuns properly and bring them and other city workers kicking and screaming into the twentieth century. Nuns' knowledge or management skills were judged in such a campaign as unfit for commodification even if their physical labor was useful.

Some sisters attempted to keep their policies consistent with their traditional approach to charitable work, and some attempted to conform to new demands. Father D. J. McMahan, supervisor of Catholic Charities, held in the aftermath of the White House Conference that sisters should "[g]ive out children as speedily as you can" in an effort to deflect charges that institutions kept them in order to obtain funding. McMahan advised that such charges "can be so much disproved by our ready activity in making families take back their children as speedily as possible and giving out others to the Home Bureau, etc., as they are sought."[16]

Some orders refused, as they had for decades, to place out children until or unless there was no chance the parents could take them back. William Doherty, who would become a leader at the city's Department of Public Charities (DPC), worked first at the Catholic Home Bureau and found that many sisters refused to comply with his efforts to place out children under their care.[17] Others, however, scurried to accommodate the Catholic Home Bureau. The Sisters of St. Joseph, who ran St. John's Home in Brooklyn, placed out brothers who had been institutionalized temporarily through their mother's hospitalization for consumption. When their brother attempted to reclaim them, Mother M. de Chantal asserted that he had "promised Sister that you would not interfere with your brothers' prospects. It is too late now. They are settled in homes only a few miles apart. If there was anyone willing to take charge of them, it should have been made known before. As they were public charges, the Catholic Home Bureau had a right to select them for places. With that we have little to do. They visit the places three times a year and see how the boys are treated. They are much better off than in the City when there are no parents to look out for them."[18]

When the brother then attempted to enlist the mayor's support in reclaiming his siblings, the DPC held that the nuns had acted appropriately and only if the Catholic Home Bureau looked positively on the brother as a guardian could the children be returned.[19] Certainly most sisters were unlikely to be as cooperative with the Catholic Home Bureau as Mother de Chantal, but in their intransigence they were also likely to be characterized as impeding progress.

Middle-class and elite Catholic women, especially those who were Irish, also began to mimic the maternalist rhetoric and organizational strategies of Protestant women of similar backgrounds. Although membership in the St. Vincent de Paul Society in New York remained overwhelmingly male, chapters in other parts of the country integrated women into the ranks of friendly visitors. In New York City, the Association of Catholic Charities was promoted as the counterpart to the society for women who did comparable visiting work.

Teresa R. O'Donohue demonstrated the degree to which the Association of Catholic Charities depended on a model derived from scientific charity perspectives. O'Donohue, corresponding secretary of the Association of Catholic Charities in New York, had joined and established herself as a leader in the Charity Organization Society by the early 1890s.[20]

She advocated that the elite grace the poor with their influence and thus mitigate class and ethnic tensions: "The labors of the Friendly Visitor seem to me to complete, assist, include, direct, and perfect them all. . . . If the happy day shall ever arrive when we shall have a sufficient number of Friendly Visitors, properly equipped, every charitable work will be strengthened a hundred fold, misery will be minimized, the hate of the anarchist may be changed into love."[21]

The Association of Catholic Charities was run from St. Rose's Settlement, where settlement workers engaged in the type of work characteristic of Protestant middle-class and elite women's voluntarism throughout the Gilded Age period. They would not give direct cash relief from the settlement but would instead help the poor locate other sources of food and clothing. Catholic settlement workers also learned how to conduct investigations using "modern" methods, to gather knowledge and statistics about people in the neighborhood in which they lived. Catholic elite women distinguished their work from that of men and used a framework historically characteristic of nonprofessional Protestant women's maternalist organizing. As O'Donohue reported, "In speaking of the Friendly Visitor, I have constantly used the pronoun She. This does not mean that men cannot undertake the work. But ordinarily, it is my judgment, that woman, with her keen eye, her knowledge of household affairs, her love for children, is the better qualified."[22]

In many respects, middle-class and elite Catholic laywomen's work in charities during the Progressive Era mimicked Protestant models for women's public authority just as Protestant settlement workers mimicked the organization and structure of Catholic convents. Accordingly, the most significant contribution that laywomen, whether middle class or elite, made to Catholic charities during this period was to offer female perspectives in public debates and policy forums.

Nowhere was that more obvious than at the National Conference of Catholic Charities, which was established in 1910. In that year, women constituted a majority of attendees although only eight Catholic sisters were present.[23] Middle-class and elite Catholic laywomen, whom male Vincentians had barred from public forums for decades, were more visible and effective at the national conference than in New York City, where Thomas Mulry and the St. Vincent de Paul Society dominated the Catholic articulation of policies.[24]

Mulry's championing of a strategy of cooperation with Protestant charitable workers met significant resistance at the national conference. McMahan heralded this new cooperative effort by stressing that Catholics needed to embrace "more preventative work" and enforce professional standards in order to provide justice rather than alms.[25] Thomas Hynes of Brooklyn disagreed. "It would apparently be inferred from the paper," he said, "that relief work is carried on by trained charity workers in a thoroughly systematized and up-to-date method, while, as conducted by Catholics, charity work moves in a cumbersome manner and is attended by antiquated, old-fashioned methods." Cautioning against denigrating the volunteer in favor of "an expert who has undergone a course of academic training and necessarily will treat the problem, practically we will admit, but from an academic point of view," Hynes maintained that such thinking ultimately valued only the elite's contribution to charitable work and undervalued the perspectives of the poor themselves.[26]

At the National Conference of Catholic Charities during its very first years, participants voiced similar criticisms of the class politics inherent in promoting professionalization. There was considerable resistance to accepting the premise of social work professionalization, namely that those who were academically trained in social work understood poverty and the poor better than those who were poor, or had been poor, themselves. Yet middle-class and elite Catholics also wanted their work to be recognized as having status and import comparable to that of Protestant professional social workers. As city governments increasingly moved toward incorporating professional standards in charities run and funded by cities, Catholics argued that they should attain the proper training in order to have access to those jobs and therefore influence welfare state formation. "If the social service phases of municipal administrations are to be part of the civil service systems," asserted one participant, "we should be prepared to have our men and women trained to take these examinations, and so well prepared that their ratings will entitle them to places on the paid administrative staff."[27]

Some Catholic women's access to these policy forums enabled them to articulate a distinctly Catholic and female perspective sorely lacking in Progressive Era New York. The single most important contribution that Catholic middle-class and elite women made at the National Conference of Catholic Charities was to express adamant and unequivocal support for mothers' pensions or public programs to provide direct cash relief for mothers in their homes. Unlike rhetoric in non-Catholic forums, Catholic women tended not to berate nuns or condemn institutionalization as a means to promote the pensions. Discussion was more likely to focus on whether the pensions would undermine public support for social insurance programs such as workmen's compensation or unemployment insurance.[28] Like Protestant and Jewish women, many Catholic female activists at the conference held that the pensions were to be "given in exchange for services being continually rendered" and therefore would not constitute a threat to programs aimed at securing a family wage for working men. But unlike Catholic women in the mid nineteenth century, they prioritized motherhood as being women's foremost contribution to the nation. Thus their rationale for pensions echoed Protestant women's use of Republican motherhood. As Mary Shinnick asserted, "The Catholic Church has always concerned herself with questions of social justice. . . . If the greatest glory of woman is motherhood and the greatest service she can render to the Nation is to train her children to become good citizens, then it is not a mark of advanced civilization in any nation to allow her to do this supremely important work in the margin of time that remains after she has used up the golden hours of the day scrubbing in a downtown office building or bending over a stranger's washtub."[29]

It was in this female-dominated national Catholic forum—not New York's forums where Protestant, Catholic, and Jewish men dominated—that Thomas Mulry ultimately broke with the "Charity Trust" and expressed support for publicly funded pensions. In 1913 he had lent support to the Charity Organization Society and the Russell Sage Foundation in opposing a New York State bill granting pensions to widows and their children.[30] At the 1914 National Catholic conference, however, such opposition to pensions was a decidedly minority opinion. Mulry had, he confessed, opposed the bill for selfish reasons:

> Unfortunately, I am one of those who have been fighting against Widows' Pensions for years. Possibly, I have my share of responsibility for having killed the bill in our legislature last year. . . . It did seem to me that our private charities should do this work rather than permit the State to do it. . . . But the help that we gave seemed so inadequate that we are obliged to confess that we might be mistaken. When the Society of St. Vincent de Paul could give only three or four dollars a week to a family, it might appear that we were repeating the story of the dog in the manger. We could not do the work ourselves and we seemed not to wish that anyone else did it.[31]

Mulry's mea culpa paved the way for the passage and allotment of widows' pensions in New York State, and, by extension, the first public outdoor relief program in New York City since the decade after the Civil War. As Mulry confessed, his resistance to pensions was never based on the "argument that the Widow's Pension hurts our institutions" but on his own relative loss of power should such funding undercut the power of those who dispensed private outdoor relief.[32] Back in New York City, the legislative committee formed to investigate the living conditions of poor widows publicized Mulry's support as being enough to turn the

tide in favor of the pensions.[33] Spearheaded by Hannah Einstein and Sophie Irene Loeb, the Widows' Pension movement in New York proved
an important forum for Jewish female activists and enabled them to
significantly undermine the power of the "Charities Trust."

Widows' Pensions

The enactment of widows' pension legislation in New York in 1915 was
understood by almost all in the Catholic and Jewish communities to be
a victory and the culmination of decades of struggle. Pensions, or cash
payments to poor mothers from public funds, had been decidedly popular
in New York City since the late 1890s, and politicians introduced and
won widespread approval for bills to fund the pensions nearly every year
since Senator John Ahearn's Destitute Mother's Bill in 1897. The Charity
Trust, however, used its legislative contacts and control over the city's
charities to stall enactment of legislation mandating that the pensions be
paid from public funds. Winning approval of the pensions legislatively,
moreover, was but the first battle; the Charity Trust attempted thereafter
to significantly undermine the intent of the legislation.

Jewish women generally found Progressive Era policy forums and
public debates to be better springboards for moral and political leadership
than Jewish institutions. Unlike most Catholic women—and certainly
unlike nuns—some Jewish middle-class or elite women had substantial access to higher education and lived within a culture that respected
and supported, at least to some degree, women being educated, speaking
publicly, and advocating social justice. Two prominent Jewish women,
Hannah Einstein and Sophie Irene Loeb, spearheaded the push toward
pensions. Einstein, a relatively wealthy German Jew, played a leadership
role in expanding Jewish women's participation in the friendly visiting
organized through the United Hebrew Charities, the Jewish corollary to
the Charity Organization Society (COS), and the St. Vincent de Paul Society. As president of the Jewish Sisterhoods of New York City, Einstein
shared with Catholic and Protestant women of similar backgrounds a
belief in a separatist strategy for women's charity work. Loeb, a Russian-
born journalist, embraced the rhetoric of social science to support her
politics. After Aaron Levy, a New York State legislator representing the
Lower East Side, was appointed chair of the New York State Commission
for Relief of Widowed Mothers, he funded Loeb's trip to Europe, where
she researched comparable pension movements and legislation in six
countries. Literally a history of such movements throughout Europe and
dependent on social science methodology and voluminous statistical evi-

dence, Loeb's final report, issued in 1914, not only formed the substance of the commission's report to the New York legislature but also became a critical resource for pension advocates throughout the United States.

Loeb and Einstein also made clear that the pensions were merely a modern form of distribution of aid that had deep roots in Jewish tradition. Most Jewish charity activists held that they had always supported pensions and that the earliest form of private mothers' pensions in the city could be traced to the Hebrew Orphan Asylum. The asylum had made "it a rule" to give cash relief directly to poor mothers rather than institutionalize or board children "unless the mother is incapable of caring for her own children by reason of physical or moral disqualifications."[34]

Jews argued, along with many Catholics, that the logic of their own system of private outdoor relief was more consistent with social insurance and entitlement programs than with the practice of Christian alms-giving or scientific charity.[35] In order to support their work on the Commission for Relief of Widowed Mothers, Einstein and Loeb invoked Jewish traditions that emphasized women and children's entitlement to such funding as well as the presumption that the funding be generous. Like other Jews in charitable work, they referenced the Talmudic and unqualified injunction to care for widows and their children. They were also likely to extend that injunction to care for single mothers in general, whether widowed, deserted, or divorced. "Such protective measures as mothers' pensions," one Jewish activist argued, "have their talmudic analogue in the *ketubah*, a written document which safeguarded the right of the wife . . . and [was] intended to care for the woman in the event of widowhood or divorce."[36] "Given a good mother there is no reason," observed Solomon Lowenstein, superintendent of New York's Hebrew Orphan Asylum and Hebrew Sheltering Guardian Society in 1910, "why she should be compelled to add the distress of breaking up her home." Moreover, aid "must be given generously. . . . The mother ought not to be compelled to engage in work that will call her away from her own home, nor be forced, in her own home, to perform so large a quantity of work as to cause her to neglect her children."[37] Private pensions, as allotted through Lowenstein's program, however, did require some measure of compliance with middle-class prescriptions for raising children.[38] Lowenstein insisted on "supervision" so as to maintain significant control over mothering performed in the home.[39]

But Loeb and Einstein's success in the pension movement was most dependent on their having created a bridge between religious rhetoric and Progressive models for state formation. At the heart of their work were "investigations," whether of pension movements in other countries or of the primary Protestant charitable organizations that had agreed in the late 1890s to give private aid to "good mothers" within their own homes. In the latter months of 1913 the commission began an investigation of those private groups, especially the COS and the Association for Improving the Condition of the Poor (AICP), which had committed themselves fifteen years earlier to caring for poor widows from private funds in an attempt to avert enactment of the Destitute Mother's Bill. The SCAA and COS had ostensibly agreed in principle that "worthy mothers," especially widows, should be supported in their own homes. The committee's investigation therefore focused not on whether charity leaders in these organizations rhetorically supported the pensions but on how the inadequacy of private payments to those deemed deserving unveiled the gap between rhetoric and practice.

By using their power and fluency in social science rhetoric, Loeb and Einstein were able to turn the tables on groups that held that investigation was the foundation of scientific charitable practices. The pair focused their state-granted investigatory powers on assessing COS and AICP case records and then showing that even when those groups identified a "worthy mother" they purposely gave only enough aid to avert starvation or homelessness. After reviewing such records in painstaking detail and acting as a sort of moral prosecutor, Loeb charged that COS policy was to keep aid meager, irregular, and short-lived but to keep supervision over families constant.[40] When COS leaders challenged the accuracy of that assertion Loeb held her ground: "I think you will find in our record . . . our members had put the question to them several times, 'if you had all the money in the world, would you treat these widows cases in the same way that you do' and they answered 'yes.'"[41]

Much of the ensuing investigation was therefore pointed at grilling COS administrators on individual cases in which aid was insufficient in quantity, cut off prematurely, or denied altogether.[42] Without the slightest sense of irony, Edward Devine complained to Hannah Einstein that "the investigation, from what I had heard, seemed to me to have been conducted in a hostile spirit" and that the COS was unfairly targeted. Devine charged sarcastically that he was "very glad to have been assured that my impression was entirely mistaken and if the Committee presses forward to a similar investigation of the minute details of the case work of the St. Vincent de Paul Societies . . . and other agencies I will be entirely convinced."[43]

The commission, however, grilled neither the St. Vincent de Paul Society nor the United Hebrew Charities in comparable fashion. Neither organization presented an argument against the principles of the pensions.

Mulry and Lee J. Frankel, head of United Hebrew Charities, had merely wanted to control the funds themselves and scurried to find some way of keeping them, and therefore control, in their hands. United Hebrew Charities, for instance, withheld support through early 1915, forming a committee headed by Frankel. As one pension supporter confided to another, "Probably this committee will come out in favor of pensions, but with the peculiar restriction that these pensions should be given through their child caring agencies—a very bad idea, indeed."[44]

Indeed, much of the former antagonism evident among groups that were primarily Catholic and Jewish and those associated with Protestant charity groups resurfaced during the mid-1910s as the campaign for widows' pensions took center stage. As Mulry and Frankel began to support enactment of the pensions, the tentative alliance between male Catholic, Jewish, and Protestant leadership began to break down.

Edward Devine of the COS, for instance, campaigned against publicly funded widows' pensions with vehemence. The pensions, he stated, were "merely a revamped and in the long run unworkable form of public outdoor relief." Unlike social insurance programs, Devine argued, "Sympathy and not the payment of a financial obligation explains it. Need and not exchange is its basis." Refusing to accept pension supporters' argument that caring for children was a service to the state and best performed by poor mothers themselves, Devine called the program "an insidious attack upon the family, inimical to the welfare of children and injurious to the character of parents."[45] Devine held, moreover, that his adversaries were "making a violent break with the historical evolution of human society" because the entire concept of supporting the least fit, in his estimation, undermined their struggle for survival. He contended that the program was a "coercive system in which all the relief funds are raised by taxation and all are distributed arbitrarily on a per capita plan without reference to individual circumstances, without reference to the thrift or efforts of the individual" and therefore "illustrating all that is most objectionable in state Socialism."[46] Leaders such as Devine ultimately could not break from a scientific charity perspective that deemed aid itself the cause of poverty or the social Darwinist foundations of such thinking.[47]

The question of who might control public funds in such a program, and whether the program would stay small or expand, continued after the bill's passage. In August 1915, John P. Mitchell, the Irish Catholic mayor of New York, appointed, among others, Sophie Irene Loeb, Hannah Einstein, and the Rev. William Courtney, supervisor of the city's Catholic Charities, to the first Board of Child Welfare. All were strong advocates of pensions and would steer the board toward more expansive allotments and less rigid criteria.[48] Others on the initial board of nine included representatives from the COS and AICP as well as John Kingsbury, current head of the DPC and also an AICP member and former secretary of the SCAA. The latter group intended to use their board positions to control the hiring of investigators, keep allotments low, and restrict access to the program.

Reminiscent of the efforts of the Charity Trust in 1898 to concede the principles of support for widows while using their control of private programs to restrict access to meaningful relief, some members of the first board initiated internecine warfare so significant that few widows received any funds at all. Although pensions were to be allocated to widows only, they had to prove that all their children were legitimate, that their husbands had been naturalized and were legal residents of New York State at the time of death. In addition, the women had to prove they were legal residents of New York City for two years before applying for aid, "needed" the money, and were "moral" and "efficient" mothers. The latter criteria, although not as bureaucratically overwhelming to poor women as the paperwork proving age, birth, marriage, and citizenship, opened a huge area of subjective evaluation, and Board of Child Welfare members fought about it continually.[49] In large part because the state controlled widows' pension legislation and the State Board of Charities was made up of a coalition of Catholics, Jews, and Protestants who supported the pensions, Loeb, Einstein, and Father Courtney held positions on the Board of Child Welfare for much of the following decade. Commissioner Kingsbury, however, was removed in 1916 by legislative mandate from Albany; the State Board of Charities insisted that the DPC should not have influence over allotment of pensions.[50]

Although some who supported pensions assumed they would lessen parental use of institutions, Catholics and Jews in charities had long held that pensions would be too restrictive to provide relief for more than a fraction of the dependent children in institutions, which the Board of Child Welfare found to be the case. The New York state law stipulated that allotments could not be more than the sum that would be paid to institutions (or $2.50 a week for each child). The presumption was that by keeping the allotment constant between the two programs the total for city expenditures would not increase. The result was, in fact, a significant expansion of allotments for dependent children because the programs had little overlap. In the first year, for instance, after a thousand families had been investigated, only 210 children had been removed from institutions through pension allotments. The city was thereby concurrently paying more than $3 million annually for dependent children's care in institutions; the $1.7 million soon allotted annually for pensions put the overall expenditure at $5 million per year in a city of slightly more than five million people. The increase in expenditures no doubt stemmed from the fact that widows who had been working to keep their children out of institutions and in their own homes were willing to apply for pensions and thus contribute to the rising total of children declared dependent.

More important, the great majority of poor parents in the city could not be aided through a program that stipulated that mothers be widows, much less naturalized citizens or long-term residents of the state and city with appropriate documentation. Requirements of the husband's naturalization and state and city residency made most immigrant mothers, including widows, ineligible.[51] Of the children committed to institutions in 1915, a great majority had parents who were immigrants.[52] They and their families were by no means less poor than those eligible for pensions. A program restricted to widows, and then only some of them, could not begin to aid those impoverished by illness, unemployment, parental desertion, divorce, alcoholism, single motherhood, or the systemic poverty in which most recent immigrants lived. Parents who found themselves in such situations continued to rely on institutionalization to get by.

The Sisters and the Scandals

Perhaps the most important byword of this new era and regime was *investigation*. Catholics in New York had historically resisted investigations of the poor for three reasons. The first was that the dominant Catholic approach in caring for the poor did not posit that individual immorality was causal in creating poverty or that aid encouraged dependency and was thus to be provided with the greatest caution. To investigate individuals or to means-test was therefore never central to how Catholics imagined ameliorating poverty. Many Protestants imagined the revolving-door policies of nuns' institutions to reflect either laziness or greediness for public funds, but Catholics understood such policies as entirely consistent with their sense of how the poor should be treated. Second, given their presumption that individual failings were not causal, the scrutiny and shaming of individuals who relied on their help was not merely superfluous but cruel. To punish the poor further for finding themselves poor was at odds with Catholic perceptions of charity; to be charitable also meant to be kind and compassionate. The third major objection focused on investigations of women's sexual transgressions. All charities for women founded and run by Catholic women religious assumed that the work did not center on attaining knowledge of the circumstances surrounding a sexual transgression. Quite the reverse, what was important was providing a space and the resources to enable women to keep those details confidential. Compassion in this case was aimed at protecting women from public shaming and, if possible, restoring women to society with reputations intact. Catholic sisters had worked for the previous half century to shield the poor from means-testing and women from public shaming. As the sisters lost status precipitously in the 1910s, however, their ability to serve as buffer was severely if not entirely diminished. Their inability to defend themselves to the public undermined the sisters' ability to defend women and the poor from similar fates. Nuns were themselves subjected to the Strong Commission's scrutiny in 1916 and 1917, a massive investigation that publicly pilloried them and their work.

The investigation of New York City's institutions by New York State gubernatorial appointee Charles H. Strong in 1916 constitutes one of the more dramatic tales of intra-bureaucratic intrigue in the history of the city's charities. The narrative tale of the "Charities Scandals" begins at the City Club, of which Strong was president and Kingsbury and Homer Folks were members. Irate at Thomas Mulry's defection to support widows' pensions, the investigation of the COS case records by the New York State Commission for Relief of Widowed Mothers, and the State Board of Charities' efforts to lessen Kingsbury's influence over the pensions, Folks colluded with Kingsbury to even the score. Kingsbury formally petitioned the governor to appoint a commission to investigate whether the State Board of Charities had exercised sufficient supervision over the city's institutions, and Folks nominated Strong to head the commission.[53]

Kingsbury had made his reputation as commissioner of public charities predominantly by building a city bureaucracy and team of investigators trained and supervised by Edward Devine. The investigators had in 1914 identified five Catholic and five Protestant institutions for dependent children as poorly managed and charged that the state board had failed in its supervisory responsibilities. By 1915 the same investigators returned to the institutions and declared them entirely compliant with city requirements for improvement. Kingsbury held that such success necessitated that the city, not the state, should thereafter assume direct responsibility for investigation. The Strong Commission was then to study whether such a transfer of authority was necessary.[54]

What began as a backroom maneuver by Folks and Kingsbury to reassert control over the city's charities spun into a maelstrom over which no one had control and which left no one unscathed. Before the end of the investigation in late spring of 1916, William Doherty, deputy commissioner under Kingsbury and a Catholic who had grown up in the

Sisters of Mercy's children's institution in Brooklyn, testified to horrific conditions in the city's Catholic institutions and recalled his experiences as "exceedingly hard." Newspapers ran innumerable headlines declaring a state of emergency, for example, "Asylum Children, Wards of the City Found in Squalor" and "Hospital Assailed as Menace to City." The Sisters of Mercy, Sisters of Charity, Dominican Sisters, and others were called to testify in public hearings at which they were accused of purposely mistreating and poorly feeding and caring for children so as to derive city revenues to help build up the coffers of the Catholic Church. After Father William Farrell issued a string of hysterical and anti-Semitic pamphlets denouncing the commission as anti-Catholic and likening the hostile interrogation of sisters to a kind of cultural rape, Kingsbury and Mayor Mitchell charged publicly that Farrell's actions constituted the church's effort to subvert democracy and the American state. When Thomas Mulry, sixty-one, died shortly after testifying in March 1916, Catholics charged that his former "friends" in the Charity Trust had, in essence, killed him. Kingsbury and Mitchell meanwhile wiretapped Father Farrell's telephone, among others, and were found out, thereby inviting their indictment, and eventual conviction, in the state's first wiretapping case.[55]

Beneath the melodrama of the scandals were Kingsbury's efforts, with the support of Mayor Mitchell and the Charity Trust, to make the city's Department of Public Charities the ultimate authority in shaping care for dependent children in New York City. He constructed the department as a professionalized and modern social work bureaucracy that had ultimate power to determine whether children could be counted as dependent on the city. If they were, the department could decide how the city would care for them. In essence, Kingsbury was charged with finally installing the kind of bureaucratic authority over dependent children's care and funding that Protestants had advocated since the mid 1880s.

Kingsbury was relatively successful in this campaign, but not because he acknowledged instituting programs resonant of those advocated by Protestant charity leaders for the preceding four decades. Rather, he was successful because he asserted through word and deed (and in blizzards of activity) that his was an entirely new project and reflective of a new age in which modern science, experts, investigation, and accumulation of scientific knowledge about poverty would provide the city, including its poor, with a wholly new system beneficial to all. The new rhetoric of Kingsbury and his supporters, the new mechanisms for investigation, and the bureaucracies to enact new policy were each dependent on some rather old ideals. But in a storm of activity and discourse that seemed nothing like before, Catholics, especially nuns, were unable to contest the new regime effectively.

At the center of Kingsbury's professionalization of staff was an entirely new investigative squadron whose credentials designated them as experts in the field of social work. In February 1915, and virtually concurrent with the passage of widows' pensions legislation, Kingsbury hired Columbia University social work professor and COS leader Edward Devine as head of the Special Bureau of Social Investigation under Kingsbury. The "social, professional or technical training of the appointees" that Devine would manage included college education, training at Columbia's School of Philanthropy under Devine, study trips in Europe "reviewing social conditions," or training in "graduate" nursing.[56] Experience in private charities was attained predominantly through work in the New York Charity Organization Society or its affiliates in other cities, the AICP, and the Russell Sage Foundation and thus was inseparable from participants' connections to and approval by the traditional Protestant charity establishment.[57]

Kingsbury's project of professionalization depended on expanding the concept of who and what should be investigated. The first and primary group was the poor themselves, especially parents who attempted to declare children dependent on the city. In this project the Special Bureau of Investigation was expanding and rationalizing work that Protestant charities had advocated for decades—investigation of the poor so as to decrease commitments. Kingsbury won approval from the Board of Estimate and Apportionment to hire new investigators by arguing that their work would decrease the city's total costs for charity, despite investigators' high individual salaries of $1,500 a year.[58] In his annual reports to the mayor, Kingsbury noted the net savings of the Special Bureau in that only about a third of the applicants were deemed poor enough to be eligible for commitment.[59]

Investigators soon found, moreover, that new coercive methods could dissuade parents from ever applying at all. Even those few deemed eligible could be required to pay for children's maintenance, relatives could often be compelled to provide cash, and parents who resisted or missed making cash payments could be prosecuted for neglect of children.[60] Threatening "aliens" with deportation, Kingsbury held, was an especially useful tactic when convincing parents to remove children from institutions or withdraw applications for aid.[61] Fully 12 percent of those who attempted to commit children as dependent in 1918 withdrew their applications, no doubt for fear of losing the children entirely or being deported themselves.[62] The DPC prominently displayed in its handbooks for investigators the federal Immigration Law of 1917, which stipulated the many categories under which immigrants could be deported. Presenting one's children for commitment could thus invite state intervention and deportation if an immigrant parent had entered the United States fewer than three years earlier or could be classified as one of many "subnormal" groups. Those included "idiots, imbeciles, feeble-minded persons, epileptics, insane persons . . . persons affected with tuberculosis or with a loathsome or dangerous contagious disease . . . persons who are found to be mentally or physically defective . . . which may affect the ability of such alien to earn a living."[63] By 1919 only a quarter of those who applied for commitment were approved, and parents had to sign a legal document and pledge compliance with provisions for payment to institutions. If the DPC deemed them to have failed in compliance, the children would be placed out or adopted, and the parents would lose all custody rights.[64]

Perhaps even more important to the ultimate success of the professionalization project was the task of convincing the public that these professionals would produce a public charitable system in which wards of the city and state would receive superior care. It was for the improvement of standards in the institutions, Folks declared in June of 1915, that a comprehensive investigation of all children's institutions was launched. The legal and practical autonomy of "forty-six different institutions, each of which is a separate corporation, self-perpetuating and substantially self-directing," Folks held, made rationalization of authority, and standardization of care, a necessity. He added, "The city had not lived up to its obligations, to say nothing of its opportunities, in exercising a wise selection in the commitment of children to institutions and thereby encouraging and, if necessary, requiring the adoption of higher standards by those whose standards may be too low."[65]

To that end, an investigating committee was formed that included initially a representative from each of the Protestant, Jewish, and Catholic communities. All three committee members had made their reputations by converting congregate institutions to the cottage plan. As Homer Folks explained in his introduction to their final report, Brother Barnabus worked at the Protectory in an experimental "cottage" branch; Ludwig Bernstein, superintendent of the Hebrew Sheltering Guardian Society, had converted a congregate institution to "a thoroughly modern, well equipped, educational and progressive cottage institution"; and R. R. Reeder had won a national reputation after publication of his *How Two Hundred Children Live and Learn*, "an exposition of cottage methods of children's institutions" from his experience as head of the New York

Orphan Asylum.[66] Both Reeder and Bernstein had received a Ph.D. in pedagogy from Columbia University. Brother Barnabus stayed on the team for only a short time, thereby refraining from contributing to the final report. Speculation grew that he was removed from the committee by the Catholic hierarchy so as to stop him from validating the criteria in the report as a "Catholic expert." He was not replaced. The DPC formally adopted the report to thereafter determine criteria used in inspections of institutions for dependent children.[67]

The committee's final report was a transitional document in the sense that it reiterated standards and inspection criteria used since the 1880s and articulated new standards reflective of "Progressive" rhetoric. Published in 1916, the report itemized inspection criteria created and used by the State Board of Charities over the previous forty years. Conditions as to physical plant, administration, sanitation, fire protection, records of children's backgrounds, degree and type of medical and dental care, food and nutrition, quarantine and hospital facilities, personal and institutional hygiene, dormitories, discipline, vocational training, social activities, and education were each delineated as appropriate for inspection, thereby codifying criteria that had from the inception of the institutional system been part of yearly inspections by the state board.

Because the committee had been formed with the assumption that the cottage system was the standard against which congregate institutions should be measured, nuns' institutions were placed in a decidedly unfavorable position. The degree to which they and all Catholic institutions had failed in this project was one of a number of reasons for poor ratings. The committee defined the "individual" development of a child, achieved through "motherly" devotion in a setting approximating the "family home," as the benchmark. Questions about educational background, moreover, assumed that institutional administrators should receive graduate training in one of a number of new fields in social science, particularly psychology and pedagogy, and that they frequently attend conferences and workshops in those disciplines.[68]

Given that Catholic nuns were likely to do poorly when judged against such standards, they were remarkably cooperative with the new investigative procedures. Kingsbury reported in 1915 that he had set up a collective meeting "with the Sisters in charge of Catholic children's institutions in the Archdiocese of New York . . . [where the] plan of inspection adopted by the Advisory Committee was outlined and criticisms and suggestions invited." Moreover, "The Sisters entered heartily into the discussions and, practically, were unanimous in expressing their willingness to cooperate with the Committee."[69] Most institutions, according to Kingsbury, "improved" by the following year in areas that had been criticized, a result that confirmed, he maintained, the wisdom of having the city thereafter assume control over investigations and relieve the state board of having to conduct investigations from Albany.[70]

Sisters in institutions had no indication that city investigators had cited problems in the institutions other than those reported to them and explicitly "fixed." Nuns were therefore as shocked as the larger city populace to hear in early 1916 that almost all Catholic institutions for dependent children had been deemed substandard and were in such "horrible" condition that the city refused thereafter to commit children to them. By the end of January 1916 the testimony of "experts" affirming these "horrible" conditions was reported daily in virtually every newspaper in the city, including the *New York Times, New York Herald, Post, Tribune, Evening Post,* and *Tablet* as well as newspapers throughout the state and the Charity Trust's *Survey,* which Devine edited.[71]

John Kingsbury's testimony early in the proceedings helped to inflate anti-institutional rhetoric to a level that was subsequently hard to control. Although Kingsbury had not actually visited any of the institutions, he claimed that all twenty-four on the list were "unfit for human habitation" and he had heard from his assistant, William Doherty, that "orphans and pigs were fed from the same bowl" and "beds were alive with vermin, . . . the heads of boys and girls were itching with uncleanliness." As Strong reported to the governor, only one institution was cited as having "vermin" in beds, although about half contained some children who had "vermin" or "nits" in their hair. As to the allegation about pigs, Strong lamented that Kingsbury's "recollection of what Doherty had reported was faulty." What Doherty had reported was that "the dining-room, after the boys had left it, looked more like a pig-pen than anything else."[72]

The press and the ensuing pamphlet wars, however, did not lend themselves to such specificity or qualifications. After Father Farrell published a letter to the governor on February 18, 1916, protesting against the charges made and the spirit of the commission, Kingsbury hired Edward Moree, a publicist for the SCAA, to collect press clippings favorable to the commission and distribute a pamphlet containing the articles in montage form. The pamphlet, six thousand copies of which were distributed, prominently displayed the newspaper clipping containing the headline "Orphans and Pigs Fed from Same Bowl" on its front cover. When later questioned by the commission about the pamphlet, Moree held that he was "extremely sorry that is there. I did not realize there was a misinterpretation of the evidence until after the thing was on the press."[73] Moree

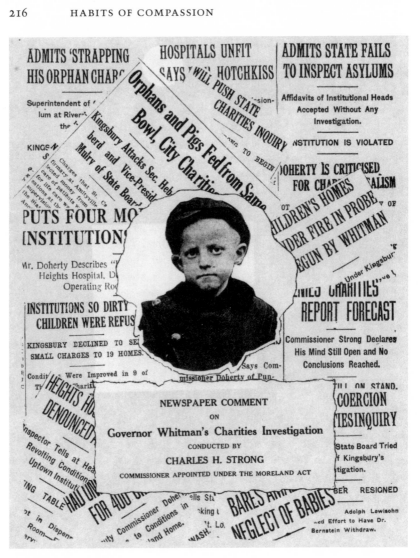

The Moree Pamphlet, from Strong Collection, courtesy of the New York State Archives.

nonetheless sent the six thousand printed copies to "prominent citizens, throughout the State."[74]

Moree's pamphlet, moreover, featured newspaper clippings containing evidence of nuns' insufficient professionalization. One from *The Sun* contained an exchange about the Sisters of Mercy's home for dependent children:

Mr. Doherty said . . . that the teachers in this Tarrytown home got only $25 a month.

"I can't get a competent cook for that," he exclaimed.

"Do you argue that because you can't get a competent cook for that sum they can't get competent teachers for $25 a month," asked Mr. Bowers.

"You're joking, Mr. Bowers," said Mr. Doherty. "If you knew anything about teaching you would know that any teachers of competence can get much more than that and would get it."[75]

The logic of professionalization reigned. If nuns were paid poorly for their work, then they must be incompetent even though vows of poverty made it inevitable that they would be paid poorly.

Catholic pamphlets issued by Father Farrell and the actions of other Catholics were no less inflammatory and distorting, thereby lending considerable credence to a generalized sense that "the Church" would stop at nothing to disguise the truth of institutional life. Whether or not the absence of Jewish institutions on the list was reflective of their presumed superiority, the use of Bernstein as a primary expert condemning Catholic institutions provided an opening for Farrell to significantly undermine the historical alliance between Catholics and Jews on these issues. Farrell accused Bernstein ("a Jew . . . born in Russia" and raised there "to manhood before coming to this country") of physically beating children and "baby-farming" infants from within his own institution.[76] Charging that the entire investigation was "anti-Catholic," he held that Doherty was a "Judas Iscariat" and that the atmosphere of the courtroom in which Catholic nuns testified was "in its essence, the same spirit the early Christians met in the circus maximus."[77]

In turn, Doherty accused both Mulry and Robert Hebberd of the state board of trying to persuade him to drop the investigation; held that Brother Barnabus was transferred to Utica by his superiors, and against his will, to keep him from contributing to the guidelines for inspection; and reported a rumor as well that Jewish community leaders had attempted to get Bernstein to resign. Catholic male leaders therefore attempted to thwart the investigation in a way that only exacerbated public scandal and encouraged many citizens to reasonably question whether they acted to cover up more egregious offenses.

Yet Farrell as well as other Catholic spokespersons did not discuss or emphasize that closing institutions would cut funding for dependent children or undermine the intent behind public support of widows' pensions (i.e., to provide the poor with access to aid without threatening parental rights). Twenty years earlier Devine and Folks would have been identified as Protestants, and the charge of anti-Catholicism would have resonated as a larger critique of Protestant policies to restrict aid to the poor and hinder the ability of Catholic communities to reproduce themselves biologically and culturally. By 1916, however, religious language no longer conveyed a complex articulation of oppositional consciousness able to reference these issues to a wider public. The controversy, moreover, could not be defined as purely religious in nature. Doherty and Mayor Mitchell were Catholic and Bernstein was Jewish, yet all condemned institutions at least as vigorously as Protestants did. Figures such as Mulry, moreover, traumatized if not actually killed by the scandals, had for decades proclaimed to the rest of the Catholic community that differences between Protestants and Catholics were merely cosmetic and alliances between the groups were warranted by common goals. The alliance among elites and across religious boundaries helped undermine a defense of institutions for dependent children as a morally just, politically desirable effort to extend aid to the poor.

By the summer of 1916 Mayor Mitchell had in the eyes of most of the city's Protestant, and some of its Jewish, elite acquitted himself of wiretapping charges in an exemplary manner. As a Catholic, yes, but an American first, he had battled the attempted seizure of an American state institution by the Catholic Church, thus averting transfer of tax money to a religious institution opposed to the fundamental principles of American democracy. On June 19 "Noted Citizens Who Back the Mayor" proclaimed their "belief in that principle . . . that all private institutions . . . be required to conform to proper standards of cleanliness, nourishment and care . . . prescribed by public authority." They stated further that "[w]e condemn the attempt of any and all representatives of such private institutions, of any religious denomination whatever, to interfere with the impartial and thorough application of that principle . . . [and] in our opinion the attempt of any one claiming to represent a religious organization to obscure the issue by an appeal to sectarian prejudices deserves emphatic condemnation."[78]

Whither the Children?

Catholic resistance to the DPC had been so disastrous that when Kingsbury announced in late 1916 that he would thereafter refuse to commit dependent children to institutions but would instead place them in foster homes "of the religious faith of their parents," Archbishop John Farley issued a pastoral letter announcing that Catholic institutions for dependent children would shortly be closed. John Kingsbury, however, panicked at the thought. He had not anticipated that he would lose the "devoted service" of hundreds of nuns, much less the use of their land and institutions. He had hired a managing bureaucracy, not people who could or would replace nuns as child-care workers. Kingsbury wrote to Archbishop Farley that he had not intended the institutions be closed but rather that they be used for a different purpose.

Kingsbury envisioned a radical recategorization of dependent children in New York into a three-tiered system in which parental and nuns' control over the fate of children was passed to the Board of Child Welfare and the DPC; closing Catholic institutions was merely a step in that process. At the apex of the new system were widows' pensions, a program Kingsbury could no longer directly control but one he wanted to remain as restricted as possible. The second was foster care, which in its incarnation under Kingsbury was a modified form of placing-out, reflective of compromises that placing-out advocates had made over previous decades. The third program advocated was permanent institutionalization for children the DPC deemed "subnormal."

Before the scandals, Kingsbury had made clear to Mayor Mitchell that he intended to move most dependent children into a foster-care system, which he characterized as reflective of the mandate from the White House Conference to keep children within a home environment. Foster care ("Boarding Out") differed from the traditional placing-out system in several respects and reflected an attempt to address long-standing criticisms of placing-out. Foster parents were to be paid for the care of children, a reform that, as Homer Folks had argued since his appointment as secretary of the SCAA in 1893, would lessen the temptation of those who housed children to exploit their labor so as to make up for the cost of their care. Foster parents, moreover, were generally presumed to be found in the city itself or within its outlying areas. Natural parents and relatives were, in keeping with the White House Conference mandate not to permanently break up families because of poverty alone, to maintain some parental rights, including visitation rights, if the child had been committed as dependent. Foster care would therefore be more profitable for the city not because payments to foster parents would be less than to institutions but because the DPC would have full charge of whether to deem applicants eligible for commitment.[79]

Because investigators had a simultaneous mandate to demand parents' direct-cash payments to the city for such care and threaten immigrant parents with deportation, Kingsbury's educated guess was that fewer parents would take such risks. "I feel it my duty to urge upon your Honor that the time has now come when the City of New York should thoroughly test the plan of placing our children in private homes," he wrote. "It is the convincing force of the idea that home life, even under some adversities, is vastly superior to institutional life for children, which has brought legislation providing for public pensions to widowed mothers in twenty-nine states of the Union."[80]

Through the scandals, Kingsbury employed age-old rhetoric about "saving children" to both condemn institutions and offer a seemingly secondary solution, a return to placing-out (or, in its modern formulation, foster care). A piece from the New York World suggested that Kingsbury's "idealism" and "common sense" had motivated him to "take at least two thousand children out of institutions and place them in the care of their mothers," but the article failed to mention that he had no plans whatsoever to give those mothers any public funding to care for their children. The article charged that institutions were responsible for "the breaking up of the family," to be corrected by a return to the placing-out system, "an old fashioned but finely beneficent mode of dealing with one of the most important social problems."[81]

Although Kingsbury had not referenced his third system publicly during the scandals, he had made clear to the Mayor before them that a relatively large number of the city's youth would not be appropriate candidates for home care, whether with their own mothers or with foster parents. He did not want to close nuns' institutions but to use the physical sites, and nuns' cheap labor, to house the "mentally deficient" then under the city's charge at Randall's Island and similar city-run poor-law institutions. Kingsbury offered an explicitly eugenics-based argument to defend the transfers—particularly to keep "sub-normal" girls from society. "Just as it is more profitable for society to care for its normal children in private homes, so it is more profitable for society to care for its feeble-minded in institutions," he wrote in early 1916. "An imbecile or moron boy on the streets, is an immediate menace to the community; an imbecile or moron girl at large on the streets, is a potential menace to succeeding generations."[82]

Under this new system Kingsbury categorized some children as eligible only for permanent institutional life, and he expected that women religious would gladly care for them. As Kingsbury explained patiently to Archbishop Farley, the DPC had succeeded in creating five thousand spaces in institutions in only six months and planned to create five thousand more. He would then begin transferring the "feeble-minded" to nuns' institutions from the newly built clearinghouse on Randall's Island, to be categorized and separated and "where they may be trained for permanent institutional life." These "defectives" would be sent to the appropriate institution, where, Kingsbury was sure, nuns would care for them as "the child's spiritual and moral welfare is uppermost in our minds." He planned on adding children more than eight years old to this group because they could not easily be put into foster care, being too hard to place. "Moreover," Kingsbury added, "there are many children slightly sub-normal—physically or morally—for whom institutional care will seem preferable to family care. . . . Then there are in this City literally thousands of children more or less mentally defective now living at home where they are handicapped, and handicapping their hard-working mothers."[83] Presumably the institutions he had characterized as "unfit for human habitation" were just fine for this group.

Kingsbury's references to "feeble-minded," "sub-normal—physically or morally," and "mentally defective" invoked the scientific rhetoric that had begun to replace the "moral" categories that during the nineteenth century had stratified the rich into the "self-reliant" and the poor into "chronic paupers," the respectable and the vicious, the moral and immoral. The normal of the twentieth century were to be distinguished from those who were subnormal and likely from racial and ethnic groups with an ostensible propensity for poverty and dependence.

As Elizabeth Lunbeck has noted, such rhetoric underlined the belief by some in the medical profession that "[c]lasses in a democracy merely reflected the unequal distribution of men's 'bodily and mental characteristics.'" Thus these "new," "objective," and "scientific" categories were inseparable from the categories of race and ethnicity. As Lunbeck observes about psychiatry in the 1910s, "Nothing about insanity was more certain than that it was dangerously on the increase, a corollary of unrestricted, largely European, immigration."[84]

The cultural and physical reproduction of new immigrants and African Americans was thereby a threat to the larger society and necessitated interventions that ranged from incarceration and institutionalization during their reproductive years to forced sterilization. The words were new, as was the scientific knowledge; the racial and ethnic groups targeted by such rhetoric were new as well. But the intent and overall logic in the system Kingsbury proposed were reminiscent of the origins of the placing-out system, which emphasized a radical undermining of the biological and cultural reproduction of the famine Irish.

A shift in control over mothering and cultural reproduction was, of course, at the heart of the new system. Only the small number of widows who could prove to investigators that they were entirely allegiant to the normative culture would have access to public funding and be able to raise their children within their homes. Other mothers poor enough to be deemed dependent by the DPC were assumed to be bad mothers and as such a threat to their children. Foster care thereby encouraged the transfer of mothering of these poor children to those the DPC deemed likely to provide normative home care. Their payment for services rendered allowed the DPC to continue monitoring and regulating mothering by investigating and regulating the homes of those who wished to visit or reclaim their children. Only the DPC could decide whether children would be returned to their parents. Having surrendered children in the first place made parents appear neglectful at the least and permanently stigmatized at most. To prove a beneficial home life required negotiating with the DPC and submitting to home inspections.

For those children whom Kingsbury envisioned would spend at least their childhoods in institutions, mothering itself was not necessary.[85] Because the children were deemed biologically inferior rather than culturally lacking, mothering and the impartation of particular values so as to reproduce the normative culture was not the point of their care by the state. In this nuns were, Kingsbury maintained, perfect workers. They provided cheap labor aimed only at securing the physical comfort and health of the children. Presumed to be deviant mothers, nuns could nonetheless devote their lives to these children without threatening the reproduction of the normative culture.

Sisters refused categorically to allow themselves or their institutions to be used in such a way. They had used the state to the degree that it suited their purposes, but many preferred to close institutions and take up other work rather than submit to their wealth and labor being used for the purposes of a political agenda at odds with their own values.[86] When and how sisterhoods closed institutions were determined by a host of circumstances. Some, like St. James run by the Sisters of Charity and St. Ann's run by the Sisters of the Good Shepherd, closed before the scandals, in 1905 and 1913, respectively.[87] Others, such as the Mercy Sisters' Tarrytown institution, were closed, ostensibly, to comply with a federal need to house soldiers during the war. Like the Good Shepherd Sisters, the Sisters of Mercy refocused efforts on adult women, whether young and working or elderly, and again relied on private funding for that work. Successive city administrations attempted to enlist sisters' care of dependent children, but nuns did not house comparable numbers of children until the depression.[88]

The scandals made clear to many, including many sisters, that their system of institutionalizing dependent children had run its course. Sisters within institutions performed an enormous amount of work under a massive bureaucracy increasingly likely to use their labor for ends the sisters never intended. Subjugated under "many masters" in the state and church, they were alienated from the work itself and apt to find themselves publicly derided for doing it at all. The largely Irish Catholic sisterhoods were more and more ethnically distinct from the children under their care. Although they might be co-religionists, the nuns were incapable of, or uninterested in, structuring their work in order to meet the needs of the larger immigrant communities of which the children were a part.

As African Americans migrated from the South during the late 1910s and 1920s and became a greater proportion of the poor, the inadequacy of the sisters' approach became glaring. A framework of religion as resistance was entirely unhelpful for this group, who were predominantly Protestant but unable to access funding under their own control. During the first few years of the Great Depression, African American poverty was so significant that Catholic institutions took in most African American children deemed by the DPC to be dependent, and the numbers of children within institutions for dependent children once again reached fifteen thousand. The strategy was merely a stop-gap until New Deal public relief programs were instituted. At that point substantial outdoor relief was again provided for the city's poor for the first time since the mid-nineteenth century. Once Aid to Dependent Children was established, all Catholic institutions for dependent children closed permanently.[89]

Investigating the Foundling

Kingsbury and his cohorts moved quickly after the scandals to an investigation of the Foundling Asylum ("Foundling Hospital"), which proved much more difficult than they had anticipated. The Foundling, as the Sisters of Charity called it, was perhaps the most universally popular institution in the city, and that popularity, and the facility's operation under legislative sanction for "abandoned infants" rather than dependent children, had kept it outside most controversies concerning public support for poor children.

Sister Irene Fitzgibbon and her colleague Sister Teresa Vincent McCrystal built the financial base of the institution in 1869 by drawing on generous public funding for children and funneling much of it into services for women. Their greatest accomplishment was to link rather than analytically or practically separate the struggles of poor women and children, and it distinguished work at the Foundling from that of the Protestant child-savers and their Catholic counterparts in children's or women's charities. At base, Sister Irene and her associates argued with ever-more sophistication that it was not possible to "save children" from infanticide, or from poverty itself, without addressing the more fundamental reasons for women's destitution and denigration. The institution received public support in part because of its approach, particularly in efforts to aid women without subjecting them to investigation, and, through it, public shaming. Kingsbury and his colleagues would eventually regret that they had not understood how important such an approach was to the city's poor women.

Because of their resistance to investigation, sisters' institutions for women had generally not fared well in the transition from private to public funding; public funding for women was almost always contingent on public investigation. Most of the funding available for women was tied to the court and criminal system, and access to it depended on complying with city investigations. In 1867 the Good Shepherd sisters, for instance, began to take in women committed through the court system, being guaranteed that the city would pay for the maintenance of each charge.[90] The sisters refused, however, to allow more than a minority of their charges to be sent by the courts. A majority of the institution's spaces were for voluntary commitment, and the convent's dependence on private, not public, funding was extended.[91] Other charities contingent on private funding and for women remained small or were closed when public funding for children's care became available.[92]

The only other order in the city to work with "fallen" women other than the Good Shepherd Sisters was the Sisters of the Divine Compassion, founded in 1886. They maintained that refusal to investigate was a critical protection against the shaming and ostracism of the larger community. The women under their care were frequently very young domestic servants who had been "seduced" by employers in rural areas and then sent to the city once pregnancy or an affair came to light within the family.[93] Mother Mary Veronica Starr, founder of the order, lamented in 1893 that women committed through the court system had to risk the humiliation that came with the city's investigation. "[T]he institutions for poor children, have become well to do since this system of committal began," she wrote. "We have plodded along, and are quite content, since it must have been God's will. Not for all the money in the world would I have a girl committed to us, when, to obtain it, she would have to declare publicly her own wrong doing. There would be little compassion in that."[94]

Certainly, the Sisters of Charity learned a great deal from their charges about circumstances that drove women to infanticide. Rather than publicizing such knowledge, however, the sisters responded by shaping the institution to provide material resources that would lessen the pressures on women to either kill or abandon children. Likely to attribute their origins and shifts in policy to the stated wishes of women who relied on their help, or to supernatural intervention, the Sisters of Charity did not claim to be shaping welfare policy but did so anyway.

As the story of the Foundling's establishment goes, Sister Irene fell ill during the cholera outbreak of 1849. During her illness she had a vision of caring for hundreds of children, and thereafter she waited patiently through her novitiate and subsequent teaching work for a chance to do so. In October of 1869 she asked a few sisters to join her in sheltering infants in a small house on Twelfth Street. Almost immediately thereafter, a woman who left her child returned to the convent, threatening suicide if she could not stay with the child. From that moment on the care of women and children was linked. News that the sisters would take in women and children spread so quickly that by January they were caring for 120 infants, receiving as many as twelve a day.[95] They placed a crib outside the convent, a bell nearby to be rung to alert them to retrieve a child. Some women, they knew, would be more likely to leave their children if they could do so unseen.

The house was entirely too small to handle the demand, and it became necessary almost immediately for the sisters to move to a larger house on Washington Square. Women who stayed at the convent were required to nurse their own and another child and in this way help lessen the mortality rate among infants left in "dying conditions" or who failed to thrive without a nurse.[96] Because of the physical limitations of the building itself, the sisters began to send most healthy infants to outside wet nurses throughout the city.

Sisters at the Foundling relied on a definition of "good mothers" that contrasted sharply with the definition offered by Protestant middle-class women of the same period. No restrictions as to race, religion, or class disqualified women for wet-nursing outside the institution or from bringing an infant into their home for the child's first two to three years. Thereby, hundreds of poor women were able to receive wages while raising their own and another child.

Using her Tammany connections, Sister Irene first incorporated the Foundling so it would be eligible for the city's 38-cent-a-day payment made to public institutions for the care of foundlings. Second, she initiated New York's first practical foster care system by giving the whole of the 38-cent daily allotment directly to outside nursing mothers, although no legislation about foster care was publicly discussed or submitted for legislative approval. As Sister Irene reported in 1873, payment to nursing mothers enabled many to perform wage work without leaving home, and thus these "good mothers" were almost exclusively poor. "Of the $115,648 expended, over $80,000 were paid to outside nurses," Sister Irene noted. "This of course is a great benefit to the poor people employed, and many families have been kept together by means of this resource. For although the sum allowed for each child is small, amounting to only $10 per month, yet this may pay the rent, and thus secure a roof for the family; which is in itself a great charity and a social benefit."[97]

In the midst of the depression of the 1870s, therefore, and with charitable resources and employment opportunities shrinking, more than a thousand poor families at a time were able to attain a modicum of financial security through wet-nursing. In contrast to middle-class definitions of "good mothering" that would have excluded women who had difficulty paying their rent, Sister Irene sought out such women and provided them with a substantial source of household income.

Reading the expansion of institutions as one of a number of ways that nuns made their agendas visible and accessible to the larger community, the Sisters of Charity's work in the Foundling Asylum from 1869 onward shows considerable change over time. To address the various problems of poor women, Sister Irene continued to expand the institution. St. Ann's Maternity Hospital was built in 1880, allowing poor women to receive care during child-bearing without paying hospital fees. St. John's Children's Hospital was built the following year, its permanent staff consisting of the best newly specialized "pediatricians" the city could supply. In addition, the sisters formed an employment agency to secure domestic service positions in which employers agreed to allow children to live with their mothers. For those who worked outside the home, Sister Irene founded St. John's Day Nursery in 1887, the first such facility in the city, to "relieve the poor struggling mothers of families from the anxiety of caring for their babies when they were compelled to go out and work."[98] Like other sisters in the city, those at the Foundling assumed that poor women would have to work and that single mothers needed help in doing so. Providing day care was but one of many ways the sisters attempted to keep families together and economically viable, and by 1910 Catholic sisters collectively ran fifteen separate day nurseries in the city—one-quarter of the total available.[99]

In the Foundling's annual reports Sister Irene used explicitly theological arguments to condemn society in general rather than unwed mothers for the shaming and social ostracism they faced. Calling the scorn of these women evidence of the "pharisaical" versus the Godly, Sister Irene was able to use ascetic selflessness to position herself and her work outside the dominant culture. "[O]n the erring woman, fall all the pain and sorrow, and (at least in the eyes of the pharisaical world) all the shame and scorn. Not so with a pitying God," Sister Irene maintained. She relied instead on "He who, when the sinful woman fell at His feet in confusion, said to her accusers, *'Let him who is without sin among you cast the first stone.'*"[100]

Sister Irene's admonition that sisters at the Foundling "live to be trusted" was as much a policy statement as a stern warning to those under her charge that a loose tongue could adversely effect the women they were attempting to aid or champion. Policy within the institution was premised on "saving" women's sexual or social reputations.[101] Within the institution itself no given names were used, and none were known to any but Sister Irene. Married women sheltered because of poverty were not in any way distinguished from those who were unmarried. The "saving" of redeemable women from "the scoffs of a wicked world" was thereby always central to policy.

Foundling policies were also organized to maximize the potential for "natural" (biological) mothers to keep their children despite poverty or social ostracism.[102] Women who decided to leave children with the sisters had three years to change their minds. After three years, the sisters would begin looking for a permanent home outside the city. In placing-out children in this way the Foundling's practices seemed to some to be comfortably close to those of Protestant reformers.[103]

Yet the Foundling, like other Catholic institutions, still held the rights of natural parents, especially mothers, to be paramount. Until 1900, moreover, they would not allow legal adoption so as to be able to remove a child from a neglectful or abusive guardian and ensure they could reunite a natural mother and child if the biological mother desired the reunion. As Sister Irene explained, "If in after life the mother is in a position to claim her child, she may always be able to do so as an exact register is kept of each child. Even should we decide to give away a child by adoption . . . we can still trace it."[104] The sisters pointed all policies toward encouraging the biological mother to claim her parental rights but feared that a child older than three or four would not be adopted. By 1919 there were 23,301 children who had been returned to parents or guardians, another 24,658 placed in homes, and approximately 3,200 who were legally adopted.[105]

Most of the difficult decisions made at the Foundling involved weighing the rights of various groups of mothers. Perhaps the hardest of the sisters' tasks was to take back a toddler or "run-around" from an outside nursing mother when the child was deemed old enough to be placed permanently in a family or the natural mother had requested the child's return. No outside nurses were allowed to keep children they raised from infancy, a stipulation the sisters believed would protect the rights of a natural mother to reclaim her child. Yet the stipulation also commodified poor women's mothering as nurses and established a competition the biological mother always won. The emotional pain that nurses endured in this arrangement was often quite palpable. The following account conveyed the difficulty of weighing the respective rights of women in such a scenario:

> A dark-haired German woman is sobbing at the doorway. "Oh, God took my baby and I cried over that, then you gave me another and now just as it can call me mamma you take it away again. Just because I am poor they think I do not know how to love," and then as she left the Sister whispered softly, "Its own mother wanted it. We had to take it away. They are going to Europe and by and by will come back with a daughter ten or fifteen years old. No one will know she was born two years sooner than they say."
>
> "And you think it is right to do that?"
>
> "Anything is right to save a woman's good name, and spare a girl the disgrace of growing to womanhood with no father. The world is hard on women, we believe in saving them through mercy, as the blessed Savior taught us."[106]

The Sisters of Charity certainly supervised the mothering of children in the care of outside nurses but did so primarily by checking the health and well-being of the infants on a monthly basis and providing material resources to aid in sufficiently clothing and feeding the children. The first Wednesday of every month was "Pay Day" at the Foundling, an event that by 1873 was held at the sisters' new institution on Sixty-eighth Street. From 7 A.M. until 5 P.M. streams of women of Irish, German, Italian, French, and African American heritage, each with an infant or toddler younger than three, would flood the surrounding neighborhood. The child was then checked by the sisters and pediatricians of their hospital for health, suitability of shoes and clothing, and general well-being. If a child was ill, he or she would be admitted to the infirmary or, after 1880, to the fully equipped children's hospital. Although men in the St. Vincent de Paul Society visited the homes of outside nurses, sisters and doctors were also required to check for signs of abuse and neglect and remove children accordingly.

The enormity of this work is hard to convey without reference to the quantities of public space and public resources used in its name. By the early 1880s the combined institutions making up the Foundling took up

The waiting room of the Foundling Asylum's Out Door Department on Pay Day. (Archives of the Sisters of Charity of New York, Mount St. Vincent)

Pay Day at the office of the Out Door Department. (Archives of the Sisters of Charity of New York, Mount St. Vincent)

all land bordering Lexington and Third Avenues from Sixty-seventh to Sixty-eighth Streets. In their first fifteen years the sisters received sixteen thousand infants. In 1880 alone, for instance, they cared for 2,488 children through outside nurses and in the institution's infant wards for sick children, in addition to 325 mothers.[107] At the May payday for outside nurses they gave out the semiannual provisions allotment for children who stayed with those women: three thousand dresses, 1,500 petticoats, two thousand shirts, a thousand pairs of drawers, two thousand stockings, two thousand diapers, a thousand pairs of shoes, five hundred cloaks, seven hundred lace caps, and three hundred hats.[108] In the conglomerate of institutions on Sixty-eighth Street daily food provisions included 250 pounds of meat, 270 loaves of bread, thirty-five pounds of butter, thirty dozen eggs, two barrels of potatoes, a barrel of sugar, 175 quarts of liquid, and fifty quarts of condensed milk.[109] Dependent primarily on city funds, the Foundling's budget from the city never dipped below a quarter-million dollars annually through 1920 and sometimes neared a half-million dollars.[110]

When the DPC turned its attention to the Foundling in late 1916 the goal was to assert control over admissions and thereby determine who among the women and children in the sisters' care were "legitimate charges." By the DPC's estimate, no payments from public funds should have been made to the institution until all women and children had been thoroughly investigated. The sisters had until this time fended off similar requests from the state board about the backgrounds of women and children under their care. As Sister Teresa Vincent explained to the state board in 1910:

> The Charter of our Institution, granted by the Legislature, carefully specifying and defining the children whom we may take and carefully defining our powers and limitation, the nature of our work depending for much of its usefulness upon its privacy, the duty we owe to the unfortunates who leave their Children with us, the duty we owe those who relying on our secrecy take Children from us by indenture or adoption, the immense amount of work we do in receiving and placing thousands of Children each year, all make those proposed rules utterly inapplicable to the New York Foundling Hospital.[111]

The DPC attempted to thwart such recalcitrance by modeling its investigation of the Foundling on the Strong investigation—examining and evaluating the institution and the sisters who ran it, the women and children who used their resources, and claiming to do so in the name of "saving children." Supervised by William Doherty, the investigative team toured the institution and the boarding homes in the fall of 1916. The investigators were generally positive about the care offered in the institution itself. Referring to the nine buildings that composed the Foundling, they reported on the "brightness of all of the rooms, the airiness and cleanliness of every hall, dormitory and kitchen. The dining-rooms of both mothers and children . . . w[ere] clean and orderly. The service was quiet and courteous, the atmosphere cheerful, and the food appetizing and well prepared."[112] Investigators also reported that the medical staff in the Foundling Hospital was highly trained and had sufficient educational credentials.

Investigators were much more critical, however, of the homes in which children were boarded, and there was profound disagreement between themselves and the sisters over what constituted "good mothering." Reporting that "[o]f the 290 nursing mothers, 278 are Italian women," they determined that "[o]f 166 boarding Homes investigated," only 36 percent were graded good, 36 percent fair, and 27 percent poor. Boarding homes merited a "poor" rating when "conditions were fundamentally wrong. In two homes, there seems ground to suspect drinking. In others the dirt and carelessness are serious. In many both sleeping conditions and feeding are altogether wrong . . . in fifty-six of these homes the family life is being carried on in four rooms. It is the exception where more than two of these are light . . . common towels and combs are the rule." Although Foundling rules stipulated that children should have their own beds, "in sixty-one of these 166 homes the New York Foundling charge was sleeping in the same bed with another child or adult."[113]

It was in assessment of their professional qualifications, however, that the sisters fared the worst. The report makes repeated reference to what were believed to be the limitations of the sisters' education and training. "The chief executive of the New York Foundling is Sister Teresa Vincent, a graduate of the Normal School of Philadelphia, 1858, and a Sister of Charity for fifty-six years" investigators reported, whereas "the boarding-out Department is in charge of Sister H. Matthew, a High School and College of Pharmacy graduate, and a Sister of Charity for thirty years."[114] "The work of the New York Foundling," investigators concluded, "is being carried on by earnest, zealous women, who are giving their lives to the welfare, as they see it, of the children under their care. They are, however, hampered by tradition. They are out of touch with conditions outside the institution, and with the more advanced standards and ideals of child-caring."[115]

The sisters' most important self-criticism was in the care of infants who were very ill. Of the 2,100 sick and dying infants received the previous year, children therefore retained in the hospital and not boarded to outside nurses, 725 died.[116] Infant mortality within the institution had been and continued to be a chronic and seemingly insurmountable problem. The Foundling sisters had attempted to combat it through hospitalizing the sickest children, but hospitalization itself facilitated the spread of contagious disease. Although sisters had reduced the level of mortality within the hospital to a quarter or a third of the sick or dying admitted, a rate much better than the city-run Infant Hospital's, no one, including the sisters, considered those rates acceptable.[117]

With a characteristic eye toward drumming up public support, Kingsbury announced in early 1917 that the DPC would thereafter control all admissions to the Foundling so as to save the city's poor from the "extreme infant mortality" evident in the institution. Using a report on infant mortality in the Foundling prepared by the Strong Commission, Kingsbury claimed that "[t]he city has . . . been in an anomalous situation. With one hand it has been spending over $225,000 a year for infant welfare work throughout the entire city; with the other it has been spending over $300,000 a year to one institution alone to perpetuate a system that facilitates the separation of infants and mothers and results in extreme infant mortality."[118] Although Bard Peck, legal counsel for the Foundling, attempted to control the effects of the publicity by challenging the numbers published, it was difficult to do so. Charles Strong apologized in a letter to Peck, claiming the numbers in his report were inflated and reflected "clerical error." Peck argued in a letter to the *Survey*, "This matter of mortality rate, however, is not the principal issue in this controversy. I give the figures above quoted merely to show that the new attitude of the DPC toward the Foundling Hospital is not justified by an excessive death rate in that institution."[119]

The primary issue, of course, was that sisters at the Foundling had—and with very little oversight—historically been able to derive public funding for women and children without investigating women under their care. Final recommendations of the investigating committee included blacklisting the boarding homes designated as poor, hiring a "trained" nurse to investigate homes in the future, and stipulating that "no child or mother shall be accepted as a city charge, unless an investigation of the mother's statement establishes her claim to such support."[120] They were dismayed to find that the sisters did not investigate their charges but rather accepted the stories of women who came to their door at face value:

> There is no effort made to find out or record any family history. Even when the mother remains for months in the institution, no record is

made of the names, the addresses of friends or relatives who may visit her. Sister Mary Fidele said that the reason no record was kept or information sought was because 'our object is to shield the girl and her family.'

There is no narrative history of the child kept in any of the departments, but all dates of placements, visits, transfers, deaths, indentures and adoptions are carefully and accurately kept in different departments, no items of statistics and for the purpose of bills and reports.

It is a social and economic injustice that mothers and babies admitted to the New York Foundling should become city charges without investigation or verification of the claims made by the mother.[121]

The sisters at the Foundling received an announcement from the DPC in early March 1917:

> First: Persons proposing children for "surrender" to the New York Foundling Hospital shall be referred to the Yorkville District Office of the Bureau of Social Investigations. . . . The surrender of no child directly to the institution shall be recognized by this Department nor shall the city accept such a child as a public charge.
>
> Second: Mothers applying for admission with their children as "accepted" cases shall be referred to the Yorkville District Office.
>
> Third: The names of women entering the institution in a pregnant condition to await confinement shall be reported to the office of the Director of the Bureau of Social Investigations, who will send a representative to interview such women in the institution. . . . Children "born in" the institution shall be accepted as public charges only in cases where their mothers shall have been previously reported to this Bureau and the decision rendered that they are proper public charges.[122]

Thus infants and mothers entering the Foundling could be considered as public charges only if they submitted to a public investigation, both of the pregnancy and of the financial status of their larger families. By April 1917 the DPC escalated the standoff by placing a member of the department in the institution itself. Thereafter, a representative of the DPC was present from 9 A.M. to 9 P.M., and mothers would need to submit to an interview with them to get within the Foundling's doors. Because the women began to arrive between 9 P.M. and 9 A.M. in order to avoid the investigators, the DPC also stipulated that sisters should make an effort "to keep the person accompanying the child at the institution until the arrival of the Department's representative on the following morning." The DPC did concede, however, that "infants abandoned on the sidewalks adjacent to the New York Foundling Hospital may be admitted to the hospital and will be committed by the Department as of the date of reception after investigation."[123]

Public outcry about the DPC's actions was evident in newspaper stories about "abandoned" infants throughout the city because investigations threatened women's privacy or took nearly a month to complete. As one source noted, "Babies now have to prove they are citizens of New York, who their parents are and that they are proper public charges before they get something to eat and a place to sleep."[124]

The great majority of mothers refused to submit to investigation. Among those who were investigated, however, Peck reported, "Nine mothers were compelled to take Court proceedings against the father against their will. Several cases were exposed to relatives of the mother through investigation." When all investigations were complete no mothers were accepted as public charges from March 1 to July 31, although nineteen of their children qualified under the provisions for dependent children. During the same period, however, the sisters accepted as private charges all of the eighty-six women the DPC rejected.[125] In one account, the "sister in charge" explained how the DPC's priorities were at odds with those of the Foundling:

> I consider that all women who have babies are good women. And I am very much afraid that this new ruling will cause mothers to leave their babies just anywhere. Even more terrible things may happen. One never knows.
>
> The mothers who come to us are just poor girls. Some of them want to keep their story from their parents. Or they may have brothers and sisters to shield. We let them stay here and take care of their babies.[126]

Sister Anna Michella complained to Mother M. Josepha about the ways in which investigations were fundamentally at odds with their mission in the Foundling. She added that the only choice was to eschew public funding altogether: "To me this is an impossibility to do and continue to preserve the confidence entrusted to us. . . . If we are going to forfeit supervision money . . . [so be it]."[127]

At base, the sisters were committed to taking in children and women without question. The DPC imagined that if it found family members who had sufficient financial resources to pay for care, it would stop the "injustice" of women and children "cheating" the system. For the Sisters of Charity, the exposure the investigation produced was an act of aggression and a greater harm to those women and children than what they were currently enduring. That they were desperate enough to be considering child abandonment made the additional aggression an act of cruelty. For the sisters, justice demanded that women be comforted not investigated, and women from families of means would often require such space and comfort as urgently as the poorest women.

Whether Catholic men in the church understood that commitment to women and children was another matter. As George Gillespie, attorney for the archdiocese, conveyed to Bard Peck in the midst of the controversy, "I am especially anxious that the Sisters show by their actions and questions that they are alive, alert, and up-to-date, and that they are not willing to permit any woman applying at the Foundling Asylum to commit a fraud on the City or to obtain the City's monies unfairly. On the other hand, I am equally anxious that the Sisters should not permit themselves to deviate one iota from the course they have heretofore followed."[128] Therein lay the quandary. Nuns were expected to uphold their own values while adapting to the city's and the larger culture's new professional models. Caught between the desire to be seen as fully assimilated and modern and true to their own mission and beliefs, nuns would travel a very hard road indeed.

In the end, sisters at the Foundling and the women in their care could be said to have won the battle. The public was decidedly on the side of the sisters, not merely because they defended all Catholics against criticism or attack but because they found the sisters' principled commitment not to punish women for their "passion and poverty" laudable. Public funding to the institution declined a bit, but private donations increased in the next several years. Sister Teresa Vincent died of heart failure on the morning of May 23, 1917, before that day's scheduled court appearance in which she was to defend the Foundling's admissions policy. Three thousand people attended her funeral at St. Patrick's Cathedral. In a sense, the proceedings did not just eulogize Sister Teresa Vincent but all "noble women" of her generation who were willing to sacrifice in the name of social justice. Mayor Mitchell and John Kingsbury were voted out of office months later, and Mitchell's successor, "Red Mike" Hylan, a Democrat, promised in his campaign to "fill the outgoing trains with 'experts.'" He was evoking a new, improved placing-out system through which investigators would be transported to homes in the Midwest.[129]

The subsequent "founding" of "Catholic Charities" in New York in 1921, and in the national arena as well, was the capstone in this drama. Fearing more scandal and anxious to appear modern, the New York diocese began to teach Catholic activists at Fordham University the fundamentals of social work and the proper modes of scientific investigation and casework.[130] Rationalizing the male hierarchy over nuns, Cardinal Patrick Hayes was celebrated for "founding" "Catholic Charities," an enormous incorporation of the discrete charities that sisters had constructed, making sure that individual deviations in sisters' approaches to social work were minimized.[131] Young Catholic women in New York and elsewhere could have access to such professional training and thus the imprimatur of expertise that would in turn allow them to enter the field of social work. In that profession they had no need to submit to the kind of ecclesiastic control that increasingly circumscribed nuns' lives.

Returning to the question of the state's immaculate conception, there are several reasons why it is imperative that historians of women in America rethink the narrative of linear progress that has thus far so influenced our understanding of gender and welfare state formation from the nineteenth through early twentieth centuries. The standard narrative attributes the enactment of widows' pensions, and their expansion in the New Deal under Aid to Dependent Children, to the activism of predominantly white, Protestant, middle-class and elite women. In advocating and directing these programs that group not only gained power for themselves in the state but also helped engineer programs for women and children. It was through such programs that they controlled conditions for mothering and thereby reproduced the dominant culture. Single poor mothers supported the programs as well, despite these controls, because they provided a means, however meager, to raise children at home and with less reliance on wage work and less fear that the children would be taken from them solely on account of their poverty. That shift toward family preservation was perhaps the single most important shift in the female-dominated trajectory of the welfare state of the twentieth century. The narrative suggests, as do innumerable historians of women, that the greater power of this relatively elite group of women in the state resulted in poor women having better access to the benefits critical to their well-being and that of their children. Kathryn Kish Sklar goes even further: "Why in the United States was so much of the path to the welfare state blazed by middle-class women?" she asks. Sklar suggests "a simple answer to that question. Women's activism was crucial because it served as a surrogate for working-class social-welfare activism."[132]

Hardly. The linear Progressive narrative above, although important in elucidating the gendered dynamics in welfare state formation, tends to elide and obfuscate class and racial dynamics. There are many truths in the progressive narrative. Elite women did turn to family preservation in the Progressive Era; they did run programs in which they championed the rights of women in the state; and as historians of women agree, they exerted power over non-elite women in the process. But the critical question is one of causation and change over time. As a linear narrative, and a Progressive one, this account tends to link poor women's well-being with the greater power and enlightenment of elite women. Change is not understood as a result of contestation, of power exerted from below as well as above. Rather, poor and working-class women are cast primarily as objects of the elite's beneficence or control, depending on whether one views the state positively or negatively.

In studying Irish Catholic nuns' role in state development it is apparent that a dialectical model is a much more appropriate lens through which to analyze causation and change over time in the female trajectory of the welfare state. Dialectics account for the range of choices created in any particular historical context and moment that derive from contestations in the larger society. Pressure from below as well as from above helps constitute and limit the choices available to certain groups, including the elite. One of the many dynamics guiding change over time that continually surprised me was that the elite almost never got what they wanted, even when their ability to exert control seemed uncontestable. Nuns and the poor were extremely creative in employing what James Scott would call the "arts of resistance."[133] Nowhere was that more apparent than in their ability to limit the choices of the elite, including elite women, so that the elite's support of family preservation became, after a half century of struggle, not only possible but also a strategy they embraced as their own. Causation in this book is therefore attributed not to the elite's greater enlightenment but to the activism and struggles of poor and working-class Catholic and Jewish women.

During the Progressive Era the debate about the "family plan" versus "institutionalization," although based on decades of Protestant-Catholic struggles over control of children, became an increasingly secularized discussion seemingly unconnected to religious, class, or cultural conflict. Protestant reformers' urgent public pleas to "get children out of institutions," once understood in the popular mind to be an assault against nuns and an effort to constrict public relief, now seemed a perfectly reasonable and humane campaign in consonance with poor people's rights. That institutionalization had been a strategy devised primarily to stop the policy of child removal, that it had been successful in doing so, and that it owed its success to the agency of working-class and poor people over decades was lost in Progressive Era discussions. Also lost was the explicit understanding that anti-institutionalization was a powerful and effective means of destroying nuns' considerable public power and credibility in welfare work and critical as well to Protestant female reformers' ability to regain the popular mandate for public mothering.

The Progressive narrative of the welfare state is dangerous in other ways as well. Nuns and other working-class women's presumption—indeed, insistence—that the poor should not be punished for poverty was never an explicit intent of Aid to Dependent Children. Rather, the thinking that presumed the poor to be dependent because of charity was incorporated into New Deal programs for women and children. Widows and an expanding group of single mothers received funds from the state not because they were "entitled" to such funding but because their children were deemed innocent of the sins, moral failings, or defects of character that presumably impoverished their mothers.[134]

Whether discussed in moral, religious, or scientific terms the premise of such funding is that adults in poverty are individually responsible for their misfortune. Thus, only a gesture of kindness toward their innocent children—"saving children"—justifies state support. That some racial and ethnic groups are disproportionately dependent on such programs convinces many that the groups are reproducing a dependent culture, a "culture of poverty," and causation in the reproduction of poverty rests in charity or welfare itself.

Such is the premise of contemporary advocates of "compassionate conservatism," which presumes reductions in aid to the poor are more "compassionate" than aid itself. Indeed, the absence of aid will inspire greater struggle on the part of the poor and greater voluntarism on the part of the better-off, thus effecting countless individual moral and religious transformations to bring the poor out of poverty. The historical primers for this movement, Marvin Olasky's *The Tragedy of American Compassion* and its more scholarly cohort, Joel Schwartz's *Fighting Poverty with Virtue: Moral Reform and America's Urban Poor*, wax eloquent on the wisdom of Josephine Shaw Lowell, Charles Loring Brace, and countless others who withheld outdoor relief, refused aid to more than a repentant handful of the poor, and resisted above all else any program that would convey to the poor that they were entitled to help.[135]

Advocating a return to the good old days when the poor had little choice but to subject themselves to individual moral reform in exchange for a pittance, Olasky and his cohorts rely on a model of social change that turns the Progressive narrative on its head. Instead of celebrating the linear progress of welfare in the twentieth century, conservatives tell the same story as Progressives but characterize it as one of declension. The poor's increased sense of entitlement to aid since the Progressive Era, especially since the New Deal, they argue, has caused and reproduced poverty. A lack of religious oversight and religious and moral reform demanded through these state programs is ostensibly the cause of the myriad social problems associated with poverty in the twenty-first century. Celebrating the end of "welfare as we know it," both Schwartz and Olasky imagine that the twentieth-century welfare state was a disastrous "detour" and that, now dismantled, it might be possible return to figures such as Brace, Lowell, and Robert Hartley as guides for shaping the "virtue" of the poor.[136]

For Olasky in particular, the fact that many people will clearly suffer in this new regime is not an unfortunate side-effect but a necessary stage. Only through suffering and shame, he maintains, will individuals be compelled to undertake a personal (and religious) transformation. Whether this will end poverty as we know it, and have known it, is less important in his estimate than whether society at large can once again coerce the poor to comply with normative standards for virtue.

The faith-based charities that Olasky and others tout as the better option than entitlement programs are those that represent, as in the nineteenth century, a particular view on poverty and charity. Catholics and Jews in this study, representing the great majority of the poor and working classes, believed with no less faith, and with absolute certainty in the confluence of their views of God and social justice, that expansive relief for the poor was a moral right and societal obligation. "Faith-based" is thus another euphemism for a return to dependence on the kinds of groups and social provisions against which the poor have always fought and a great percentage of the faithful have always condemned.

It is the persistence and harmfulness of the belief that poverty in America is caused by the individual moral failings of the poor that may constitute the greatest defeat of the Irish Catholic sisters who constructed charitable systems in New York City. Closing their institutions, being publicly pilloried for their work and thereby erased from memory as actors in shaping the state, were but some of the many crosses they expected to bear. Yet their work for many years was a brick-and-mortar testament to their values: The poor should not be punished for poverty, parents should be helped in raising their children, and women should be aided because in the end the world is unjust. The sisters did not imagine they could effect a perfect society, but they did imagine that compassion for people who struggled in this imperfect world was the higher road.

NOTES

Abbreviations

AANY   Archives of the Archdiocese of New York
AICP   Association for Improving the Condition of the Poor
AFGS   American Female Guardian Society
AMSV   Archives of the Sisters of Charity of New York at Mount
          St. Vincent
ASDC   Archives of the Sisters of Divine Compassion, White Plains, N.Y.
ASGS   Archives of the Sisters of the Good Shepherd, Jamaica,
          Queens, N.Y.
ASMNY   Archives of the Sisters of Mercy, Dobbs Ferry, N.Y.
CAS   Children's Aid Society
DPC   Department of Public Charities
NYCMA   New York City Municipal Archives
RCOA   Roman Catholic Orphan Asylum
SCAA   State Charities Aid Association
SPCC   Society for the Prevention of Cruelty to Children
SVOP   St. Vincent de Paul Society

Introduction

The quotation in the epigraph is from T. S. Eliot, *Four Quartets* (New York: Harcourt and Brace, 1943).

1. Throughout this work I refer to Catholic women in religious institutes as "women religious," "sisters," and "nuns," thereby reflecting common usage but not canon law, which stipulated that only enclosed women religious be referred to as nuns.

2. *New York Times,* Aug. 17, 1896, 6; *New York Herald Tribune,* Aug. 18, 1896.

3. Mary Peckham Magray, *The Transforming Power of the Nuns: Women, Religion, and Cultural Change in Ireland, 1750–1900* (New York: Oxford University Press, 1998); Suellen Hoy, "The Journey Out: The Recruitment and Emigration of Irish Religious Women to the United States, 1812–1914," *Journal of Women's History* 6 (Winter–Spring 1995): 64–88.

4. Mary Ewens, *The Role of the Nun in Nineteenth-Century America* (1971, repr. Salem, N.H.: Ayer Publishers, 1984), 86, 201, 252.

5. *The Catholic Almanac for 1848* (Baltimore: F. Lucas, Jr., 1849): 180–81; *Hoffmann's Catholic Directory, Almanac and Clergy List* (Milwaukee: Hoffmann Brothers, 1898), 98–104.

6. A sizable literature on the availability of this option nationwide makes evident that poor parents used a variety of institutions to rear children temporarily through the Gilded Age period. See especially Patricia Kelleher, "Maternal Strategies: Irish Women's Headship of Families in Gilded Age Chicago," *Journal of Women's History* 13 (Summer 2001): 80; Timothy Hasci, *Second Home: Orphan Asylums and Poor Families in America* (Cambridge: Harvard University Press, 1997); Matthew Crenson, *Building the Invisible Orphanage: A Prehistory of the American Welfare System* (Cambridge: Harvard University Press, 1998); Nurith Zmora, *Orphanages Reconsidered: Child Care Institutions in Progressive Era Baltimore* (Philadelphia: Temple University Press, 1993); and Elizabeth Lasch-Quinn, "The Kindness of Strangers," *New Republic*, Dec 28, 1998, 46.

7. Hon. Bird S. Coler, Comptroller of the City of New York, "Municipal Subsidies to Private Charities," *The St. Vincent de Paul Quarterly* 4 (1899): 300, 304, 306. In 1899 New York City expended approximately $3.1 million per year on charities, of which approximately $2.2 million went to dependent children. The closest city charitable expenditures in 1899 were those of Baltimore, which allotted $227,000.

8. Among the best work on women and the state in the period covered are Robin Muncy, *Creating a Female Dominion in American Reform, 1890–1935* (New York: Oxford University Press, 1991); Linda Gordon, *Pitied but Not Entitled: Single Mothers and the History of Welfare* (New York: Free Press, 1994); Molly Ladd-Taylor, *Mother-Work: Women, Child Welfare, and the State, 1890–1930* (Urbana: University of Illinois Press, 1994); Kathryn Kish Sklar, *Florence Kelly and the Nation's Work: The Rise of Women's Political Culture, 1830–1900* (New Haven: Yale University Press, 1995); Gwendolyn Mink, *The Wages of Motherhood* (Ithaca: Cornell University Press, 1996); Joanne Goodwin, *Gender and the Politics of Welfare Reform: Mother's Pensions in Chicago, 1911–1929* (Chicago: University of Chicago Press, 1997); and Theda Skocpol, *Protecting Soldiers and Mothers: The Political Origins of Social Policy in the United States* (Cambridge: Harvard University Press, 1992).

9. A wonderful exception to this trend is Kathy Peiss, *Cheap Amusements: Working Women and Leisure in Turn-of-the-Century New York* (Philadelphia: Temple University Press, 1985).

10. See especially Evelyn Brooks Higgenbotham, *Righteous Discontent: The Women's Movement in the Black Baptist Church* (Cambridge: Harvard University Press, 1993); Suzanne Lebsock, *The Free Women of Petersburg: Status and Culture in a Southern Town, 1746–1860* (New York: W. W. Norton, 1984); Deborah Gray White, *Ar'n't I a Woman? Female Slaves in the Plantation South* (New York: W. W. Norton, 1985); Paula Giddings, *When and Where I Enter: The Impact of Black Women on Race and Sex in America* (New York: Bantam Books, 1985); Albert Raboteau, *Slave Religion: The Invisible Institution in the Antebellum South* (New York: Oxford University Press, 1978); and Lawrence Levine, *Black Culture, Black Consciousness: Afro-American Folk Thought from Slavery to Freedom* (New York: Oxford University Press, 1977).

11. See especially Chandra Mohanty, "Under Western Eyes: Feminist Scholarship and Colonial Discourses" (citing Marnia Lazreg, "Feminism and Difference: The Perils of Writing as a Woman on Women in Algeria," *Feminist Issues* 14 [Spring]: 81–107), 72–73, 62–63, and Mohanty, "Cartographies of Struggle: Third

World Women and the Politics of Feminism," both in *Third World Women and the Politics of Feminism,* edited by Chandra Talpade Mohanty, Ann Russo, and Lourdes Torres (Bloomington: Indiana University Press, 1991); Catherine Hall, "Feminism and Feminist History," in *White, Male and Middle Class: Explorations in Feminist History* (Cambridge: Polity Press, 1992), 1–40; Edward Said, Introduction to *Orientalism* (New York: Random House, 1979), 1–28; Evelyn Accad, "Sexuality and Sexual Politics: Conflicts and Contradictions for Contemporary Women in the Middle East," in *Third World Women,* edited by Mohanty, Russo, and Torres, 251–67; Valentine M. Moghadam, "Revolution, Islam and Women: Sexual Politics in Iran and Afghanistan," in *Nationalisms and Sexualities,* edited by Andrew Parker et al. (New York: Routledge, 1992), 424–46; and Arlene MacLeod, "Hegemonic Relations and Gender Resistance: The New Veiling as Accomodating Protest in Cairo," *Signs* 17 (Spring 1992): 533–57.

12. This introduction is not intended to be a thorough discussion of all the historiographic literature that has influenced me and the framework of this project. For a detailed discussion of the larger fields of immigrant, Catholic, women's, and welfare history with which this work engages, see Maureen Fitzgerald, "Irish-Catholic Nuns and the Development of New York City's Welfare System, 1840–1900," Ph.D. diss., University of Wisconsin-Madison, 1992.

Perhaps the most compelling work on relationships between female reformers and women of nondominant groups includes Theda Perdue, *Cherokee Women: Gender and Culture Change, 1700–1835* (Lincoln: University of Nebraska Press, 1998); Peggy Pascoe, *Relations of Rescue: The Search for Female Moral Authority in the American West, 1874–1939* (New York: Oxford University Press, 1990); and Karen Anderson, *Changing Woman: A History of Racial Ethnic Women in Modern America* (New York: Oxford University Press, 1996).

13. Among the literature on Catholic sisters that has been critical to my understanding of their collective and distinctive histories are Ewens, *The Role of the Nun;* Mary J. Oates, "Organized Voluntarism: The Catholic Sisters in Massachusetts, 1870–1940," *American Quarterly* 30 (Winter 1978): 652–80; Mary Oates, "'The Good Sisters': The Work and Position of Catholic Churchwomen in Boston," in *Catholic Boston: Studies in Religion and Community, 1870–1970,* edited by Robert E. Sullivan and James M. O'Toole (Boston: Archdiocese of Boston, 1985), 171–200; Mary DeCock, "Turning Points in the Spirituality of an American Congregation: The Sisters of Charity of the Blessed Virgin Mary," *U.S. Catholic Historian* 10 (Spring 1992): 59–69; Carol K. Coburn and Martha Smith, *Spirited Lives: How Nuns Shaped Catholic Culture and American Life, 1836–1920* (Chapel Hill: University of North Carolina University Press, 1999); JoAnn Kay McNamara, *Sisters in Arms: Catholic Nuns through Two Millenia* (Cambridge: Harvard University Press, 1996); Margaret Susan Thompson, "Discovering Foremothers: Sisters, Society, and the American Catholic Experience," and "Philemon's Dilemma: Nuns and the Black Community in Nineteenth-Century: Some Findings," both in *The American Catholic Religious Life: Selected Historical Essays,* edited by Joseph M. White (New York: Garland Publishing, 1988), 81–96; and Diane Batts Morrow, *Persons of Color and Religious at the Same Time: The Oblate Sisters of Providence, 1828–1860* (Chapel Hill: University of North Carolina University Press, 2002).

14. Two sophisticated studies of Catholic charities have put the development

of Catholic charities in a national context and in relation to the larger welfare system: Mary J. Oates, *The Catholic Philanthropic Tradition in America* (Bloomington: Indiana University Press, 1995), and Dorothy M. Brown and Elizabeth McKeown, *The Poor Belong to Us: Catholic Charities and American Welfare* (Cambridge: Harvard University Press, 1997). See also Susan S. Walton, *To Preserve the Faith: Catholic Charities in Boston, 1870–1930* (New York: Garland Publishing, 1993), and Marian J. Morton, "The Transformation of Catholic Orphanages: Cleveland, 1851–1996," *Catholic Historical Review* 88 (Jan. 2002): 65–89. Several studies on Catholic charities were published in the late Progressive Era through the mid-twentieth century and feature nuns' institutions prominently. The critical works include John O'Grady, *Catholic Charities in the United States* (1930, repr. New York: Arno Press and the New York Times, 1971); Francis E. Lane, *American Charities and the Child of the Immigrant: A Study of Typical Child Caring Institutions in New York and Massachusetts Between the Years 1845 and 1880* (Washington: Catholic University of America, 1932); and George Paul Jacoby, *Catholic Child Care in Nineteenth-Century New York* (Washington: Catholic University of America, 1941).

15. Suellen Hoy, "Walking Nuns: Chicago's Sisters of Mercy," in *At the Crossroads: Old Saint Patrick's and the Chicago Irish,* edited by Ellen Skerrett (Chicago: Loyala University Press, 1997), 30. Skerrett notes that Jane Addams seemed oblivious to the sisters and larger Catholic culture in the vicinity of Hull-House. Ellen Skerett, "The Irish of Chicago's Hull-House Neighborhood," in *New Perspectives on the Irish Diaspora* (Carbondale: Southern Illinois University Press, 2000), 189–222.

16. Linda Gordon has found that her sample of white female leaders in national welfare reform from the 1890s through the mid twentieth century contains a majority of women who worked in New York City's charities in the Progressive Era and during the 1920s. Linda Gordon, "Black and White Visions of Welfare: Women's Welfare Activism, 1890–1945," *Journal of American History* 78 (Sept. 1991): 572.

Chapter 1: Republican Mothers and Brides of Christ

The quotation in the epigraph is from Mary Condren, *The Serpent and the Goddess: Women, Religion and Power in Celtic Ireland* (San Francisco: HarperSanFrancisco, 1989), 78.

1. Bruce Lincoln, "Culture," in *A Guide to the Study of Religion,* edited by Willi Braun and Russell T. McCutcheon (New York: Cassell, 2000), 410, 409–22.

2. Benedict Anderson, *Imagined Communities: Reflections on the Origins and Spread of Nationalism* (London: Verso Books, 1991).

3. Anderson, *Imagined Communities.*

4. [Mother Mary Teresa] Austin Carroll, *Leaves from the Annals of the Sisters of Mercy,* 4 vols. (New York: Catholic Publication Society, 1889), 3: 203–13.

5. Kerby A. Miller, *Emigrants and Exiles: Ireland and the Irish Exodus to North America* (New York: Oxford University Press, 1985), 21.

6. William V. Shannon, *The American Irish* (New York: Collier Books, 1963), 21; Miller, *Emigrants and Exiles,* 21–23.

7. Kevin Whelan, "The Catholic Church in County Tipperary, 1700–1900," in *Tipperary: History and Society, Interdisciplinary Essays on the History of an Irish County*, edited by William Nolan (Dublin: Geography Publications, 1985), 218–19.

8. David W. Miller, "Irish Catholicism and the Great Famine," *Journal of Social History* 9 (1975): 81–98.

9. Evelyn Brooks Higgenbotham, *Righteous Discontent: The Women's Movement in the Black Baptist Church* (Cambridge: Harvard University Press, 1993).

10. Kevin Whelan, "The Regional Impact of Irish Catholicism, 1700–1850," in *Common Ground: Essays on the Historical Geography of Ireland*, edited by W. J. Smyth and Kevin Whelan (Cork: Cork University Press, 1988), 253–77.

11. S. J. Connolly, *Priests and People in Pre-Famine Ireland, 1780–1845* (Dublin: Gill and Macmillan, 1982), 272–78, 60–73; Jay Dolan, *The American Catholic Experience: A History From the Colonial Times to the Present* (New York: Doubleday, 1985), 164; Miller, *Emigrants and Exiles*, 21–25, 88–101; Dennis J. Clark, "The Irish Catholics: A Postponed Perspective," in *Immigrants and Religion in Urban America*, edited by Randall M. Miller and Thomas D. Marzik (Philadelphia: Temple University Press, 1977), 53, 56–57.

12. Carroll, *Leaves from the Annals*, 3: 206; Miller, *Emigrants and Exiles*, 54, 27–101, passim; Gearóid Ó Tuathaigh, *Ireland before the Famine, 1798–1848* (Dublin: Gill and Macmillan, 1972).

13. JoAnn Kay McNamara, *Sisters in Arms: Catholic Nuns through Two Millenia* (Cambridge: Harvard University Press, 1996).

14. Much of my understanding of Irish convents in the nineteenth century has been gained through working with Mary Peckham Magray, to whom I owe a great debt. Mary Peckham Magray, *The Transforming Power of the Nuns: Women, Religion, and Cultural Change in Ireland, 1750–1900* (New York: Oxford University Press, 1998), 8–9 passim.

15. Caitriona Clear, *Nuns in Nineteenth-Century Ireland* (Dublin: Gill and MacMillan, 1987), 101; Maria Luddy, "Women and Philanthropy in Nineteenth-Century Ireland," Ph.D. diss., University College, Cork, 1989, 35–36; Mary L. Peckham, "Reemergence and Early Development of Women's Religious Orders in Ireland, 1770–1850," *Women's History Working Papers Series*, no. 3, 1990.

16. Clear, *Nuns in Nineteenth-Century Ireland*, 105.

17. Magray, *The Transforming Power of the Nuns*, 41–45, 9. In 1800 there were only a hundred nuns in all of Ireland, just 5 percent of the church's workforce. By 1850 there were roughly 1,500, representing 40 percent of the church's workforce. Most were in active sisterhoods that founded and staffed educational and charitable institutions throughout Ireland.

18. Miller, *Emigrants and Exiles*.

19. Carroll, *Leaves from the Annals*, 3: 207.

20. Julia McKenna was sent immediately to the Brooklyn Sisters of Mercy.

21. Carroll, *Leaves from the Annals*, 3: 216.

22. Carl Wittke, *The Irish in America* (Baton Rouge: Louisiana State University Press, 1956), 89.

23. James Olson, *Catholic Immigrants in America* (Chicago: Nelson-Hall, 1987), 29. For discussions of the Irish immigrant population increase relative to

the national Catholic population see Gerald Shaughnessy, *Has the Immigrant Kept the Faith? A Study of Immigrants and Catholic Growth in the United States, 1790–1920* (New York: Mcmillan, 1925), 126–46, 154; and James E. Roohan, *American Catholics and the Social Question, 1865–1900* (New York: Arno Press, 1976), 5–6.

24. Jay Dolan, *The Immigrant Church: New York's Irish and German Catholics, 1815–1865* (Baltimore: Johns Hopkins University Press, 1975), 22. Germans, whose immigration rate surpassed that of the Irish in the 1850s, accounted for one-quarter of the parishes throughout the city in 1865 although the German population represented no more than one-seventh of the total Catholics in the city. Neither Italian nor African American Catholics established their own parishes in the city until much later in the century (24–25). The Irish kept the city's 1,500 black Catholics out of English-language Catholic parishes, and African Americans as a group instead attended the French St. Vincent de Paul parish until 1883. Yet the great majority of New York's black population belonged to Protestant churches.

25. John Francis Maguire, *The Irish in America* (1868, repr. New York: Arno Press and the New York Times, 1969), 361–69; Katherine E. Conway, *In the Footprints of the Good Shepherd: New York, 1857–1907* (New York: Convent of the Good Shepherd, 1910), 45; Hasia Diner, *Erin's Daughters in America: Irish Immigrant Women in the Nineteenth Century* (Baltimore: John Hopkins University Press, 1983), 130. See also Suellen Hoy, "The Journey Out: The Recruitment and Emigration of Irish Religious Women to the United States, 1812–1914," *Journal of Women's History* 6 (Winter-Spring 1995): 64–88.

26. Jay Dolan, *Catholic Revivalism: The American Experience, 1830–1900* (Notre Dame, Ind.: Notre Dame University Press, 1978), 207.

27. Dolan, *The American Catholic Experience*, 192.

28. Lyndal Roper, *The Holy Household: Women and Morals in Reformation Augsburg* (New York: Oxford University Press, 1989); Clarissa Atkinson, *The Oldest Vocation: Christian Motherhood in the Middle Ages* (Ithaca: Cornell University Press, 1991).

29. I use the terms *Anglo* and *white* here as racial tags for the Protestant, native-born, middle-class group I discuss throughout and distinguish them from African American, middle-class Protestants or German middle-class Protestants. Reference to Protestant middle-class Americans should hereafter be assumed to mean white and native-born unless otherwise noted.

30. Nancy Cott, *The Bonds of Womanhood: "Woman's Sphere" in New England, 1780–1835* (New Haven: Yale University Press, 1977); Ann Douglas, *The Feminization of American Culture* (New York: Knopf, 1977); Linda K. Kerber, *Women of the Republic: Intellect and Ideology in Revolutionary America* (Chapel Hill: University of North Carolina, 1980); Jeanne Boydston, *Home and Work: Housework, Wages, and the Ideology of Labor in the Early Republic* (New York: Oxford University Press, 1990); Paula Baker, "The Domestication of Politics: Women and American Political Society, 1780–1920," *American Historical Review* 89 (June 1984): 620–47.

31. "As a subversive reformation of the self's relation to family and the family's position in society," Jenny Franchot has argued, nineteenth-century "convents . . . challenged middle-class Protestant boundaries between public and private."

Franchot, *Roads to Rome: The Antebellum Encounter with Catholicism* (Berkeley: University of California Press, 1994), 126–27

32. Preface to Maria Monk, *Awful Disclosures of the Hotel Dieu Nunnery* (1836, repr. Hamden: Archon Books, 1962), 1.

33. Ray Allen Billington, *The Protestant Crusade, 1800–1860: A Study of the Origins of American Nativism* (New York: Rinehart, 1938), 68–76, 85–90, 99–108, 310–11, 315, 348, 361, 366, 412–16; Monk, *Awful Disclosures*, passim; Joseph G. Mannard, "The 1839 Baltimore Nunnery Riot: An Episode in Jacksonian Nativism and Social Violence," *Maryland Historian* 11 (1980): 13–27; Mary Ewens, *The Role of the Nun in Nineteenth-Century America*, (1971, repr. Salem, N.H.: Ayer Publishers, 1984) 183–200; Ray A. Billington, "The Burning of the Charlestown Convent," *New England Quarterly* 10 (June, 1937): 4–24; John Talbot Smith, *The Catholic Church in New York* (New York: Hall and Locke, 1905), 139.

34. Ewens, *The Role of the Nun*, 157–58.

35. Ray Allen Billington, "Introduction: The *Awful Disclosures* in Historical Perspective," in Monk, *Awful Disclosures*, passim. Billington calls the book "the most influential single work of anti-Catholic propaganda in America's history." Monk herself met with a bitter end after being exposed as a fraud. She died in a prison on Blackwell's Island after being arrested for picking pockets at a brothel in the Five Points District. Billington, *The Protestant Crusade*, 99–108; Ray A. Billington, "Maria Monk and Her Influence," *Catholic Historical Review* 22 (Oct., 1936): 283–96; Smith, *The Catholic Church in New York*, 1: 132–39; Nancy Lusignan Schultz, *Fire and Roses: The Burning of the Charlestown Convent, 1834* (Boston: Northeastern University Press, 2000).

36. Ewens, *The Role of the Nun*, 164–65, 145–96.

37. Gerda Lerner, *The Grimké Sisters from South Carolina: Rebels against Slavery* (Boston: Houghton Mifflin, 1967); Ellen Carol DuBois, *Feminism and Suffrage: The Emergence of an Independent Women's Movement in America, 1848–1869* (Ithaca: Cornell University Press, 1978); Aileen Kraditor, *The Ideas of the Woman Suffrage Movement, 1890–1920* (New York: Columbia University Press, 1965); Nancy Hewitt, *Women's Activism and Social Change in Rochester, New York, 1822–1872* (Ithaca: Cornell University Press, 1984).

38. On how much, or little, marriage law changed over the course of the century, even after passage of the Married Women's Property Acts, see Joan Hoff, *Law, Gender and Injustice: A Legal History of U.S. Women* (New York: New York University, 1991), 121–24; Michael Grossberg, *Governing the Hearth: Law and the Family in Nineteenth-Century America* (Chapel Hill: University of North Carolina Press, 1985); and Nancy F. Cott, "Giving Character to Our Whole Polity: Marriage and the Public Order in the Late Nineteenth Century," in *U.S. History as Women's History: New Feminist Essays*, edited by Linda Kerber et al. (Chapel Hill: The University of North Carolina Press, 1995), 107–21.

39. John Francis Richmond, *New York and Its Institutions, 1609–1871* (New York: E. B. Treat, 1871), 346.

40. Applications for the Sisters of Mercy of New York, Archives of the Sisters of Mercy, Dobbs Ferry, N.Y. (hereafter ASMNY).

41. See, for instance, a very strong work explicating Catholic women's victimization: Uta Ranke-Heinemann, *Eunuchs for the Kingdom of Heaven: Women, Sexuality, and the Catholic Church* (New York: Doubleday, 1990).

42. Rosemary Ruether, "Mothers of the Church: Ascetic Women in the Late Patristic Age," in *Women of Spirit: Female Leadership in the Jewish and Christian Traditions*, edited by Rosemary Ruether and Eleanor McLaughlin (New York: Simon and Schuster, 1979), 72.

43. Ruether, "Mothers of the Church." Conversions from Quakerism and Scotch Presbyterianism occurred in 1857 and 1859, respectively (ASMNY).

44. "Notes from the Annals of St. Catherine's Convent of Mercy" and "Foundation," both ASMNY.

45. "Applications for Admittance," ASMNY.

46. Ibid.

47. Reprinted in Carroll, *Leaves from the Annals*, 3: 148.

48. K. H. Connell, *The Population of Ireland, 1750–1845* (New York: Oxford University Press, 1950); Robert Kennedy, *The Irish: Emigration, Marriage and Fertility* (Berkeley: University of California Press, 1973); C. M. Arensberg and S. T. Kimball, *Family and Community in Ireland*, 2d ed. (Cambridge: Harvard University Press, 1968); Diner, *Erin's Daughters in America*, 6–7.

49. See also Janet Nolan, *Ourselves Alone: Women's Emigration from Ireland, 1885–1920* (Lexington: University Press of Kentucky, 1989).

50. J. J. Lee, "Women and the Church since the Famine," in *Women in Irish Society: The Historical Dimension*, edited by Margaret MacCurtain and Donncha Ó Corráin (Westport: Greenwood Press, 1979), 37–45; Kennedy, *The Irish*, 72–73; K. H. Connell, "Peasant Marriage in Ireland after the Great Famine, *Past and Present* 12 (1957): 76–91; Diner, *Erin's Daughters*, 7–29.

51. Miller, *Emigrants and Exiles*, 346. In 1840 there was only one priest for every three thousand Catholics in Ireland; in 1860, one for every 1,500; and by 1900 there was one priest for every nine hundred. David W. Miller, "Irish Catholicism and the Great Famine," *Journal of Social History* 9 (1975): 81–98; Emmet Larkin, "The Devotional Revolution in Ireland," *American Historical Review* 77 (June 1972): 627, 649, 651, 625–52.

52. Whether, or to what degree, the famine represented a culmination of economic patterns evident in the pre-famine era or a radical break from those patterns is still a matter of lively debate among historians of Ireland. See, for example, S. J. Connolly, "'A Nation of Beggars'? Priests, People and Politics in Famine Ireland, 1846–52," *Victorian Studies* 39 (Winter 1996): 205.

53. Some argue that this is still the case in Ireland. See, for instance, Jenny Beale, *Women in Ireland: Voices of Change* (Bloomington: Indiana University Press, 1987), 85–105, passim.

54. I emphasize "extant" and "accessible" because to say that no evidence to which I had access proved the existence of lesbian relationships in convents in no sense proves or implies that none existed. Rosemary Curb and Nancy Manahan, eds., *Lesbian Nuns: Breaking Silence* (Talahassee: Naiad Press, 1985); John Boswell, *Christianity, Social Tolerance and Homosexuality: Gay People in Western Europe from the Beginning of the Christian Era to the Fourteenth Century* (Chicago: University of Chicago Press, 1980); Bernadette J. Brooten, *Love betweeen Women: Early Christian Responses to Female Homoeroticism* (Chicago: University of Chicago Press, 1996).

55. Sister Philippa to Archbishop Michael Corrigan, Dec. 3, 1885, C-10, Archives of the Archdiocese of New York (hereafter AANY).

56. "Notes from the Annals of St. Catherine's Convent of Mercy," passim, ASMNY.

57. Sister Philippa to Archbishop Michael Corrigan, Dec. 3, 1885, C-10, AANY.

58. Carroll, *Leaves from the Annals,* 3: 150; "Notes from the Annals of St. Catherine's Convent of Mercy," ASMNY.

59. Sister Marie De Lourdes Walsh, *The Sisters of Charity of New York, 1809–1959,* 3 vols. (New York: Fordham University Press, 1960), 3: 64–88.

60. Carroll, *Leaves from the Annals,* 3: 220.

61. Magray, *The Transforming Power of the Nuns,* 36–37.

62. Hoff, *Law, Gender and Injustice,* 87–90.

63. Catherine E. Beecher to Sarah Buckingham Beecher, Aug. 20, 1843, reprinted in *The Limits of Sisterhood: The Beecher Sisters on Women's Rights and Woman's Sphere,* edited by Jeanne Boydston, Mary Kelley, and Anne Margolis (Chapel Hill: University of North Carolina Press, 1988), 239–40. Thanks to Jeanne Boydston for mentioning this citation.

64. Boydston, Kelly, and Margolis, eds., *The Limits of Sisterhood,* 110.

65. Walsh, *The Sisters of Charity of New York,* 1: 140–41, 1: 150, 1: 154. On recruitments through select schools, see "Notes from the Annals of St. Catherine's Convent of Mercy," ASMNY. For examples of women entering after having lived in charitable institutions, see Walsh, *The Sisters of Charity of New York,* 3: 26, 3: 49, 3: 14–16, 3: 218.

66. Sister Mary Madeline Tobin to Archbishop John Hughes, May 15, 1862, A-16, AANY.

67. Sister Mary of St. Patrick to Archbishop Michael Corrigan, Feb. 12, 1889, C-21, AANY.

68. "Notes from the Annals of St. Catherine's Convent of Mercy," 1867, ASMNY.

69. Ibid., 1850, 1851, 1852, 1888, all ASMNY. On class in Irish convents, see Caitriona Clear, "Walls within Walls: Nuns in Nineteenth Century Ireland," in *Gender in Irish Society,* edited by Chris Curtin, Pauline Jackson, and Barbara O'Connor (Galway: Galway University Press, 1987), 134–49.

70. Magray, *The Transforming Power of the Nuns,* 42–44.

71. "Notes from the Annals of St. Catherine's Convent of Mercy," 1883, ASMNY.

72. "Notes from the Annals of St. Catherine's Convent of Mercy," 1878, ASMNY; *Acts of Chapter, St. Catherine Convent, Madison Avenue, New York,* ASMNY.

73. "Work Schedules," ASMNY.

74. Elaine Pagels, *Adam, Eve, and the Serpent* (New York: Random House, 1988), 78.

75. *Annals of the Sisters of Mercy,* 1857, ASMNY.

76. Carroll, *Leaves from the Annals,* 171–72.

77. Ewens, *The Role of the Nun,* 135.

78. Ibid., 46–47. The constitution further allowed for flexibility by stating explicitly that "[t]here will be adopted such modifications in the Rules as the difference of country, habits, customs, and manners may require." "Constitution of the Sisters of Charity in the United States of America," reprinted in Walsh, *The Sisters of Charity of New York,* 1: 19. The importance of the problem of financing, moreover, becomes clear when we consider that the most common alternative to running an academy was the use of slave labor. The Sisters of Charity were

one of only eight Catholic women's religious orders to survive through the early nineteenth century and the only one that did not depend on slave labor to bring in a profit for use by the convent (Ewens, *The Role of the Nun*, 68). The other seven orders that survived and used slave labor to do so are the Carmelites, Loretto Sisters, Visitandines, Nazareth Sister of Charity, Dominicans, Sacred Heart nuns, and New Orleans Ursulines.

79. Walsh, *The Sisters of Charity of New York*, 1: 59, 1: 62–63.

80. Sister Mary Madeline Tobin to Archbishop John Hughes, May 15, 1862, A-16, AANY.

81. "Notes from the Annals of St. Catherine's Convent of Mercy," 1890, ASMNY.

82. Sister M. Dolorita to Archbishop Michael Corrigan, "Corpus Christi," undated, C-26, AANY.

83. The election of community officers was democratic although limited only to those who had made their final vows, thereby eliminating novices and postulants from elections that took place at "chapter" meetings. Officers were usually elected every three years by a majority vote of vowed sisters in the order. As in many other women's orders, moreover, a woman could remain mother superior for only two terms. She then still held the title *mother* but retained none of its formal authority. For the range of elective practices by convents in the United States, see Ewens, *The Role of the Nun*, passim. See also Elizabeth Kolmer, "Women Religious in the United States: A Survey of Recent Literature," *U.S. Catholic Historian* 10, nos. 1–2 (1992): 87–92.

84. How local hierarchies were replicated differed for specific orders. In some, a mother superior and possibly an assistant mother, bursar, and mistress of novices would be elected by all professed nuns of the local order, or they would be appointed to the positions by their superiors in the order and would have authority over their local convent. In others, head sisters or sisters superior would run specific institutions, but entire hierarchies were not replicated.

85. For the Sisters of Mercy and the Sisters of Charity, a majority of professed sisters' support in the chapter meeting was necessary for the convent's officers to assume leadership. See, for instance, E. McCabe, Bishop of Dublin, Sisters of Mercy, to Archbishop Michael Corrigan, Feb. 14, 1881, AANY.

86. "Notes from the Annals of St. Catherine's Convent of Mercy," 1867, ASMNY.

87. "Notes from the Annals of St. Catherine's Convent of Mercy," 1851, 1855, 1856, 1863, 1865, ASMNY.

88. "Notes from the Annals of St. Catherine's Convent of Mercy," 1864, ASMNY; Francis McNeirny, Bishop of Albany, to Archbishop Michael Corrigan, April 20, 1888, C-16, AANY.

89. John Mullaly to Archbishop McCloskey, May 4, 1876, A-28, AANY.

90. Mother Mary Augustine McKenna to other Sisters of Mercy, 1873, reprinted in Carroll, *Leaves from the Annals*, 215.

91. Ibid., 209.

92. Ibid.

93. The notable exceptions to this rule were women who became nuns after they converted from Protestantism. Among those most visible in public contestations, and deemed "feminist" by historians, were figures such as Mary Francis Cusack, an upper-middle-class convert.

94. Sister Francis Cecilia Conway, "Notes on Foundling," Archives of the Sisters of Charity of New York at Mount St. Vincent. Sister Francis Conway worked with Sister Irene at the Foundling from 1890 to 1896.

95. Officially termed the Public School Society, the early public school system was developed from what had been a Quaker school in the early century. "The Act Incorporating the Public School Society, April 9, 1805," in Robert H. Bremmer, *Children and Youth in America: A Documentary History* (Cambridge: Harvard University Press, 1970), 1: 255–56.

96. *Twenty-seventh Annual Report of the Trustees of the Public School Society of New York* (New York, 1832), 14–16, reprinted in Bremmer, *Children and Youth in America*, 1: 260.

97. Ibid.

98. Joseph J. McCadden, "Bishop Hughes versus the Public School Society of New York," *Catholic Historical Review* 50 (1964): 188, 189, 193, reprinted from William Oland Bourne, *History of the Public School Society of the City of New York* (New York: W. Wood, 1870), 180–86; Carl F. Kaestle, *The Evolution of an Urban School System: New York City, 1750–1850* (Cambridge: Harvard University Press, 1973), 145–48. Governor William H. Seward's message to the New York State Legislature, 1842, reprinted in Bremmer, *Children and Youth in America,* 1: 464.

99. Diane Ravitch, *The Great School Wars: New York City, 1805–1973* (New York: Basic Books, 1974), 51–52.

100. Stanley Nadel, *Little Germany: Ethnicity, Religion and Class in New York City, 1845–1880* (Urbana: University of Illinois Press, 1990); Miller, *Emigrants and Exiles*, 26–101, 193–279.

101. *Twenty-seventh Annual Report of the Trustees of the Public School Society of New York*, 14–16, reprinted in Bremmer, *Children and Youth in America,* 1: 260.

102. Miller, *Emigrants and Exiles*, 76.

103. McCadden, "Bishop Hughes," 193.

104. Ravitch, *The Great School Wars*, 46–50.

105. John Hughes to Unnamed Bishop, New York, Aug. 27, 1840, photostat in the Brown Collection, AANY, reprinted in McCadden, "Bishop Hughes," 195.

106. Dolan, *The Immigrant Church*, 108. By 1844 Bible reading was excluded from thirty-one schools in the city. Billington, *The Protestant Crusade*, 155.

107. "Dr. Cummings of St. Stephen's started a school in the basement of his new church, found it practically impossible to meet expenses, and solemnly marched his children to the nearest public school, where he had made arrangements for their admission; greatly to the disgust and indignation of his bishop [Hughes], with whom he lost favor entirely." Smith, *The Catholic Church in New York*, 1: 187.

108. Dolan, *The Immigrant Church*, 111, 105–6. Jay Dolan estimates the Catholic school population at twelve thousand. Between 1840 and 1850 fifty-six new Catholic secondary schools for girls were opened in New York City; by 1866 there were in addition sixty secondary schools for boys. A Catholic internal report estimated that approximately twenty thousand pupils were reached in the forty-four parochial schools and twenty large "school houses" in 1866 ("Parochial Schools, Asylums, Hospitals, circa 1866," A-29, AANY). The percentage of Catholic children educated in New York Catholic schools in 1867 rested somewhere between

17 percent and 33 percent of the Catholic school-age population. See also Selma Berrol, "Who Went to School in Mid-Nineteenth Century New York? An Essay in the New Urban History," in *Essays in the History of New York City: A Memorial to Sidney Pomerantz,* edited by Irwin Yellowitz (Port Washington: Kennikat Press, 1978), 43–60.

109. Walsh, *The Sisters of Charity of New York,* 1: 102–3, 112–14.

110. Joseph B. Code, "Bishop John Hughes and the Sisters of Charity," *Miscellenea Historica* (1949): 6. Code reprints most of the varied correspondence relating to this controversy but with little comment.

111. Father Deluol to Bishop Hughes, June 17, 1846, reprinted in John Hassard, *Life of the Most Reverend John Hughes, D.D., First Archbishop of New York* (New York: D. Appleton, 1866), 291–93.

112. In the negotiations prior to accepting the management of the half orphan asylum in New York, the Sisters of Charity had objected that caring for both boys and girls in the institution was inconsistent with their rule. Yet in the end, and with no other sisterhood to do the work, they agreed to care for both sexes and ignore their rule on this point. Walsh, *The Sisters of Charity of New York,* 1: 81–83; Ewens, *The Role of the Nun,* 125–26.

113. Father Deluol to Bishop Hughes, June 17, 1846, reprinted in Hassard, *Life of the Most Reverend John Hughes,* 291–93.

114. Code, "Bishop John Hughes," 7, 9–10; Father Deluol to Bishop Hughes, June 17, 1846.

115. Hassard, *Life of the Most Reverend John Hughes,* 290–92.

116. Ibid., 291–93, 294; Walsh, *The Sisters of Charity of New York,* 1: 134, 1: 121.

117. Nicholas O'Donnell to Mother Etienne Hall, Brooklyn, Aug. 28, 1846, in Code, "Bishop John Hughes," 32–33.

118. Louis Regis Deluol to John Hughes, Emmitsburg, June 26, 1846, in Code, "Bishop John Hughes," 26.

119. John Hughes to Louis Regis Deluol, New York, June 20, 1846, in Hassard, *Life of the Most Reverend John Hughes,* 294–96.

120. John Hughes to Mother Etienne Hall, New York, Aug. 1, 1846, in Code, "Bishop John Hughes," 30.

121. Mother Etienne to John Hughes, Emmitsburg, Aug. 3, 1846, in Hassard, *Life of the Most Reverend John Hughes,* 298–99.

122. John Hughes to Sister Rosalia Green [Visitatrix], New York, Aug. 24, 1846, in Hassard, *Life of the Most Reverend John Hughes,* 299–300.

123. John Hughes to Samuel Eccleston, New York, Oct. 20, 1846, in Code, "Bishop John Hughes," 36.

124. Louis Regis Deluol to John Hughes, Baltimore, Dec. 4, 1846, in Code, "Bishop John Hughes," 39.

125. Code, "Bishop John Hughes," 33–40. Hughes negotiated with Archbishop Eccleston of Baltimore from September through November of 1846.

126. Walsh, *The Sisters of Charity of New York,* 1: 149.

127. Ibid., 1: 148–49.

128. George Ellington, *The Woman of New York; or, The Underworld of the Great City* (1869, repr. New York; Arno Press, 1972), 620.

129. Dolan, *The Immigrant Church,* 111, 105–6; Berrol, "Who Went to School?" 43–60.

130. The Sisters of Charity of Emmitsburg took steps immediately to fully affiliate with the Daughters of Charity in France in order to avert further splits in the order. In Cincinnati, however, seven sisters refused to affiliate and formed their own community under direction of the city's bishop. Ewens, *The Role of the Nun*, 129.

131. The Nazareth Sisters of Charity in Nashville, for instance, were urged to separate into a new diocesan community under the bishop's control after a priest complained about Nazareth motherhouse's decision to withdraw sisters from his church choir without his consent. Ibid., 129.

132. Ibid., 130.

133. "Notes from the Annals of St. Catherine's Convent of Mercy," 1873, ASMNY. Try as they might, Sisters of Mercy were not united nationally until 1929.

134. Robert Emmett Curran, *Michael Augustine Corrigan and the Shaping of Conservative Catholicism in America, 1878–1902* (New York: Arno Press, 1978).

135. Ewens, *The Role of the Nun*, 253.

Chapter 2: Good Girls, Bad Girls, and the Great Hunger, 1845–70

The quotation in the epigraph is from "Thoughts for the Women of the Times," *Catholic World* 14 (1871–72): 470–71.

1. Kerby Miller, *Emigrants and Exiles: Ireland and the Irish Exodus to North America* (New York: Oxford University Press, 1985), 294–98 and appendix tables 3–10, 573–80.

2. Hasia Diner's thesis on the contours of an Irish Catholic sex/gender system in America has been a starting point for my research on nuns and single women in New York City. Yet while I agree with her thesis on most points, I disagree with Diner's assumption that "Irish women rarely crossed the line when it came to sexual deviance. . . . In Ireland, illegitimacy was virtually unknown, and prostitution extremely rare." Diner, *Erin's Daughters in America: Irish Immigrant Women in the Nineteenth Century* (Baltimore: Johns Hopkins University Press, 1983), 136–37. See also Janet Nolan, *Ourselves Alone: Women's Emigration from Ireland, 1885–1920* (Lexington: University Press of Kentucky, 1989). On American and British single women, see Joanne Meyerowitz, *Women Adrift: Independent Wage Earners in Chicago, 1880–1930* (Chicago: University of Chicago Press, 1988), xviii; and Martha Vicinus, *Independent Women: Work and Community for Single Women, 1850–1920* (Chicago: University of Chicago Press, 1985).

3. Carol Groneman Pernicone, "'The Bloody Ould Sixth': A Social Analysis of a New York City Working-Class Community in the Mid-Nineteenth Century," Ph.D. diss., University of Rochester, 1973, 12; Diner, *Erin's Daughters*, 31.

4. Numbers from Miller, *Emigrants and Exiles*, 582, appendix, table 13. The total number of immigrants from Connaught from 1851 to 1910 was 701,572, with 371,917 of them women.

5. Mary Cullen estimates that married women regularly contributed from 15 to 25 percent of a family's cash earnings when the husband was fully employed off the farm and 35 percent when the husband's employment was irregular. Cullen, "Breadwinner and Providers: Women in the Household Economy of Labour-

ing Families 1835–6," in *Women Surviving,* edited by Maria Luddy and Cliona Murphy (Dublin: Poolbeg Press, 1989), 99.

6. John Francis Maguire, *The Irish in America* (1868, repr. New York: Arno Press and the New York Times, 1969), 208.

7. Pernicone, "'The Bloody Ould Sixth,'" 145–47; Alan L. Olmstead, *New York City Banks, 1819–1861* (Chapel Hill: University of North Carolina Press, 1976), 51. Christine Stansell has concluded that female servants were "the only women workers who saved money" in antebellum New York. Stansell, *City of Women: Sex and Class in New York* (Urbana: University of Illinois Press, 1987), 157.

8. Robert Ernst, *Immigrant Life in New York City, 1825–1863* (New York: Columbia University Press, 1949), 66.

9. Ernst, *Immigrant Life,* 219; Stansell, *City of Women,* 156–57.

10. Pernicone, "'The Bloody Ould Sixth,'" 166.

11. Carol Groneman, "Working-Class Immigrant Women in Mid-Nineteenth-Century New York: The Irish Woman's Experience," *Journal of Urban History* 4 (May 1978): 260.

12. *New York Times,* Nov. 10, 1853. For an extended discussion of sewing women in New York City through the antebellum period, see Stansell, *City of Women,* 105–29.

13. The New York Association for Improving the Condition of the Poor (AICP), the premier private charity in the city, claimed to provide outdoor relief primarily for Irish male laborers and Irish washerwomen and sewers. Sewing women were so poor through the winter of 1857 that the AICP provided support for a third of all women in the city claiming to support themselves by the needle. *Fifteenth Annual Report of the Association for Improving the Condition of the Poor,* 1858, 36–37; *New York Daily Tribune,* June 8, 1853; Stansell, *City of Women,* 111.

14. Ernst, *Immigrant Life,* appendix 1, 185–214, 69–76, passim.

15. Diner, *Erin's Daughters,* 71.

16. On services for women in Ireland, see Maria Luddy, "Women and Philanthropy in Nineteenth-Century Ireland," Ph.D. diss., University College, Cork, 1989, passim; and "Notes from the Annals of St. Catherine's Convent of Mercy" and "Foundation," both in the Archives of the Sisters of Mercy, Dobbs Ferry, N.Y. (hereafter ASMNY).

17. The monetary support the church gave to the project would, in Hughes's words, constitute a "shield to protect the purity and innocence of the poor, virtuous, and destitute daughters of Ireland arriving in this city, toward whom as far as their means will allow, the Sisters of Mercy fulfill the office of guiding and guardian angels in every respect." Archbishop John Hughes to Robert Emmet, Nov. 1848, in John Hassard, *Life of the Most Reverend John Hughes, D.D., First Archbishop of New York* (New York: D. Appleton, 1866), 309.

18. "Notes from the Annals of St. Catherine's Convent of Mercy" and "Foundation," ASMNY.

19. Archbishop John Hughes to Miss Harriet Lane, Nov. 23, 1859, A-4, Archives of the Archdiocese of New York (hereafter AANY); "History of the Sisters of Mercy in New York," Nov. 1850, A-16, AANY.

20. Archbishop John Hughes to Miss Harriet Lane, Nov. 23, 1859, A-4, AANY.

21. Helen Sweeney, *The Golden Milestone: 1846–1896* (New York: Benzinger Bros., 1896), 20.

22. Miller, *Emigrants and Exiles*, 300, 199–200, 295–96.

23. "Notes from the Annals of St. Catherine's Convent of Mercy," 1858, ASMNY. Devotional prayer groups were particularly popular among Irish Catholic women; a majority (more than 60 percent) of the total sodalities organized in nineteenth-century America were exclusively for women, whereas fewer than one-quarter were exclusively male. Ann Taves, *The Household of Faith: Roman Catholic Devotions in Mid-Nineteenth-Century America* (Notre Dame: University of Notre Dame Press, 1986), 18, see also table 5.

24. "History of the Sisters of Mercy in New York," Nov. 1850, A-16, AANY.

25. J. R. Bayley, *History of the Catholic Church, New York* (New York: Catholic Publication Society, 1870), 135–36.

26. Archbishop John Hughes to Miss Harriet Lane, Nov. 23, 1859, A-4, AANY.

27. Henry J. Common and Hugh N. Camp, *The Charities of New York, Brooklyn and Staten Island* (New York: Hurd and Houghton, 1868), 501.

28. Faye E. Dudden, *Serving Women: Household Service in Nineteenth-Century America* (Middletown: Wesleyan University Press, 1983), 65–71.

29. George Ellington, *The Woman of New York; or, The Underworld of the Great City* (1869, repr. New York; Arno Press, 1972), 621.

30. Ellington, *The Woman of New York;* "Notes from the Annals of St. Catherine's Convent of Mercy," 1847–60, ASMNY.

31. [Mother Mary Teresa] Austin Carroll, *Leaves from the Annals of the Sisters of Mercy* (New York: Catholic Publication Society, 1889), 3: 151.

32. Carroll, *Leaves from the Annals*, 3: 151.

33. "Notes from the Annals of St. Catherine's Convent of Mercy," 1847–60, ASMNY; *Freeman's Journal*, Nov. 5, 1859, 5.

34. Carroll, *Leaves from the Annals*, 3: 175.

35. Ibid., 3: 172–75.

36. Warnings against the "seduction" by wealthier men who would be reluctant to marry poor women are prominent throughout the prescriptive literature. See, for instance, Mary Sadlier, *Bessy Conway; or, The Irish Girl in America* (New York: D. and J. Sadlier, 1863), 138.

37. Carroll, *Leaves from the Annals*, 3: 179.

38. Ibid., 3: 179.

39. Ibid.

40. Maguire, *The Irish in America*, 314–15.

41. Ibid., 315.

42. Ibid., 319.

43. Ibid., 319–20.

44. George Deshon, *Guide for Catholic Young Women, Especially for Those Who Earn Their Own Living* (New York: Catholic Book Exchange, 1897), 249; Maguire, *The Irish in America*, 338.

45. "Reverend Father Preston as Chaplain to the Convent of the Sisters of Mercy," in Archives of the Sisters of the Divine Compassion, White Plains, N.Y. (hereafter ASDC).

46. "Reverend Father Preston as Chaplain to the Convent of the Sisters of Mercy," ASDC.

47. "Applications for Admission to the Convent of Mercy," 1848, ASMNY.

48. Sadlier, *Bessy Conway*, 262.

49. Ibid., 263.

50. Deshon, *Guide for Catholic Young Women*, 271.

51. The spelling is Sadlier's (*Bessy Conway*, 273).

52. Deshon, *Guide for Catholic Young Women*, 300.

53. "Thoughts for the Women of the Times," *Catholic World* 14 (1871–72): 470–71.

54. "The Right Training of Women," *Freeman's Journal*, Aug. 27, 1859, 5.

55. Deshon, *Guide for Catholic Young Women*, 282.

56. In his study of Transfiguration Parish, Jay Dolan has argued that the death rate of the Irish in the 1850s was twice that of the Germans in the parish. Among the residents of "Sweeney's Shambles" in the Sixth Ward, one-fifth of all the adults died in thirty-two months. Jay Dolan, *The Immigrant Church: New York's Irish and German Catholics, 1815–1865* (Baltimore: Johns Hopkins University Press, 1975), 39; Stansell, *City of Women*, 199; Pernicone, "'The Bloody Ould Sixth,'" 59; Miller, *Emigrants and Exiles*, 319, 506.

57. The majority (59 percent) of laboring Irish worked in occupations that had always been unskilled—carting, day labor, and seasonal farm labor for men and domestic service for women. Another 26.2 percent worked in occupations that had recently been proletarianized into unskilled factory work (the sewing trades, printing, and hat making). Comparing the class structure of German-born and Irish-born workers in New York City, Germans—and, of course, native-born—workers were more likely to be artisans or proprietors than the Irish. Although a majority (63.6 percent) of German workers were employed in positions for the unskilled in 1855, those positions had been, for the most part, recently de-skilled from artisanal crafts. Amy Bridges, "Becoming American: The Working Classes in the United States before the Civil War," in *Working-Class Formation: Nineteenth-Century Patterns in Western Europe and the United States*, edited by Ira Katznelson and Aristide R. Zolberg (Princeton: Princeton University Press, 1986), 157–96, see especially 172, table 5.1. See also Ernst, *Immigrant Life*, appendix 1, 185–214, 69–76, passim; and Pericone, "'The Bloody Ould Sixth,'" 8, 101–2.

58. In her study of the Sixth Ward census of 1855, Carol Groneman found that at least 44 percent of Irish women in the ward worked; moreover, 35 percent of Irish women over forty were also wage-earners, although percentages decreased with age. Carol Groneman, "'She Earns as a Child—She Pays as a Man': Women Workers in a Mid-Nineteenth-Century New York City Community," in *Immigrants in Industrial America*, edited by Robert Ehrlich (Charlottesville: University Press of Virginia for the Eleuthenian Mills-Hagley Foundation and Balch Institute, 1977), 35.

59. Numbers taken from "Population," in U.S. Census Bureau, *Eighth Census of the United States* (Washington: U.S. Census Bureau, 1860), 609.

60. Sadlier, *Bessy Conway*, 282–83.

61. Ibid., 225–26.

62. Ibid., 135–36, 162–64.

63. Ibid., 227.

64. Deshon, *Guide for Catholic Young Women*, 14–15.

65. *Annual Report of the Governors of the Almshouse* (New York: George F. Nesbitt, 1849–59); *Annual Report of the Commissioners of Public Charity and Correction of the City of New York*, 1860–90. The city department overseeing public charities changed its name three times in the nineteenth century, from

Governors of the Almshouse, Commissioners of Public Charities and Correction (1860–96) to Department of Public Charities (1896–1936). Annual reports were found at New York City's Municipal Library.

66. *Second Annual Report of the Commissioners of Public Charities and Correction of the City of New York*, 1860, 122–27.

67. Ibid.; Deshon, *Guide for Catholic Young Women*, 203–4.

68. Timothy Gilfoyle, *City of Eros: New York City, Prostitution, and the Commercialization of Sex, 1790–1920* (New York: W. W. Norton, 1992), 61; William Sanger, *The History of Prostitution: Its Extent, Causes, and Effects throughout the World* (New York: Harper, 1859).

69. Barbara Hobson, *Uneasy Virtue: The Politics of Prostitution and the American Reform Tradition* (Chicago: University of Chicago Press, 1990), 35. As Marilynn Wood Hill points out, it is difficult to assess exactly what proportion of all prostitutes were Irish, yet she perhaps underestimates Irish women's participation when relying on census estimates. Their exclusion from brothels and relegation to streetwalking makes census estimates necessarily unreflective of Irish prostitutes' experience. For a larger discussion of the varying estimates of racial and ethnic breakdowns, see Marilynn Wood Hill, *Their Sisters' Keepers: Prostitution in New York City, 1830–1870* (Berkeley: University of California Press, 1993), 52–58; see also Gilfoyle, *City of Eros*, 61–62.

70. K. H. Connell, "Illegitimacy before the Famine," in Connell, *Irish Peasant Society: Four Historical Essays* (New York: Oxford University Press, 1968), 51–86.

71. Michel Foucault, *Discipline and Punish: The Birth of the Prison* (New York: Vintage, 1995).

72. "And even Irish Catholics . . . seem generally to have been immune to the conception of irredeemable female transgression," Stansell asserts, "(perhaps because the American church had not yet embarked on the surveillance of sexual mores for which it later became so well known)." Stansell, *City of Women*, 180.

73. Deshon, *Guide for Catholic Young Women*, 232.

74. Maria Luddy, "Prostitution and Rescue Work in Nineteenth-Century Ireland," in *Women Surviving*, edited by Maria Luddy and Cliona Murphy (Dublin: Poolbeg Press, 1990), 51, 51–84.

75. Sadlier, *Bessy Conway*, passim.

76. As Hughes wrote in 1848, "The *men* of Ireland, on their own soil, had rendered the protection of a shield unnecessary. This unhappily is not the case of the women of Ireland arriving in this city, young, pure, innocent, unacquainted with the snares of the world, and the dangers to which poverty and inexperience would expose them in a foreign land." Archbishop John Hughes to Robert Emmet, Nov. 1848, reprinted in Hassard, *Life of the Most Reverend John Hughes*, 309.

77. Maguire, *The Irish in America*, 181–82, 212–13, 339–40.

78. Ibid., 341–42.

79. Ibid., 342.

80. Gilfoyle, *City of Eros*, 68–69.

81. Hill, *Their Sisters' Keepers*, 86–89.

82. Gilfoyle, *City of Eros*, 62–64.

83. Lori D. Ginzberg, "'Moral Suasion Is Moral Balderdash': Women, Politics, and Social Activism in the 1850s," *Journal of American History* 73, no. 3 (1986): 601–22.

84. Carroll Smith-Rosenberg, "Beauty, the Beast, and the Militant Woman: Sex Roles and Sexual Standards in Jacksonian America," *American Quarterly* 23 (Fall 1971): 562–84.

85. *Five Points Monthly Record* (New York, 1854), 113–16, reprinted in Robert H. Bremner, *Children and Youth in America: A Documentary History*, 2 vols. (Cambridge: Harvard University Press, 1970), 1: 421–23.

86. *Twenty-third Annual Report of the Association for Improving the Condition of the Poor,* 1866, 37.

87. *Annual Report of the Association for Improving the Condition of the Poor,* 1852, 36, 1856, 26, and 1860, 50–51.

88. "Women's Protective Emigration Society," Archives of the New York Historical Society.

89. Data about foreign-born nativity became available in 1860 when just over thirty-nine thousand were committed to the Tombs. *Annual Report of the Commissioners of Public Charities and Correction of the City of New York,* 1860, 73–75, 1865, 4–7, 12, and 1870, 323–24, 329. German women accounted for 7 percent, and native-born women represented 15 percent, of the female prison population. "Population," in *Eighth Census of the United States,* 1860, 609, cited in Ernst, *Immigrant Life,* 198. Figures on native-born black women in the city prison population are unavailable for 1860, but in 1850, 1855, and 1865, black, native-born women accounted for 8 percent, 4 percent, and 3 percent, respectively, of the city prison's female inmates. I would assume that their proportion in reference to their own community did not decrease but that the greater numbers of foreign-born women in the city grew at a higher rate. While the percentage of Irish-born women in the city's female prisons fell in 1865 and 1870 to 59 percent and 49 percent, the native-born female prison population grew in tandem. It seems reasonable to conclude that many who were counted as native-born in 1870 had Irish-born parents. *Annual Report of the Commissioners of Public Charities and Correction of the City of New York,* 1860, 73–75, 1865, 4–7, 12, and 1870, 323–24, 329.

90. *Annual Report of the Commissioners of Public Charities and Correction of the City of New York,* 1860, 73–75, 1865, 4–7, 12, and 1870, 323–24, 329; see also *Annual Report of the Police Magistrates Courts of the City of New York,* 1875–1900. Whereas the city penitentiary for women remained small through the antebellum period, incarcerating only a few hundred women each year, the city prison and workhouse expanded to accommodate more than thirty-six thousand people annually by 1855, a third of whom were women. *Second Annual Report of the Governors of the Almshouse,* 1850, 50–53; *Seventh Annual Report of the Governors of the Almshouse,* 1855, 80–81.

91. *Annual Report of the Police Magistrates Courts of the City of New York,* 1874, 16–17.

92. Gilfoyle, *City of Eros,* 164.

93. Sanger, *The History of Prostitution,* 559. Gilfoyle, *City of Eros,* 164–67, 62.

94. Deshon, *Guide for Catholic Young Women,* 203–4.

95. Ibid., 230, 229.

96. Mother M. Magdalene Clover, "Narration of the Opening of the New York House," Archives of the Sisters of the Good Shepherd, Jamaica, Queens, N.Y. (hereafter ASGS).

97. Archbishop John Hughes, pastoral of 1854, reprinted in *The Complete Works of the Most Rev. John Hughes, D.D.,* compiled by Lawrence Kehoe (New York: Published for the compiler, 1865), 2: 727.

98. The first Good Shepherd Convent in New York was started at Fourteenth Street in a house rented by Mrs. Ripley for $1,000 per year. Katherine Conway, *In the Footprints of the Good Shepherd: New York, 1857–1907* (New York: Convent of the Good Shepherd, 1907), 73.

99. Sister Mary Magdalene to Archbishop Hughes, Good Shepherd Convent, New York, Feb. 12, 1859, AANY.

100. Mother Mary Magdalene Clover, "Narration of the Opening of the New York House," ASGS.

101. On descriptions of life and reformation within the House of the Good Shepherd, see Conway, *In the Footprints of the Good Shepherd,* passim; Ellington, *The Women of New York,* 623–33.

102. Conway, *In the Footprints of the Good Shepherd,* 73.

103. Sanger, *The History of Prostitution,* passim.

104. Sisters of the Good Shepherd, New York Convent, to Motherhouse, Angiers, France, Dec. 20, 1867, ASGS.

105. Conway, *In the Footprints of the Good Shepherd,* 3.

106. Archbishop John Hughes to Levi S. Ives, June 19, 1863, Archives of the Sisters of Charity of New York at Mount St. Vincent (hereafter AMSV).

107. Archbishop John Hughes to Levi S. Ives, June 11, 1863, A-4, AANY.

108. "Report of the Supervisor of the Bureau of Admissions and Discharges," *Fifteenth Annual Report of the New York Catholic Protectory,* 1878, 126.

109. Rev. Michael Nash S.J. to Archbishop Corrigan, Feb. 1, 1891, C-28, AANY.

Chapter 3: Placing-Out and Irish Catholic Cultural Reproduction, 1848–64

The quotations in the epigraphs are from Lucy Ellen Guernsey, *Irish Amy* (New York: American Sunday-School Union, 1853), 18–19, and John Francis Maguire, *The Irish in America* (1868, repr. New York: Arno Press and the New York Times, 1969), 519–20.

1. The first census to fully list nationalities among the population of New York City was the New York State Census of 1855. For total population growth for Manhattan, see Robert Ernst, *Immigrant Life in New York City, 1825–1863* (New York: Columbia University Press, 1949), 191 (on the percentage of the foreign-born in New York City see 193). For the percentage of African Americans in the city, see Carol Groneman Pernicone, "The 'Bloody Ould Sixth': A Social Analysis of a New York City Working-Class Community in the Mid-Nineteenth Century," Ph.D. diss., University of Rochester, 1973, 35.

2. Ernst, *Immigrant Life,* 29–35; Francis E. Lane, *American Charities and the Child of the Immigrant: A Study of Typical Child Caring Institutions in New York and Massachusetts between the Years 1845 and 1880* (Washington: Catholic University of America, 1932), 18–21.

3. Ernst, *Immigrant Life,* 129–34; Lane, *American Charities,* 18–19; George

Paul Jacoby, *Catholic Child Care in Nineteenth Century New York* (Washington: Catholic University of America, 1941), 21. On the city's long battle with the commissioners of emigration, see *Seventh Annual Report of the Commissioners of Public Charities and Correction of the City of New York*, 1865, xi–xix. The commissioners of emigration were the objects of constant criticism from immigrants and other reformers. Irish Democrat Mike Walsh voiced complaints about the vested interests of the commissioners' employment agency and the treatment of women "forcibly shoved out like dogs" for refusing the first offer of a job at low wages. Other reformers complained throughout the 1850s that the majority of those who relied on city and private charity were foreigners and therefore should be relieved by the commissioners and that the commissioners' failure to screen out pauper immigrants adequately would eventually destroy New York City's charitable systems. In fact, however, the resources available to the commissioners were completely inadequate to the task. The flood of impoverished immigrants into New York City could hardly be stemmed by a small commission. Immigrants and poverty would be a constant theme for the city's reformers throughout the century. The belief that one small group could take care of the problem adequately was abandoned by the mid-1850s. The federal government assumed regulatory jurisdiction over immigration and established a welfare fund to provide for immigrants after their arrival through the Immigration Law of 1882. John Higham, *Strangers in the Land: Patterns of Nativism, 1860–1925* (New York: Atheneum, 1978), 43–44.

4. David Rothman, *Discovery of the Asylum: Social Order and Disorder in the New Republic* (Boston: Little, Brown and Company, 1971), passim.

5. *Second Annual Report of the New York Association for Improving the Condition of the Poor*, 1845, 14–17 (1845–1938 available on microfilm at the New-York Historical Society).

6. *Annual Report of the New York Association for Improving the Condition of the Poor*, 1851, 18, 1858, 37, and 1860, 49–52.

7. *Seventeenth Annual Report of the New York Association for Improving the Condition of the Poor*, 1860, 51.

8. *Fifteenth Annual Report of the New York Association for Improving the Condition of the Poor*, 1858, 37.

9. New York City Almshouse Residents

	1850	1855	1860
Irish	1,464 (62%)	1,949 (63%)	2,524 (61%)
German	94 (4%)	148 (5%)	261 (6%)
Native-born	545 (23%)	773 (25%)	985 (24%)
Other	252 (11%)	226 (7%)	359 (9%)
Totals	2,355	3,096	4,129

Sources: *Second Annual Report of the Governors of the Almshouse*, 1850, 21; *Seventh Annual Report of the Governors of the Almshouse*, 1855, 1; *Second Annual Report of the Commissioners of Public Charities and Correction of the City of New York*, 1860, 12.

10. *Seventeenth Annual Report of the New York Association for Improving the Condition of the Poor*, 1860, 48.

11. Bellevue Hospital: Admissions

	1850	1855	1860
Irish	2,596 (70%)	4,242 (74%)	6,998 (66%)
German	175 (5%)	281 (5%)	823 (8%)
Native-born	647 (17%)	856 (15%)	1,925 (18%)
Other	310 (8%)	376 (6%)	805 (8%)
Totals	3,728	5,755	10,551

Sources: *Second Annual Report of the Governors of the Almshouse,* 1850, 29; *Seventh Annual Report of the Governors of the Almshouse,* 1855, 21; *Second Annual Report of the Commissioners of Public Charities and Correction of the City of New York,* 1860, 40.

Lunatic Asylum: Admissions

	1850	1855	1860
Irish	199 (51%)	178 (48%)	190 (47%)
German	51 (13%)	63 (17%)	83 (21%)
Native-born	97 (25%)	78 (21%)	85 (21%)
Other	44 (11%)	52 (14%)	43 (11%)
Totals	391	371	401

Sources: *Second Annual Report of the Governors of the Almshouse,* 1850, 91; *Seventh Annual Report of the Governors of the Almshouse,* 1855, 103; *Second Annual Report of the Commissioners of Public Charities and Correction of the City of New York,* 1860, 170.

12. Ernst, *Immigrant Life,* 56.

13. Robert Hartley, *Seventeenth Annual Report of the New York Association for Improving the Condition of the Poor,* 1860, 49, 51.

14. *Fifteenth Annual Report of the New York Association for Improving the Condition of the Poor,* 1858, 37.

15. *Eighth Annual Report of the New York Association for Improving the Condition of the Poor,* 1851, 18; see also *Seventh Annual Report of the New York Association for Improving the Condition of the Poor,* 1850, 23–25.

16. *Eighth Annual Report of the New York Association for Improving the Condition of the Poor,* 1851, 19.

17. Seth Koven and Sonya Michel, "Motherworlds," in *Mothers of a New World: Maternalist Politics and the Origins of Welfare States,* edited by Seth Koven and Sonya Michel (New York: Routledge, 1993), 2.

18. German women who supported the Nazis, for instance, used precisely the same linkage between their duties as mothers and citizens to emphasize their importance in cultural reproduction and thereby help legitimate eugenics policies and, ultimately, the Holocaust itself. Gisela Bock, "Equality and Difference in Nationalist Socialist Racism," in *Feminism and History,* edited by Joan Wallach Scott (New York: Oxford University Press, 1996), 267–90; Gisela Bock and Pat Thane, Introduction, in *Maternity and Gender Policies: Women and the Rise of the European Welfare States, 1880s–1950s,* edited by Gisela Bock and Pat Thane (New York: Routledge, 1991), 1–20; Gisela Bock, "Antinatalism, Maternity and Paternity in National Socialist Racism," in *Maternity and Gender Policies,* 233–

55; Eileen Boris, "The Power of Motherhood: Black and White Activist Women Redefine the 'Political,'" and Sonya Michel, "The Limits of Maternalism: Policies toward American Wage-Earning Mothers during the Progressive Era," both in *Mothers of a New World: Maternalist Politics and the Origins of Welfare States,* edited by Seth Koven and Sonya Michel (New York: Routledge, 1992), 213–45, 277–320; Geraldine Heng and Janadas Devan, "State Fatherhood: The Politics of Nationalism, Sexuality, and Race in Singapore," *Nationalisms and Sexualities* edited by Andrew Parker et al. (New York: Routledge, 1993), 343–64.

19. *Twentieth Annual Report of the American Female Guardian Society,* 1854, 8.

20. Reprinted in *Twentieth Annual Report of the American Female Guardian Society,* 1854, 9.

21. Jacoby, *Catholic Child Care,* 79.

22. Carroll Smith-Rosenberg, *Religion and the Rise of the American City: The New York Mission Movement, 1812–1874* (Ithaca: Cornell University Press, 1971), 190, 217.

23. *Nineteenth Annual Report of the American Female Guardian Society,* 1853, 11.

24. "An Act to Provide for the Care and Instruction of Idle and Truant Children, Passed April 12th, 1853," reprinted in the *Twenty-first Annual Report of the American Female Guardian Society,* 1855, 45.

25. *Thirteenth Annual Report of the New York Association for Improving the Condition of the Poor,* 1856, 41.

26. Rothman, *Discovery of the Asylum,* 221–24. John Williams of the Boston Children's Mission, moreover, had also suggested prior to Brace's emergence that reformers in eastern cities attempt to organize elaborate systems for taking poor children off city streets and placing them in Protestant homes. Miriam Z. Langsam, *Children West: A History of the Placing Out System of the New York Children's Aid Society* (Madison: University of Wisconsin Press, 1964), 18. More recent discussions of Charles Loring Brace are in Stephen O'Connor, *The Orphan Trains: The Story of Charles Loring Brace and the Children He Saved and Failed* (New York: Houghton Mifflin, 2001); Timothy J. Gilfoyle, "Street-rats and Guttersnipes: Child Pickpockets and Street Culture in New York City, 1850–1900," *Journal of Social History* 37 (Summer 2004): 853–82; and Clay Gish, "Rescuing the 'Waifs and Strays' of the City: The Western Emigration Program of the Children's Aid Society," *Journal of Social History* 33 (Fall 1999): 121–31.

27. Rothman, *Discovery of the Asylum,* 213–20, on the House of Refuge.

28. *Twenty-fourth Annual Report of the American Female Guardian Society,* 1858, 7–8.

29. "Report of the Select Committee appointed to visit Charitable Institutions supported by the State," Senate Document 8, New York State, Jan. 9, 1957, 98.

30. The first Catholics to be active in groups such as the Charity Organization Society did not join them until the 1880s.

31. The Catholic Union later claimed credit for the Freedom of Worship Bill of 1888. Catholic Union of New York, *The Persistent Violation by the Managers of the House of Refuge,* pamphlet, New York, 1882.

32. Langsam, *Children West,* 46.

33. *Twenty-first Annual Report of the American Female Guardian Society*, 1855, 6.

34. Charles Loring Brace, *The Dangerous Classes of New York and Twenty Years' Work among Them* (1872, repr. Washington: National Association of Social Workers, 1973), 75–76.

35. *Twentieth Annual Report of the American Female Guardian Society*, 1854, 8.

36. *Second Annual Report of the Children's Aid Society*, 1855, 8.

37. Ronald Takaki, *A Different Mirror: A History of Multicultural America* (Boston: Little, Brown, 1993), 162. There is, of course, growing sophistication in studies of ethnic whiteness and race and change over time. See especially Matthew Jacobson, *Whiteness of a Different Color: European Immigrants and the Alchemy of Race* (Cambridge: Harvard University Press, 1998); Alexander Saxton, *The Rise and Fall of the White Republic: Class Politics and Mass Culture in Nineteenth-Century America* (London: Verso, 1990); and David Roediger, *The Wages of Whiteness: Race and the Making of the American Working Class* (London: Verso, 1991).

38. *First Annual Report of the Children's Aid Society*, 1854, 12.

39. A discussion of Native American children boarding in missionary families appears in Linda Clemmons, "'We Find It a Difficult Work': Educating Dakota Children in Missionary Homes, 1835–1862," *American Indian Quarterly* 24 (Fall 2000): 570. The Dawes Act of 1887 helped rationalize these programs and set up a national network of boarding schools. Michael C. Coleman, *American Indian Children at School, 1850–1930* (Jackson: University Press of Mississippi, 1993); Robert A. Trennert Jr., *The Phoenix Indian School: Forced Assimilation in Arizona, 1891–1935* (Norman: University of Oklahoma Press, 1988).

40. *From Cherry Street to Green Pastures: A History of the Colored Orphan Asylum at Riverdale on Hudson*, pamphlet, Schomberg Collection, New York Public Library; see also "Report of the Select Committee Appointed to Visit Charitable Institutions Supported by the State," Senate Document 8, New York State, Jan. 9, 1957, 100; and Vincent Harding, *There Is a River: The Black Struggle for Freedom in America* (New York: Vintage Books, 1981), 140, 158, 160, 194, 117–39. See also Marian J. Morton, "Institutionalizing Inequalities: Black children and Child Welfare in Cleveland, 1859–1998," *Journal of Social History* 34 (Fall 2000): 141–62.

41. "An Act to Provide for the Care and Instruction of Idle and Truant Children, Passed April 12th, 1853," reprinted in the *Twenty-ninth Annual Report of the American Female Guardian Society*, 1863, 45.

42. *Tenth Annual Report of the Children's Aid Society*, 1863, 5–6. Farmers were often happy to pay the $10 for each child they took from the society, sometimes more if the child was strong and healthy and less if weak, a practice that, as Catholics pointed out, made the system roughly comparable to slave auctions. John Francis Maguire, *The Irish in America* (1868, repr. New York: Arno Press and the New York Times, 1969), 519.

43. *Fourth Annual Report of the Children's Aid Society*, 1857, 6–7.

44. *Third Annual Report of the Children's Aid Society*, 1856, 8, emphasis in the original.

45. Paul S. Boyer, *Urban Masses and Moral Order in America, 1820–1920* (Cambridge: Harvard University Press, 1978), 96, 99, 100.

46. *Fourth Annual Report of the Children's Aid Society,* 1857, 8.

47. *Second Annual Report of the Children's Aid Society,* 1855, 8.

48. *First* through *Tenth Annual Report of the Children's Aid Society,* 1853–62, passim.

49. *Ninth* and *Tenth Annual Report of the Children's Aid Society,* 1861–62.

50. "Mr. John Francis Maguire, M.P.," *Harper's Weekly,* March 30, 1867, 194.

51. Christine Stansell, *City of Women: Sex and Class in New York* (Urbana: University of Illinois Press, 1987). Although I am in many respects indebted to Stansell's analysis of the growth of the placing-out movement in the 1850s, my analysis differs from hers in two primary ways. First, while Stansell sees it as a male-run movement that middle-class or elite white women did not support and eventually contested, I posit that women were quite central to child removal and placing out. Second, Stansell assumes (211) that the Irish did not resist. Not only did they resist but they were also quite successful in doing so.

52. *Fifth Annual Report of the Children's Aid Society,* 1858, 4. Similar rhetoric is apparent in the reports of the AFGS. *Twentieth Annual Report of the American Female Guardian Society,* 1854, 11.

53. *Third Annual Report of the Children's Aid Society,* 1856, 9, 5; Boyer, *Urban Masses and Moral Order,* 101.

54. *Sixth Annual Report of the Children's Aid Society,* 1859, 69.

55. On references to drunken mothers in CAS reports see, for instance, *Annual Report of the Children's Aid Society,* 1860, 49, 61, 1861, 42–45, and 1863, 13, 16.

56. *Annual Report of the Children's Aid Society,* 1856–62.

57. *Twentieth Annual Report of the American Female Guardian Society,* 1854, 11, emphasis in the original.

58. Guernsey, *Irish Amy,* 14.

59. Ibid., 136.

60. Ibid., 139.

61. Ibid., 312.

62. "Notes from the Annals of St. Catherine's Convent of Mercy," Archives of the Sisters of Mercy, Dobbs Ferry, N.Y.

63. [Mother Mary Teresa] Austin Carroll, *Leaves from the Annals of the Sisters of Mercy* (New York: Catholic Publication Society, 1889), 194–97. Of the many resources of the famine Irish perhaps none was so powerful as a sense of humor, and nuns were as likely to delight in laughter as any of their Irish cohorts. Despite the unthinkable scope of work the Mercy Sisters did each day to imagine them as endlessly solemn and self-important is to do them an injustice. When novices at the convent, for instance, became too visibly guilty over a mistake, Mother Mary O'Connor was known to start what amounted to water fights with the convent's holy water (Carroll, *Leaves from the Annals,* 196). To create a good, funny story out of the stuff of tragedy and hardship was to connect with the larger Irish community in a common pursuit. "Dark" Irish humor, often incomprehensible to those outside the community, often proved the most critical, and affordable, staple of Irish daily sustenance.

64. *Thirteenth Annual Report of the New York Association for Improving the Condition of the Poor,* 1856, 25.

65. Ibid., 25–26.

66. Lawrence Kehoe, comp., *The Complete Works of the Most Rev. John Hughes, D.D.* (New York: Published for the compiler, 1865), 2: 692.

67. John Hughes to Rev. George Haskins, Sept. 30, 1858, A-3, Archives of the Archdiocese of New York (hereafter AANY).

68. James Roohan, "American Catholics and the Social Question," Ph.D. diss., Yale University, 1952, 208–9; Kerby A. Miller, *Emigrants and Exiles: Ireland and the Irish Exodus to North America* (New York: Oxford University Press, 1985), 334.

69. Archbishop John Hughes to Mr. R. Coddington, March 31, 1858, A-2, AANY.

70. David A. Gerber, *The Making of an American Pluralism: Buffalo, New York, 1825–1860* (Urbana: University of Illinois Press, 1989), 311–17.

71. Archbishop Hughes, "Orphan Asylum: Pleas for State Aid to Orphan Asylum," undated, A-17, AANY.

72. Mary Ann Sadlier, *Willy Burke; or, The Irish Orphan in America* (New York: D. J. Sadlier Press, 1845); n.a., *The Blakes and the Flanigans* (New York: D. J. Sadlier Press, 1856); Colleen McDannell, "'The Devil Was the First Protestant': Gender and Intolerance in Irish Catholic Fiction," *U.S. Catholic Historian* 8 (Winter–Spring 1989): 54, 51–65.

73. St. Patrick's (the Roman Catholic Orphan Asylum) contained 910 orphans and was run by the Sisters of Charity and understood to be Irish. St. Joseph's Orphan Asylum was run by the Sisters of Notre Dame, understood to be German, and contained 189 orphans; St. Vincent de Paul contained 107 orphans and although run by the French contained many non-Irish and non-German orphans of divergent nationalities and ethnicities. "Parochial Schools, Asylums, Hospitals, ca. 1866," A-29, AANY.

74. *Thirteenth Annual Report of the Children's Aid Society,* 1866, 42.

75. Philip Hosay, "The Challenge of Urban Poverty: Charity Reformers in New York City, 1835–1890," unpub. diss., University of Michigan, 1969, 100–102, 124–27.

76. Iver Bernstein, *The New York City Draft Riots: Their Significance for American Society and Politics in the Age of the Civil War* (New York: Oxford University Press, 1990), 8.

77. *Twentieth Annual Report of the New York Association for Improving the Condition of the Poor,* 1863, 19–20; Catherine Ross, "Society's Children: The Care of Indigent Youngsters in New York City, 1875–1903," Ph.D. diss., Yale University, 1978, 8–10.

78. For discussions of nuns' Civil War service, in particular that of the New York Sisters of Mercy and Charity, see, for instance, George Barton, *Angels of the Battlefield: A History of the Labors of the Catholic Sisterhoods in the Late Civil War* (Philadelphia: Catholic Art Publishing, 1897); Helen Sweeney, *The Golden Milestone: 1846–1896* (New York: Benzinger, 1896), 69–83; and Mary Ewens, *The Role of the Nun in Nineteenth Century America* (1971, repr. Salem, N.H.: Ayer Publishers, 1984), 223–51.

79. On the Irish, Catholic, and Irish Catholic press and abolitionism, see Carl Wittke, *The Irish in America* (Baton Rouge: Louisiana State University Press, 1956), 126–34, 144–45; and Noel Ignatiev, *How the Irish Became White* (New York: Routledge, 1995).

80. Bernstein, *The New York City Draft Riots*, 18.

81. Ibid., 36–37.

82. Ibid., 21.

83. Wittke, *The Irish in America*, 146; Bernstein, *The New York City Draft Riots*, 24

84. Bernstein, *The New York City Draft Riots*, 39–40; Wittke, *The Irish in America*, 146.

85. Eric Foner, *Reconstruction: America's Unfinished Revolution, 1863–1877* (New York: Harper and Row, 1988), 32–34; Adrian Cook, *The Armies of the Streets: The New York City Draft Riots of 1863* (Lexington: University Press of Kentucky, 1974); Brother Basil Leo Lee, F.S.C., *Discontent in New York City, 1861–1865* (Washington: Catholic University of America Press, 1943).

86. Bernstein, *The New York City Draft Riots*, 62.

87. *Eleventh Annual Report of the Children's Aid Society*, 1864, 4, 5, 10.

88. Sister Marie De Lourdes Walsh, *The Sisters of Charity of New York, 1809–1959* (New York: Fordham University Press, 1960), 3: 38.

89. Hughes did not sanction the establishment of the laity-controlled Catholic Protectory until after the Christian Brothers, the only male order he could recruit for work with boys, explicitly asked not to be given powers of legal incorporation or property ownership. Brothers of the Christian Schools to Archbishop Hughes, Feb. 2, 1859, A-13, AANY; see also "Prospectus for Industrial School for Orphan Boys," 1861, A-6, AANY; "A Short Sketch: The New York Catholic Protectory," in *National Conference of Charities and Correction* (Boston: Printed for the Committee on the History of Child-Saving Work by Geo. H. Ellis, 1893), 8.

90. Hughes initially objected when he found that the board had already asked the Sisters of the Good Shepherd to work with girls in the institution. As he wrote, "No one has spoken or written to me. . . . But I have discovered incidentally that [the Board], with, no doubt, the best intentions, have interfered in a way which as Archbishop of New York, I cannot permit or tolerate. The Sisters as are called the Good Shepherd have their own works. It is mine to guide them in the execution of it. But no interference with them or any other Religious Community can be permitted by me." Archbishop John Hughes to Levi S. Ives, June 19, June 10, 1863, both in the Archives of the Sisters of Charity of New York at Mount St. Vincent.

91. "Appeal," *First Annual Report of the New York Catholic Protectory* (West Chester: The Protectory, 1864), 15–16 (available at the New York Public Library). Here as elsewhere it is evident, and I agree with Matthew Jacobson (*Whiteness of a Different Color*, 49) that Irish Catholics referenced their racial distinctiveness from Anglo-Saxons as a point of pride not just as a complaint against exclusion by the British or Americans from the Anglo-Saxon category of race.

92. Levi Silliman Ives, *Church and State Charities Compared, with Special Reference to the System of New York State Charities, Lectures 1 and 2* (New York: Edward Dunigan and Brother James B. Kirker, 1857), 50 (available at the New York Public Library).

93. Levi Silliman Ives, "The Protection of Catholic Children: A Lecture Delivered at Cooper Institute, November 23, 1864," in *First Annual Report of the New York Catholic Protectory*, 1864, 78.

94. "The meeting of these mothers and their children . . . can hardly ever be

forgotten by those who witnessed it." *Homeless Child and Messenger of St. Joseph's Union*, 1: 1877, cited in Jacoby, *Catholic Child Care*, 163.

95. Maguire, *The Irish in America*, 515.

96. Ives, "The Protection of Catholic Children," 78.

97. Ibid., 78, 75.

98. *First Annual Report of the New York Catholic Protectory*, 1864, 43.

Chapter 4: Saving Children from the Child-Savers, 1864–94

The quotations in the epigraphs are from Robert Hartley, *Twenth-fourth Annual Report of the New York Association for Improving the Condition of the Poor*, 1867, 39–40, and Isaac Hecker, "Public Charities," *Catholic World* 17 (April 1873): 4.

1. Hartley, *Twenty-fourth Annual Report*, 40–41. For a larger discussion of "alien" voting rights in late-nineteenth-century industrial cities, see Martin Shefter, "Trade Unions and Political Machines: The Organization and Disorganization of the American Working Class in the Late Nineteenth Century," in *Working-Class Formation: Nineteenth-Century Patterns in Western Europe and the United States*, edited by Ira Katznelson and Aristide R. Zolberg (Princeton: Princeton University Press, 1986), 210, 197–276.

2. Hartley, *Twenty-fourth Annual Report*, 39–40; *Twenty-sixth Annual Report of the New York Association for Improving the Condition of the Poor*, 1869, 27.

3. After the war, some Catholics urged elite Catholic women to provide a counterpoint to Protestant maternalist organizing by mimicking their voluntarist associations. Appeals to laywomen to undertake charity work are rife throughout literature directed at middle- and upper-class Catholics in this period. "The Sanitary and Moral Condition of New York City" and "The Rights of Catholic Women," both in *Catholic World* 7 (1868): 566, 846–48; "Who Shall Take Care of the Poor? Parts 1 and 2" and "The Charities of New York," both in *Catholic World* 8 (1868–69): 703–16, 734–40, and 279–85.

4. *New York City Society of St. Vincent de Paul: Report of the Superior Council, Report for 1864* (New York: E. B. Clayton's Sons, 1865), 23, 7.

5. The Catholic Union became the Catholic Club during the 1880s. John Talbot Smith, *The Catholic Church in New York* (New York: Hall and Locke, 1905), 1: 321–24; *Constitution and By-Laws of the Catholic Union Circle of New York* (New York: Edward H. Coffin, 1873). The group claimed credit for two pieces of legislation related to charitable work through the late nineteenth century: the religious clause of the Children's Law of 1875 and the Freedom of Worship Bill of 1888.

6. "Notes from the Annals of St. Catherine's Convent of Mercy," 1864, Archives of the Sisters of Mercy, Dobbs Ferry, N.Y. (hereafter ASMNY).

7. Ibid.

8. Ibid.

9. "Notes from the Annals of St. Catherine's Convent of Mercy," 1865, ASMNY.

10. "Notes from the Annals of St. Catherine's Convent of Mercy," 1867, ASMNY.

11. New York state appropriated $2.2 million during his term from 1869 to 1870—as much as for the seventeen years before 1869. John W. Pratt, "Boss Tweed's Public Welfare Program," *New York Historical Society Quarterly* 45 (Oct. 1961): 409, 410.

12. Emma Brace, ed., *The Life of Charles Loring Brace* (New York: Arno Press, 1976), 306; *Nineteenth Annual Report of the Children's Aid Society,* 1872, 37.

13. *Minutes of the Board of Apportionment of the City and County of New York* (New York: 1871–73), 20–22 (available at the New York Public Library).

14. The Roman Catholic Orphan Asylum, for instance, received the $10,000 it requested. St. Joseph's Children's Home under the direction of the Sisters of Mercy received $3,000 although they had requested nothing. In contrast, the Protestant-run Juvenile Asylum, Howard's Home, and Children's Fold were deprived of excise funds altogether, while the Five Points Mission and American Female Guardian Society had their funding cut to $2,000 and $6,000, respectively. Ibid., 159–63.

15. "Our Established Church," *Harper's Weekly,* July 3, 1869, 423; "Union of Church and State in New York," *Harper's Weekly,* May 16, 1868, 307; "Church and State," *Harper's Weekly,* Feb. 19, 1870, 121–22. If Thomas Nast was Harper's most avidly anti-Catholic cartoonist, Eugene Lawrence was his counterpart on the editorial page. Eugene Lawrence, "Modern Monks and Nuns," *Harper's Weekly,* Jan. 16, 1875, 66–68.

16. *Catholic Almanac for 1848* (Baltimore: F. Lucas Jr., 1848), 180–84. Twenty Sisters of Charity worked in orphan asylums, and seven Sisters of Mercy worked with single women and prisoners. *Sadlier's Catholic Almanac and Ordo, 1865* (New York: D. and J. Sadlier, 1865), 93–94.

17. Sister Marie De Lourdes Walsh, *The Sisters of Charity of New York, 1809–1959,* 3 vols. (New York: Fordham University Press, 1960), 3: 52–56.

18. *Minutes of the Board of Apportionment of the City and County of New York,* 1871, 62, 151.

19. "Notes from the Annals of St. Catherine's Convent of Mercy," 1864, ASMNY.

20. Mrs. R. B. Connolly to Sister Irene, Dec. 8, 1869, Feb. 8, 1870, Archives of the Sisters of Charity of New York at Mount St. Vincent (hereafter AMSV).

21. Theda Skocpol, *Protecting Soldiers and Mothers: The Political Origins of Social Policy in the United States* (Cambridge: Harvard University Press, 1992), 98.

22. "Advisory Committee," 1874, AMSV.

23. *Report of the Special Committee,* New York Catholic Protectory, Feb. 11, 1867, AMSV.

24. *Minutes of the Board of Apportionment of the City and County of New York,* 1871, 74.

25. *Minutes of the Board of Apportionment of the City and County of New York,* 1871, 62, 151; John Francis Richmond, *New York and Its Institutions, 1609–1871,* (New York: E. B. Treat, 1871), 353, 359, 345–46; Board of United Charities, *Handbook of the Benevolent Institutions and Charities of New York for 1876,* 34–35.

26. Hecker, "Public Charities," 13.

27. Michael A. Gordon, *The Orange Riots: Irish Political Violence in New York City, 1870 and 1871* (Ithaca: Cornell University Press, 1993), 206–8.

28. The Committee of Seventy, the membership of which was male, organized passage of a new city charter through state legislation in order to nullify the home rule charter Tweed had used to gain control over city appropriations. The new charter, which would remain in force from 1873 to 1897, decreased city officials' abilities to raise taxes or incur debt, restricted the mayor from firing department heads without the governor's approval, and made Tammany a more powerful broker in connecting city and state legislation. Gordon, *The Orange Riots*, 200–201.

29. Martha Branscombe, *The Courts and the Poor Laws in New York State: 1784–1929* (Chicago: University of Chicago Press, 1943), 147; David M. Schneider and Albert Deutsch, *The History of Public Welfare in New York State, 1867–1940* (Chicago: University of Chicago Press, 1941), 20–24.

30. For a discussion of Josephine Shaw Lowell's career and the connections she drew among the State Charities Aid Association (SCAA), state board, and Charity Organization Society, see Joan Waugh, *Unsentimental Reformer: The Life of Josephine Shaw Lowell* (Cambridge: Harvard University Press, 1997), 113–14, 129, 154–59, 160–61, passim.

31. Lori D. Ginzberg, "A Passion For Efficiency: The Work of the United States Sanitary Commission," in *Women, Families, and Communities: Readings in American History*, edited by Nancy A. Hewitt (Glenview: Scott, Foresman, 1990), 1: 202–16; Lori Ginzberg, *Women and the Work of Benevolence: Morality and Politics in the Northeastern United States, 1820–1885* (New Haven: Yale University Press, 1990); David Rothman, *Conscience and Convenience: The Asylum and its Alternatives in Progressive America* (Boston: Little, Brown, 1980), 313.

32. On scientific charity, see, for instance, Paul Boyer, *Urban Masses and Moral Order in America, 1820–1920* (Cambridge: Harvard University Press, 1978), 143–53; Walter I. Trattner, *From Poor Law to Welfare State: A History of Social Welfare in America*, 3d ed. (New York: Free Press, 1984), 77–107; and Michael B. Katz, *In the Shadow of the Poorhouse: A Social History of Welfare in America* (New York: Basic Books, 1986), 58–83.

33. Boyer, *Urban Masses and Moral Order*, 103.

34. For a particularly insightful discussion of the assumptions about culture and biology in nineteenth-century discourse, see Peggy Pascoe, "Miscegenation Law, Court Cases, and Ideologies of 'Race' in Twentieth Century America," *Journal of American History* 83 (June 1996): 44–69.

35. Charles S. Hoyt, "The Causes of Pauperism," in *Tenth Annual Report of the State Board of Charities of the State of New York* (Albany: Weed and Parsons, 1877), 97–98.

36. *Seventh Annual Report of the State Charities Aid Association* (New York: Cushing, Bardesa, 1879), 2.

37. William Letchworth, *Proceedings of the Convention of the Superintendents of the Poor of the State of New York Held in Rochester, New York, Tuesday and Wednesday, June 9th and 10th, 1874* (Rochester: Evening Express Printing, 1874), 10, reprinted in Katz, *In the Shadow of the Poorhouse*, 107 (a longer discussion of family breakup policy in this period appears on 106–9).

38. *Twenty-first Annual Report of the Children's Aid Society*, 1874, 5–7, 10.

39. Schneider and Deutsche, *The History of Public Welfare in New York State*, 37.

40. *Thirty-second Annual Report of the New York Association for Improving of the Condition of the Poor*, 1875, 35–41.

41. *Twenty-first Annual Report of the Children's Aid Society*, 1874, 5–7, 10; see also Charles Loring Brace, *The Dangerous Classes of New York and Twenty Years' Work among Them*, (1872, repr. Washington: National Association of Social Workers, 1973), 388, 389, 387; and Brace, ed., *The Life of Charles Loring Brace*, 333–34.

42. Schneider and Deutsche, *The History of Public Welfare in New York State*, 20.

43. Ibid., 35–36.

44. Ibid., 46–48.

45. *Sixteenth Annual Report of the Commissioners of Public Charities and Correction of the City of New York*, 1875, viii–ix.

46. Hecker, "Public Charities," 10. The Children's Aid Society further listed "4,026 persons sent to West" for 1876 alone. Board of United Charities, *Handbook of the Benevolent Institutions and Charities of New York for 1876*, 26–27; John Rose Greene Hassard, *Grants of Land and Gifts of Money to Catholic and Non-Catholic Institutions in New York Compared: Which Church Does the State and City Support?* (New York: Catholic Publication Society, 1879), passim.

47. According to the city's 1876 charities *Handbook*, the American Female Guardian Society listed its first object as "reception of friendless children and transmission to country homes." The Five Points House of Industry listed its object similarly: "Providing of temporary and permanent homes for friendless children." *Handbook of the Benevolent Institutions and Charities of New York for 1876*, 26–27, 29–31; Hecker, "Public Charities," 8–10.

48. *Report of the Howard Mission*, 1876, cited in Francis E. Lane, *American Charities and the Child of the Immigrant: A Study of Typical Child Caring Institutions in New York and Massachusetts between the Years 1845 and 1880* (Washington: Catholic University of America, 1932), 51–52.

49. On the national movement to bring children out of almshouses, see John O'Grady, *Catholic Charities in the United States* (1930, repr. New York, Arno Press and the New York Times, 1971), 95–97; and Katz, *In the Shadow of the Poorhouse*, 107–9.

50. *Fourth Annual Report of the State Charities Aid Association of New York*, 1876, 18.

51. *Fifth Annual Report of the State Charities Aid Association of New York*, 1877, 1–2.

52. Ibid.

53. Schneider and Deutch, *The History of Public Welfare in New York State*, 63.

54. Ibid.

55. Ibid.

56. Ibid.

57. *Sixth Annual Report of the State Charities Aid Association of New York*, 1878, 7, 38.

58. Peter Guilday, *The National Pastorals of the American Hierarchy (1792–1919)* (Westminster, Md.: Newman Press, 1954), 216–17.

59. Reprinted in John Francis Maguire, *The Irish in America* (1868, repr. New York: Arno Press and the New York Times, 1969), 517.

60. Mrs. C. Spaulding, for 'Home Managers,' AFGS, to Mr. Wilson, May 14, 1874, reprinted in John Hassard, "Specimen Charities," *Catholic World* 21 (June 1875): 300–301.

61. Hassard, "Specimen Charities," 300–301.

62. Hecker, "Public Charities," 5.

63. Ibid., 4.

64. "Who Shall Take Care of the Poor?" 712.

65. Augustine Hewit, "The Duties of the Rich in Christian Society," *Catholic World* 14 (1872): 579.

66. Hecker, "The Charities of New York," 282–83; see also "The Sanitary and Moral Condition of New York City," 557, 561–66; and "The Homeless Poor of New York City," *Catholic World* 16 (1872–73): 206–12.

67. "Who Shall Take Care of the Poor?" 706–7.

68. Hewit, "The Duties of the Rich," 579.

69. "Who Shall Take Care of the Poor?" 704.

70. Ibid.

71. Ibid.

72. P. C. Dooley, "Report of the Supervisor of the Bureau of Admissions and Discharges," *Fifteenth Annual Report of the New York Catholic Protectory* (West Chester: The Protectory, 1877), 70, 72 (available at Columbia University).

73. The Protectory was restricted since its earliest days to sheltering only those committed directly through the courts, although it had been founded to take transfers from other institutions as well as direct commitments by parents. In its first five years the board spent $469,034, while only $164,807 was received from public funds. The remaining $300,000 was derived from private donations, fairs, and the labor of children within the institution. Richmond, *New York and Its Institutions,* 353; *Twelfth Annual Report of the New York Catholic Protectory* (West Chester: The Protectory, 1875), 402.

74. Henry Jas. Anderson, President, Board of Managers, and Sister Mary Helena, both *Eleventh Annual Report of the New York Catholic Protectory* (West Chester: The Protectory, 1874), 360, 368.

75. William P. Letchworth, "Homes of Homeless Children," from *Ninth Annual Report of the New York State Board of Charities,* 1876, 365, repr. as Letchworth, *Homes for Homeless Children: A Report on Orphan Asylums and Other Institutions for the Care of Children* (Albany: Weed and Parsons, 1876).

76. "Notes from the Annals of St. Catherine's Convent of Mercy," 1872, ASMNY.

77. The Asylum of St. Vincent De Paul was established in 1859 and in 1875 was run by fourteen sisters of the Religious Order of the Marianites of the Holy Cross. St. Joseph's Orphan Asylum was incorporated in 1859 and run in 1875 by fifteen sisters of the Order de Notre Dame. In 1875 only twenty-one of the 123 children in St. Vincent de Paul's Orphan Asylum were full orphans, the remainder being half orphans or destitute. In the same year, 126 of the two hundred children in St. Joseph's Orphan Asylum for German children had either one or both parents living. Letchworth, "Homes of Homeless Children," 202–4, 359–61, passim.

78. *Roman Catholic Orphan Asylum, Minutes of the Board of Managers,* May 3, 1874, cited in George Jacoby, *Catholic Child Care in Nineteenth-Century New York* (Washington: Catholic University of America, 1941), 110.

79. *Roman Catholic Orphan Asylum, Minutes of the Board of Managers,* March
1, 1874, cited in Jacoby, *Catholic Child Care,* 103.

80. Letchworth, "Homes of Homeless Children," 259.

81. "Notes from the Annals of St. Catherine's Convent of Mercy," 1876,
ASMNY.

82. "Notes from the Annals of St. Catherine's Convent of Mercy," 1877,
ASMNY.

83. *Sixth Annual Report of the State Charities Aid Association of New York,*
1878, 123.

84. Josephine Shaw Lowell, "Report on the Institutions for the Care of Destitute
Children of the City of New York," in *Nineteenth Annual Report of the New
York State Board of Charities,* 1886, 22; *Report of the State Board of Charities
in Relation to Private Charitable Institutions in New York City,* 1881, Assembly
Document 41 (Albany: Weed and Parsons, 1881), 23.

85. The institutions include the St. Joseph's Industrial Home directed by the
Sisters of Mercy and having charge of 867 children in 1880; St. Stephen's Home
directed by the Sisters of Charity and having charge of 309 children in 1880; St.
Joseph's Asylum for German children directed by the Sisters of Notre Dame and
having charge of 282 children in 1880; and St. Ann's Home run by the Sisters of
the Good Shepherd (no exact figures for this year). *Report of the State Board of
Charities in Relation to Private Charitable Institutions in New York City,* 23.

86. These institutions included the Asylum of the Third Order of the Sisters
of St. Dominic (1877), St. Joseph's Home of the Missionary Sisters of the Third
Order of St. Francis (1879), the Dominican Convent of Our Lady of the Rosary
(1879), and St. James Home (1879), from Lowell, "Report on the Institutions for
the Care of Destitute Children of the City of New York," 167.

87. Ibid., 165–66, passim. Figures are from *Report of the State Board of Charities in Relation to Private Charitable Institutions in New York City.* The figure
for Catholic institutions included the total inmates for the Asylum of the Sisters
of St. Dominick, the Asylum of St. Vincent de Paul, the Institution of Mercy, the
Missionary Sisters of St. Francis, the Mission of the Immaculate Virgin, St. James
Home, and St. Stephen's Home. Protestant or secular institutions included the
American Female Guardian Society, and the Home for Fallen and Friendless Girls
(the Association for the Benefit of Colored Orphans was excluded). Jewish institutions included the Ladies Deborah Nursery and the Hebrew Sheltering Guardian
Society, established in 1878 and 1879 respectively. Payments for the Protectory
and the Foundling Asylum were made under separate provisions for reformatories
and foundling hospitals, the institutions receiving in 1880 $234,054 and $236,086
respectively from state, counties, and cities. By 1880 Catholic institutions so
dominated the system that of a total of 2,906 children for whose maintenance
institutions received funding, Catholics sheltered 2,383 (82 percent), Protestant
or secular organizations sheltered 213 (7 percent), and Jewish institutions cared
for 310 (10 percent).

88. Sister M. Ulrica, "Report of the Directress of the Female Department,"
Ninth Annual Report of the New York Catholic Protectory, 1872, 280; Casimir
Villeneuve, "Report of the Superintendent of the Bureau of Admissions and Discharges," *Twenty-first Annual Report of the New York Catholic Protectory,* 1884,
346.

89. This number is exclusive of the Foundling Asylum. Lowell, "Report on the Institutions for the Care of Destitute Children of the City of New York," 1886, passim.

90. When the Mercy Sisters learned that the Protectory could not accommodate all dependent boys in the city over nine, they built a separate institution for them in Balmville, refusing "to send them to the different Judges who committed them as many of them had sisters amongst the girls." "Notes from the Annals of St. Catherine's Convent of Mercy," 1878, ASMNY; Jacoby, *Catholic Child Care*, 223, 225–27, 231–32.

91. *Statistics Related to the Support of Children at Public Expense in Private Institutions in New York City*, Document 63 (New York: State Charities Aid Association, 1894), 5.

92. Ibid., 13.

93. Address of Right Rev. D. J. McMahon [*sic*], supervisor of Catholic Charities, Archdiocese of New York, in *Proceedings of the Conference on the Care of Dependent Children*, Jan. 25, 26, 1909 (Washington: Government Printing Office, 1909), 98.

94. *Annual Report of the New York Catholic Protectory*, 1890–98, passim; *The New York Catholic Protectory: A Short Sketch* (West Chester: The Protectory, 1885), 51–54.

95. Letchworth, "Homes of Homeless Children," 194. Sister Agnes Muldoon, for instance, in charge of St. Joseph's Industrial School, claimed in 1875, "We place them where we think they will be most likely to succeed, and watch over them afterward. . . . A girl well trained [on a sewing machine] can earn $9 or $10 a week. The last two that left us get $10 a week." Ibid., 259.

96. *Rules of the St. Vincent de Paul Society* (New York: D. and J. Sadlier, 1862), 19.

97. Brother Justin to Henry Hoguet, Manhattan College, Oct. 13, 1887, Archives of the Archdiocese of New York (hereafter AANY).

98. P. C. Dooley, "Report of the Bureau of Admissions and Discharges," *Sixteenth Annual Report of the New York Catholic Protectory*, 1879, 127.

99. *Roman Catholic Orphan Asylum, Report for 1881*, 15, cited in Jacoby, *Catholic Child Care*, 113.

100. P. C. Dooley, "Report of the Supervisor of the Bureau of Admissions and Discharges," *Fourteenth Annual Report of the New York Catholic Protectory*, 1877, 70.

101. P. C. Dooley, "Report of the Supervisor of the Bureau of Admissions and Discharges," *Seventeenth Annual Report of the New York Catholic Protectory*, 1880, 171.

102. Henry Hoguet, *Sixteenth Annual Report of the New York Catholic Protectory*, 1879, 99. In the late 1850s, the Roman Catholic Orphan Asylum sent out circulars to farming communities and advertised in the Catholic *Freeman's Journal*, noting that "[a]pplications from farmers, whether for boys or girls, will have preference over all others." Jacoby, *Catholic Child Care*, 117–18.

103. Henry Hoguet and Board of Managers of the Protectory to Archbishop McCloskey, Feb., 1878, A-29, AANY.

104. Mother Ambrosia to the Executive Committee, New York Catholic Protectory, May 10, 1880, AMSV.

105. *Thirtieth Annual Report of the New York Catholic Protectory*, 1893, 12–13.

106. Jacoby, *Catholic Child Care*, 108.

107. Mother Regina Lawless to P. C. Dooley, March, 1878, AMSV.

108. Ibid.

109. P. C. Dooley, "Report of the Superintendent of the Bureau of Admissions and Discharges," *Sixteenth Annual Report of the New York Catholic Protectory*, 1879, 171.

110. P. C. Dooley, "Report of the Superintendent of the Bureau of Admissions and Discharges," *Seventeenth Annual Report of the New York Catholic Protectory*, 1880, 221.

111. *Twenty-second Annual Report of the New York Catholic Protectory*, 1885, 425.

112. *Nineteenth Annual Report of the New York Catholic Protectory*, 1882, 303, 333.

113. *Twenty-sixth Annual Report of the New York Catholic Protectory*, 1889, 606.

114. Casimir Villeneuve, "Report of the Superintendent of Bureau of Admissions and Discharges to the Board of Managers," *Twenty-second Annual Report of the New York Catholic Protectory*, 1885, 380.

115. *Sadliers' Catholic Directory, Almanac, and Ordo for the Year of Our Lord 1874* (New York: D. and J. Sadlier, 1874), 87–93; *Sadliers' Catholic Directory, Almanac, and Ordo for the Year of Our Lord 1884* (New York: D. and J. Sadlier, 1884), 145–54; *Hoffmann's Catholic Directory, Almanac* (Milwaukee: Hoffmann Bros., 1886), 91–96.

116. "Notes from the Annals of St. Catherine's Convent of Mercy," 1867, ASMNY.

117. Walsh, *The Sisters of Charity*, 1: 217.

118. "Notes from the Annals of St. Catherine's Convent of Mercy," 1872, ASMNY.

119. Numbers of servants, officers, and religious were tabulated from individual reports on institutions for dependent children for the year, 1886, from Lowell, "Report on the Institutions for the Care of Destitute Children of the City of New York," 1886, passim.

120. Ibid.

121. *Second Annual Report of the New York Catholic Protectory*, 1865, 59–60.

122. [Mother Mary Teresa] Austin Carroll, *Leaves from the Annals of the Sisters of Mercy* (New York: Catholic Publication Society, 1889), 199.

123. After the destruction of the girls' buildings at the Protectory in 1872, the girls' department occupied temporary frame buildings for two years. In 1877 Mother Mary Regina complained that they were still in use because of the Protectory's $200,000 debt. *Fourteenth Annual Report of the New York Catholic Protectory*, 1877, 64. For the Dominican Sisters' use of tents see Lowell, "Report on the Institutions for the Care of Destitute Children of the City of New York," 227.

124. Ibid., 209–10.

125. Jacoby, *Catholic Child Care*, 169–70.

126. Lowell, "Report on the Institutions for the Care of Destitute Children of the City of New York," passim.

127. *Association for Befriending Children*, pamphlet ca. early 1870s, Archives of the Sisters of the Divine Compassion, White Plains, N.Y. (hereafter ASDC). Native-born Father Thomas Preston, who was an especially active adviser to the order, was also an early member (1885) of the Charity Organization Society. Mary J. Oates, *The Catholic Philanthropic Tradition in America* (Bloomington: Indiana University Press, 1995), 51.

128. Mother Veronica wrote to an SPCC administrator suggesting that a mother of a child "comes to see her occasionally and does not appear to be an altogether desirable Guardian for a girl of this age." Mother M. Veronica, R.S.C. to Mr. E. Fellows Jenkins, Supv., May 28, 1895, Good Counsel Farm, White Plains, N.Y., ASDC. In another instance Mother Veronica also resisted returning a child to her mother, who had visited for ten years but was "a drunkard, and an altogether irresponsible person." Mother M. Veronica to Mr. E. Jenkins, Supv., n.d., ASDC. In 1900 an Italian mother attempted to reclaim her children, but the sisters refused; when one of the children died following the mother's visit, she sued the institution. Documents related to the Cappilero case, ASDC.

129. The contrast also begs the question of the influence of ethnicity and class versus religion. The predominantly native-born Sisters of Divine Compassion tended both to be more critical of poor parents, and yet more sympathetic to "fallen women," than was true of most Catholics.

130. Both the Deborah Nursery and the Hebrew Sheltering Guardian Society were founded in 1879 to take in destitute Jewish children under the provisions of the Children's Law. Lowell, "Report on the Institutions for the Care of Destitute Children of the City of New York," 219, 224–25.

131. Myer Stern, "Shall State Aid Be Withdrawn from Denominational Institutions?" in *Catholic Charities and the Constitutional Convention of 1894 of the State of New York: Report to the Committee on Catholic Interests of the Catholic Club* (New York: J. J. O'Brien and Son, 1894). Perhaps in part because of a limited workforce, children from the Hebrew Orphan Asylum, Hebrew Sheltering Guardian Society, and Deborah Nursery and Child's Protectory were sent to public schools daily, therefore lessening the degree to which Jewish children were segregated from the native-born culture. Catherine J. Ross, "Society's Children: The Care of Indigent Youngsters in New York City, 1875–1903," Ph.D. diss., Yale University, 1978, 103–4; Lowell, "Report on the Institutions for the Care of Destitute Children of the City of New York," 219.

132. Stern, "Shall State Aid Be Withdrawn?" 7.

133. *Report of the State Board of Charities in Relation to Private Charitable Institutions in New York City, 1881*, 38–49.

134. Ibid., 26, 7.

135. *New York Times*, Dec. 29, 1874.

136. *Annual Report of the Society for the Prevention of Cruelty to Children of the City of New York*, 1875–1902, passim; see also Ross, "Society's Children," 25.

137. *Report of the State Board of Charities in Relation to Private Charitable Institutions in New York City, 1881*, 27.

138. Homer Folks, *The Care of Destitute, Neglected and Delinquent Children* (New York: Macmillan, 1902), 173–75.

139. "Report of the Standing Committee on Dependent and Delinquent Children," *Nineteenth Annual Report of the State Board of Charities,* 1886, 159–62.

140. Martha Branscombe, *The Courts and the Poor Laws,* 365; *Nuns of the Order of St. Dominick v. Long Island City,* N.Y.S. 415 (1888).

141. Josephine Shaw Lowell, *Public Relief and Private Charity* (New York: G. P. Putnam's Sons, 1884), 74–75, 71, 85.

142. Josephine Shaw Lowell to Archbishop McCloskey, Dec. 5, 1885, A-28, AANY.

143. Archbishop Corrigan to Josephine Shaw Lowell, July 7, 1885, C-18, AANY.

144. "A Report on the Administration of Charities and Correction in the City of New York," *Charities Reform Committee,* State Charities Aid Association Document 46, 17; *Fifteenth Annual Report of the State Charities Aid Association,* 1887, 18.

145. "Address of Rev. James King," in *Catholic Charities and the Constitutional Convention of 1894 of the State of New York: Report to the Committee on Catholic Interests of the Catholic Club,* 19.

146. Frederic Coudert, transcript of testimony, *Catholic Charities and the Constitutional Convention of 1894,* 13.

147. Louis Bliss, transcript of testimony, *Catholic Charities and the Constitutional Convention of 1894,* 6.

Chapter 5: "The Family" and "the Institution"

The quotations in the epigraphs are from Elias L. Trotzkey, *Institutional Care and Placing-Out: The Place of Each in the Care of Dependent Children* (Chicago: Marks Nathan Jewish Orphan Home, 1930), and Mrs. Dorsey to the Mayor of New York, April 22, 1897, RG 0–15, SWL-36, New York City Municipal Archives (hereafter NYCMA).

1. Raymond Williams, *Keywords: A Vocabulary of Culture and Society* (New York: Oxford University Press, 1976), 144–45.

2. Robert Emmett Curran, *Michael Augustine Corrigan and the Shaping of Conservative Catholicism in America, 1878–1902* (New York: Arno Press, 1978), 173–75; see also Stephen Bell, *Rebel, Priest and Prophet: A Biography of Dr. Edward McGlynn* (New York: Robert Schalkenbach Foundation, 1968).

3. "Remarks," *St. Vincent de Paul Quarterly* 3 (1898): 124, 125; Curran, *Michael Augustine Corrigan,* 44–45, 116.

4. James E. Roohan, *American Catholics and the Social Question, 1865–1900* (New York: Arno Press, 1976); Eric Foner, "Class, Ethnicity, and Radicalism in the Gilded Age: The Land League and Irish America," in *Politics and Ideology in the Age of the Civil War* (New York: Oxford University Press, 1980), 150–200.

5. Henry Hoguet to Archbishop Michael Corrigan, Dec. 5, 1886, C-9, Archives of the Archdiocese of New York (hereafter AANY).

6. Ibid.

7. Edward McGlynn to Archbishop Michael Corrigan, Dec. 20, 1886, reprinted in Curran, *Michael Augustine Corrigan*, 217.

8. Archbishop Michael Corrigan to Bishop Bernard McQuaid, Jan. 17, 1887, Archives of the Diocese of Rochester, reprinted Curran, *Michael Augustine Corrigan*, 221–22.

9. Curran, *Michael Augustine Corrigan*, 222.

10. Mother Ambrosia to Archbishop Michael Corrigan, April 9, 1887, C-14, AANY.

11. Ibid.

12. Council Book, April 5, Aug. 25, 1887, Archives of the Sisters of Charity of New York at Mount St. Vincent's (hereafter AMSV). Thanks to Sister Anne Courtney for providing this citation.

13. Roohan, *American Catholics*, 439.

14. James J. Hennesey, *American Catholics: A History of the Roman Catholic Community in the United States* (New York: Oxford University Press, 1981), 215.

15. From the 1890 Census, Federal, cited in Philip Hosay, "The Challenge of Urban Poverty: Charity Reformers in New York City, 1835–1890," unpub. Ph.D. diss., University of Michigan, 1969, 207–10.

16. *Annual Report of the Department of Public Charities of the City of New York for 1915*, 128.

17. On Italian conflicts with an Irish-dominated church, see Silvano Tomasi, *Piety and Power: The Role of the Italian American Parishes in the New York Metropolitan Area, 1880–1930* (Staten Island: Center for Migration Studies, 1975); Robert Anthony Orsi, *The Madonna of 115th Street: Faith and Community in Italian Harlem, 1880–1950* (New Haven: Yale University Press, 1985); Mary Elizabeth Brown, "The Making of Italian-American Catholics: Jesuit Work on the Lower East Side, New York, 1890s-1950s," *Catholic Historical Review* 73 (April 1987): 195–210.

18. Archbishop Michael Corrigan to Peter Paul Cahensly, July 22, 1891, Center for Migration Studies, cited and reprinted in Brown, "The Making of Italian-American Catholics," 197–98.

19. Stephen Michael DiGiovanni, "Mother Cabrini: Early Years in New York," *Catholic Historical Review* 77 (Jan. 1991): 56–57.

20. *Twenty-third Annual Report of the Society for the Prevention of Cruelty to Children of the City of New York*, 27; Catherine J. Ross, "Society's Children: The Care of Indigent Youngsters in New York City, 1875–1903," Ph.D. diss., Yale University, 1978, 45.

21. *Twentieth Annual Report of the New York Catholic Protectory*, 1882, 290.

22. Unlike studies of Irish "whiteness," the evidence in this study points to the terms *American* and *foreigner* as being the significant lever the Irish used to subjugate others.

23. DiGiovanni, "Mother Cabrini," 65–66.

24. Sister Marie De Lourdes Walsh, *The Sisters of Charity of New York, 1809–1959* (New York: Fordham University Press, 1960), 3: 9–11.

25. Walsh, *The Sisters of Charity*, 3: 9–11. DiGiovanni, "Mother Cabrini," 67.

26. DiGiovanni, "Mother Cabrini," 68–69.

27. Josephine Shaw Lowell to the State Board of Charities, July 6, 1889, reprinted in William Rhinelander Stewart, *The Philanthropic Work of Josephine Shaw Lowell* (New York: Macmillan, 1911), 250–51.

28. James J. Traynor to Archbishop Michael Corrigan, May 7, 1892, C-30, AANY. Traynor referred to the SPCC as "Mr. Gerry's people."

29. Myer Stern, "Shall State Aid Be Withdrawn from Denominational Institutions?" in *Catholic Charities and the Constitutional Convention of 1894 of the State of New York: Report to the Committee on Catholic Interests of the Catholic Club,* June 1894, 5.

30. Stern, "Shall State Aid Be Withdrawn?" 4–5. A board member of the Hebrew Orphan Asylum declared in 1899 that while "It is our privilege . . . to welcome them, . . . it is also our duty to assimilate them to our language and civilization . . . and thus protect our own repute as loyal and good citizens." *Hebrew Orphan Asylum, Annual Report,* 1899, 33–34.

31. Lee Frankel, chair, "Report of the Committee on Dependent Children," *Proceedings,* Second Biennial Meeting of the National Conference of Jewish Charities, Detroit, Michigan, May 26–28, 1902 (hereafter Second Conference of Jewish Charities).

32. Reena Sigman Friedman, *These Are Our Children: Jewish Orphanages in the United States, 1880–1925* (London: Brandeis University Press, 1994); see also Hyman Bogen, *The Luckiest Orphans: A History of the Hebrew Orphan Asylum of New York* (Urbana: University of Illinois Press, 1992).

33. Friedman, *These Are Our Children.* Through the turn of the century, religious and cultural training in Jewish institutions reflected these tensions. At one national conference of Jewish charity organizers in 1901, some leaders blamed orthodoxy for the destitution of the larger community. One author held, for instance, that orthodox tendencies to have large families, stop work to pray several times a day, and refuse to work on the Sabbath were practices that made the orthodox unemployable and hopelessly destitute. Morris Goldstein, "Causes of Poverty and the Remedial Work of Organized Charity," *Proceedings,* Second Conference of Jewish Charities, reprinted in *Trends and Issues in Jewish Social Welfare, 1899–1958,* edited by Robert Morris and Michael Freund (Philadelphia: Jewish Publication Society of America, 1966), 54–55.

34. Harold Silver, "The Russian Jew Looks at Charity," in *Trends and Issues,* edited by Morris and Freund, 59; Friedman, *These Are Our Children,*145.

35. On the argument put forth by the Evangelical Alliance, see, for instance, "Address of Rev. James King," in *Catholic Charities and the Constitutional Convention of 1894 of the State of New York: Report to the Committee on Catholic Interests of the Catholic Club,* 19. For Catholic arguments, see Frederic Coudert, *Catholic Charities and the Constitutional Convention of 1894,* 13; and Louis Bliss, *Catholic Charities and the Consistutional Conventon of 1894,* 20.

36. Eldridge T. Gerry, "The Commitment of Dependent Children in New York County, in *Proceedings of a Conference on the Care of Dependent and Delinquent Children in the State of New York, November 14, 15, 16, 1893,* State Charities Aid Association (hereafter SCAA) Document 59 (New York: State Charities Aid Association, 1894), 51, 62.

37. Josephine Shaw Lowell, "Report on the Institutions for the Care of Des-

titute Children of the City of New York," in *Nineteenth Annual Report of the New York State Board of Charities*, 1886, passim; Joseph Choate, in *Catholic Charities and the Constitutional Convention of 1894 of the State of New York: Report to the Committee on Catholic Interests of the Catholic Club*, 199.

38. Choate, *Catholic Charities and the Constitutional Convention of 1894*, 3–4.

39. Ibid., 1–4. Louisa Schuyler claimed that Choate had submitted and won approval for the exact statement the SCAA had proposed in anticipation of the convention. Louisa Lee Schuyler, *Charities Article of the Revised Constitution of the State of New York, Adopted November 6, 1894*, SCAA Document 62, 2–3.

40. Schuyler, *Charities Article*, 7–8.

41. Despite Schuyler's assurances that "autocratic" authority did not exist; the city's institutions felt the sting of the new amendment immediately. Because the amendment, which became effective January 1, 1895, stipulated that institutions must comply with rules of the State Board before public appropriations could be made, the city comptroller asked the board to send him those rules to ensure compliance. Because the rules did not yet exist, the comptroller refused to sanction appropriations. Through the following months a morass of bureaucratic chaos kept the institutions from receiving funds. The comptroller did not release any monthly payments of the total $1.5 million budgeted for the city's institutions until April 4, thereby sending many institutions into financial crisis. *Minutes of the Board of Estimate and Apportionment of the City of New York* (New York: M. B. Brown Printing, 1895), 134–36. Some accused the State Board of purposely not complying with the provisions of the law by not making rules in order to cut funding immediately. In January 1895, State Board President William R. Stewart convened a meeting of the representatives of Catholic institutions, the SCAA, SPCC, State Board, and others to negotiate the rules. The policies that Lowell and the SCAA suggested were predictable: immediate placement of all institutionalized children into public schools, decreased commitments, annual inspections of parents' homes, and hiring paid examiners for regulation of and compliance with the rules. Ross, "Society's Children," 172–79; William Rhinehart Stewart Collection, box 18, letterbook 4, New York Public Library.

42. S. C. Croft, Department of Public Charities of the City of New York, Commissioner's Office, to Hon. William R. Stewart, State Board of Charities, Jan. 22, 1897, RG 0-15, 90-SWL-7, New York City Municipal Archives (NYCMA hereafter).

43. Katherine Hall to Hon. Silas C. Croft, President, Department of Public Charities of the City of New York, Sept. 22, 1897, RG 0-15, 90-SWL-7, NYCMA.

44. *Thirty-first Annual Report of the New York State Board of Charities*, 1898, pt. 1, 125–27.

45. *Annual Report of the State Charities Aid Association of New York*, 1905–6, 1913, appendix. The number of committals stayed high primarily because parents continued to declare their children dependent, and when faced with the option of doing so through the city or through the SPCC, they chose the latter, a group far less committed to means-testing applicants to assess their ability to support their children. Because the state amendment had not divested the SPCC of its power to commit, the State Board of Charities then argued that it must have regulatory powers over the SPCC lest the sentiment of the amendment be undermined by SPCC practices. In 1898 the SPCC won a suit against the State

Board, maintaining autonomy from the board in its commitment work because it was not incorporated as a charitable institution and thereby not subject to legislation pertaining to charities. The SPCC thereafter used its legal authority to administer a committal system parallel to, and much more generous than, that regulated by city or state.

46. Elizabeth McKeown and Dorothy M. Brown, "Saving New York's Children," *U.S. Catholic Historian* 13 (Summer 1995): 83–84; John O'Grady, *Catholic Charities in the United States* (1930, repr. New York: Arno Press and the New York Times, 1971), 255–56.

47. O'Grady, *Catholic Charities in the United States*, 256.

48. *New York City: Society of St. Vincent de Paul: Report of the Superior Council, 1864–1902* (New York: E. B. Clayton's Sons, 1894), 54. Mulry was, of course, not alone in attempting to emulate Protestant culture by accepting its standards for charitable work, distancing himself from the Catholic poor, or seeking the approval and acceptance of well-born Protestants. One St. Vincent de Paul chapter reported in the same year, for instance, that "[a]fter accomplishing very little by moral suasion, we hit upon a plan to make these people live up to their faith. We told them that unless they attended Mass every Sunday their grants would be cut off." Ibid., 68.

49. Robert W. Hebberd to Homer Folks, Nov. 4, 1897, Homer Folks Collection, Rare Book and Manuscript Library, Columbia University (hereafter Folks Collection).

50. Robert W. Hebberd to Homer Folks, Nov. 21, 1897, Folks Collection.

51. Ibid.

52. Thomas M. Mulry to Homer Folks, April 9, 1897, Folks Collection.

53. Josephine Shaw Lowell to Gertrude Rice, Nov. 20, 1901, Folks Collection.

54. Thomas Mulry to Homer Folks, Nov. 9, 1899, Folks Collection.

55. Homer Folks to Hon. Seth Low, Nov. 22, 1901, Folks Collection.

56. Gertrude Rice to Seth Low, Nov. 22, 1901, Folks Collection.

57. Gertrude Rice to Homer Folks, Dec. 20, 1901, Folks Collection.

58. John Rodrigue, New York Protectory Office, Broom Street, to Archbishop Corrigan, March 11, 1891, C-27, AANY.

59. John Crane to Archbishop Corrigan, Jan. 16, 1891, C-27, AANY.

60. Sister Jerome to Archbishop Corrigan, July 29, 1891, C-26, AANY.

61. George Robinson, "Care of Destitute and Delinquent Children," *St. Vincent de Paul Quarterly* 4 (1899): 36–39.

62. Mother Mary Veronica, "Brief Review of Seven Years," 1902, Archives of the Sisters of the Divine Compassion, White Plains, N.Y. (hereafter ASDC).

63. Lowell, "Report on the Institutions for the Care of Destitute Children in the City of New York," 199.

64. Ibid. Comments on nuns appear throughout the report.

65. *Annual Report of the State Charities Aid Association of New York, 1888,* 11.

66. J. S. Lowell, "Dependent Children in New York County," in *Proceedings of a Conference on the Care of Dependent and Delinquent Children in the State of New York, November 14, 15, 16, 1893* State Charities Aid Association Document 59 (New York: State Charities Aid Association, 1894), 38–39; Walter I. Trattner,

From Poor Law to Welfare State: A History of Social Welfare in America, 3d ed. (New York: Free Press, 1984), 100.

67. Lowell, "Dependent Children in New York County," 138 (quotation), 282.

68. Sophie E. Minton, "Family Life versus Institution Life," *Report of the Committee on the History of Child Saving*, 1893, Twentieth National Conference of Charities and Correction, 46–47. Minton was using the words of a Protestant matron in an orphan asylum in South Australia to make her point

69. Edmond J. Butler, executive secretary of the Catholic Home Bureau for Dependent Children, New York City, while speaking favorably on placing-out and legal adoption, also deplored the attacks on institutions: "During a period of more than forty years in which the writer has been in personal contact with directors of institutions he has never met one who did not hold that a normal family home is the best place for a dependent child." From *Foster-home Care for Dependent Children*, U.S. Department of Labor, Children's Bureau Publication 136, 34, cited in Trotzkey, *Institutional Care and Placing-Out*, 6.

70. Gerry, "The Commitment of Dependent Children in New York County," 57.

71. "Address of Right Rev. D. J. McMahon [*sic*], Supervisor of Catholic Charities, Archdiocese of New York," *Proceedings of the Conference on the Care of Dependent Children, January 25, 26, 1909* (Washington: Government Printing Office, 1909), 98. Although an average for all, some institutions, such as the Protectory, were down to an average eleven-month stay. George Robinson, President, the New York Catholic Protectory, to Hon. George B. McClellan, New York City, Feb. 13, 1908, RG 0-15, MGB-70, NYCMA.

72. Thomas Mulry, "Care of Dependent Children," read at the National Conference of Charities, New York City, 1898, and reprinted in *St. Vincent de Paul Quarterly* 3 (1898): 197.

73. Katherine Conway, *In The Footprints of the Good Shepherd: New York, 1857–1907* (New York: Convent of the Good Shepherd, 1907), 30.

74. The Sisters of the Divine Compassion to Commissioner Scanlan, State Board of Charities, April 12, 1902, ASDC.

75. Mother Mary Veronica to Mrs. dePeyster, April 30, 1900, ASDC.

76. Mother Mary Veronica Starr to Josephine Shaw Lowell, Chairman of the Committee on Dependent Children, Charity Organization Society, May 16, 1900, ASDC.

77. "The Public Support of Dependent Children in Private Institutions," in *Proceedings of a Conference on the Care of Dependent and Delinquent Children in the State of New York, November 14, 15, 16, 1893*, State Charities Aid Association Document 59 (New York: State Charities Aid Association, 1894), 168, 159–70.

78. Minton, "Family Life versus Institution Life," 51–52.

79. Ibid., 52.

80. Josephine Shaw Lowell to the State Board of Charities, 252.

81. William Riordan, *Plunkitt of Tammany Hall: A Series of Very Plain Talks on Very Practical Politics* (New York: Penguin Books, 1995), 48.

82. Josephine Shaw Lowell, *Public Relief and Private Charity* (New York: G. P. Putnam's Sons, 1884), 74, 100–103.

83. John Ahearn to Mayor William L. Strong, April 18, 1897, RG 0–15, 90–SML-6, NYCMA.

84. Ibid.

85. Ibid.

86. Ibid.

87. Ibid. On the larger movement nationwide to provide veterans' benefits to veterans and their families, see especially Theda Skocpol, *Protecting Soldiers and Mothers: The Political Origins of Social Policy in the United States* (Cambridge: Harvard University Press, 1992), 102–51.

88. Unsigned to Hon. William L. Strong, May 3, 1897, RG 0-15, 90-SML-6, NYCMA.

89. Sarah Lynch to W. L. Strong, April 22, 1897, RG 0-15, SWL-36, NYCMA.

90. Mrs. Robert Smith to William L. Strong, April 22, 1897, RG 0-15, SWL-36, NYCMA.

91. Mrs. Peterson to Mayor Strong, April 22, 1897, RG 0-15, SWL-36, NYCMA.

92. T. S. Ring to Mayor Strong, April 23, 1897, RG 0-15, SWL-36, NYCMA.

93. Clara Jackson to Mayor Strong, RG 0-15, SWL-36, NYCMA.

94. Homer Folks to Mayor Strong, April 10, 1897, RG 0-15, 90-SMC-6, NYCMA.

95. Josephine Shaw Lowell to Strong, April 22, 1897, RG 0-15, 90-SML-6, NYCMA.

96. *Sixteenth Annual Report of the Charity Organization Society of New York*, 10–11, reprinted in Eve P. Smith, "The Failure of the Destitute Mother's Bill: The Use of Political Power in Social Welfare," *Journal of Sociology and Social Welfare* 14 (June 1987): 63–87.

97. William R. Stewart to Hon. William L. Strong, April 21, 1897, RG 0-15, 90-SML-6, NYCMA.

98. Kate Hall to Hon. William L. Strong, April 21, 1897, RG 0-15, 90-SWL-6, NYCMA.

99. Ross, "Society's Children," 182–85.

100. The SPCC's opposition, moreover, may have been decisive in the bill's demise, but opposition was not based on scientific charity principles. Rather, perhaps with a view toward the pending litigation by which it claimed independence from the State Board of Charities, the SPCC maintained that its legal duties to apportion public funds as suggested in the bill "do not properly come within its corporate functions." Fellow Jenkins, Secretary, New York Society for the Prevention of Cruelty to Children, "Resolution," April 14, 1897, RG 0-15, 90-SML-36, NYCMA.

101. Smith, "The Failure of the Destitute Mother's Bill," 67.

102. Homer Folks to Hon. William Strong, April 22, 1897, RG 0-15, 90-SML-6, NYCMA.

103. Mary Vida Clark, "Supervision of Children Placed in Families," May 9, 1900, *Thirty-fourth Annual Report of the New York State Board of Charities,* Senate Document 26, 795–96.

104. Ross, "Society's Children," 187–88.

105. "Remarks," *St. Vincent de Paul Quarterly* 4 (1899): 50.

106. Ross, "Society's Children," 158.

107. *Catholic Home Bureau Report,* Sept. 13, 1913, 1915, MS-E6, AANY.

108. "Dependent Children in New York City with Special Reference to the Work of the Committee on Dependent Children of the Charity Organization Society," *Charities* 7 (1901): 369–73.

109. Josephine Shaw Lowell, "Children," in William Rhinelander Stewart, *The Philanthropic Work of Josephine Shaw Lowell* (New York, 1911), 268–76, reprinted in Robert H. Bremner, *Children and Youth in America: A Documentary History* (Cambridge: Harvard University Press, 1970), 2: 350–51.

110. "Dependent Children in New York City with Special Reference to the Work of the Committee on Dependent Children."

111. Josephine Shaw Lowell to Gertrude Rice, Nov. 20, 1901, Folks Collection.

112. *Thirty-second Annual Report of the State Charities Aid Association of New York,* 1905, 11, 12.

113. *Thirty-third Annual Report of the State Charities Aid Association of New York,* 1906, 12–13.

114. Edward T. Devine, "The Breaking Up of Families," *Proceedings of the New York State Conference of Charities and Correction at the First Annual Session, May 21–23, 1900,* New York Senate Documents 26 (Albany: James B. Lyon, State Printer, 1901), 75.

115. Edward Butler, "Discussion of 'The Breaking Up of Families,'" in *Proceedings of the New York State Conference of Charities,* 79–82.

116. Ibid., 75, 84.

117. "Proceedings of an Informal Conference on Various Matters of Present Interest Relating to Charities in New York City, May, 1900," *Annual Report of the New York State Board of Charities,* 1901, Senate Document 26, pt. 1, 867, 868, 869.

118. "Proceedings of an Informal Conference on Various Matters," 808.

119. Ibid.

120. Devine, "The Breaking Up of Families," 77.

121. O'Grady, *Catholic Charities in the United States,* 268–69.

122. Homer Folks, Hastings Hart, John Glenn, Thomas Mulry, Edward Devine, Julian Mack, Charles Birtwell, Theodore Dreiser, and James West to President Theodore Roosevelt, "Request for the President to Call the Conference," Dec. 22, 1908, reprinted in *Proceedings of the Conference on the Care of Dependent Children, January 25, 26, 1909* (Washington: Government Printing Office, 1909).

123. *Proceedings of the Conference on the Care of Dependent Children,* 16.

124. Ibid., 149.

125. Ibid., 42, 73, 77. Other Catholics from New York, including male religious such as the Rev. William J. White, supervisor of Catholic Charities in Brooklyn, held that the best means of combating child dependency was to support organized labor so workers had sufficient benefits and wages to get them through periods of depression, unemployment, sickness, or general misfortune.

126. Ibid., 95.

127. Ibid., 53.

128. Ibid., 97.

129. Mark Carnoy, *The State and Political Theory* (Princeton: Princeton University Press, 1984), 70.

130. Arlene MacLeod, "Hegemonic Relations and Gender Resistance: The New Veiling as Accomodating Protest in Cairo," *Signs* 17 (Spring 1992): 555.

131. Michael B. Katz, *In the Shadow of the Poorhouse: A Social History of Welfare in America* (New York: Basic Books, 1986), 125, 118–21, 124–27. Historians' characterizations of the White House Conference and its rejection of institutions overwhelmingly agree with Katz. See, for example, David J. Rothman, *Conscience and Convenience: The Asylum and Its Alternatives in Progressive America* (Boston: Little, Brown, 1980), 208–9; and Molly Ladd-Taylor, *Mother-Work: Women, Child Welfare, and the State, 1890–1930* (Urbana: University of Illinois Press, 1994), 137.

Chapter 6: The Immaculate Conception of the Welfare State, 1895–1920

The quotations in the epigraphs are from D. J. McMahan, Supervisor of Catholic Charities in New York, to Sister Superior, Jan. 30, 1909, Archives of the Sisters of Charity of New York at Mount St. Vincent (hereafter AMSV), and Mother Mary Veronica, "Brief Review of Seven Years," ca. 1900, Archives of the Sisters of the Divine Compassion, White Plains, N.Y. (hereafter ASDC).

1. Cited in Stella Margetson, *Leisure and Pleasure in the Nineteenth Century* (New York: Coward-McCann, 1969), 104.

2. Barbara Melosh, *"The Physician's Hand": Work Culture and Conflict in American Nursing* (Philadephia: Temple University Press, 1982), 30.

3. Gordon Atkins, "Health, Housing and Poverty in New York City, 1865–1898," Ph.D. diss., Columbia University, 1947, 94–101; quotation from Mrs. Elizabeth C. Hobson, *Recollections of a Happy Life* (New York: G. P. Putnam's Sons, 1916), 108–9.

4. State Charities Aid Association (hereafter SCAA), *A Century of Nursing, by a Member of the Hospital Committee*, Document 1, 1873, 23–28, 33–36, 48, 27. References to the relatively low class status of nuns are pervasive in the pamphlet: "Like all religious organizations the German orders include women of education of superior social grade, but the preponderating number of deaconesses at Kaiserwerth . . . are of the grade from which domestic servants come." Ibid., 34

5. Some historians of American women have studied women's settlements of the late nineteenth and early twentieth centuries and mentioned that their social organization was not entirely different than that of Catholic convents. Kathryn Kish Sklar, "Hull House in the 1890s: A Community of Women Reformers," in *Unequal Sisters: A Multicultural Reader in U.S. Women's History,* edited by Ellen Carol Du Bois and Vicki L. Ruiz (New York: Routledge, 1990), 110.

6. In Robin Muncy's discussion of Hull-House in Chicago, she stresses the tendency of settlement workers to refer to each other as "sisters," to assess the application of a worker for indications of "settlement spirit," to guide the "sister" through periods of postulancy and "novitiate," and then decide collectively whether she would become fully "ordained." Women who lived outside the settlement but supported its work were referred to as "lay sisters." The private donations of women outside the settlement, as well as the settlement workers' personal wealth, were used to finance charitable projects and collective

living space. Robin Muncy, *Creating a Female Dominion in American Reform, 1890–1935* (New York: Oxford University Press, 1991), 4–23, passim.

7. Suellen Hoy, "Walking Nuns: Chicago's Sisters of Mercy," in *At the Crossroads: Old Saint Patrick's and the Chicago Irish,* edited by Ellen Skerrett (Chicago: Loyala University Press, 1997), 30. Skerrett notes that Jane Addams seemed oblivious to the sisters and larger Catholic culture in the vicinity of Hull-House. Ellen Skerett, "The Irish of Chicago's Hull-House Neighborhood," in *New Perspectives on the Irish Diaspora* (Carbondale: Southern Illinois University Press, 2000), 189–222; see also Suellen Hoy, "Caring for Chicago's Women and Girls: The Sisters of the Good Shepherd, 1859–1911," *Journal of Urban History* 23 (March 1997): 260.

8. Mother Mary Veronica, "Address to the Catholic Girls' Club, September 15, 1902," cited in Sister Mary Teresa, RDC, *The Fruit of His Compassion: The Life of Mother Mary Veronica, Foundress of the Sisters of the Divine Compassion* (New York: Pageant Press, 1962), 461.

9. Molly Ladd-Taylor, *Mother-Work: Women, Child Welfare, and the State, 1890–1930* (Urbana: University of Illinois Press, 1994), 4. Robin Muncy continues, "Given the particular construction of gender at the turn of the century, female professionals could succeed in satisfying their needs for respect, autonomy, and effectiveness only at the expense of other women" (*Creating a Female Dominion,* xv).

10. James Mohr, *Abortion in America: The Origins and Evolution of National Policy, 1800–1900* (New York: Oxford University Press, 1978); Barbara Ehrenreich and Deidre English, *Witches, Midwives, and Nurses: A History of Women Healers* (Old Westbury: Feminist Press, 1973), passim.

11. Eldridge T. Gerry, "The Commitment of Dependent Children in New York County," in *Proceedings of a Conference on the Care of Dependent and Delinquent Children in the State of New York, November 14, 15, 16, 1893,* State Charities Aid Association Document 59 (New York: State Charities Aid Association, 1894), 62; "Remarks of Hon. William Allen Butler," and "Agument of Mr. George Bliss," both in *Catholic Charities and the Constitutional Convention of 1894 of the State of New York: Report to the Committee on Catholic Interests of the Catholic Club,* passim; Mary J. Oates, *The Catholic Philanthropic Tradition in America* (Bloomington: Indiana University Press, 1995), 21–22.

12. Mary Hayes, "The Founding Years of Trinity College: A Case Study in Christian Feminism," *U.S. Catholic Historian* 10, nos. 1–2 (1992): 79–86.

13. Muncy, *Creating a Female Dominion,* 4.

14. An excellent anthology on the origins and significance of Catholic women's higher education is *Catholic Women's Colleges in America,* edited by Tracy Schier and Cynthia Russett (Baltimore: Johns Hopkins University Press, 2002). On the role of sisterhoods in founding and administering Catholic women's colleges, see especially, Monika Hellwig, "Colleges of Religious Women's Congregations: The Spiritual Heritage," Kathleen A. Mahoney, "American Catholic Colleges for Women: Historical Origins," and Mary J. Oates, "Sisterhoods and Catholic Higher Education, 1890–1960," all in *Catholic Women's Colleges,* 17–24, 25–54, 161–94.

15. Various applications to the Sisters of Mercy, Archives of the Sisters of Mercy, Dobbs Ferry, N.Y.

16. Rev. D. J. McMahan, Supervisor of Catholic Charities in New York, to Sister Superior, Jan. 30, 1909, AMSV.

17. Dorothy M. Brown and Elizabeth McKeown, *The Poor Belong to Us: Catholic Charities and American Welfare* (Cambridge: Harvard University Press, 1997), 43.

18. Mother M. de Chantal, Supt., Sisters of St. Joseph, St. John's Home, 992 St. Mark's Ave., Brooklyn, N.Y., to Master Anthony Finch, May 5, 1914, RG 0-15, MJP-132, New York City Municipal Archives (hereafter NYCMA).

19. J. McKee Borden, Secretary, Department of Public Charities of the City of New York to Mrs. Andres, May 15, 1914, RG 0-15, MJP-132, NYCMA.

20. Brown and McKeown, *The Poor Belong to Us*, 28.

21. Teresa R. O'Donohue, "The Friendly Visitor," *Proceedings, First National Conference of Catholic Charities*, Sept. 25–28, 1910, Catholic University of America, Washington, D.C., 151.

22. Ibid., 154.

23. Oates, *The Catholic Philanthropic Tradition in America*, 75, 76.

24. Ibid., 80–87 (on Catholic women's lay organization and professionalization); Brown and McKeown, *The Poor Belong to Us*, 73–76. Both works discuss and analyze the larger national Catholic contexts before the 1920s. Although they have distinct emphases, both are excellent at illuminating the tensions and difficulties of the Catholic Charities consolidation movement.

25. Msgr. D. J. McMahan, in *Proceedings, First National Conference of Catholic Charities*, Sept. 25–28, 1910, Catholic University of America, Washington, D.C.

26. Thomas Hynes, in *Proceedings, First National Conference of Catholic Charities*, Sept. 25–28, 1910, Catholic University of America, Washington, D.C., 114.

27. Mrs. J. M. Molamphy, in *Proceedings, Fourth National Conference of Catholic Charities*, Sept. 19, 1916, Catholic University of America, Washington, D.C., 370.

28. Mary Shinnick, "Pensioning of Widows," *Proceedings, Second National Conference of Catholic Charities*, Sept. 23, 1912, Catholic University of America, Washington, D.C., 123.

29. Shinnick, "Pensioning of Widows," 125.

30. Robert Hebberd, in *Proceedings, Third National Conference of Catholic Charities*, Sept. 1914, Catholic University of America, Washington, D.C., 149–51.

31. Thomas Mulry, in *Proceedings, Third National Conference of Catholic Charities*, 1914, Catholic University of America, Washington, 154–55.

32. Mulry, in *Proceedings, Third National Conference*.

33. Richard Neustadt to Mr. McCabe, City Editor, *New York American*, Dec. 23, 1914, A3106-78, New York State Archives, Albany (hereafter NYSA).

34. Solomon Lowenstein, "A Study of the Problem of Boarding Out Jewish Children and of Pensioning Widowed Mothers," *Proceedings*, Second Biennial Meeting of the National Conference of Jewish Charities, Detroit, Michigan, May 26–28, 1902 (hereafter *Proceedings* of the Second Conference of Jewish Charities), 206–11, reprinted in Robert H. Bremner, *Children and Youth in America: A Documentary History* (Cambridge: Harvard University Press, 1970), 329.

35. Abraham Cronbach, "What Makes Jewish Social Work 'Jewish'? Historical Aspect," *Jewish Social Service Quarterly* 6 (Sept. 1930): 3–5. Based on the Talmudic tradition of regular sharing of crops with the poor of any society, Myer Stern held in 1894 that "it is . . . commanded to the Jews that when they have garnered their harvest, the gleaning and the corner of the field should be left for the poor and the stranger." Myer Stern, "Hebrew Institutions for Dependent Children in New York City," in *Proceedings of a Conference on the Care of Dependent and Delinquent Children in the State of New York, November 14, 15, 16, 1893*, State Charities Aid Association Document 59 (New York: State Charities Aid Association, 1894), 47, 46–50.

36. Cronbach, "What Makes Jewish Social Work 'Jewish'?" 3–5.

37. Lowenstein, "A Study of the Problem of Boarding Out Jewish Children and of Pensioning Widowed Mothers," 218–19, 229–34, reprinted in Bremner, *Children and Youth in America*, 355–57.

38. Rent money was given with the stipulation that women must move themselves and their children to a "better neighborhood," preferably suburban, which in the early twentieth century included Queens and the Bronx. Ibid.

39. "The friendly visitor, sympathetic, tactful, with a knowledge of good housekeeping, can be of invaluable service to her. In addition to assisting in the expenditure of funds and the management of the family budget, she may find work to do in advice concerning the preparation of foods and the foods to be used; the cleanliness of children, their schooling and amusement. With proper supervision, I believe this kind of work can become extremely valuable; without it, I am convinced that it can result only in failure." Ibid., 356.

40. Sophie Irene Loeb, "Report of Proceedings of Executive Session of the Commission on Relief for Widowed Mothers," Nov. 13, 1913, A3106-78, folder 11, 586, NYSA.

41. Loeb, "Report of Proceedings of Executive Session."

42. Commission on Relief for Widowed Mothers, Transcripts of Hearings, 1913–14, Oct. 30–Dec. 13, 1913, A3106-78, NYSA.

43. Edward Devine to Hannah Einstein, Nov. 15, 1913, A3106-78, NYSA.

44. Richard Neustadt to Dr. John Lovejoy Elliott, Hudson Guild, Jan. 29, 1915, A3106-78, NYSA.

45. Edward T. Devine, "Pensions for Mothers," *American Labor Legislation Review* 3 (1913): 193–99, reprinted in Bremner, *Children and Youth in America*, 377.

46. Devine, "Pensions for Mothers," 379.

47. As Robert DeForest declared when questioned by the commission: "I think such pensions would be hurtful to the community because they would lead people to rely upon the government instead of upon themselves. They would increase dependency and pauperism." Aaron J. Levy, Chairman, Commission on Relief for Widowed Mothers, to Hon. Robert W. DeForest, President, Charity Organization Society, March 12 1914, A3106-78, NYSA.

48. William H. Matthews, "Report of Work of the Board of Child Welfare of the City of New York, for the Twelve Months Ending August 6, 1916," RG 0-15, MJP-161, NYCMA.

49. The legislation stipulated that the nine members of the city's Board of Child Welfare, three of whom had to be women, would be appointed by the mayor.

Operating independently of the city's Department of Public Charities, the board would have sole charge over the administration of pensions. Mayor Mitchell, as well as his commissioner of public charities, John Kingsbury, had been opposed to Widows' Pensions legislation, particularly to the provision that the board operate independently of the DPC. Matthews, "Report of Work."

50. Sophie Irene Loeb, *Everyman's Child* (New York: Century, 1920), 73–74.

51. Matthews, "Report of Work," 8.

52. *Annual Report of the Department of Public Charities of the City of New York for 1915*, 128.

53. Robert Hebberd charged that this was retribution for the Pension Commission's treatment and publicity of the Charity Organization Society. Paul S. Blakely et. al., *A Campaign of Calumny: The New York Charities Investigation* (New York: America Press), 12, 14.

54. This narrative, as well as the analysis that follows, is largely pieced together from the voluminous collection of the Strong Commission, NYSA, including a large scrapbook of newspaper accounts (A0017). Some of the transcript of both the Strong Commission testimony, which neared nine thousand pages, and the prosecution of John P. Mitchell and John Kingsbury, is still restricted under the provisions of the Moreland Act. Some of the critical report and pamphlet literature includes *Report of Charles H. Strong, Commissioner to Examine into the Management and Affairs of the State Board of Charities, the Fiscal Supervisor and Certain Related Boards and Commissions to Govenor Whitman*, Oct. 25, 1916, and *The Answer of the State Board of Charities to the Report . . . of Commissioner Charles H. Strong, under the Provisions of the Moreland Act* (Albany: J. B. Lyon, 1916). The following pamphlets were all issued in the spring of 1916: *Newspaper Comment on Governor Whiteman's Charities Investigation Conducted by Charles H. Strong, Commissioner Appointed under the Moreland Act* (hereafter "Moree Pamphlet"); *Extract from the Testimony before the Strong Commission of E. A. Moree, Employed by the State Charities Aid Association. . .* ; W. B. Farrell, *"Charity for Revenue": . . . Mr. R. R. Reeder's Interview in* The World. *. . . a Reply*; William B. Farrell, *How the Strong Commission Has Discredited Itself*; William B. Farrell, *A Public Scandal: The Strong Commission*; Msgr. Dunn to the Noted Citizens Who Back the Mayor; and Paul S. Blakely et al., *A Campaign of Calumny: The New York Charities Investigation* (New York: America Press). Other analyses of the Strong Commission and the scandals include Brown and McKeown, *The Poor Belong to Us*, 42–50; Oates, *The Catholic Philanthropic Tradition in America*, 72; Matthew A. Crenson, *Building the Invisible Orphanage: A Prehistory of the American Welfare System* (Cambridge: Harvard University Press, 1998), 284–305; and John F. McClymer, "Of 'Morning Glories' and 'Fine Old Oaks': John Purroy Mitchell, Al Smith, and Reform as an Expression of Irish-American Aspiration," in *The New York Irish*, edited by Ronald H. Bayor and Timothy J. Meagher (Baltimore: Johns Hopkins University Press, 1996), 380–84.

55. Ibid.

56. John Kingsbury to Hon. John Purroy Mitchel, Mayor, City of New York, Oct. 16, 1914, RG 0-15, MJP-132, NYCMA.

57. Kingsbury claimed that he had identified "men and women who had had experience in approved social work" by "enlist[ing] the cooperation of the executives of the Charity Organization Society of New York, the Brooklyn Bureau of

Charities, the New York Association for Improving the Condition of the Poor," the Brooklyn ACIP, the SCAA, and the Russell Sage Foundation. John Kingsbury to Hon. John Purroy Mitchel, Mayor, City of New York, Oct. 16, 1914, RG 0-15, MJP-132, NYCMA. In his study of "social workers" in New York, Edward Devine explicitly excluded "Roman Catholic" because so few of them employed salaried workers. Edward T. Devine and Mary Van Kleek, *Positions in Social Work: A Study of the Number, Salaries, Experience and Qualifications of Professional Workers in Unofficial Social Agencies in New York City, Based upon an Investigation made by Florence Woolston for the New York School of Philanthropy and the Intercollegiate Bureau of Occupations* (New York: New York School of Philanthropy, 1916), 15–18, 1–55.

58. The effect of the investigators' work, Kingsbury claimed, resulted in a net savings to the city of $100,000 in 1914, their first year under his command. John Kingsbury to Hon. John Purroy Mitchel, Mayor, City of New York, Oct. 16, 1914, RG 0-15, MJP-132, 5, NYCMA. For a comparative framework of social workers' salaries in the city, see Devine and Van Kleek, *Positions in Social Work.*

59. John Kingsbury to Hon. John Purroy Mitchel, Mayor, City of New York, Oct. 16, 1914, RG 0-15, MJP-132, NYCMA.

60. Ibid.

61. Ibid.

62. *Annual Report of the Department of Public Charities of the City of New York, 1918,* 36.

63. *Handbook of the Bureau of Social Investigations of the Department of Public Charities of New York City, 1917,* 56–57.

64. *Annual Report of the Department of Public Charities of the City of New York, 1918,* 33–36; *Annual Report of the Department of Public Charities of the City of New York, 1919,* 31–32.

65. Homer Folks, Introduction, in William J. Doherty, Ludwig B. Bernstein, and R. R. Reeder, *Child-Caring Institutions: A Plan of Inspection—Questions, Suggestions, and Standards* (New York City: Department of Public Charities of the City of New York, 1916), 8.

66. Folks, Introduction, 8–9.

67. Doherty, Bernstein, and Reeder, *Child-Caring Institutions.*

68. Investigators were asked to reply to the following questions: "Does the appearance of children indicate repression or freedom?"; "How much actual individual supervision is exercised over the children? Indicate the number of governors or governesses employed for units of 50 children." "Ideals" of each institution were measured accordingly: "What attitude does the institution take concerning the child? Does it view him as an individual. . . ? Are the children the mere pawns forming some ulterior purpose of the institution and not themselves the real ends developed and conserved?" "Is the institution getting anywhere in its service to the children, or does it fill in a sort of indifferent section of their young lives, beginning with no fixed program and ending with no definite results?" Ibid.

69. *Annual Report of the Department of Public Charities of the City of New York for 1915,* 60.

70. Ibid., 45–59.

71. "Scrapbook of the Strong Investigations," NYSA.

72. "Report of Charles H. Strong, Commissioner to Examine into the Manage-

ment and Affairs of the State Board of Charities, the Fiscal Supervisor and Certain Related Boards and Commissions to Governor Whitman," Oct. 25, 1916, 111–13, 114.

73. *Extract from the Testimony before the Strong Commission of E. A. Moree*, 6724.

74. Ibid.

75. Reprint of article from the *New York Sun*, Feb. 9, 1916, Moree Pamphlet.

76. Farrell, *A Public Scandal*, 5–7.

77. William B. Farrell, *How the Strong Commission Has Discredited Itself*, Feb. 24, 1916, 16, 13.

78. Reprinted in *Msgr. Dunn to the Noted Citizens.*

79. Kingsbury reported that the proportion accepted had been reduced by the end of 1915 to 31 percent of those who applied. *Annual Report of the Department of Public Charities of the City of New York for 1915*, 126.

80. Ibid., 14–15.

81. Moree Pamphlet.

82. *Annual Report of the Department of Public Charities of the City of New York for 1915*, 14–15.

83. John Kingsbury to Archbishop John Cardinal Farley, March 3, 1917, AMSV.

84. Elizabeth Lunbeck, *The Psychiatric Persuasion: Knowledge, Gender and Power in Modern America*, (Princeton: Princeton University Press, 1994), 64, 122.

85. After the Strong investigation, Kingsburg made his larger plan more visible to the public. "The Department of Public Charities is attempting to prevent the propagation of feeble-minded children by segregating in the city and various state institutions women of child-bearing age and men who are likely to transmit weak mental traits." *Humanizing the Greater City's Charity: The Work of the Department of Public Charities of the City of New York* (New York: Public Welfare Committee, 1917), 103–4.

86. The city administration under John Hylan in the early 1920s was likely to see the new foster care system as providing inferior care and thus worked hard to enlist the Sisters again in housing children. *New York City Department of Charities, Annual Report for 1921*, 6.

87. Sister Marie De Lourdes Walsh, *The Sisters of Charity of New York, 1809–1959* (New York: Fordham University Press, 1960), 3: 30.

88. On the closing of the Tarrytown institution and the opening of the Reginia Angelorium and Devin Home, see Katherine Burton, *His Mercy Endureth Forever* (Tarrytown: Sisters of Mercy, 1946), 21–31.

89. On closing St. Agatha's and the Catholic Protectory in 1938, see Walsh, *The Sisters of Charity*, 3: 116–19, 3: 50.

90. *Annual Report of the Police Magistrates Courts of the City of New York*, 1867–90.

91. In 1893 and 1894, for instance, the Good Shepherd Sisters counted only $23,923 from the city in a total budget of $133,133. The remainder was earned through machine work, laundry, fine sewing, and altar beads made in the House of the Good Shepherd, as well as from small donations. *Annual Report for 1893 and 1894, House of the Good Shepherd, New York City*, E-7, AANY.

92. Maureen Fitzgerald, "The Perils of Passion and Poverty: Women Religious

and the Care of Single Women in New York City, 1845–1890," *U.S. Catholic Historian* 10 (1992): 45–58.

93. "Reports, Association for Befriending Children and Young Girls, 1870–1871," ASDC.

94. Mother Mary Veronica Starr to Miss Binsse, March 14, 1893, ASDC.

95. Mother Jerome, Mount St. Vincent, to Archbishop John McCloskey, Jan., 1870, A-20, AANY.

96. *Annual Report of the Foundling Asylum of the Sisters of Charity of the City of New York* (West Chester: New York Catholic Protectory, 1870–74).

97. *Annual Report of the Foundling Asylum,* 1873, 8.

98. Foundling Asylum Scrapbook, undated newspaper clipping from the year 1887, AMSV.

99. At least a quarter of the sixty-seven day nurseries in New York City in 1917 were run by nuns. *Handbook of the Bureau of Social Investigations of the Department of Public Charities of New York City,* 1917, 68–69. Available at Columbia University.

100. *Annual Report of the Foundling Asylum,* 1881, 11.

101. On the question of "redeeming" pregnant women, see especially Rickie Solinger, *Wake Up Little Susie* (New York: Routledge, 2000).

102. *Annual Report of the Foundling Asylum,* 1873–90.

103. On controversies generated by the Foundling's placements, see Linda Gordon, *The Great Arizona Orphan Abduction* (Cambridge: Harvard University Press, 1999).

104. *Annual Report of the Foundling Asylum,* 1873, 8.

105. Walsh, *The Sisters of Charity,* 3: 82.

106. Undated, uncited newspaper clipping, "Founding Asylum Scrapbook," AMSV.

107. *Annual Report of the Foundling Asylum,* 1881, 15.

108. "Healthy and Happy Babies," Foundling Asylum Scrapbook, n.d., AMSV.

109. Herbert Burdett, in *The Illustrated American,* May 17, 1890, 310.

110. "Foundling Asylum" file in "Charities," AANY.

111. Sister Teresa Vincent, Directress and Treasurer, to Hon. R. Hebberd, Se., State Board of Charities, October 11, 1910, AMSV.

112. "Report of the Inspection of the Boarding-out and Placing-out Work of the New York Foundling Asylum," [dates of Inspection, Nov. 21, Dec. 13, 1916], AMSV, 20.

113. "Report of the Inspection," 23, 5, 66, 67.

114. Ibid., 69–70.

115. Ibid., 8.

116. Ibid., 3.

117. *Annual Report of the Foundling Asylum,* 1870–1917.

118. "Family Trees for New York Foundlings," *Survey,* March 17, 1917, 698.

119. Charles H. Strong to Bard L. Peck, Esq., March 12, 1917, AMSV; Bard L. Peck, Counsellor at Law, to the Editor of *The Survey,* March 1917, AMSV; "Family Trees for New York Foundlings," 698; Bard Peck, Esq., "In the Matter of the Controversy between the New York Foundling Hospital and the Commissioner of Charities of the City of New York," AMSV.

120. "Report of the Inspection of the Boarding-out and Placing-out Work of the New York Foundling Asylum," 7.

121. Ibid., 40. "Of the children admitted with their mothers and surrendered by their mothers there is no history available, as the statements made by the mothers were not verified in any way. The mothers were asked their names, addresses (which were not insisted upon), age, birthplace, name and age of child. The children's birth records are not looked up, and there is no proof that either mother or child are proper charges of the City. The Sisters state that married women are not allowed to surrender their babies, but there is no investigation made of the woman's statement." Ibid., 3. The investigators included Mary V. Bolton, Bessi de Koster, Della A. Fergus, E. M. Haughwout, Bertha E. Tomlinson (supervisor of inspection), and Nellie Wise.

122. Peck, "In the Matter of the Controversy," AMSV.

123. A. M. Wilson, Director, Bureau of Social Investigations, DPC, to Sister Anna Michella, April 5, 1917, AMSV.

124. "Babies Unaided If Not Citizens," Foundling Asylum Scrapbook, 1917, AMSV.

125. Peck, "In the Matter of the Controversy," 3–4, 1–2.

126. "Babies Unaided If Not Citizens."

127. Sister Anna Michella, Foundling Asylum, to Mother M. Josepha, April 18, 1917, AMSV. She added, "The representatives who are here from 9 A.M. to 9 P.M. are a great strain and I fail to see much results, they are very slow in accepting cases and I see very little confidential work being done."

128. George Gillespie to Bard L. Peck, Esq., April 9, 1917, AMSV.

129. *Annual Reports of the New York Founding Asylum, 1916–17, 1920–21,* E-10, AANY; Walsh, *The Sisters of Charity.* The quotation is in McClymer, "Of 'Mornin' Glories,'" 388. Hylan's administration continually ridiculed the "experts" they believed "on the pretext of improving methods of private child-caring institutions . . . rudely invaded their premises, employed outside and unsympathetic investigators to make surveys, broke up their customs, flouted their religious convictions, and finally presented reports of their activities that were grossly unfair." *New York City Department of Charities, Annual Report for 1921,* 5.

130. Brown and McKeown, *The Poor Belong to Us,* 74–75.

131. Oates, *The Catholic Philanthropic Tradition in America,* 75–76, 71–97.

132. Kathryn Kish Sklar, "The Historical Foundations of Women's Power in the Creation of the American Welfare State, 1830–1930," in *Mothers of a New World: Maternalist Politics and the Origins of Welfare States,* edited by Seth Koven and Sonya Michel (New York: Routledge, 1993), 44.

133. James Scott, *Domination and the Arts of Resistance: Hidden Transcripts* (New Haven: Yale University Press, 1990).

134. Linda Gordon, *Pitied but Not Entitled: Single Mothers and the History of Welfare* (New York: Free Press, 1994).

135. Marvin Olasky, *The Tragedy of American Compassion* (Washington: Regnery Publishing, 1992); Joel Schwartz, *Fighting Poverty with Virtue: Moral Reform and America's Urban Poor, 1825–2000* (Bloomington: Indiana University Press, 2000).

136. Schwartz, *Fighting Poverty with Virtue,* xix.

INDEX

Associate Professor MAUREEN FITZGERALD
teaches in the Department of Religious Studies
at the College of William and Mary, where she is
also director of undergraduate studies for the
American Studies Program

Women Doctors in Gilded-Age Washington: Race, Gender, and
Professionalization   *Gloria Moldow*

Friends and Sisters: Letters between Lucy Stone and Antoinette Brown
Blackwell, 1846–93   *Edited by Carol Lasser and Marlene Deahl Merrill*

Reform, Labor, and Feminism: Margaret Dreier Robins and the Women's
Trade Union League   *Elizabeth Anne Payne*

Private Matters: American Attitudes toward Childbearing and Infant
Nurture in the Urban North, 1800–1860   *Sylvia D. Hoffert*

Civil Wars: Women and the Crisis of Southern Nationalism
George C. Rable

I Came a Stranger: The Story of a Hull-House Girl   *Hilda Satt Polacheck;
edited by Dena J. Polacheck Epstein*

Labor's Flaming Youth: Telephone Operators and Worker Militancy,
1878–1923   *Stephen H. Norwood*

Winter Friends: Women Growing Old in the New Republic, 1785–1835
Terri L. Premo

Better Than Second Best: Love and Work in the Life of Helen Magill
Glenn C. Altschuler

Dishing It Out: Waitresses and Their Unions in the Twentieth Century
Dorothy Sue Cobble

Natural Allies: Women's Associations in American History
Anne Firor Scott

Beyond the Typewriter: Gender, Class, and the Origins of Modern
American Office Work, 1900–1930   *Sharon Hartman Strom*

The Challenge of Feminist Biography: Writing the Lives of Modern
American Women   *Edited by Sara Alpern, Joyce Antler,
Elisabeth Israels Perry, and Ingrid Winther Scobie*

Working Women of Collar City: Gender, Class, and Community in
Troy, New York, 1864–86   *Carole Turbin*

Radicals of the Worst Sort: Laboring Women in Lawrence, Massachusetts,
1860–1912   *Ardis Cameron*

Visible Women: New Essays on American Activism   *Edited by
Nancy A. Hewitt and Suzanne Lebsock*

Mother-Work: Women, Child Welfare, and the State, 1890–1930
Molly Ladd-Taylor

Babe: The Life and Legend of Babe Didrikson Zaharias   *Susan E. Cayleff*

Writing Out My Heart: Selections from the Journal of Frances E. Willard,
1855–96   *Edited by Carolyn De Swarte Gifford*

U.S. Women in Struggle: A *Feminist Studies* Anthology   *Edited by
Claire Goldberg Moses and Heidi Hartmann*

In a Generous Spirit: A First-Person Biography of Myra Page
Christina Looper Baker

Mining Cultures: Men, Women, and Leisure in Butte, 1914–41
Mary Murphy

Gendered Strife and Confusion: The Political Culture of Reconstruction
    Laura F. Edwards
The Female Economy: The Millinery and Dressmaking Trades, 1860–1930
    Wendy Gamber
Mistresses and Slaves: Plantation Women in South Carolina, 1830–80
    Marli F. Weiner
A Hard Fight for We: Women's Transition from Slavery to Freedom in
    South Carolina   *Leslie A. Schwalm*
The Common Ground of Womanhood: Class, Gender, and Working
    Girls'Clubs, 1884–1928   *Priscilla Murolo*
Purifying America: Women, Cultural Reform, and Pro-Censorship
    Activism, 1873–1933   *Alison M. Parker*
Marching Together: Women of the Brotherhood of Sleeping Car Porters
    Melinda Chateauvert
Creating the New Woman: The Rise of Southern Women's Progressive
    Culture in Texas, 1893–1918   *Judith N. McArthur*
The Business of Charity: The Woman's Exchange Movement, 1832–1900
    Kathleen Waters Sander
The Power and Passion of M. Carey Thomas   *Helen Lefkowitz Horowitz*
For Freedom's Sake: The Life of Fannie Lou Hamer   *Chana Kai Lee*
Becoming Citizens: The Emergence and Development of the California
    Women's Movement, 1880–1911   *Gayle Gullett*
Selected Letters of Lucretia Coffin Mott   *Edited by Beverly Wilson
    Palmer with the assistance of Holly Byers Ochoa and Carol Faulkner*
Women and the Republican Party, 1854–1924   *Melanie Susan Gustafson*
Southern Discomfort: Women's Activism in Tampa, Florida, 1880s–1920s
    Nancy A. Hewitt
The Making of "Mammy Pleasant": A Black Entrepreneur in Nineteenth-
    Century San Francisco   *Lynn M. Hudson*
Sex Radicals and the Quest for Women's Equality   *Joanne E. Passet*
"We, Too, Are Americans": African American Women in Detroit and
    Richmond, 1940–54   *Megan Taylor Shockley*
The Road to Seneca Falls: Elizabeth Cady Stanton and the First Woman's
    Rights Convention   *Judith Wellman*
Reinventing Marriage: The Love and Work of Alice Freeman Palmer and
    George Herbert Palmer   *Lori Kenschaft*
Southern Single Blessedness: Unmarried Women in the Urban South,
    1800–1865   *Christine Jacobson Carter*
Widows and Orphans First: The Family Economy and Social Welfare
    Policy, 1865–1939   *S. J. Kleinberg*
Habits of Compassion: Irish Catholic Nuns and the Origins of the Welfare
    System, 1830–1920   *Maureen Fitzgerald*

The University of Illinois Press
is a founding member of the
Association of American University Presses.

Composed in 9.5/12.5 Trump Mediaeval
by Jim Proefrock
at the University of Illinois Press
Manufactured by Sheridan Books, Inc.

University of Illinois Press
1325 South Oak Street
Champaign, IL 61820-6903
www.press.uillinois.edu